Great Thinkers and Doers

THE BLACK PRESS IN AMERICA SERIES
Kim Gallon and E. James West, Series Editors

From *Freedom's Journal* to the digital age, Black-owned and -oriented publications have provided a critical voice for Black communities. From arts and culture to civil rights, from public health to diasporic politics, the Black Press—a term most commonly applied to the shared coverage of Black newspapers and magazines—has given form and focus to all aspects of Black life. This groundbreaking series provides a home for Black Press scholarship and the nascent field of Black Press Studies. It is rooted in and helps to extend the work of the Black Press Research Collective, a leading hub for curating and producing knowledge about the Black Press in and beyond the United States.

Great Thinkers and Doers

Networking Black Feminism in the Black Press, 1827–1927

Teresa Zackodnik

Johns Hopkins University Press
Baltimore

© 2025 Johns Hopkins University Press
All rights reserved. Published 2025
Printed in the United States of America on acid-free paper

9 8 7 6 5 4 3 2 1

Johns Hopkins University Press
2715 North Charles Street
Baltimore, Maryland 21218
www.press.jhu.edu

Library of Congress Cataloging-in-Publication Data

Names: Zackodnik, Teresa C., author.
Title: Great thinkers and doers: Networking Black feminism in
    the Black press, 1827–1927 / Teresa Zackodnik.
Description: Baltimore : Johns Hopkins University Press, 2025. |
    Series: The Black press in America series | Includes bibliographical
    references and index.
Identifiers: LCCN 2024042582 | ISBN 9781421451961 (hardcover) |
    ISBN 9781421451978 (ebook)
Subjects: LCSH: African American press—History. | African American
    women—Press coverage. | Reporters and reporting—United States—
    History. | African American women—Intellectual life—History.
Classification: LCC PN4882.5 Z33 2025 | DDC 071.308996073—
    dc23/eng/20241216
LC record available at https://lccn.loc.gov/2024042582

A catalog record for this book is available from the British Library.

Special discounts are available for bulk purchases of this book. For more information, please contact Special Sales at specialsales@jh.edu.

EU GPSR Authorized Representative
LOGOS EUROPE, 9 rue Nicolas Poussin, 17000, La Rochelle, France
E-mail: Contact@logoseurope.eu

Contents

	Acknowledgments	*vii*
	Introduction. "In anything relating to our people, I am insensible of boundaries"	1
1	Recirculation and African American Feminisms	23
2	Making Place: Black Women's Politics and Letters to the Editor	52
3	Geographies of Racialization, Occupation, and Refusal in the *Southern Workman*	83
4	Feminist Black Internationalism in *The Crisis* and *Negro World*	119
5	Intermedial Fugitivity and the "New Negro" Woman in *The Colored American Magazine*	155
	Coda. The New Underground Railway	186
	Appendix. African American Literary Societies and Lyceums	*201*
	Notes	*235*
	Bibliography	*293*
	Index	*335*

Acknowledgments

Funding from the Social Sciences and Humanities Research Council paid for graduate student research assistance and made archival research possible at the Wisconsin Historical Society, Madison; the Library of Congress; the Schomburg Center for Black Life and Culture at the New York Public Library; the Southern California Library for Social Studies and Research; the University of Oregon; and the special collections at the University of Delaware. I thank my students at the University of Alberta for stimulating conversations in courses during the years this book was developing and my fellow conference goers for their questions and insights at meetings where I presented my early thinking on the project. Deep gratitude is due to E. James West and Kim Gallon for their work to create the Johns Hopkins book series New Directions in Black Press Studies and to relaunch the Black Press Research Collective. This came at an important time for me and, I'm sure, for others.

For her detailed and extensive research assistance that supported much of this project, I thank Dr. Melissa Stephens. I also thank Dr. Jackie Baker, Dr. Karen Engle, and Bradley Lafortune for their research assistance during their former lives as graduate students. For their work producing data visualizations, I thank Bamdad Aghilidehkordi and Nicholas van Orden. And I thank Nicholas van Orden both for thinking with me about data visualization tools and for our collaboration on a conference paper that furthered my own thinking as represented here. Any errors in data upon which the geospatial visualizations in this book are based are my own. Any limitations in the appendix result from my own research and from the issues inherent in optical character recognition.

Parts of chapter 2 that involve visualizing the locations and political focus of Black feminisms appeared in a special issue of *a/b: Auto/biography Studies* edited by Kimberly Blockett. I thank her for the bar her own research set for work on early Black women writers and the edition's anonymous reviewers for helping me sharpen this work. Some of my preliminary work with the *Southern Workman* (much of it not represented here) appeared online in *Commonplace* 15, no. 2

(January 2015), and I am grateful for Anna Mae Duane's keen editorial questions that helped sharpen my thinking. An earlier version of some of the research in chapter 4 was published in *Modernisms/modernity*, and I thank the anonymous reviewers and special issue editors Ann Ardis and Patrick Collier for their incisive critique that helped me further develop this work. Research from which chapter 5 developed was published in the special issue of *American Periodicals* guest edited by Joycelyn Moody and Eric Gardner, whose editorial work furthered my thinking in important ways and whose research has been a touchstone for the field of Black periodical studies.

Personal support is the reason why any research project gets done, and this book is no different. Joycelyn Moody's model as a researcher of early African American women writers, her sharpness as a reader and thinker, her guidance and mentorship as an editor of the Transitions in American Literature series at Cambridge University Press, and her generous friendship were all gifts that helped propel me forward and sustained me at some challenging times. Jacqueline Emery's enlivening collaboration with me on *The Southern Workman*, in work unrelated to this project, was a wonderful reminder that this periodical is an important resource for anyone studying Indigenous or African American intellectuals, activists, writers, and artists. For her support of this work as a generous and incisive reader, I thank my longtime friend Susan Hamilton, who is an ocean away in miles but near in heart. For buoying me more than they know through a book that has been a long time coming, I thank Jackie Baker, C J Bogle, Michael Bucknor, Beth Capper, Danielle Fuller, Corrinne Harol, Louise Harrington, Sherrill Johnson, Mike Litwack, Keavy Martin, Orly Lael Netzer, Julie Rak, Carol Ann Sabean, Mark Simpson, and Christine Stewart. For their steady love, I thank my sister Nadine Zackodnik, my brother-in-law Al, my nephews Owen and Milo, and my dear David Gader. As always, I am so very grateful for my daughter Rose, who has always clarified for me what matters in this life.

Great Thinkers and Doers

Introduction

"In anything relating to our people, I am insensible of boundaries"

In 1864, Edmonia Highgate left her home in Syracuse to teach freedpeople in Norfolk, Darlington, New Orleans, and Lafayette Parish at schools sponsored by the American Missionary Association (AMA). In the spring of 1869, Highgate wrote the editor of the *National Antislavery Standard* from Jackson, Mississippi, where her sister Carrie was stationed as an AMA teacher. She shared the news that she had attended a literary society at which "several selections from Whittier and Frances E. W. Harper were rendered by these laundresses, cooks, porters, waiters, etc., with a pathos that told truly that the rhymed story was their own."[1] Highgate was offering more than local color. The earliest Black papers, *Freedom's Journal* (New York, NY; 1827–1829) and *The Colored American* (New York, NY; 1837–1842), had actively supported literary societies as central to a politics of racial uplift.[2] In 1837, the *Colored American* pronounced that literary societies were "of more importance than any others in the present age of Societies and Associations" and urged African Americans to "'cultivate a reading disposition' as the foundational step toward a long process of elevation and communal self-determination."

A decade earlier, *Freedom's Journal* had published similar enjoinders that lauded literary associations as a "well-known method to remove the evil . . . [and] create a spirit of emulation, and, of course, a disposition for reading which would tend to mature the judgment and expand the mind."[3] As Elizabeth McHenry has established, African American literary societies were the "intellectual centers for an increasingly unified and politically conscious" Black public that called for a "substantive democracy."[4] African Americans continued to see literary societies as central politically and to see the literary as part of a respectability politics that centered the moral and religious as late as the 1880s, when the African Methodist Episcopal (AME) Church called for the increase of its "Bethel Literaries . . . accumulating all over the country." As a result, the church would come to be seen as a literary center and "not only a moral and religious" one.[5]

Black literary societies were also distinctive sites for women's literary production and political participation. Women's literary societies were organized as early as men's. For example, the Young Ladies Literary Society of Lynn, Massachusetts—which formed "to meet once a week, to read in turn to the society, works adapted to virtuous and literary improvement"—was founded in 1827, and the Reading Room Society for Men of Color was founded in Philadelphia in 1828.[6] "Since the late 1820s," Martha Jones writes, "women had been taking pen in hand and shaping the debates" as members of such societies.[7] From 1830 through the 1850s, the number of Black women's literary societies was double that of those reserved for male membership in many places.[8] This evidence makes clear that Black women mobilized the political activism and strategies that literary societies made possible.

These societies offered outlets for Black women's creative and political writing. They were socially acceptable venues for discussing and debating concerns that affected their communities and they created an important sense of women's collectivity. The earliest documented Black female literary societies provided their members with venues in which "to practice and perform literacy and allowed them to experiment with voice and self-representation in ways that approximated the ideals of civic participation."[9] Mutual benevolent societies and literary societies also fostered women's activism and leadership. Many African American women who entered the abolition movement, for example, did so by first affiliating with such societies, where they acquired public speaking and leadership skills.

Through literary societies, women were also essential readers of and anonymous and pseudonymous contributors to the radical abolitionist and early Black press. Frances Smith Foster has established that "by 1827, when public education for men was scant and for women almost nonexistent, enough African-American women could and did read newspapers that their interests affected the papers' content. (In fact, from the first issues, some women writers appeared as subjects and as contributors.)"[10] African American women and the literary societies they founded or quickly came to dominate were crucial in establishing and sustaining a Black press that they also recognized as an important tool in their developing politics.

The early Black press and the radical abolitionist press testify to the importance of women's literary societies to Black communities and to their development out of the female mutual benevolent or mutual aid associations established in the late eighteenth century. Erica Dunbar suggests the Female Benevolent Society of St. Thomas (1793) is "perhaps the oldest women's philanthropic organization on record."[11] That society took on or aborbed the "welfare functions of the Free African Society."[12] *Freedom's Journal* published the proceedings of female benevolent association meetings, which were an early form of Black women's political culture and often provided women a conduit for participating in public politics through reform work. Such societies enjoyed wide community approval and support.[13] As James and Lois Horton have established, "Black women not only contributed to the welfare of their community" but also "participated in the political discourse of the day" through benevolent societies and associations, "a role unfamiliar to most American women of the time."[14]

In Philadelphia, where the African American population tripled from 1800 to 1830, the Reading Room Society for Men of Color was established in 1828, the Philadelphia Female Literary Society in 1831, and the Female Minerva Literary Association in 1833.[15] These literary societies were clearly fostered by a strong culture of mutual aid and benevolent association work among women, who also outpopulated men in the city at a ratio of 1.43 to 1 in 1830. From the mid-1820s through the early 1830s, Black women established sixty of the eighty mutual benefit societies that operated in Philadelphia.[16] By 1838, the city had 119 mutual benefit societies, "more than half of which were female associations, and women made up nearly two-thirds of the membership of all benefit societies."[17] Black newspapers frequently reported on the growth of African American communities for their readers, and the *Colored American* noted that "by fall of 1841, African American Philadelphia [had] 16 churches, 21 schools . . . 6 literary and debating societies, 3 moral reform societies, 2 lyceums, and 2 weekly newspapers."[18] By the late 1840s, the number of literary and debating societies and lyceums had grown to 106.[19]

Women did not always see literary societies as succeeding benevolent associations in a linear trajectory of civic participation, and the operations of literary societies were often not distinct from mutual aid or benevolent associations. For example, Boston's Afric-American Female Intelligence Society was led by Elizabeth Riley, who went on to lead that city's Colored Female Union benevolent society.[20] Women's benevolent societies fostered and at times also operated as literary societies, a fact that gendered literary character as a political strategy. In

Salem, Massachusetts, the Colored Female Religious and Moral Society "offered weekly prayer, religious conversation, profitable reading, and friendly advice along with sickness and death benefits to members" for yearly dues of 52 cents.[21] The African Dorcas Associations and Female Dorcas Societies in the Northeast were benevolent organizations that supplied children attending the African Free Schools with clothing and destitute and sick members with financial aid, but they were also strong monetary supporters of the Black press and seedbeds for female literary societies. In November 1837, Charles Ray, coeditor of the *Colored American* along with Philip Bell and Samuel Cornish, wrote that the Female Dorcas Society of Buffalo had donated $10 "toward the Editor's Salary . . . [and] incidental expense of the paper."[22] Similarly, the New York Female Literary Society held fairs in the late 1830s to support the *Colored American*.[23]

Reports indicate that the "mental feasts" women's literary societies offered were held in benevolent societies such as the Dorcas associations.[24] In April 1837, the *Colored American* reported on the Troy African Female Benevolent Society, founded four years earlier, which was also a literary society that read "compositions . . . written by the younger members of the Society." This society may well have predated the Troy Debating Society, the Troy Literary Society, and the Troy Mental and Moral Improvement Society, all of which Dorothy Porter documents as established "before 1837" in a Black community that numbered roughly four hundred people.[25] In 1847, Troy hosted the National Convention of Colored Citizens, at which a national Black press was debated and strongly supported by Henry Highland Garnet. Garnet had delivered the radical "An Address to the Slaves of the United States" at the 1843 Buffalo convention, the writing of which his wife, Julia Williams, is said to have had a hand in.[26] Julia Williams was active in the Female Benevolent Society of Troy and, with a group of Syracuse women, raised funds in 1849 to support the *Impartial Citizen* (Syracuse, NY; Boston, MA; 1849–1850).

Benevolent societies flourished and maintained significant savings for mutual aid and benevolence drawn from membership fees, and like women's literary societies, they remained active through the nineteenth century, "multipl[ying] by the thousands" after Emancipation.[27] For example, by the late 1870s, Black women in Richmond had organized twenty-five benevolent associations and a division of the Independent Order of St. Luke, founded in 1867 by formerly enslaved Mary Prout in Baltimore. In 1899, the Order of St. Luke was taken on by Maggie Lena Walker, who led it to "100,000 members in twenty-eight states" by 1920. The order created the St. Luke Penny Savings Bank; the *St. Luke Herald* (Richmond, VA; 1902–1931), a weekly paper; a department store; funding for scholarships; and a school for girls. The order also campaigned for woman suffrage, against lynching, and for the desegregation of public transportation.[28] Benevolent societies were not only venues for Black women to actively support their communities and to sustain mutual support among women, but they worked in ways related to African American female literary societies as outlets for Black women's creative and political writing, as acceptable venues for discussing concerns affecting the community and women within it, and as spaces of female collectivity. Shirley Logan argues that these organizations sanctioned women's "increased community activism" along a spectrum, ranging from the rationale that "rhetorical skills would help women have a greater moral influence" in their families to using female literary societies as "training grounds for, if not sites of," political activism such as antislavery work.[29]

We are only beginning to build a sense of the extent to which women founded literary societies. We do not yet fully appreciate their longevity and geographical reach, which went well beyond the Northeast, nor their role in Black women's politics and the development of the Black press. Scholarship on Black women's literary societies tends to focus on the urban Northeast, particularly Boston's Afric-American Female Intelligence Society (AAFIS founded in 1832), where Maria Stewart delivered her first public address, and the Philadelphia Female Literary Association (founded in 1831), whose members included Grace Bustill Douglass, Sarah Douglass, Harriett Forten Purvis, and Sarah Forten. This is arguably the case because William Lloyd Garrison published both content written by members of the Philadelphia Female Literary Association in *The Liberator*'s Ladies' Department and circulated Stewart's writings and addresses.[30] But a wealth of historical African American newspapers provide evidence of women's literary societies and the over 1,000 Black literary societies and lyceums organized in forty-two states, Liberia, Canada, and Haiti from the late 1820s through the 1950s (see the appendix). Black literary societies open to female membership were established as early as 1827 in Maine and Massachusetts and they grew through the 1830s not only in the urban Northeast in Pennsylvania, New York, Connecticut, New Jersey, and Rhode Island, but also in Maryland and Washington, DC.[31] By the 1840s, Black literary societies existed in Ohio, and by the 1850s they were active in Canada West, Louisiana, and California. Black literary societies and lyceums were very active in Kansas for thirty years, with the state counting nearly 200 in operation from 1880 to 1910. To appreciate the strength of turn-of-the-century organizing in Kansas, a useful comparator is New York, where

131 Black literary societies were organized over some eighty years from 1826 to 1903.[32] These societies, in other words, were not only organized outside the Northeast but were most active in areas that have not yet been studied.

Most of the recognizable Black female activists of the nineteenth and early twentieth centuries were members of and addressed literary societies, making them crucial for understanding early African American feminisms. Sarah Mapps Douglass, Sarah Forten, Maria Stewart, and Elizabeth Jennings were all active in Northeast literary associations in the 1830s, and they all pursued feminist black nationalist arguments in the work they published in newspapers at the time.[33] Ida B. Wells participated in two Memphis literary societies: one that met at the Vance Street Christian Church and produced their own paper, the Memphis *Evening Star*, which gave Wells her first editorial position; and the other, in the late 1880s, that held its meetings at the LeMoyne Normal Institute. She credited her membership in these societies with the development of her career as a public speaker, journalist, and editor.[34] Charlotte Forten Grimké welcomed Anna Julia Cooper to her "at home" literary society in Washington, DC, in the late 1880s.[35] Cooper was a member of the Oberlin Ladies' Literary Society when she pursued her MA studies in the early 1880s, and later she was a member of both the Bethel Literary and Historical Association and the Book Lovers Club in Washington, DC. Cooper wrote what is now regarded as the prototypical Black feminist manifesto, *A Voice from the South* (1892); she cofounded the National League of Colored Women in 1892; and she addressed the 1893 World's Congress of Representative Women in Chicago ("Women's Cause Is One and Universal") and the First Pan-African Conference in London in 1900 ("The Negro Problem in America").

Cooper also addressed Washington's Bethel Historical and Literary Society in the spring of 1902.[36] Founded by Bishop Daniel Payne in 1881 through the Union Bethel AME Church, the society hosted the nation's Black intellectuals, educators, and activists. The Bethel was a prominent society in which women had leadership roles and was covered widely in the Black press.[37] As early as 1884, it also operated as a model for AME Church Bethel literaries that were growing across the nation. In the late 1890s, both the *Colored American* and the *Christian Recorder* (Philadelphia, PA; Nashville, TN; 1852–) reported that the Bethel Historical and Literary Society drew as many as 800 to its "big meetings."[38] Mary Ann Shadd Cary and Mary Church Terrell were also members of and gave addresses at the Bethel. In the spring of 1888, Shadd Cary invited "leading members" of the American Woman Suffrage Association to the Bethel; Susan B. Anthony and Frederick Douglass addressed those gathered at this meeting.[39] Terrell became the society's first female president in 1892.[40] She was also the first president of the National Association of Colored Women's Clubs (NACWC), which she cofounded with Harriet Tubman, Margaret Murray Washington, Frances Harper, and Ida B. Wells in 1896. Terrell was active in temperance, a founding member of the National Association for the Advancement of Colored People (NAACP), and a member of and frequent speaker for the National American Woman Suffrage Association (NAWSA), and she represented American women at the 1904 International Council of Women in Berlin. She also financially backed the *Colored American* (Washington, DC; 1893–1904), owned by Edward Elder Cooper (founder of the Indianapolis *Freeman*) and wrote its Women's World column under the pseudonym Euphemia Kirk. Terrell published under both this pseudonym and her own name in the Black press and in white-owned and white-edited papers.[41]

From the late 1880s through the turn of the twentieth century, Black feminists such as Fannie Jackson Coppin,[42] Frances Harper,[43] Carrie Clifford,[44] Lucy Craft Laney,[45] Coralie Franklin Cook,[46] Lucy Moten,[47] Ida Gibbs,[48] Hallie Quinn Brown,[49] Ida B. Wells, Nannie Helen Burroughs,[50] and Mattie Bowen[51] addressed the Bethel Historical and Literary Society.[52] These women hailed originally from the North, the South, and the Midwest, and had been born with either free or enslaved status. In other words, the values, opportunities, and training that literary societies offered were not regionally bound.[53] Coralie Franklin Cook was a member of the Book Lover's Club in Harper's Ferry, West Virginia, before migrating to Washington, DC, and Nannie Helen Burroughs organized the Harriet Beecher Stowe Literary Society at M Street High School after migrating from Virginia to Washington, DC. All were active in a range of other political organizations, such as Black women's clubs; suffrage organizations; the NAACP and its precursor, the Niagara Movement; the Colored Woman's League; and the pan-African congresses.

Maritcha Lyons and Frances Harper crossed paths at the Brooklyn Literary Union (1866) in the late 1890s, where Harper gave a speech on November 15, 1892, entitled "Enlightened Motherhood."[54] With Victoria Earle Matthews, Lyons spearheaded the evening at Lyric Hall in October 1892 that raised funds for the publication of Ida B. Wells's anti-lynching pamphlet *Southern Horrors*. The event spurred Matthews and Lyons to organize the Woman's Loyal Union of New York City and Brooklyn (1892), which petitioned Congress in 1894–1895 to investigate lynching. Lyons also debated Wells at the Brooklyn Literary Union.[55] In the fall of 1902, Harper addressed the Boston Literary and Historical Association (founded in

1901), which counted Pauline Hopkins, novelist and editor of *The Colored American Magazine* (Boston, MA; New York, NY; 1900–1909) from 1900 to 1904, as a founding member.[56]

Most of the Black feminists who addressed literary societies at the turn of the century had also been members of literary societies as their networked activism developed and, through their activity in Black women's clubs, they were part of a formally organized feminist movement that "used literacy to create gendered spaces of collaborative agency."[57] For example, Sara Iredell Fleetwood, who led the movement to integrate Black women in the nursing profession, was a founding member of the Ladies Union Association (1863), a relief organization for Civil War soldiers. She was also a leader in the Washington Monday Night Literary Club and in the Migonette Club, the women's literary society at M Street High School. She cofounded the Colored Women's League (1892), whose leadership included Josephine B. Bruce, Anna Julia Cooper, Mary Jane Patterson, and Anna E. Murray; she was a speaker at the National League Convention; she was a member-delegate of the NACWC; and she was a member of the National Association for the Relief of Destitute Colored Women and Children (founded 1863), as were Elizabeth Keckley and Frederick Douglass.[58] The club movement raised funds for community institutions through literary societies,[59] recommended readings to women, and organized book clubs and lyceums. Some Black women's clubs grew directly out of women's literary societies, such as the N. U. G. Club of Salina, Kansas, which was originally the N. U. G. Literary Society (see the appendix), and the Indianapolis Woman's Improvement Club, which was originally organized as a literary club in 1903 by Lillian Thomas Fox, the first Black reporter for the *Indianapolis News*.[60] Literary societies and lyceums were spaces where women's education was debated, even while they functioned to increase women's activist literacy and to broaden the capacity of community-based education. And many took the names of Black feminists, thereby marking their place within that activist tradition, such as the Silone Yates Literary Society of Olathe, Kansas; the Frances Harper Literary Society of Savannah, Georgia (founded 1900); the Lucy Laney Lyceum of Charleston, South Carolina; and the Ida B. Wells Literary Society of Indianapolis (1895).[61]

Understanding that literary societies functioned as training grounds for Black feminist activists while fostering and sustaining the fledgling Black press calls us to revise the notion that early Black feminism had a local effect bound by state or region (with the exception of a handful of nationally known figures) or that Black feminism had limited impact until the national club movement developed. Through the symbiotic relationship between the Black press and literary societies, early Black feminism was networked and national, transnational, and international in its reach. For example, *Freedom's Journal* distributed its "more than eight hundred issues . . . published each week" through "a network that included forty-seven authorized agents and extended from Waterloo, Ontario, to rural North Carolina, from Port-au-Prince to Liverpool to Richmond, Baltimore, and New Orleans."[62] The *A.M.E. Church Review* (Philadelphia, PA; Nashville, TN; Atlanta, GA; 1884–), in which women such as Fannie Barrier Williams, Mary V. Bass, and Mary Church Terrell published, claimed a reach that extended "to all parts of the United States, to Europe, Asia and Africa, to Canada, Nova Scotia, Bermuda, St. Thomas, British Guiana, Haity, San Domingo, and St. Croix."[63] And the San Francisco *Elevator* (1865–1898), which women's associations financially supported and which published the work of contributors such as Jennie Carter, had agents in British Columbia, Panama City, Idaho Territory, Nevada, and Oregon and "boasted of official distributors in Asia and a clientele spread over the entire Pacific" from 1865 to 1872.[64]

The Black press, which aimed to foster a national Black collectivity from its inception in 1827 with the publication of *Freedom's Journal*, relied on Black women's organizational, political, intellectual, and textual labor.[65] As Kim Gallon's overview of the Black press outlines, early newspapers such as the *Weekly Advocate* (New York, NY; 1837), later known as the *Colored American*; *Freedom's Journal*; and *The North Star* (Rochester, NY; 1847–1851) promoted a respectability politics in which women "disproportionately shouldered the duty" to conduct themselves and to promote moral values that would advance "racial progress" toward "full acceptance into the American project."[66] In addition to being the subjects of such a politics promoted in the Black press, women were also recognized by editors as their staunchest supporters because they were both avid readers and skilled organizers who conducted fund-raising campaigns to buoy fledgling newspapers. Frances Smith Foster documents that "by 1827 . . . enough African-American women could and did read newspapers that their interests affected the papers' content."[67] By the late nineteenth century, the Black press was catering to a female readership with women's columns, such as the Cleveland *Gazette*'s For the Fair Sex and Gossipy Notes on Matters Dear to the Average Feminine Heart, and with columns written by female journalists, such as Catherine Casey's and Mary Bolton's Our Women's Column in the *Christian Recorder*, Gertrude Mossell's columns for *The New York Age* (1887–1953), the *New York Freeman* (1884–1887), and *The Indianapolis World* (1883–1932); Florence Williams's The Ways of the World in *The New York Age*; Carrie Clifford's Of Interest to Women in *Alexander's Magazine* (Boston,

MS; 1905–1909); and Lillian Lews's columns in the *Washington Bee* (1882–1922), the *Boston Advocate* (1885–187?), and the *People's Advocate* (Washington, DC; 1876–1890). Women were financially underwriting the Black press with fund-raising fairs and donation campaigns in the early nineteenth century and with distribution networks and financial support from beauty culturalists in the early twentieth century.[68] Lucille (Green) Randolph, a graduate of Madame C. J. Walker's Leila Beauty College, financially backed her husband's socialist magazine *The Messenger* (New York, NY; 1917–1928) and distributed it from her Harlem beauty salon while using her earnings to pay its debts.[69] Walker and A. Philip Randolph also collaborated with other activists in founding the International League for Darker Peoples, and she facilitated the political organizing of beauty culturalists through the Madam C. J. Walker Hair Culturalists Union of America (1916) and its annual conventions.[70] Walker also provided financial support to Marcus Garvey's *Negro World* (New York, NY; 1918–1933), which advertised beauty products to readers along with movement-sponsored fashion shows and beauty contests. Beauty culturalists, models of Black entrepreneurship, formed a strong base of female membership in the Garvey movement.

Even though male editors recognized that women were key to Black press viability and the politics it promoted and even though women financed Black periodicals and underwrote Black press content and distribution through the literary societies they organized and dominated in membership, very few studies have focused on women and the Black press. Black periodical studies has produced richly detailed periodical-centric and editor-centric studies—all of which are valuable and unquestionably necessary. But such a focus also intersects with the gendering of nineteenth- and early twentieth-century newspaper work and the rarity of women in editorial roles, an intersection that inadvertently has remained quiet on the relation between Black women and the Black press.[71] Although editors took significant risks to found newspapers and magazines that benefited their immediate and broader communities, managing them often at great personal expense, they had little power to make them sustainable. Black press sustainability hinged on readers and subscribers, and Black women together with the community institutions they made possible were essential to a paper's viability.

What would centering Black women mean to Black press studies? This book proposes that recalibrating our understandings of the relation between the Black press and Black women's political and community organizing promises to help us better apprehend how important women were to this media phenomenon in its first 100 years. Despite their underrepresentation in the public records and the leadership of both the Black press and Black public politics, women are overrepresented in mutual benevolent, moral improvement, and literary societies that functioned as community centers of political, oratorical, and print culture work.[72] Sustained and sustaining collectivizing work was undertaken in these sites, and the forms of activism they supported predate by a century or more political formations such as the colored convention movement, which has long been credited with midwiving the Black press. A focus on these locations of Black collective praxis also brings into view a co-constitutive model of relation between the Black press and Black feminisms, each shaping and fostering the other. We can see just how pivotal Black women were in the development and viability of the Black press when we shift the frame of inquiry from the lives, politics, and management of particular periodicals—or the *what* of the Black press—to a focus on *how* the Black press was networked with community organizations and its affordances used.

The stories we tell of the Black press need to account for both the networked literary and benevolent societies in which Black women were dominant and the labors of Black women as readers, content producers, advertisers, and editors at both the column and periodical level. To do so calls us to think in interconnected ways about Black women's political culture and activism, about Black readers and the communal reading that lyceums and literary societies promoted, about the political consciousness members of those societies could acquire through the debates and lectures they sponsored and the production of publishable work they encouraged, and about the opportunity the Black press offered readers to enter Black print space and share in work toward achieving communal goals. Such an accounting promises to significantly enrich Black press studies.

Women's crucial role in developing and sustaining the Black press during its first century has been either vastly underestimated or largely ignored. As Martin Dann observed, the Black press was "one of the most potent arenas in which the battle for self-definition could be fought and won. . . . Indeed, black papers were usually the only source of information about the repression of the black community." The Black press rivaled only the church in its centrality to nineteenth-century Black politics and communities. Histories of its development have long cited the Black convention movement as its birthplace, those "more than 200 state and national Colored Conventions . . . held between 1830 and the 1890s," at which "an organized political response to American racism" in the form of a Black nationalist politics was formulated.[73] These conventions were led by men, many of whom were or became editors of the emergent Black press. Colored convention movement leaders did not begin seating women as delegates until the 1850s, and then they seated only "a handful."[74] Locating the birth of the Black press primarily or solely in that movement and its delegates thus excludes or marginalizes women in early Black press studies. However, foundational and new work focused on early Black print culture, African American readers and literary societies, the colored convention movement, and Black women's political culture have together laid essential groundwork for better understanding that women were crucial in several ways to the development and viability of the Black press.

In her definitive work on early African American print culture, Frances Smith Foster reminded us that "the definitions and assumptions with which one begins have a significant influence upon the story one finds." Her assertion that "early African-American print culture . . . is virtually synonymous with the Afro-Protestant press," led to an ongoing recovery of writing in Black periodicals that has changed how we study and understand nineteenth-century African American literature.[75] Yet Foster also made clear that Black print emerged from and developed within organized collectives, particularly the benevolent and mutual aid societies that were established "much earlier than the late eighteenth century," the "multicolony networks of friends and acquaintances," and the "organized literary circle[s]" that shared original literary "productions" among their members.[76] Foster called scholars of Black print to focus beyond the local and the regional on activist and literary networks across these scales.

We know from the work of Elizabeth McHenry on Black readers that such collectivities continued into the nineteenth century and operated at the same time that the colored convention movement (1830–1899) was gathering Black leaders from across the nation to debate issues relevant to Black communities. That centralized and formally organized Black political movement also raised the political necessity of a Black press. P. Gabrielle Foreman has recently underscored that the colored convention movement had a "collective, geographically expansive, and distributed structure and ethos" that informed a "foundational literary and organizing mode." The study of that movement through this lens promises to reframe understandings of "early Black print culture, Black organizing, and Black authorship."[77] Yet since the organizational collectives of literary societies were active across the country for decades beyond the colored convention movement; were accessible to all regardless of textual literacy or formal education; and were communally based but regionally and nationally networked by the Black press, which they directly supported through contributor content, circulation nodes, and direct subscription, they form a significant vector in a complex networking of political labor that made Black press emergence not only possible but viable over time. Indeed, it was "no coincidence that the rise of the African American press paralleled the development of literary societies and literary culture" and that the deeper networking of the two was operative in much more than "northern antebellum Black communities."[78]

Martha Jones's groundbreaking history of Black feminist activism in the nineteenth century, *All Bound Up Together*, conceptualized Black public culture as the "inter-relatedness of various sites of African American life" in which "a broad array of intellectual currents" flourished in "the many communal associations" fostered by "churches, political organizations, secret societies, literary clubs, and antislavery societies." Not limited to these structures, "public culture also encompassed a realm of ideas, a community of interpretation, and a collective understanding of the issues of the day."[79] Through a framework that sees public activism as shaped by intertwined and overlapping political sites and modes of debate and activism, Jones's work called us to reconsider highly gendered dichotomies that both simplify and misrepresent the development and operation of politics in Black communities, such as private versus public and politically marginalized versus institutionally organized paradigms.[80] Extending the foundation laid in the work of scholars such as Shirley Wilson Logan and Frances Smith Foster, McHenry's study of literary societies as sites of political debate argued that for women they functioned as political training grounds and that they mobilized "the pursuit of literary character" as a political strategy available to all Black community members regardless of their textual literacy.[81]

The insights of Foster, Jones, and McHenry inform the insights of The Colored Conventions Project led by Foreman, which "seeks to address—or redress—the exclusion and erasure from convention proceedings of Black women who were partners in this organizing history" through their "intellectual and infrastructure-building labor."[82] The project has documented a "veritable who's who of nineteenth-century Black print pioneers [who] served as committee chairs and speakers"[83] at conventions. Fully one-third of named attendees and organizers "had been or would become involved in [periodical] editorship" by the 1850s.[84] Such facts serve as a basis for the well-established assertion that the colored convention movement midwived the Black press.[85] Yet Foreman also sketches the contours of a decades-long synergistic relation between the movement and the "literary [and] 'moral improvement' society meetings" that "spread the word" on issues to be debated at conventions and asserts that the founding of those societies "overlapped directly with the early national conventions . . . until 1835."[86] Taken together, the work of these Black feminist scholars and others has made clear that the environment in which the Black press emerged was complex and that future work must dig deeper into what appear to be parallel and overlapping sites of Black politics and communal life if Black women's political labors and the effects of those labors on the Black press are to be understood.

Great Thinkers and Doers argues that the Black periodical press was viable because of the significant organizational, political, emotional and intellectual labor women undertook in mutual benevolent societies, literary societies and lyceums. It also argues that the relation developed between the Black press and Black feminisms was co-constitutive, each enabling and shaping the other. As a media form with characteristics, practices, and genres, the Black periodical can be understood as a constitutive technology for Black feminisms. As readers, editors, advertisers, and contributors to the Black press, Black women used press seriality, reprinting, page layout, press forms, and illustration in deliberate ways to gain a national, transnational, and international reach for Black feminisms. As they did so, they shaped Black press forms, fostered Black press sustainability, and networked Black collectivist political sites with and through the Black press, thus shaping what Black periodicals offered their readers.

The Black press can be approached as more than an archive of early Black print culture or of Black feminist content, in other words, by considering how readers, column writers, contributors, advertisers, and editors used the media form, its particular genres, and its journalistic practices. The importance of doing so is underscored by Jonathan Senchyne's observation that "information labor . . . tends to disappear behind the information it transmits."[87] Consequently, I take up Dallas Liddle's encouragement to "follow the genre" as a methodology for periodical study. This method can reveal something of how and why Black women used press forms in ways that differ from or exceed usual journalistic or editorial practice. Liddle's questions are incisive: "What does the genre do, exactly, and what does that function lead the periodical to do? As we search for a better model for understanding the periodical press, those are surely the questions to ask."[88] Considering how Black feminist uses of press genres disrupted standard practice is crucial, given that Black women's entry into the print public sphere was not an individualist act underwritten by the economic, as Benedict Anderson's print-capitalism thesis would have it; instead, it was an achievement of "positive collective incorporation" for African Americans that was underwritten by the social.[89] The dual disruption early Black feminists pose to both standard journalistic practice in their own day and to commonplace assertions in periodical studies in our day is unsurprising given that their mobilization of Black periodicals for liberatory and collectivist purposes had to contend with a legacy of enslavement, liberal individualism, and racial capitalism that was facilitated by and financially enabled both the media form in the United States and the ongoing functioning of white supremacist settler colonialism.[90]

Studying the co-constitutive relation between the Black press and Black feminisms also requires attending to the broader media ecology through which the Black press developed and was networked. Black women's organizational and leadership skills multiplied the number of literary and benevolent societies across the country, and for more than a century those societies produced and sustained a readership, subscribers, financial supporters, content producers, distribution nodes, and a mode of circulation for the Black press. These societies reached out across the nation and into geographies that were central to imaginings of Black freedom, such as Canada West, Liberia, and Haiti. Black press editors understood the importance of these societies to African Americans and thus to the viability of their papers, devoting space on the page to their founding and activities.

Further study of the importance of literary and benevolent societies to the Black press, particularly in its first century, is made newly possible by the digitization of historical Black newspapers. Even though such digitization projects have made for an incomplete and often paywalled compendium of newspapers published by and for African Americans, they have much to offer our developing understanding of both Black public culture, as Martha Jones defines it, and conditions of possibility for the Black press. Black women also translated the commitments of a broader Black collective that was debated in such societies to varied forms of politics in the nineteenth and early twentieth centuries, including those centered on abolition, temperance, woman's rights, suffrage, anti-lynching, desegregation of public transportation, Black nationalism and internationalism, critiques of racial capitalism, and the multipronged activism the Black women's club movement pursued.

Understanding a media ecology, as Ann Ardis stressed when she raised its importance for periodical study, "depends . . . on scrupulous attention to both the materiality of print and its intermedial relationships with other communication technologies—even when, especially when, we allow historical data to 'disrupt and reconfigure' long standing historical generalizations . . . and conceptual or theoretical or genre paradigms."[91] An attention to the media ecology in which both the Black press and Black feminisms developed informs my approach in at least three ways: in the larger inquiry posed by the book that suggests that a focus on Black women will disrupt and reconfigure the stories we tell about the

Black press, Black public politics, and Black organizing; in the conceptual paradigm of Black feminist recirculation that looks at how literary societies mobilized the intermedial relation of the oratorical to the print-textual; and in the method I employ of following the genre and attending to the affordances of the periodical in order to understand how the Black press and Black feminisms were co-constituted, even as the media form's ability to adequately represent Black life and imagined Black futures was necessarily under question. My methodology suggests and models reading protocols that tend to diverge from those operative in the field of periodical studies. I also take seriously Carla Peterson's call for scholars to employ an "approach that encourages speculation and resists closure," an approach necessary for studying the lives and work of Black women in the nineteenth century given the lack of documentation that makes "speculation . . . the only alternative to silence, secrecy and invisibility."[92] *Great Thinkers and Doers* is organized around broad areas of concern that would benefit from further attention in both Black press and periodical studies: Black press viability and its conditions; the politicization of press genres and practices to meet the needs of Black public politics, including Black feminisms; and the disruptions that race and racialization pose to the media form and its affordances. I offer suggestions toward what is ultimately a beginning, and begin we must with a renewed focus on Black women in future considerations of how the Black press operated and was used by the people it sought to represent.

Black Press Viability

Nineteenth-century Black newspapers struggled with near-constant financial precarity. Often in print for short periods of time, sometimes for as little as a month, Black papers depended on advance subscription while editors worked to strengthen circulation figures that could ensure ongoing publication or generate advertising sales and revenue.[93] As William Still's 1855 letter to Mary Ann Shadd, editor of the *Provincial Freeman* (Windsor, Toronto, Chatham, Canada West; 1853–1860), highlights, their viability was fragile: "How you have thus long and well succeeded, to me is a matter of wonder. As I glance over the wrecks which have marked the career of not a few of the 'sterner sex' . . . in almost every instance those enterprises have hopelessly failed ere they had existed twelve months—indeed most of them before six months."[94] Shadd kept the *Provincial Freeman* in print for an astounding seven years when, as Jane Rhodes observes, "the only black newspapers that survived this period in the United States were those with strong support from white abolitionists and philanthropists, like *Frederick Douglass'*

Paper [Rochester, NY; 1851–1860], or from established institutions, like the A.M.E. Church."[95] Distribution was also challenging, since venues such as "periodical depots, book stores, and street vendors," were "closed to Black periodicals" in a racially segregated media economy.[96] Through their organization of and participation in literary, moral improvement, and benevolent societies, Black women directly supported the Black press with written content, with a ready readership who did not need to be textually literate, with funds they raised to financially support Black papers and their editors, and with organizations that could function to distribute Black periodicals in their communities. Members of such societies might first encounter a newspaper at their meetings, where they also became familiar with particular titles, and societies would adopt a paper as their "organ." For any Black periodical, growing the readership could increase both per-copy circulation figures and subscription rates, both of which were necessary if a paper was to be viable. For example, the *Christian Recorder*'s weekly production cost estimates in 1865 indicate the need for over 4,000 paid subscriptions or "over 173,000 single-copy sales."[97]

Nineteenth-century Black newspapers typically offered their readers local news and (if their circulation was large enough) correspondent columns with news from other cities or states alongside "clipped" or reprinted content from their exchanges with papers that were owned and edited by both white and Black colleagues. The practice of agreeing to send or exchange free copy of one's paper with another editor formed the basis of reprinting, "offer[ing] editors across the nation local news and commentary they might otherwise never see." Editors also listed their exchanges, since they offered "reputational value."[98] Local news was often focused on local organizations—literary societies, fraternal orders, schools, churches—and social happenings, through which editors pursued a strategy of increasing local circulation by naming community members and community associations.[99] Some early Black newspapers, such as the New York–based *Colored American*, focused their local and regional news content largely on literary and benevolent societies, and societies tended either to adopt a newspaper as their "chief organ" or to create their own paper.[100]

As McHenry has documented, African American literary societies were multifaceted in both their actions and effects. "They organized discussion groups and supported libraries and reading rooms. Some instructed beginning readers, while others supported those more advanced. Literary societies planned reading lists and schedules; they provided regular opportunities for authors to 'publish' original literary creations and for audiences to encourage, discuss, and criticize their ideas and presentation."[101] At their meetings one could expect to hear members read aloud both these original pieces and published newspaper content. Many a Black paper filled a regular column or more with content created in these spaces or with reports on their gatherings.[102]

Literary societies and lyceums were also sites through which Black women mobilized a praxis of recirculation. As chapter 1 argues, recirculation was a central tool of early Black feminism. This practice was more than reprinting, repurposing, or making a text move again beyond its originally intended circulatory network or in a form that was different from the original.[103] Rather, Black feminists engaged in a deliberate and self-reflexive circulation of both oral and written texts through the feedback loop they established between literary societies and the Black press these societies fostered. In turn, the Black press was able to tap into the circulatory matrix that developed out of the communal reading practices in these societies to reach a community of readers they may not have otherwise reached. Black feminists used recirculation with a political intent and effect that exceeded reprinting as a journalistic practice and enabled Black women's politics at times to "go viral."

Literary societies were active into the mid-twentieth century. They were networked both geographically and with formal political organizations; and for at least a century, literary societies maintained vital links to a Black press that enabled this networking and that they, in turn, sustained financially. Through the literary societies Black women often organized and dominated in membership, they did more than simply support the Black press as readers or as members of societies that made the emergent Black press possible and viable. Black women also understood that their politics could be advanced through the symbiotic relation between those societies and the Black press.

Politicizing Press Genres

Much as literary societies functioned as political training grounds for Black women, operating as a sort of gateway to political debate and expression as I establish in chapter 1, periodicals offered genres that functioned as gateways to public presence in print. Letters to the editor were a gateway genre for Black women in the early Black press, as evidenced by their use. Because African Americans entered the public sphere through social and collectivist forms of incorporation, I suggest in chapters 2 and 3 that studying their letters to the editor call for different reading protocols than are typically used for this press genre. Together, taking this genre as a gateway press form for Black women and reading it as registering collective concerns motivates these chapters' consideration of how such letters made Black place by asserting Black presence.

Chapter 2 argues that working in Black periodical studies with a key institution of American democracy and the public sphere, as letters to the editor are often understood, requires protocols of reading that bring collective relations and communal interests to the surface.[104] Data visualization is one such practice that can demonstrate why shifting away from the print-capitalism thesis or reading this press form as serving the individual—whether editor or reader—would mean that we stop reaffirming liberal individualism as a technology of white supremacy and settler colonialism. This chapter maps the national reach of Black feminist politics from 1827 through the mid-1870s and argues that Black women's letters to the editor function as what Judith Madera calls a "circulating commons" that enabled Black feminism to be organized "by the circulation of discourse."[105]

Chapter 3 turns the focus to the *Southern Workman* (Hampton, VA; 1872–1939), which was produced by freedpeople and captive Indigenous students resident at Hampton Normal and Agricultural Institute. Letters to the editor written by Hampton students and graduates, however primed their writing may have been by school authority figures, contest notions of mobility and autonomy underwriting investments in liberal ideas of freedom that existed in name only for all but those privileged by the settler-colonial state at the time. To apprehend Black and Indigenous uses of this press form as challenges to white supremacist settler-colonial space-as-possession, a reading protocol that focuses on collectives and collective place making in print is again required, together with a close-reading protocol of what such letters communicated. My reading of Indigenous and African American students' and graduates' letters in this chapter takes seriously that Black feminist politics as social justice struggle develops not only through a co-constitutive relation with the Black press but also in the context of the US nation-state's foundational and formative exercise of genocide and slavery as "interrelated fatalities."[106]

Periodical Disruptions

Reading for collective concerns matters to Black periodical scholarship, which has underscored the role of the Black press in facilitating an imagining of collective relations that were not confined to the nation-state,[107] that were "mobile, continually transforming,"[108] and that were theorized as practices of citizenship.[109] Black women's politicizing of press forms and practices not only pursued Black collective interests and aims but were disruptive in their collectivizing effect. Their harnessing of the media's seriality for their politics of recirculation and their collectivizing of an individualist genre such as the letter to the editor continued in Black women's early twentieth-century innovations with the column that I examine in chapter 4. The development of women's columns and advertising that targeted women are often cited in periodical scholarship as evidence that editors were keenly aware of women readers as a vital part of their market and one they courted actively. But these developments have a distinctive resonance where the Black press is concerned because of the intersection of sociopolitical, media, and economic phenomena. Established historiographies of African American feminism, the Black press, Black women's journalism, and cultures of Black internationalism each emphasize that the early twentieth century was a pivotal moment. The growth of the Black press, African American labor and migration, the Black women's club movement, and the nationalisms and allied internationalisms that emerged from World War I entailed unique conditions for each, but rarely are these developments considered together, even though they clearly intersect in the praxis of Black women. To consider that intersection, chapter 4 focuses on the columns that Jessie Fauset edited in the NAACP's magazine *The Crisis* (New York, NY; 1910–) and Amy Jacques Garvey edited in the UNIA's newspaper *Negro World*.

Fauset's and Jacques Garvey's columns disrupted the expected practices of that press genre in order to pursue the imperatives of adversarial internationalisms. Fauset's reprinting and juxtaposition in layout and Jacques Garvey's collage column, which called for reader collaboration and drew on reprinting, placed the conditions of "the Negro" in an international frame, heightened their readers' political consciousness while shifting its spatial orientation, and internationalized Black feminisms. Their innovations expanded the geopolitics of the interracial and Black nationalist movements that their periodicals represented and underscored the inextricable links between race-based oppression, capitalism, patriarchy, and the rise of new nationalisms. Each did much more than steady the rudder at these periodicals while their male editors, W. E. B. Du Bois and Marcus Garvey, were overseas or incarcerated.

Chapter 5 continues to explore how Black female editors pursued a praxis of disruption by examining Pauline Hopkins's editorial work from 1900 to 1904 at *The Colored American Magazine*. To do so, this chapter returns to the slave system's foundational underwriting of the periodical as a media form in the United States. The logics and rhetorics of slavery advertising that the newspaper as a media form depended on from its inception posed particular challenges to the liberatory possibilities Black editors, readers, artists and journalists could realize through its pages. Yet periodical studies has not adequately acknowledged or grappled with this fact, even though many working in the field think carefully about the ways newspapers and magazines can be used to articulate, shape, and mobilize Black politics in varied locations and time periods. This is arguably part of a larger tendency, sharply observed by Brigitte Fielder and Jonathan Senchyne, of "book history and studies of print and digital cultures to ignore their intersections with race and, more specifically, with African American craft and expression."[110] Such intersections are a pressing issue for American periodical studies, all the more so at a time when the field more broadly has been pursuing questions of a common methodology and how to more deeply theorize its objects of study. Chapter 5 proposes that the inflection of such questions through a future-oriented and digital vocabulary has risked ignoring the disruptions Black geographies and Black temporality pose to liberal and neoliberal possessive and extractive logics and epistemologies. Attention to those disruptions instead suggests that we consider how Black periodicals and their editors may have pursued a double rendition of economies of representation and trafficking, such that representing African Americans in their full humanity and achievement necessarily carried with it the legacy of the media's imagery once designed to secure their enslaved status. To do so will raise hard but vital questions for the reliance of periodical studies on a print-capitalism understanding of the media form or its theorizing that the primary drivers of print were economic.

Pauline Hopkins's editorial choices, including the deliberate intermediations she mobilized between *The Colored American Magazine*'s cover design, its content, and its photographic illustration, encouraged readers to consider how social understandings that facilitated projects of domination were scripted through press genres and racializing press iconography. In particular, her series of "race women" portraits pointedly countered New Negro politics and investments and used technological advancements, such as photographic reproduction and illustration, at the same time she called for attention to both the media form's persisting logics and an enduring racial capitalism.

Conductors on the New Underground Railway

Great Thinkers and Doers closes with attention to financial viability as it impacts the realization of Black feminist and leftist political aims by focusing on Charlotta Bass's editorship of the *California Eagle* (Los Angeles, CA; 1879–1966) from 1912 to 1951 and placing it in conversation with Beatrice Cannady's editorship of the Portland *Advocate* (1903–1936) from 1912 to 1933. The hallmarks of Bass's political work seem as attuned to our own climate as they were to mid-twentieth-century Los Angeles and well worth studying for that alone. With Bass at the helm, the *Eagle* was the largest Black weekly on the West Coast. By the 1940s, it was also under federal surveillance as a subversive influence because of her political campaigns and her allyship with Latinx Angelinos and agricultural laborers in the state. Bass had proven that her columns and the newspaper itself could be very effective tools for mobilizing citizens, workers, and voters. The *Eagle* had also become a stone that threatened to sink Bass by May 1948, when the Los Angeles Newspaper Guild informed her of complaints that she was underpaying some staff and violating guild hiring practices. The book's larger questions of how Black women pursued collectivist politics in and through the Black press and how Black press viability was affected by their labors are central in Bass's editorial career. As Bass said in her regular column On the Sidewalk in 1941, marrying liberatory politics with newspaper work meant one had to be "prepared to have their heads cracked, their hopes frustrated, and their financial strength weakened."[111] Turning to her work alongside Cannady's enables us to consider the challenges Black women faced politically and financially as businesswomen in Black media, which in turn will impact how we understand Black women to be a force in the Black press.

Chapter One

Recirculation and African American Feminisms

In early December 1893, *The Parsons Weekly Blade* (Parsons, KS; 1892–1900) reprinted "An Able Paper by Mrs. Pryor Read Before the Bishop Worthington Lyceum," which originally ran in the Omaha *Enterprise* (1893–1914). Readers in Parsons, Kansas, and throughout the *Blade*'s circulation network were clearly interested in goings-on in a Nebraska literary society, judging from the two columns of four above the fold given to this address.[1] In her speech, Mrs. Pryor indicted African American men for insulting their mothers: "What is the matter with women of the Negro race who have toiled from morn till night, that you sons might learn to wield the pen which you now use as an instrument of attack upon her?" Pryor did not let up: "If you would spend less of your time standing on the corner with your hands in your pockets, blowing some political horn . . . and more of your time with your families, perusing with them the best books and papers obtainable . . . you would see less to find fault with." Her defense of Black womanhood touted exemplary models: "Franc[e]s E. W. Harper, A. E. Johnson, Prof. Mary V. Cook, Misses Ida B. Wells, V[ictoria] E[arle] Matthews, Lillian Lewis, A[melia] L. Tilghman, Henrietta Vinton Davis, Martha B. Briggs—deceased, Hallie Q[uinn] Brown, Katie D. Chapman, and a host of others whom I might mention[,] but time bids me hasten."[2] Of the eleven women Pryor lauded, seven were journalists, editors, or both (Johnson, Cook, Wells, Matthews, Lewis, Tilghman, and Chapman); five were nationally and internationally famous as public speakers, writers, and activists (Harper, Wells, Matthews, Davis, and Brown); and all would be said now to be feminist in their politics and their activist commitments to woman's rights, suffrage, education, Black nationalism, and the Black women's club movement.

In that roll call, Pryor reminded her audience that the Black press, literary societies, and Black feminisms were inextricably linked. A year after Pryor's 1893 address, Ida B. Wells visited Omaha to organize an Anti-Lynching League branch.[3] Wells's career as an internationally recognized anti-lynching activist was made possible because Black feminists such as Victoria Earle Matthews, Maritcha Lyons, Susan Smith McKinney, Gertrude Mossell, and Josephine St. Pierre Ruffin had galvanized Black women through New York literary societies to raise over $600 to support Wells's spring 1893 anti-lynching lecture tour in the United Kingdom and the resumption of the *Free Speech and Headlight* in Memphis (1888–1892), the offices of which a white mob, angered by Wells's editorials, had burned to the ground.[4] In 1895, Omaha's Ella Mahammitt was elected vice-president representing the West of the newly formed National Federation of Afro-American Women; she would edit the *Enterprise* after her husband purchased it in 1896.[5] These links between Pryor's address to the Bishop Worthington Lyceum in Omaha, its recirculation in the Black press, and the feminist political organizing that swirled around it is far from coincidental; rather, they manifest the circulatory matrix through which both the Black press and Black feminisms were continuing to develop.

Black women formed the bedrock of both African American literary societies and the fledgling Black press. From the appearance of the earliest Black and abolitionist papers onward, Black women made use of the press in distinctive ways to create and galvanize publics for their concerns and to supply newspapers with a range of content, including addresses such as Pryor's. They did so through literary societies and lyceums that created a nexus of orality, reading, and print publication linking African American communities across the nation, a nexus that also mobilized the Black feminist practice of recirculation. Black women used recirculation, enabled by a feedback loop established between literary societies and the abolitionist and Black presses, to pursue their politics on diverse issues such as education, colonization and emigration, labor, and Black nationalism. Black feminism was networked through its co-constitutive relation with the Black press, and recirculation enabled Black feminism to go viral at times. This chapter argues that as readers and writers, African American women played a foundational role in the development and sustainability of the Black periodical press; that they did so through their membership in literary societies and their politicized use of the press, in particular their use of recirculation; and that an analysis of this co-constitutive relation between the Black press and Black feminism is long overdue.

For Black feminist politics, the collectivizing "literary character" promoted by literary societies was key, as was their value of shared reading that meant "the power of formal or individualized literacy" was not prioritized over knowledge held and shared within the community.[6] Widely conceived to include both reading and listening to texts read aloud, literary societies did not require members to be textually literate and they were not restricted to a Black elite, as Frances Smith Foster, Shirley Logan, and Elizabeth McHenry have stressed. In fact, the oral presentation of texts was central to the program of any literary society, and Black literary societies were open to all. The praxis of literary societies linked the twinned rhetorical forces of nineteenth-century American civic life—oratory and print—in the development of Black politics generally and Black feminism particularly. As Maisha Fisher clarifies, for African American communities, "orality is a major force for literacy."[7]

This imbrication of oratory and print also highlights the importance of recirculation for the development of Black women's political culture in the early decades of the nineteenth century. I use the term "recirculation" to distinguish these women's deliberate and self-reflexive circulation of texts from literary societies through the Black press and back into literary societies as distinctive from the journalistic practice of reprinting.[8] I also use recirculation to mean more than circulating texts through informal networks of readers, clipping texts for scrapbooks or memory books, or repurposing or excerpting one text within another, each of which is an operative definition of the term for other scholars working in Black print culture studies.[9] Recirculation as a central tool of early Black feminism is more than making a text move again beyond its originally intended circulatory network or its originally intended form, which is understood as remediation. Rather, Black feminists deliberately cultivated a feedback loop and circulatory matrix *for political purposes* between African American literary societies and the Black press they fostered, which developed out of communal reading practices that gave African Americans ways to participate in the political debates directly affecting them, regardless of whether they were textually literate or not. Recirculation enabled Black feminist politics and publics at a time when African Americans were barred from full participation in the democratic public life of the nation and when that national public was hostile not only to Black freedom and its exercise but to Black life itself.

Black women's literary societies cultivated the recirculation of writings, lectures, and addresses outward from their organizations to newspapers that published them. These published pieces were then circulated back into other literary societies, where they were read to new audiences. Those new audiences might debate what they read orally or in print and the results of such debate could circulate again in published form through other newspapers and literary societies. This feedback loop between literary societies and the newspaper press enabled recirculation, which not only amplified a developing Black feminist politics but also constituted what Dilip Parmeshwar Gaonkar and Elizabeth Povinelli call a "circulatory matrix . . . through which new discursive forms, practices, and artifacts carry out their routine ideological labor of constituting subjects who can be summoned in the name of a public or a people."[10] The result was the naturalization of Black feminist thought and argument and the active creation of a public for whom such texts were recognizable within a political culture that called women to listen to, read, debate, or create their own "original productions."

Given that the earliest African American women's literary societies also provided the abolitionist and Black press with content, these were also sites through which women quickly came to apprehend the press as an important political tool and to use what Michael Warner calls its "reflexivity in the circulation of texts among strangers." The readers of their "original contributions" became "a social entity," a public that comes to "exist *by virtue of being addressed*."[11] Notably for these women, the distinctly African American communal reading practice of sharing printed texts orally together with the circulatory matrix formed between women's literary societies and the press meant they could capitalize upon "the sense that ongoing discussion [was] unfold[ing] in a sphere of activity."[12] Black women harnessed that circulatory matrix not only to recirculate their politics but also to actively shape "new forms of subjectivity and identity" for women in their communities.[13] In doing so, they exercised what Warner has called a "new, creative, and distinctly modern mode of power," the "projection of a public" for whom women came to be seen as necessary political agents.[14]

Recirculation: Making Black Feminist Publics

African American feminists understood their use of recirculation as a constitutive act. They capitalized on the ways African Americans readers used the press. Frankie Hutton estimates that the circulation of most Black newspapers from 1827 to 1860 ranged from 1,500 to 3,000, but the actual readership of such papers was "considerably wider," due to the prevalent practice of sharing newspapers within a community. Some editors of Black papers at this time estimated that for every "100 copies of the paper" an average of "1,000 readers" existed who were accessing the paper through local lending practices.[15] Communal reading was particularly common in the South, where newspapers were routinely read aloud to people gathered in barbershops.[16] African American communities across the country "did not valorize the power of formal or individualized literacy over communal knowledge."[17] As a correspondent for the *Christian Recorder* (Philadelphia, PA) wrote in 1877 from St. Joseph, Missouri, "Fathers and mothers that cannot read, when the day's work is done, press the school children or some friend into service and the *Recorder* is read in the family circle. The sayings of the different writers are commented on, the news is discussed, and pleasant, instructive evenings are spent."[18] Circulating texts through shared or communal reading practices did more than broaden the audience they reached, it contributed to even as it was fostered by Black collectivist politics and horizontal relations.

The circulation enabled by these communal reading practices was part of a media environment that included what Meredith McGill has called an American "culture of reprinting," in which texts "achieve[d] a remarkable mobility across elite and mass-cultural formats" and across regions of the nation. Periodicals actively exchanged and reprinted material ranging from literature to news items (both national and foreign), often stripped of signature and offered anonymously, in an elaborate market of unauthorized republication that was driven by republican values of decentralized power and the democratization of knowledge. But perhaps the most noteworthy effect of reprinting was its elevation of "local affairs to national prominence, which gave "writing by socially marginal authors a powerful cultural presence."[19]

Black feminists who saw the press as an important political tool used its reflexivity, which Michael Warner conceives of as "developed . . . through reviews, reprintings, citations, controversies. These forms single out circulation both through their sense of temporality and through the way they allow discourse to move in different directions." For Warner, the "punctual rhythm of circulation" produces a sense of vital debate, and that sense of debate was particularly heightened for Black communities by both the overlap of a national culture of reprinting with communal reading practices and the symbiotic relation of literary societies and the Black press.[20] Together such reflexivity offered Black feminists the unprecedented opportunity and means to create both a public and a politics that were national and at times international in scope. Here theories of circulation prove helpful for understanding texts and their circulation as not simply communicating arguments or positions but as actively making and shaping a politics. For Benjamin Lee and Edward LiPuma, "circulation and exchange have been seen as processes that *transmit* meanings, rather than as constitutive acts in themselves."[21] Understanding early Black feminism as co-constitutive with the Black press entails understanding recirculation both as deliberately mobilized by Black feminists to create publics and as capable of shaping these publics to be self-aware of their position within a larger whole. It is far from coincidental that this is analogous to the ways that theories of periodical and newspaper readership have posited a shared readerly self-consciousness constituted by the regular rhythm of sitting down to read the paper.[22] In that sense, recirculation as a series of repeated acts shaped Black feminist consciousness just as it enabled Black feminists to shape both a Black public consciousness and the Black press itself. Black feminists' advocacy of women's education and emigration in the Black and radical abolitionist press further clarifies these connections upon which activists such as Sarah Mapps Douglass, Sarah Forten, and Maria Stewart capitalized.

Women's Education: "Time for us to be up and doing"

Education not only drew women to literary societies but was one of the earliest communal values Black women advocated for through the circulatory matrix that linked their societies and the Black press. In the late summer of 1827, Amy Matilda Cassey, a founding member of the Philadelphia Female Literary Association (PFLA) and Philadelphia's Gilbert Lyceum (1841), signed herself "Matilda" in a letter to *Freedom's Journal* that argued for women's education. Cassey's circle included reformers such as "[William Lloyd] Garrison, James McCune Smith, Lucy Stone, William Whipper, Sarah Mapps Douglass, Sarah Forten, Frederick Douglass, Margaretta Forten, Robert Purvis, Rebecca Buffum, and Wendell Phillips."[23] "Matilda's" letter opens by indicting the paper for not having "said sufficient upon the education of females," a daring move given that at this time *Freedom's Journal* was publishing pieces chastising women who did not hold their tongues.[24] She continued, "I hope you are not to be classed with those who think that our mathematical knowledge should be limited to '*fathoming the dish-kettle*,' and that we have acquired enough of history, if we know that our grandfather's father lived and died." In what would become a refrain in women's contributions to the press and to their literary societies, "Matilda" argued that a woman's influence over children and spouse "demands that our minds should be instructed and improved with the *principles of education and religion*. . . . There is a great responsibility resting somewhere, and it is time for us to be up and doing."[25] Cassey's letter raised the topic of Black women's education for a readership that editors John Russwurm and Samuel Cornish were actively cultivating as a national collective: "It is our earnest wish to make our Journal a medium of intercourse between our brethren in the different states of this great confederacy."[26] She did so two years before David Walker cast the acquisition of learning by African Americans as a radically emancipatory and threatening act in his *Appeal*, writing that "the bare name of educating the coloured people scares our cruel oppressor almost to death."[27]

Women such as "Beatrice" similarly argued before their literary societies that "woman has a high destiny to fulfill" in "the domestic circle . . . requir[ing] extensive exertions . . . call[ing] for strict attention, on her part to the benefits of a good education."[28] Signing herself A., Sarah Forten published a contribution to the PFLA in *The Liberator* (Boston, MA; 1831–1865) that couched the value of a "well educated female" in an "influence" and "power" she characterized as "absolute."[29] Forten, under her pen names A., Ada, and Magawisca, contributed "over a dozen poems and essays to several different newspapers between 1831 and 1837."[30] In the fall of 1837 and at the age of eleven, Elizabeth Jennings delivered from memory her mother's essay "On the Improvement of the Mind" at the third anniversary of the Ladies' Literary Society of New York, which her mother Elizabeth Jennings Sr. had cofounded. The *Colored American* (New York, NY; 1837–1842) reprinted it, along with the meeting's order of exercises and a recommendation to enroll in the society: "Now is a momentous time, a time that calls us to exert all our powers, and among the many of them, *the mind is the greatest*," she argued. "Why sleep thus? Awake and slumber no more—arise, put on your armor, ye daughters of America, and stand forth in the field of improvement. . . . The mind is powerful, and by its efforts your influence may be as near perfection."[31] These women were joined by others whose contributions to their literary societies were published by *The Liberator* in the 1830s.[32] Women's education was not raised in Black public politics until 1834, when delegates to the annual colored convention in New York praised Prudence Crandall for converting her Canterbury, Connecticut, school to a high school for Black "ladies and misses" after white parents pulled their daughters from the school because Crandall had enrolled a Black pupil.[33]

Maria Stewart, hailed as the first American woman orator, joined these calls for women's education. Born with free status, Stewart was indentured until the age of fifteen. Her husband, shipping agent Thomas Stewart, was an associate of David Walker and died under mysterious circumstances in 1829, leaving Stewart to be "swindled . . . out of her inheritance" by white businessmen and forced to return to domestic service.[34] While supporting herself, Stewart wrote what scholars have taken to be her first published essay, "Cause for Encouragement." "Cause" was, in fact, a letter to the editor written in response to the *Liberator*'s "account of the 'Second Annual Convention of the People of Color,' held in Philadelphia June 4–15, 1832." It critiqued a political event and movement, open only to Black men at the time, that sought to establish the Black press as an arm of Black public politics.[35] Women's literary societies were also playing an important role in the emergence of women in the newspaper press through this genre, supporting them as they wrote letters or "communications" to newspaper editors. The PFLA was the seedbed for Sarah Forten's March 14, 1831, letter under the pen name Magawisca to Garrison, who published it under the title "The Abuse of Liberty." The same is true of Sarah Mapps Douglass's "Extract from a Letter," signed with her pen name Sophanisba, which appeared immediately under Stewart's "Cause for Encouragement."[36] Both bore the notation "For the Liberator."

If we recenter African American literary societies in their foundational and sustaining role in Black periodical culture and keep in sight that these societies were predominantly female spaces and political training grounds, the importance of understanding someone like Maria Stewart as influenced by this becomes clear. Although at present we know that Stewart joined a literary society in New York City after she left Boston in 1833, it is worth considering that she may well have belonged to one during the late 1820s and early 1830s or to a benevolent or antislavery society, as she was becoming highly visible politically.[37] Michelle Garfield's contention that "the rise of the black intellectual and literary movement" was facilitated by the constellation of *Freedom's Journal* (1827–1829), David Walker's *Appeal* (1829), and Stewart's *Religion and the Pure Principles of Morality* (1831) is very helpful in understanding the co-constitutive relation between Stewart's activism, the Black press, Black print culture, and literary societies.[38]

David Walker acted as the Boston agent for *Freedom's Journal*, a paper that had the full support of the Massachusetts General Colored Association, which met in his apartment at 81 Joy Street until 1830, when the Walkers moved out and their friends, Stewart and her husband, took up residence.[39] Walker's pamphlet was an incendiary publication not simply because he found ways to smuggle it into the proslavery South but also because the Southern press wrote about its covert circulation, raised anxiety over its ability to foment rebellion, and thereby performatively created the very public it worried Walker's pamphlet would galvanize. It is striking that Stewart's public career began when three factors arguably enabled her notoriety: Walker's pamphlet had already achieved a sort of viral effect; literary societies were very quickly establishing the imbrication of reading, oratory, and writing for Black women's politics; and women in those societies and in print were consistently advocating for Black women's education.

Women such as Amy Matilda Cassey, Maria Stewart, and Elizabeth Jennings Sr. argued for women's education by positioning their political intervention as the result of their readerly disposition and by amplifying their individual signatures or voices as collective. One way they did so was to echo phrasing in a sort of call-and-response across their work. As Martha Jones has observed, Stewart echoed Cassey's sarcasm—Black women limited to "fathoming the dish-kettle"—when in 1831 she scoffed at Black women being "compelled to bury their minds and talents beneath a load of iron pots and kettles."[40] In her 1832 "Cause for Encouragement," Stewart wrote Garrison using another sarcastic domestic metaphor for Black women's condition: "Many bright and intelligent ones are in the midst of us; but because they are not calculated to display a classical education, they hide their talent behind a napkin."[41] We might also hear an echo of Cassey's "principles of education and religion" in Stewart's *Religion and the Pure Principles of Morality*. And in 1837, Jennings Sr. echoed Stewart's 1831 call "O you daughters of Africa, awake! awake! arise! no longer sleep nor slumber, but distinguish yourselves. Show forth to the world that ye are endowed with noble and exalted faculties" with her "Why sleep thus? Awake and slumber no more." Letters Black women wrote to newspaper editors may well have been composed in the collaborative environment of literary societies, such as the letter "A Colored Lady in Medford" wrote on slavery that was published in *The Liberator* in April 1831, or the letter May wrote on emancipation that was published in late October 1832.[42] Letters to the editor effectively stage civic debate by presenting a position on an issue, assuming and thereby performatively creating an engaged public through the act of address.[43] These women's letters created the authority they claimed for Black women's voices and civic identity within the larger collective.

A letter like Maria Stewart's "Cause," which advocated for women's education as she centered religion in the work of racial uplift, repeated a refrain offered in newspapers such as the *Colored American* and *Freedom's Journal* that promoted literary societies as routes to self-improvement and to corrective Black representation, both of which were understood as essential to race advancement and abolition. A "Short Address; Read at a 'Mental Feast,' by a Young Lady of Color," was published in the May 11, 1833, edition of *The Liberator*, a year after Stewart's "Cause." It argued that in order "to elevate our condition, and alleviate our brethren in bondage from the bitter and galling yoke," all African Americans—including women called to "arise . . . and resolve"—must be educated or "enlighten[ed] in literature and knowledge."[44] By stressing women's intelligence despite their lack of access to formal education, these women implicitly raised and answered the question of where they might develop that intelligence. As McHenry has contended, "Before formal education opportunities became available for Black women, literary societies served as [an] . . . invaluable means of educating Black women beyond what was considered their 'proper sphere.'"[45] Female literary societies were another way to consider Stewart's napkin and Cassey's dish kettle: they provided the cover for Black women's education when political organizations such as the Black convention movement were focused on formal education for Black men.[46]

Such calls for women's education developed in women's literary societies and moved outward through the circulatory matrix that continued to grow between newspapers and literary societies, joining women's letters, addresses, and poetry on emancipation and slavery that were part of a larger collective discourse on freedom and the rights of "the race" pursued in women's literary societies.[47] When these calls for women's education were recirculated in *Freedom's Journal*, they reached a national and transnational readership. In the *Colored American*, they reached "at least eighteen hundred" subscribers and "more than ten thousands" of readers in the Caribbean Basin and the United States ("more than three-fourths [of] . . . our own people"). In *The Liberator*, they reached a predominantly Black readership, since 80 percent of its initial 450 subscribers were free African Americans and Black "organizations, churches, [and] societies,"[48] including readers from the eastern United States, up the coast to New Brunswick, and across the Atlantic into the United Kingdom.[49]

Garrison, who envisioned *The Liberator* as a forum for Black activists and an interracial political coalition, represented the free Northern African American community as organized and politically active by reporting on their meetings. But calls for Black women's education also reached readers in the South. Garrison made a deliberate use of reprinting to heighten the sense of his paper's impact, as Henry Mayer documents: "Southern editors not only saw the paper but reprinted material from it—accompanied by bitter condemnation—which was then picked up by other papers and eventually worked over again by Garrison in a lively cycle that . . . enabled *The Liberator* to make a noise out of proportion to its size or subscription base."[50] In fact, as Augusta Rorbach notes, he sent *The Liberator* to Southern papers to fuel this cycle.[51] By the time Stewart's letter calling for Black women's access to education was published in the paper, the effects of the *Liberator*'s virality were evident. Georgetown had passed a law prohibiting free African Americans from picking up copies of the paper at the post office and imposed a

$25 fine and thirty days' imprisonment for those who did so. If unable to pay the fine, they would be "sold into slavery for four months." The *National Intelligencer* (Washington, DC; 1800–1870) called for the paper's suppression. A Raleigh, North Carolina, jury indicted Garrison and his partner Isaac Knapp for distributing incendiary material. A vigilance association in Columbia, South Carolina, posted a $1,500 reward for whites found circulating the paper, and the Georgia legislature offered a $5,000 reward for Garrison's arrest. Garrison received death threats both from the South and from within New England.[52]

Stewart wrote "Cause for Encouragement" to Garrison only a month after he had published Black women's contributions to the PFLA in the Ladies' Department of *The Liberator* and had called for "the colored ladies of other places to go and do likewise."[53] The second volume of *The Liberator* expanded the paper, partly by giving "increasing prominence to women's voices, both Black and white" precisely because female literary and antislavery societies provided him with the content to fill that additional space. Sarah Mapps Douglass, Sarah Forten, and other Black women published anonymously and under multiple pseudonyms in the paper, signing themselves Bera, Anna Elizabeth, Ella, Beatrice, Zoe, Woodby, Sophanisba, Zillah, Ada, A., and Magawisca.[54] Newspapers such as *The Liberator*, the *Colored American*, and *Freedom's Journal* were an early part of what Shirley Logan documents as a system of "direct link[s] between these societies and various publication venues" that by the late nineteenth century meant that "a paper presented at a literary society meeting might be published in a newspaper or by the society itself or . . . be developed into a book for even wider distribution."[55] This imbrication of oratory and print, literary society and newspaper that Black women were establishing from the late 1820s through the 1830s became commonplace by the close of the century.

Enlisting in "the holy warfare": Emigration Debates and Black Nationalism

Debates over emigration and assertions of Black nationalism were central to African American conceptualizations of and claims to home and national belonging. These notions were necessarily future oriented in their imagining otherwise, and they are often misunderstood as largely the purview of male political leaders and writers. Yet in the spring of 1832, Maria Stewart addressed Boston's Afric-American Female Intelligence Society (AAFIS) in a speech that focused on women's roles in Black nationalist efforts. The address, published in *The Liberator* on April 28, 1832, has been characterized as the beginning of a "fatal rhetorical miscalculation"[56] that "exacted a high personal cost" and eventually led to Stewart being run out of the city.[57] However, debating Black nationalist politics was far from unusual in women's literary societies at the time. Sarah Mapps Douglass published "Moonlight" under her pseudonym "Zillah" in the Ladies' Department of *The Liberator* two weeks before Stewart's address appeared in the paper. One of those "original piece[s]" that members of the PFLA "put anonymously into a box, and afterwards criticised by a committee," Mapps Douglass's "Moonlight" offered a subtle Black nationalist argument against emigration and colonization.[58] Born with free status in Philadelphia on September 9, 1806, Mapps Douglass was a cofounder of the PFLA and a member of the interracial Philadelphia Female Anti-Slavery Society (PFASS) at a time when attending abolition meetings was "a life-threatening activity."[59] During the 1820s, she operated a school for African American children in Philadelphia subsidized by the PFASS. In 1853, she ran "the girls' department of the Institute for Colored Youth, and "between 1855 and 1858 she took the medical course" at the "Ladies' Institute of Pennsylvania Medical University."[60] Contemplating the death of friends in her 1832 *Liberator* publication "Moonlight," Mapps Douglass recalled her "happy schooldays,— my school companions. . . . O, my heart! where are they now? Two or three have left their native city for a foreign land; others have passed away." Likening emigration to death, she closed with her understated hope that African Americans would yet become citizens of the nation rather than be forced to establish colonies in foreign lands: "Hope whispers,—'The time is not far distant, when the wronged and enslaved children of America shall cease to be a "by-word and a reproach" among their brethren.'"[61]

Mapps Douglass joined a debate already underway in her own literary society and in the press. On January 28, 1832, Garrison had published a PFLA member's contribution to the box signed "A Colored Female of Philadelphia" that advocated emigration to Mexico or Upper Canada over Africa, framing the choice as in keeping with "the sentiments of some of my Trenton brethren." This anonymous member thought that "attach[ing] ourselves to a nation already established . . . in this hemisphere" was an advantage and lauded emigration as the exercise of "republicanism" and "independence" made "manifest." She advocated for emigration to Mexico in particular, noting that its climate and soil would "contribute to our wealth" and, in turn, enable African Americans to "become a people of worth and respectability." Mexico also promised "the rapid growth of amalgamation amongst" its "eight millions of colored, and one million of whites," which she argued had "every probability" of "becom[ing] one entire colored nation."[62] *The Liberator* then published a series of responses to this member from the PFLA box in its August 1832 edition.

Within the communal spaces of literary societies, women explored a range of sites for reimagined and realized Black freedom and belonging. In late July 1832, *The Liberator* published an extract from a letter Sarah Mapps Douglass wrote as Zillah to a friend debating emigration to Upper Canada. "You do not agree with me in regard to emigration. Would that I had eloquence enough to convince you that I am right!" she wrote. "If we should bend our steps to Hayti, there is no security for life and property. . . . If we go to Mexico, it is the same there. Why throw ourselves upon the protection of Great Britain, when thousands of her own children are starving? Do you suppose she can feel more love for us than she does for her own?"[63] Haiti had sought to attract African American immigration since 1804. By 1818, the Haitian government was offering African Americans land and paid passage, and in the 1820s, Jonathan Granville, a charismatic Haitian military officer, lectured to Black audiences through the American Northeast and the upper South on the advantages of Haitian emigration. The Haitian Emigration Society was formed in Philadelphia in 1824, and by the 1830s some 8,000 to 13,000 African Americans had emigrated to Haiti, only to face illness and hardship. By the early 1830s, when Sarah Mapps Douglass and other women were writing on emigration for their literary societies and *The Liberator*, the disappointments of Haitian emigration and opposition to the American Colonization Society meant that debates over emigration and colonization had become highly charged. Some African Americans were participating in colonization in Liberia, yet reports raised fears that their health was endangered. Upper Canada, which was said to have a healthier climate, emerged as a viable alternative and it was seriously discussed at the national Black conventions in the early to mid-1830s. Some Black leaders feared that emigration to Canada would create the perception that the fight for Black rights had been relinquished. Nonetheless, from the 1830s through the 1860s, 40,000 African Americans emigrated to Canada, more than emigrated to either Haiti or Africa. This was only a small proportion of the free Black population of the United States, however, and the vast majority remained.[64]

Members of women's literary societies, including Mapps Douglass, were well-informed voices within a rapidly developing debate about emigration and colonization. As "Zillah," she wrote one of a series of responses that PFLA members produced to "A Colored Female of Philadelphia," which *The Liberator* published on August 18, 1832. Finding Haiti and Canada unsuitable colonies for African Americans and rejecting emigration altogether, Mapps Douglass invoked God as ordaining that African Americans remain in their "own, native land," much as Maria Stewart fused her social gospel with her Black nationalist arguments: "I firmly believe it is his will that we remain. I would not give up this belief for a thousand worlds. . . . Cease, then, to think of any other city of refuge. Listen to the voice of our dear Redeemer! . . . 'Fear not, little flock; it is your Father's good pleasure to give you the kingdom.'" Mapps Douglass referred to "the approval of Heaven," "the Rock of Ages," "our dear Redeemer" and the Father in her short, four-paragraph response.[65] She contributed regularly to the Ladies' Department throughout 1832, signing her contributions Zillah and Sophanisba, and she contributed as Zillah to *The Emancipator* (New York, NY; Boston, MA; 1833–1850) in 1833. She published under her own name in the *Pennsylvania Freeman* (Philadelphia, PA; 1838–1854) in the late 1830s; the *National Anti-Slavery Standard* (New York, NY; Philadelphia, PA; 1840–1870) and Frederick Douglass's *North Star* in the 1840s and 1850s; the *Anglo-African Magazine* (New York, NY; 1859–1860) in the late 1850s; and in *The Liberator* in 1863.[66]

Maria Stewart's Black nationalist politics and religious rhetoric were not unusual in women's literary societies. It is quite possible that her ideas and her rhetoric took shape through the growth and influence of such societies as the AAFIS in Boston, which hosted her in the spring of 1832. Established in September 1831, the AAFIS collected both monthly and yearly dues for "the purchasing of books, the hiring of a room and other contingencies," including aid to any member experiencing "any unforeseen and afflictive event." The group's constitution was published across two columns in the Ladies' Department of *The Liberator* on January 7, 1832, immediately above an extract from Stewart's first tract, *Religion and the Pure Principles of Morality*, titled "Mrs. Steward's [sic] Essays." Its preamble read:

> Whereas the subscribers, women of color of the Commonwealth of Massachusetts, actuated by a natural feeling for the welfare of our friends, have thought fit to associate *for the diffusion of knowledge, the suppression of vice and immorality, and for cherishing such virtues as will render us happy and useful to society*, sensible of the gross ignorances under which we have too long labored, but trusting, by the blessing of God, we shall be able to accomplish the object of our union—we have therefore associated ourselves under the name of the Afric-American Female Intelligence Society.[67]

Through its listing of acceptable activities and interests and its specification of how membership dues would be used, the AAFIS constitution marks the links between women's literary and benevolent societies that centered community welfare, both economic and moral, and community service rendered in the name of womanly virtue. Rather than declaring that its female members pursued the *acquisition* of knowledge, the association facilitated the *diffusion* of knowledge in the community: it "rented halls and sponsored lectures by William Lloyd Garrison" and others, and promoted "abolitionist debates, dramatic readings, fund-raising . . . reading rooms, and other community welfare projects." The fact that its members did not participate in public debates or lectures" tells us something of both the response to Stewart's address and how she presented herself.[68]

From the fall of 1832 to her farewell address in late September of 1833, Stewart took to Boston platforms. Her *Religion and the Pure Principles of Morality, The Sure Foundation on Which We Must Build* (1831), which sold for six cents and was published by Garrison about five months before her lecture at the AAFIS, was advertised in October 1831 and excerpted in *The Liberator* on January 7, 1832, where it appeared immediately under the AAFIS constitution. Stewart closed *Religion and the Pure Principles of Morality* dramatically with this selfless declaration: "I have never taken one step, my friends, with a design to raise myself in your esteem, or to gain applause. But what I have done, has been done with an eye single to the glory of God, and to promote the good of souls." She continued: "I have neither kindred nor friends. I stand alone in your midst, exposed to the fiery darts of the devil, and to the assaults of wicked men. But though all the powers of earth and hell were to combine against me, though all nature should sink into decay, still I would trust in the Lord, and joy in the God of my salvation."[69] In her AAFIS address, Stewart again presented herself as a martyr: "I have enlisted in the holy warfare, and Jesus is my captain; and the Lord's battle I mean to fight, until my voice expire in death. I expect to be hated of all men, and persecuted even unto death, for righteousness and the truth's sake."[70] In fact, she repeated these invocations so often that they became a hallmark of her lectures and writing. She cultivated the persona of a holy warrior serving the divine will of God and Black liberationist politics. While Stewart may have done this to protect her Black female peers in the AAFIS from community censure by association—she was a lone figure, not connected to that female collective—she also worked to direct that negative attention toward her political ends, marking her awareness of the rhetorical force of recirculation.

Stewart's deliberate courting of notoriety for its use in heightening the recirculation of her work is rooted in her appropriation of masculine political address. Eddie Glaude notes that religion was central to Black politics and in particular to Black nationalism in the early nineteenth century, when "the nation [was] imagined not alongside religion but precisely *through* the precepts of Black Christianity. . . . Out of Black religious life emerged a conception of Black national identity." For antebellum Northern African Americans, political discourse and "political languages were tied to a Black Christian imagination."[71] More than a matter of rhetorical style, Stewart's social gospel was firmly in step with male-dominated political debate and her militancy was conventionally masculine.

Stewart opened her lecture to the AAFIS with a statement that cohered with the group's constitutional focus on virtue, morality, and humility: "Religion is held in low repute among some of us; and purely to promote the cause of Christ, and the good of souls, in the hope that others more experienced, more able and talented than myself might go forward and do likewise." But in just two sentences she moved to a fiery jeremiad that ran for paragraphs, indicting the Black community for working against its own interests and the African American clergy for failing to "faithfully discharge their duty" by hiding "the truth . . . from our eyes" in order to keep the peace "when there was no peace." Stewart claimed "our own color are our greatest opposers," then quickly moved to the Black nationalist call for community solidarity and collective uplift that was also ringing out in the Black convention movement: "Unless the rising generation manifest a different temper and disposition towards each other from what we have manifested, the generation following will never be an enlightened people. We this day are considered as one of the most degraded races upon the face of the earth. It is useless for us any longer to sit with our hands folded, reproaching the whites; for that will never elevate us."[72] Patrick Rael has noted that in the antebellum North, "theodicy and jeremiads" were "meld[ed] . . . with important principles of nationalism" in the rhetoric of Black leaders that "told African American northerners they were part of a special community with a divine mission."[73] Stewart's movement in this address from a focus on religion to an indictment of the clergy and on to a call for Black collectivity indicates her appropriation of a Black nationalist politics, making her closing even more outrageous than her claim to be "fired . . . with a holy zeal" to call her community to account for their "envious and malicious disposition." She ended by exhorting the women of the AAFIS to form the backbone of a renewed Black nationalism: "O woman, woman! Upon you I call, for upon your exertions almost entirely depends whether the rising generation shall be any thing more than we have been or not. O woman, woman! Your example is powerful, your influence great; it extends over your husbands and your children, and throughout the circle of your acquaintance."[74] Stewart closed with a Black nationalist call for collectivity and racial uplift that depended on woman's influence.

This is a move that scholars have characterized as well beyond the comfort zone of her audience.[75]

Yet Stewart was deliberate in all she did. She knew she would cause a stir in Boston and presented herself as a lone and world-weary martyr to the Black nationalist cause, one whose "soul has been so discouraged within me, that I have almost been induced to exclaim, 'Would to God that my tongue hereafter might cleave to the roof of my mouth and become silent forever!'" In this closing she invited her female listeners at the AAFIS to indict and martyr her, and then she took the text of her address to Garrison's *Liberator* offices. He published it on April 28, 1832, with a header that read, "It is proper to state that the Address of Mrs. Stewart, in our Ladies' Department to-day, is published *at her own request, and not by desire of the Society* before whom it was delivered."[76] Stewart recirculated her lecture as the anomalous and independent act of a marginal figure in a paper she knew would reach most Black Bostonians, Black communities in the Northeast, and an anxious Southern reprinting circuit. Stewart took her politics viral. She made the role of women in Black nationalism newsworthy beyond Boston by using recirculation and the notoriety of Garrison's paper and personal reputation in ways that benefited both her political work and *The Liberator*. Marilyn Richardson has noted that advertising the lectures of a Black woman and printing them along with her essays gave Garrison items of "news in and of themselves" as well as "strong statements in support of his publication's stands."[77]

Stewart very clearly set in motion a political program that marks her understanding of recirculation, using the nexus that had already developed between literary societies and the newspaper press. At times, this took the form of direct references to the media form and its affordances or to the ways it would equip its readers with knowledge. She began her political program with a strong statement on the powers of the press in *Religion and the Pure Principles of Morality* in the fall of 1831: "This is the land of freedom. The Press is at liberty. Every man has a right to express his opinion." In her Franklin Hall lecture on September 21, 1832, she positioned herself as a newspaper reader, thereby claiming to have the authority to debate colonizationists on African American character and capability: "I observed a piece in the *Liberator* a few months since, stating that the colonizationist had published a work respecting us, asserting that we were lazy and idle. I confute them on that point." And in her African Masonic Hall lecture on February 17, 1833, she reminded her audience of her first tract, quoting it while calling them to action: "God will surely raise up those among us who will plead the cause of virtue and the pure principles of morality more eloquently than I am able to do."[78]

Stewart's choices evidence a deliberate program of recirculation. She followed Garrison's printing and advertising of *Religion and the Pure Principles of Morality* in the fall of 1831 and his excerpting of it in the January 7, 1832, issue with the publication and sale of her ten-cent tract *Meditations*, which was advertised in the March 31, 1832, issue. This was followed with her publication of the AAFIS lecture in the April 28, 1832, issue of *The Liberator*.[79] Stewart's letter to the editor, "Cause for Encouragement," was then published in *The Liberator* in July 1832, followed by her September 21, 1832, Franklin Hall address, printed again "By Request" in the paper on November 17 that year. Publication of her February 27, 1833, African Masonic Hall address (in two installments) also ran "By Request," a consistent notation making clear that Garrison did not solicit them but that they were published on Stewart's initative.[80] The paper then ran advertisements of public lectures she planned to give in Boston in the spring and fall of 1833.[81] Stewart made the most controversial Black-supported abolitionist paper in circulation central to a multifaceted program of recirculation.

Even appearing to have been run out of Boston seems to have worked well for Maria Stewart if we understand recirculation as foundational to her Black feminist politics. Stewart left Boston in 1833 for New York City, where she remained active in reform and Black feminist politics by joining the Ladies' Literary Society of New York.[82] Alexander Crummel recalled "listening, on more than a few occasions, to some of her compositions and declamations" produced for that society.[83] She continued to lecture and be visible in the press after she left Boston. Her 1835 "*Productions of Mrs. Maria W. Stewart* was advertised in Boston and elsewhere" and after she moved to Baltimore in 1852, she became a regular contributor to the *Repository of Religion and Literature, and of Science and Art* (Indianapolis, IN; 1858–1863), published for the literary societies of the AME church's Baltimore, Indiana, and Missouri Conferences.[84] One of these contributions, published as "The Proper Training of Children" in the January 1861 issue, was originally a lecture she had given in November 1860 as part of the Ladies Literary Festival at the St. James Protestant Episcopal Church in Baltimore.[85] The *Repository*, "twenty-two pages, bound . . . and small enough to fit conveniently in a pocket," cultivated literary societies as a subscription base and "printed addresses given by women before small groups, especially literary societies."[86] One of its regular columns was the Young Ladies' Lecture Room.[87] McHenry characterizes the magazine as "providing the individual reader with opportunities to engage in a communal model of literary activity," citing its founding editor Elisha Weaver's claim that

Repository readers would become "'fit for society, [and] better neighbors in any community.'"[88]

Stewart also continued to have a presence in *The Liberator*. Abolitionist William C. Nell wrote to the paper on March 5, 1852, recalling that in the early 1830s, "Mrs. Maria W. Stewart—fired with a holy zeal [—delivered] . . . public lectures [that] awakened an interest acknowledged and felt to this day."[89] Stewart had this letter reprinted in the 1879 edition of her collected works, *Meditations from the Pen of Mrs. Maria W. Stewart*, which she financed with her hard-won war veteran widow's pension of $8 a month. The effect was to suggest that she had never left the minds of reform-minded Bostonians during the more than forty years since her controversial lectures in that city. *Meditations* was advertised in the *People's Advocate*, a Washington, DC, paper and sold for thirty-five cents a copy.[90] When she died in 1879, that Black weekly devoted "thirty inches of its front page" to Stewart.[91]

Maria Stewart crafted a lone martyr persona in Boston at the beginning of her career that in many ways scholars have adopted with little question. Yet the afterlife of her work in Boston signals the likelihood that her orations there had been developed in women's literary societies and mutual aid associations, collective sites that continued to be of value to her in New York and Baltimore. Rather than an isolated individual pursuing an unusual politics, Stewart was one participant among many and her work was possible not only because it was shared by other women who had been making related arguments through literary societies that we can document since 1827 but also because women's societies—both benevolent and literary—had been training grounds for their communally oriented political work as early as the eighteenth century, as Frances Smith Foster reminds us.[92] Her career as a reader, writer, and orator may be one of the best known, but its development in women's literary societies is far from unique. In Stewart's very deliberate labors we see the seeding of a Black feminist politics of recirculation.

Turn-of-the-Century Black Feminisms and Recirculation

Recirculation was operative in the activism of the most well-known Black feminists in the nineteenth and early twentieth centuries. By that time, Black feminist recirculation practices were driven toward both newspaper and alternative print formats such as the pamphlet, enabling the dissemination of extended political articulation. Frances Harper was already nationally recognized as a galvanizing public speaker when she gave her lecture "Enlightened Motherhood" to the Brooklyn Literary Union on November 15, 1892, which was then recirculated in pamphlet form.[93] Harper's practices of recirculation date back to at least August 1854 with what is known as her first public address, "The Elevation and Education of Our People" in New Bedford, Massachusetts. She recirculated this speech in the first edition of *Poems on Miscellaneous Subjects* as an essay titled "The Colored People in America," just as she did her address "Christianity," which she first delivered in Boston in September 1854.[94] Due to Harper's national reputation as a lecturer, activist, and writer, much of her oratory recirculated in the abolitionist and Black press in transcribed or excerpted form or was recirculated as essays in *The Liberator*, the *National Anti-Slavery Standard*, the *Anti-Slavery Bugle* (New Lisbon, OH; 1845–1861), the *Christian Recorder*, *Frederick Douglass' Paper*, the *Anglo-African Magazine*, the *Weekly Anglo-African* (New York, NY; 1859–1861), the *A.M.E. Church Review*, and the *Woman's Journal* (Boston, MA; 1870–1931) from the mid-1850s through the late 1890s.[95] Harper's awareness of the affordances offered by the newspaper press may have developed at home. Her uncle, Rev. William Watkins Sr.—who signed himself the "Colored Baltimorean" as a correspondent for *The Genius of Universal Emancipation* (Baltimore, MD; Hennepin, IL; 1826–1839), *Freedom's Journal*, the New York *Colored American*, and *The Liberator*—raised Harper after she was orphaned at the age of three with his wife, Henrietta Russell Watkins. Their son, Harper's cousin William J. Watkins Jr., was an associate editor of *Frederick Douglass' Paper* in the 1850s.[96]

In the 1890s, Victoria Earle Matthews's uses of recirculation may well have been influenced by her journalistic career.[97] A nationally sought-after newspaper correspondent, Matthews wrote as Victoria Earle for the *National Leader* (Washington, DC; 1888–1889), the Detroit *Plaindealer* (Detroit, MI; 1883–1894), the *Southern Christian Recorder* (Little Rock, AR; Nashville, TN; 1886–1952), the *Boston Advocate* (Boston, MA; 1885–1887?), the *Washington Bee*, the *Richmond Planet* (Richmond, VA; 1883–1938), the American *Catholic Tribune* (Cincinnati, OH; Detroit, MI; 1886–1897), the *Cleveland Gazette* (Cleveland, OH; 1883–1945), the *New York Globe* (1880–1884), the *New York Age*, the *New York Enterprise*, Ringwood's *Afro-American Journal of Fashion* (Cleveland, OH; 1891–1894), the *A.M.E. Church Review*, and the *Woman's Era* (Boston, MA; 1894–1897). She recirculated "The Value of Race Literature," an address for the First Congress of Colored Women at Berkeley Hall in Boston on July 30, 1895, as a twenty-three-page pamphlet and self-published "The Awakening of the Afro-American Woman," which she delivered at the Annual Convention of the Society of Christian Endeavor in San Francisco on July 11, 1897, as a twelve-page pamphlet in 1897.[98]

Matthews was also instrumental in organizing the support of 250 Black women from New York, Boston, and Philadelphia who gathered on October 5, 1892, at Lyric Hall in New York to hear Ida B. Wells deliver a speech on lynching that was based on her seven-column exposé in the June 25, 1892, edition of the *New York Age*. Wells recirculated that address as the pamphlet *Southern Horrors: Lynch Law in All Its Phases*, for which Frederick Douglass wrote an introduction, and had New York Age Print publish it by the end of October 1892. She also recirculated "Lynch Law," a chapter she wrote for the pamphlet *The Reason Why the Colored American Is Not in the World's Columbian Exposition* (1893) with Frederick Douglass, Irvine Garland Penn, and Ferdinand Barnett, as part of her pamphlet *A Red Record* (1894). Wells's notoriety and her UK anti-lynching tours of 1893 and 1894 resulted in her speeches being recirculated as excerpts in papers such as the *Birmingham Daily Post*, the *Birmingham Daily Gazette*, the *New York Times*, the *Hawaiian Gazette* (Honolulu, HI; 1865–1918), the *Commercial Appeal* (Memphis, TN; 1841–), the *Cleveland Gazette*, and the *American Citizen* (New York, NY; 1802–1810).[99]

Anna Julia Cooper, much like Wells, Matthews, and Harper, recirculated her public addresses, some of which appeared in her feminist manifesto *A Voice from the South, by a Black Woman of the South* in 1892. She self-published the manifesto through the Aldine Publishing House in Xenia, Ohio, and sold it for $1.25 a copy. Cooper first recirculated one of these speeches, "The Higher Education of Women," which she delivered at the invitation of Howard University alumni to an American Conference of Educators convention on March 25–27, 1890, in the April 1891 edition of the Woman's Department of the *Southland* magazine (Winston-Salem, NC; 1890–1891), which she coedited.[100] She then recirculated this speech as chapter 2 of *A Voice from the South*, which also included "Womanhood: A Vital Element in the Regeneration and Progress of a Race," first delivered as "The Colored Woman of the Country" to the "convocation" of African American clergy of "the Protestant Episcopal Church at Washington, DC, 1886," according to Cooper's own notation for the speech in *A Voice from the South*. This address was reported by the Indianapolis *Freeman* (1884–1927) as "the most notable paper of the week. . . . one of the brightest, deepest, sweetest and tenderest efforts we have heard in years." Louise Hutchinson documents that Cooper had delivered it "many times before both black and white audiences."[101] In 1913, Cooper self-published *The Social Settlement: What It Is, and What It Does* as a pamphlet through the Murray Brothers Press in Washington, DC, after it had first circulated in the *Oberlin Alumni Journal* earlier that year. Her public addresses were frequently recirculated in the Black press.[102]

Contemporaries of Matthews, Wells, and Cooper, such as Mary Church Terrell, Fannie Barrier Williams, and Margaret Murray Washington, also employed similar recirculating techniques that we can see as ultimately developing from Maria Stewart's multilevel program of public address, newspaper recirculation, and pamphlet publication. Fannie Barrier Williams recirculated "The Intellectual Progress of the Colored Women of the United States since the Emancipation Proclamation," delivered to the Congress of Representative Women at the World's Congress Auxiliary of the World's Columbian Exposition in May 1898, as a self-published pamphlet.[103] Margaret Murray Washington's "We Must Have a Cleaner 'Social Morality,'" delivered on September 12, 1898, at Charleston's Old Bethel AME Church to a "large assemblage" of Black women, was recirculated in the *Charleston News and Courier* (1873–1991) a day later.[104] And Mary Church Terrell's address "Progress of Colored Women" before the National Woman Suffrage Association at the Columbia Theater in Washington, DC, on February 18, 1898, was recirculated in the *Washington Bee*, the *Colored American* (Washington, DC), and the *Broad Ax*. Terrell then self-published her remarks as a fifteen-page pamphlet with the *Colored American* coverage as a preface.[105] She also recirculated parts of her address to the International Council of Women in Berlin in 1904, titled "The Progress and Problems of Colored Women," by writing "The International Congress of Women" for the October issue of *Voice of the Negro* (Atlanta, GA; Chicago, IL; 1904–1907).[106] These are the most recognizable Black feminists of the nineteenth and early twentieth centuries who were practicing recirculation, with several pursuing a program of self-publication. All of these women, like Stewart, Cassey, Forten, Jennings Sr., and Mapps Douglass before them, are documented as addressing and having been members of lyceums and literary societies.

"Girls, the race question hangs on you": The Black Press and Thriving Literary Societies

Although Elizabeth McHenry has suggested that "in the aftermath of the failure of Reconstruction," literary societies in the North were reorganized to become "the staging ground for Black communities' increased activism," they had always functioned in this way.[107] Erica Ball has documented that in the 1830s and 1840s, literary societies were sites where African Americans learned to practice "living an antislavery life" by acquiring education, studying conduct manuals, and attending to their moral development alongside other aspects of self-improvement.[108] The *Colored American* (New York, NY) reported that literary societies were working in cooperation with benevolent and church societies to send delegates to organizations such as the annual council of the Philadelphia Association for the Moral and Mental Improvement of the People, which incorporated in 1835. The association was one of the most prominent vigilance committees that aided self-emancipated African Americans and prevented their recapture, but that was not their sole focus. In 1839, the association's council resolved to have "each church and society" of Philadelphia "appoint three persons" to "form a Board of Education"; resolved to "view as it ever has done, with disgust and indignation, the scheme of the American Colonization Society"; and recommended to "our people the propriety of extending their aid and patronage in support of those papers whose columns are opened for the defence of human rights."[109] In other words, their politics were strongly aligned with the Black feminist activism in *The Liberator*'s pages that emerged from Black women's literary societies.

Although Black women in New York City criticized all-male associations such as the Odd Fellows and the Masons for pushing out literary societies in the mid-1850s, lyceums and literary societies continued to thrive across the country, fostering various forms of political organizing, including the Black women's club movement.[110] By the 1890s, literary societies were active in anti-lynching work in response to a call from the Black press.[111] That call had first been issued in the 1830s: "Girls[,] the race question hangs on you."[112] From 1891 through at least 1916, the Kansas Interstate Literary Association drew Kansas and Missouri literary societies as well as "doctors, lawyers, editors, poets, teachers, professors" to its annual multiday gatherings that discussed "affairs of nation, of thought." These annual meetings were covered in Black papers across the nation.[113] In the early twentieth century, literary societies sent delegates to annual meetings of the National Independent Political League, as did churches, lodges, and equal rights associations.[114]

Just as women attendees of the colored conventions "sustained the movement" with monetary donations in the 1850s, women's literary societies were financially supporting the Black press from the early to mid-nineteenth century.[115] The New York Female Literary Society held fairs in the late 1830s to support the *Colored American*, and in 1848 Sarah Mapps Douglass helped found the all-Black Women's Association of Philadelphia to financially support "Frederick Douglass's call for Black nationalism."[116] The preamble of its constitution stressed "self-elevation" and "self-exertion" alongside a program of fundraising . . . that would "support . . . the Press and Public Lecturers devoted to the Elevation of the Colored People."[117] Just a year later, Black women in Syracuse, including Julia Williams Garnet and Caroline Storum Loguen, formed the Provisional Committee that financially supported Samuel Ringgold Ward's weekly *Impartial Citizen*.[118] Julia Williams Garnet, the wife of Henry Highland Garnet, was a member of the Boston Female Anti-Slavery Society, and Caroline Storum Loguen, with her husband Jermain, ran an Underground Railroad station in their Syracuse home that helped roughly 1,500 people on their self-emancipation journeys. Maria Stewart was part of a New York women's North Star Fair Association that raised funds so the "truths" Frederick Douglass's *North Star* offered "may penetrate every corner of that *den of oppression* [the South]." These women stressed the centrality of a community-sustained press to Black collectivist politics, asserting that "every person must be convinced of the power of the press, and should therefore, exert their utmost influence to sustain it."[119] Mary Still, who was a sales agent for the *Christian Recorder* from 1862 to at least 1864, wrote its editor Elisha Weaver in the spring of 1861 to offer him $20 that had been raised by women through the Female Union Publication Society of the AME Church to keep the paper "in circulation."[120] In 1866, women in Cincinnati held a fair to raise funds for the *Christian Recorder* so "that type and a printing press may be obtained."[121] And in the West, the Ladies' Pacific Accumulating Society of San Francisco formed the "Elevator Aid Association" to financially support Phillip Bell's *Elevator* (San Francisco, CA). As F. H. Grice wrote to the paper in October 1868, "*our ladies show far more interest in sustaining the press*, and they intend to continue their benevolent undertaking in aid of a journal which fearlessly vindicates our rights, not as a distinct race, but as American citizens."[122] The paper's circulation had grown beyond San Francisco by February that year, when "Mary" wrote the editor from Sacramento to "assure you the women have always felt an interest in your paper." She also made clear that women were providing content as well as financial backing for the *Elevator*. "The ladies do not neglect you as literary contributors, and I know they will not neglect you as financial contributors. . . . Let every woman forward a dollar" to "aid in the noble enterprise."[123] The Black press of California developed from its literary societies: the Athenaeum of San Francisco, organized in 1853, founded both a library "of 800 volumes and periodicals and magazines" and the city's first Black newspaper, *Mirror of the Times* (1857–1862). Four years later, the *Mirror* "listed agents in cities and towns throughout California."[124]

However fragile the links between literary societies and newspapers, they were fundamental. As papers or literary societies folded and others were established in their stead, those links were remade. Reports of literary societies and lyceums in the Black press make clear that the co-constitutive connections between them functioned as a regenerating network for each beyond the location or base of either. That networked relation remained alive and well during the 1890s, even though scholars assert that this is the decade when literary societies were in decline.[125] The network of literary societies and newspapers enabled Black feminisms to be national and mobile rather than fixed and bound to a community or region. The column Our Journalists and Literary Folks in the Indianapolis *Freeman* offered brief reports on schools, editors, newspapers, and literary societies, and papers such as *The Topeka Plaindealer* (Topkea, KS; 1900–1932) and the *New York Globe* (New York, NY; 1880–1884), the *New York Freeman*, and the *New York Age* carried reports of lyceums and literary societies across the country from the 1880s through the 1930s.[126] In the early 1890s, the *Parsons Weekly Blade* (Parsons, KS; 1892–1901) promoted literary societies in ways similar to the *Colored American* in the late 1820s and early 1830s: "more good literary societies among our people will serve as invaluable means to improvement.... We must study; we must read more and more every day."[127] From the 1880s through the 1930s, Kansas was home to the most literary societies of any state in the nation (see the appendix). Instead of concentrating in cities, they formed along the rail lines that facilitated newspaper and periodical distribution (figure 1.1).

How many Black women readers fueled the unprecedented growth of the Black press in the 1880s and 1890s is as difficult to determine as the total readership of such papers. Given that in these decades Black papers hired African American women to write Women's Departments and published women's letters to the editor, essays, and articles, it is clear that editors courted a female readership. T. Thomas Fortune employed Gertrude Mossell and Florence Williams to write columns for the *New York Freeman* and *New York Age*, respectively, in the 1880s. Lillian Lews (writing under the pen names Bert Islew, Lillial Akbeeta, and Kewus) wrote a column titled They Say for the *Washington Bee* in 1889 and 1900, and Ella V. Chase Williams wrote the paper's Our Women column in 1896–1897 while she was also a columnist for the *Boston Advocate* and the *People's Advocate* (Alexandria, VA; Washington, DC).[128] Papers such as the Indianapolis *Freeman* ran several columns to appeal to women readers, such as Woman's World, What Our Women Are Doing (edited by Grace Lucas Thompson), For and About Women, Our Women, Women's Work and Play, and Woman's Work and Interest (edited by Mme. Sylvia Sherry) in 1884–1927. The Detroit *Plaindealer* initially offered Woman's Work and Ways as a fashion column from November 1891 to the end of September 1892, but thereafter and until 1895 that column focused on Black women's accomplishments and their political meetings. The women's

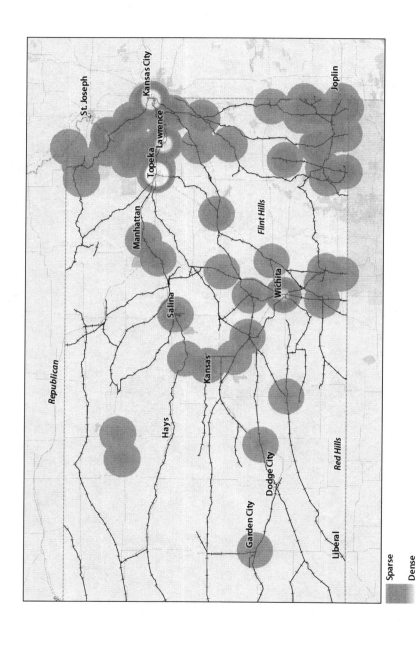

Figure 1.1. Kansas Literary Societies and Lyceums, 1880–1939 heat map. Produced by Teresa Zackodnik in ArcGIS using a base layer created by the Bureau of Transportation Planning, Kansas Department of Transportation.

column of the *Huntsville Gazette* (1879–1894), titled In Woman's Behalf, promoted suffrage, women's education, and women's employment and frequently quoted from or reprinted content from suffragist and abolitionist Lucy Stone's woman's rights periodical, the *Woman's Journal*. The Afro-Protestant press also ran women's columns in these decades: the *Christian Recorder* offered readers Our Women's Column in the late 1870s through the 1880s; Mary Virginia Cook Parrish (whose pseudonym was Grace Ermine) wrote the Women's Department of the *American Baptist* (Louisville, KY; 1878–1988) in the late 1880s; and Sarah Dudley Pettey authored the bimonthly Woman's Column in *The Star of Zion* (Charlotte, NC; 1876–), an African Methodist Episcopal Zion paper, beginning in 1896.[129]

Reports on literary societies continued to be offered into the twentieth century by newspapers such as the *Washington Bee*, the Indianapolis *Freeman*, the *Illinois Record* (Springfield, IL; 1897–1899), the *Cleveland Gazette*, *The Topeka Plaindealer*, the *Huntsville Gazette*, and the *Dallas Express* (Dallas, TX; Houston, TX; 1893–1970).[130] as literary societies and lyceums continued to be founded or, like the Garrison Lyceum in Boston and the Memphis Lyceum, were reorganized.[131] Clearly, these societies, their communal reading practices, and the Black feminist recirculation they mobilized remained central to Black communities as the Black press exploded; announcements of their activities were a constant in newspaper pages. Although scholars of the lyceum movement among white Americans credit it with creating the environment necessary to sustain a newspaper press, scholars of the Black press tend to tie its development to growth in alphabetical literacy among African Americans, to technological advances that reduced publication costs, and to African American migration.[132] Insufficient attention has been paid to the literacy rates of women migrants, and to literary societies as integral to advancements in alphabetical literacy, a developing readership for the Black press, and the financial viability, circulation, and distribution of newspapers.

Just as the Colored Reading Society of Philadelphia subscribed to *Freedom's Journal* and *The Genius of Universal Emancipation* as early as 1828,[133] literary societies subscribed to an official or chief organ in the 1880s and 1890s and thereby sustained papers such as the *Weekly Pelican* (New Orleans; 1886–1889), the *Huntsville Gazette*, the *New York Age*, and the Indianapolis *Freeman*.[134] Josephine St. Pierre Ruffin's monthly, *The Woman's Era* (Boston, MA; 1894–1898)—touted as the first periodical published for and by Black women—like its early nineteenth-century predecessors, offered "bulk rates to organizations whose members resold the paper [to] raise funds" and used the reports of activities supplied by benevolent societies such as the Working Woman's League of Providence, Rhode Island, as content.¹³⁵ The Black women's club movement, formed from the federations of clubs that began as literary societies, saw founding their own periodicals as central to their political aims. For example, at its 1897 meeting in Nashville, the NACWC established both "a formal structure and a communications network in the publication of the *National Notes* [Washington, DC; 1897–]" and the Mississippi State Federation of Colored Women's Clubs "actively communicated their goals and projects" in *The Woman's Herald* (Gloster, MS; 1908–?), including "quality childcare, an African American history curriculum, proper medical care facilities, improved conditions for Black domestic workers, and the care of children and adults with disabilities."¹³⁶

We are only beginning to understand that Black literary societies extended well beyond the Northeast corridor and the early to mid-nineteenth century. Taking as foundational the link between literary societies and newspapers alters both the geographical and temporal frames that are predominant in scholarship. The Black press continued to report on literary societies and lyceums not only in the United States but also in Haiti and Liberia in the 1880s and 1890s, indicating that "literary character" continued to strongly propel a vision of Black freedom.¹³⁷ Such reporting gave Black papers such as the Indianapolis *Freeman*, the *Savannah Tribune* (Savannah, GA; 1876–1878, 1886–1960), *The Topeka Call* (Topeka, KS; 1893–1898), *The Plaindealer* (Topeka, KS; 1899–1958), and *The Western Outlook* (San Francisco, CA; Oakland, CA; 1894–1928) content, readerships, distribution outlets, and subscribers. Editors of papers such as the Indianapolis *Freeman*, *The New York Freeman*, *The Topkea Plaindealer*, *The New York Globe*, and the *New York Age* clearly understood that carrying news of literary societies—both locally and from across the country, in regular columns or prominently on the front page—could cultivate a subscription base fostered by communal organizations. Their value is marked by the fact that this practice continued as newspapers were sold from one editor to another.¹³⁸ Lyceums and literary societies also continued to produce their own periodicals in these decades, including the *Gleaner* (Fort Scott, KS), published by the Fort Scott Lyceum; *St. Matthew's Lyceum Gazette* (Detroit, MI), edited by Mary E. Lambert; and the Lincoln Lyceum's *Lincoln Gazette* (Lincoln, NB), edited by Moses Alton and Sarah Butler.¹³⁹ All were following a tradition that included the Galbraith Lyceum's paper the *Lyceum Observer* (Baltimore, MD; 1863–186?), now known as the first newspaper published for and by African Americans in Baltimore.¹⁴⁰

In Colorado, Montana, Florida and other states, literary societies were only beginning to be established in the mid- to late 1890s. In Langston, Oklahoma,

Bessie Floyd Dungee started the Literatae Club, women students in the Teacher's College founded the Phyllis Wheatley Club, and women such as Metella Clement, Nettie Carlisle, and Mrs. J. E. Robinson" were contributors to the *Langston City Herald* (Langston City, Oklahoma Territory; 1891–1902) in the mid-1890s, which also served as contact for membership to "a society to benefit needy girls in the county" they had organized. In Boley, Oklahoma, the Boley Ladies Industrial Club, which was founded in 1908 "to serve social, economic and benevolent needs," also founded the Boley Public Library.[141] Thriving lyceums and literary societies in Georgia, Illinois, Kansas, Missouri, Pennsylvania, New York, Colorado, Tennessee, and Texas continued into the early twentieth century. In Arkansas, such societies were active in the early 1950s, while in North Carolina, home to some of the oldest Black literary societies such as the Priscilla Art and Literary Club of Charlotte, these organizations operated into the late 1980s.[142]

Although the networking of Black women's community and political organizations, literary societies, and newspapers has long been overlooked, its importance to both the development of Black feminism and the Black press is abundantly clear. Little would have been possible for the Black press without the women who formed literary societies and sustained newspapers from the 1830s and beyond with content, readers, and direct financial aid. In turn, that networked relation between literary societies and newspapers was leveraged to enable the recirculation of Black feminist content, which created the conditions for Black women's politics to be organized neither "by a place or an institution" nor by leaders, as we conventionally think of political movements, "but by the circulation of discourse."[143] For our understanding of Black feminism, attention to the circulatory matrix forged between literary societies and the Black press is essential; for our understanding of how the Black press was founded and sustained, such attention is both long overdue and revolutionary.

Chapter Two

Making Place

Black Women's Politics and Letters to the Editor

> People who do not control physical places often construct discursive spaces as sites of agency, affiliation, and imagination.
>
> —GEORGE LIPSITZ

In his scholarship on the *Christian Recorder*, Eric Gardner suggests that for Black women, subscribing to a newspaper "was arguably a kind of gateway act in their struggles for print presences." If subscribing was a gateway act for Black women as individuals, we might say that the letter to the editor established a critical mass of their voices. For women, both acts could lead to their names appearing in print, marking the female subscriber or letter writer as a citizen in at least two ways: "as a citizen of a specific locale" and "as a citizen in terms of commerce, speaking materially of either class position or of class aspirations" evidenced in their ability and decision to take, read, write to, or have read to them a newspaper.[1] Black women such as Amy Matilda Cassey, Sarah Mapps Douglass, Sarah Forten, and Maria Stewart, whose politics were co-constituted through the circulatory nexus that linked literary societies and the Black press, used this press form as early as the 1830s to voice their collectivizing assertions on women's education and emigration.

Often writing a letter to the editor was a Black woman's first step into the print public sphere. While *The Liberator* was a primary location for published letters in the 1830s, women such as Sarah Mapps Douglass and Susan Paul also wrote to the *National Anti-Slavery Standard* in the 1840s; and by the 1850s and 60s, Mary Ann Shadd (Cary by 1856), Charlotte Forten, Laura Haviland, Sarah Parker Remond, Frances Harper, Harriet Jacobs, Elizabeth Jennings Jr., Sojourner Truth, Sattira Douglass, and Harriet Tubman were writing or dictating letters to the editors of the *Voice of the Fugitive* (Windsor, ON; 1851–1854), *The Liberator*, *Frederick Douglass' Paper* (Rochester, NY; 1851–1660), the *Anti-Slavery Advocate*, the *Provincial Freeman*, the *Anti-Slavery Bugle*, the *New York Tribune*, the *Pacific Appeal* (San Francisco, CA; 1862–1880) the *National Anti-Slavery Standard*, the *Weekly Anglo-African*, the *Christian Recorder*, and the Boston *Commonwealth* on issues such as emigration and colonization, the abolition of slavery, the free labor movement, the Civil War, Black enlistment, supporting the freedpeople, and racial segregation on public transportation.

As was the case for Maria Stewart, Black women's letters to the editor have been mistaken for or came to form the basis of extended print forms such as pamphlets or essays. For example, Charlotte Forten's "Life on the Sea Islands," published in *The Atlantic Monthly* (Boston, MA; Washington, DC; 1857–) in two parts in 1864, had its origin not only in Forten's private journals but also in letters she wrote to the editors of the *Boston Evening Transcript* (Boston, MA; 1872–1941), the *Salem Register* (Salem, MA; 1841–1903), and the *Liberator* from the Sea Islands of South Carolina in late 1862.[2] In the late 1880s, Forten was still writing letters to the editor, such as the one she sent *The Evangelist* (New York, NY; 1856–1869) to correct misrepresentations of race relations in New England. She reminded readers of Connecticut's "'Black Law' . . . forbidding any person to establish in the state any school, academy, or literary institution for the instruction or education of colored person[s] who are not inhabitants of the State, without the consent in writing . . . of a majority of the civil authority, and also of the select men of the town, in which such school . . . is situated"; and of the destruction of the New England school that had admitted Henry Highland Garnett. Nonetheless, African Americans in New England were educated and worked as lawyers, justices of the peace, and judges, and sat as members of state legislatures.[3]

By the 1860s and 1870s, some women moved from penning letters to the editor to becoming regular correspondents for papers such as the *Christian Recorder*, as Gardner's research establishes was the case for Annie M. Smith, a teacher and secretary of the majority-female Freedmen's Aid Society in Xenia, Ohio; Edmonia Highgate of Syracuse, New York, whose mobility I explore in more detail in this chapter; Sallie Daffin, a schoolteacher who was a graduate of Philadelphia's Institute for Colored Youth; and Lizzie Hart of Morrow, Ohio. Jennie Carter of Nevada City, California, writing under the pen names Mrs. Ann J. Trask and Semper Fidelis, made a similar transition in the pages of the San Francisco *Elevator* at this time, as did Elizabeth Jennings Jr., whose legal battle against segregation in streetcars resulted in the publication of her letters on colonization as a correspondent for the *Pacific Appeal* in the winter of 1862.[4] Many Black feminists continued to use letters to the editor for activist work from the 1870s through the early twentieth century. Mary Ann Shadd's "Trade for our Boys," which offered an account of the National Labor Convention that was held in Washington, DC, on December 6–8, 1872, was written as a letter to the editor of the *New National Era* (Washington, DC; 1870–1874). In the mid- to late 1880s, Ida B. Wells wrote letters to the editors of the *New York Freeman* and *The Evening Scimitar* (Memphis, TN; 18??–1904) on Black political rights, the failure of the Republican and Democratic Parties to protect them, and racialized violence in the South. Mary Church Terrell wrote letters to the editor frequently, including in 1907 and 1908 to correct the media's misrepresentation of her speeches on Black women's safety in domestic labor positions in the South.[5]

Newspapers have offered a letter to the editor section as a public forum for debate for as long as they have circulated. In fact, Teresa Strouth Gaul and Sharon Harris suggest that "letters are the foundational genre of American journalism."[6] Yet how we study this press form and what we argue its uses signify tends to center individualism as a political value. The consequences of this tendency for understanding Black feminisms as well as African Americans' use of this press form are significant. Media historians and periodical studies scholars regard letters to the editor as a constructed press form through which editors shape or consolidate perceptions of their publications. Even though media historians and journalism studies and periodical studies scholars acknowledge that editors are highly selective as they carefully manage this section of the paper, they also continue to read letters to the editor as "a key institution of the public sphere" in which "democracy blossoms because regular citizens" are empowered to enter into "public democratic debate."[7] Underwritten by the print-capitalism thesis and the Habermasian ideal of the public sphere as accessible, transparent, and disinterested, these rather different understandings of letters to the editor emphasize the individual—whether controlling editor or empowered reader—and the capital each asserts, both economic and cultural.[8]

In contrast, work in Black print culture studies and Black periodical studies underscores the ways that collectivity formed the core of how Black readers, editors, and writers understood the affordances of print media. In her work on early African American print culture, Joanna Brooks argues that "Blacks entered the public sphere, not with the negative identity of the disinterested individual citizen, but through positive *collective* incorporation."[9] Eric Gardner maintains that African Americans used letters to the editor as a "central mode for defining and redefining community and nation."[10] Both scholars are part of a broader academic understanding of the Black press as collectivist in conception and praxis that includes Gordon Fraser's understanding of Black newspapers as facilitating "a quasi-national collectivity" not only imaginatively but through its technologies that networked editors, writers, printers, readers and agents, and Benjamin Fagan's framing of the Black press as a central site for imagining collective relations that were not confined to the nation-state. Derrick Spires contends that African Americans theorized Black citizenship in print as "a relation created by and practiced between members of a community."[11] As what he calls "both archive and repertoire," spaces of Black print were understood as activist in the nineteenth century.[12] P. Gabrielle Foreman would term these spaces of "collective address" that were crucial to a "culture of writing that valued collaboration, incorporation, and reach—rather than singular authorship." Black print culture's collectivist praxis and ethos emerged from and helped sustain nineteenth-century Black activism that strove, as Foreman puts it, "to make real an enlivened notion of Black freedom's relationship to participatory democracy embodied in collective, as much as individual, Black agency and rights."[13]

Attention to the collective is crucial not only for understanding the work of Black women's letters to the editor within that wider frame of Black collective relations but also for understanding the operations of racialization as assemblages or unequal formations that position collectives forcefully and violently within social, political, and material orders foundational to American liberal democratic individualism and the white supremacist settler colonialism that authors it.[14] Saidiya Hartman argues that through a "burdened individuality," African Americans were subjugated, not freed, as the nation displaced its "responsibility for providing and ensuring the rights and privileges conferred by the Reconstruction Amendments" onto freedpeople, who were required "to prove their worthiness for freedom."[15] African Americans were forced and later coerced into participating in white supremacist settler colonialism, first through the racial capitalism of the plantation system and then on land they farmed as sharecroppers or as homesteaders who had migrated into newly opened territories and the West. As Jodi Byrd, a member of the Chickasaw Nation, has pointed out, racialization licensed settler expansion into Indigenous territories by "turning indigeneity into a 'racial' category" and in doing so attempted to enforce individualism as a mode of relationality upon Indigenous peoples in order to equate "the distinctions of indigenous nations as sovereign and independent with that of every other racialized and diasporic arrival to be mediated within U.S. citizenry."[16] In other words, working with a central institution of American democracy and the public sphere, as letters to the editor are often understood, requires us to acknowledge that the scholarly investment in reading this press form as serving the individual—whether editor or reader—rests on settler colonialism's interrelated technologies of theft and exploitation of Indigenous territory and African arrivants, the violent and ongoing genocide of Indigenous peoples and the attempted dehumanization of African Americans, and the racialization of space and movement.[17]

This chapter works with a combination of close reading and geospatial data visualizations in order to explore alternative ways of reading letters to the editor that illuminate the distinctive political uses African American women made of that press form in the nineteenth century. What might change if we were to read letters to the editor less for ways they serve either the individual letter writer or the needs of the editors who publish them and more for the ways they mark collective conditions and aspirations or for the ways they mark what Henri Lefebvre foregrounds as counterspace practices that contest notions of space as transparent and what Ashon Crawley attends to as practices of making, not taking?[18] Data visualizations, as a protocol of reading, can assist in recalibrating the tendency to focus on letters to the editor as serving the individual, which is of particular importance when we study the use of a press form by people whose histories include coercion to liberal individualism and liberal democratic citizenship as well as the violent denial of autonomy in the choice to move and in the choice to remain in place and in relation to place.[19] This chapter's premise is that interscale reading—a combination of close reading and data visualization—can enable us to read letters to the editor as a collective and collectivizing form. I pursue that premise in at least two ways. First, in order to map the national reach of Black feminist politics, I elaborate on chapter 1's assertion that Black feminism is organized and sustained not by leader, place, or institution but by recirculation facilitated by Black women's collective organizing.[20] Second, I attend to how this may shift long-standing scholarly assumptions about the registration of Black political desire in print. However much we cannot take letters to the editor as individual readers' unfettered contributions to democratic debate and must, in turn, acknowledge the editorial hand that mediated which letters made it to print, we also cannot ignore the genre or continue to read it in mutually exclusive ways. As Eurie Dahn puts it, such "letters tell us something real about the periodical's self-positioning as well as the different subject positions that the periodical's readers hold or repudiate."[21] Readers were clearly using this press form, and editors were repeatedly inviting them to do so because this content was of interest to others.

The Power for Doing Good

The effects of women such as Mapps Douglass and Stewart taking positions on emigration and Black nationalism in the radical abolitionist and Black press early in the nineteenth century can be seen in the work of journalists and editors that followed them, such as Mary Ann Shadd.[22] Before she left the United States for Canada West in the early fall of 1850, believing this to be the most viable destination for Black emigration, Shadd, like Stewart, was first published with a letter to the editor. In her January 25, 1849, letter to Frederick Douglass's *North Star*, she wrote from her home in Wilmington, Delaware, on improving the condition of free Blacks in the North. Her letter indicted the Black community's central political institution, the Black church, by charging that its clergy were "corrupt . . . sapping our every means, and . . . inculcating ignorance as a duty." She could have gone without saying that, in this controversial accusation as "in anything relating to our people, I am insensible of boundaries," but she was not one to hold back.[23] In a move uncannily similar to Stewart's political program, Shadd's late January 1849 letter to the editor was published in the March 23, 1849, edition of the *North Star* and formed part of her self-published twelve-page pamphlet, *Hints to the Colored People of the North*, which sold for twelve and a half cents.[24] *Hints* had already been promoted by Black nationalist Martin Delany prior to its publication. In his January 16, 1849, letter to the *North Star* published in the column In the Lecturing Field, he wrote of convening meetings in Wilmington, Delaware, on December 25 through 30, 1848, at which Shadd rose to "declar[e] that the subject on which [he] spoke was 'the very food for which the people's minds in Wilmington were starving to death.'" Delany then noted she was the author of a pamphlet "now in press on the elevation of our people," which he had had "the pleasure of examining . . . in manuscript . . . and [took] pleasure in . . . recommending . . . as a creditable production." He wrote that *Hints* would be available at the "bookstore and anti-slavery office of G. W. Goines, 198 S. Sixth street, Philadelphia, also at the grocery store of A. J. Williams, French st. [sic], Wilmington, Delaware." Four months later, Douglass published a letter to the editor dated April 23, 1849, signed J. B. Y. from Philadelphia, that offered a review of sorts and excerpts from Shadd's *Hints* while also bemoaning that the press had offered neither recognition nor mention of it.[25]

As Carla Peterson has pointed out, the emigration debates of the 1850s "replayed in similar terms" those of the 1830s and reconsidered the viability of African colonization as well as Haitian and Canadian emigration in the face of legal developments such as the Fugitive Slave Law of 1850, the Kansas-Nebraska Act of 1854, and the Dred Scott decision of 1857.[26] Women were more publicly involved in the 1850 emigration debates, as Martha Jones documents. "Nearly one-quarter (39 of 171) of the 'executive delegates'" were women at the 1854 National Emigration Convention of Colored People that Martin Delany convened in Cleveland, where "Canadian activist Mary Bibb was elected vice president, and four additional women served as members of the finance committee."[27] The women delegates of this convention were instrumental in its ninth resolution, which declared that "the work of elevation among us cannot be complete until the education of our sons and daughters . . . have been fully accomplished, thereby fitting them for many high positions in society, either in their places of choice as emigrants, or otherwise."[28] Shadd attended the 1855 National Convention of Colored Men in Philadelphia as an elected member and delivered "one of the best speeches" of the convention with her remarks on emigration to Canada West.[29] This convention was the first that included "women's trades in its statistical records and acknowledge[d] their role in the marketplace."[30] Yet in 1849, Shadd's *Hints* was so controversial that it did not sell. In it she contended that "our people . . . make a grand display of ourselves," leaving African Americans open to the "contempt" of "our avowed enemies and pretended friends." She believed the situation was so serious that it was alienating antislavery supporters: "Our true friends are sad at heart because of our weakness—this 'grasping at straws.'" *Hints* stirred the ire of Black Philadelphians who knew of Shadd's pamphlet even if they refused to buy it, and they certainly "would not have had it as a gift."[31]

In 1852, Delany again called attention to *Hints* as "an excellent introduction to a great subject" written by a "peculiarly eccentric" young woman in his *Condition, Elevation, Emigration, and Destiny of the Colored People of the United States.*[32] Although it appeared years after *Hints* had failed, Delany's mention served as free advertising for Shadd just as her second pamphlet appeared in June of 1852, titled *A Plea for Emigration; or Notes of Canada West in its Moral, Social and Political Aspect: with Suggestions Respecting Mexico, West Indies and Vancouver's Island for the Information of Colored Emigrants*. Given that they favored different destinations—Delany favored Central or South America and Shadd preferred Canada West—Delany appeared to be plugging the competition, even though, as Jane Rhodes notes, he also seemed to be unaware that Shadd had published a new emigration pamphlet the same spring that he published *Condition*.[33] *A Plea for Emigration*, a forty-four-page pamphlet, sold for twelve and a half cents and was both advertised in and subject to petty review by the *Voice of the Fugitive*, in which Henry Bibb noted its printing errors and disapproved of Shadd's decision to have it printed in Detroit. And like *Hints* before it, *A Plea for Emigration* was essentially ignored by the American Black and abolitionist press.[34] Nonetheless, Shadd worked to link her new pamphlet to the affordances of the newspaper press, albeit with a greater degree of control than she had exercised with *Hints*. Two months after establishing the *Provincial Freeman* on March 24, 1853, she began a lecture tour of Canada West and the northeastern United States both to attract subscribers and educate potential Black emigrants, "selling *A Plea* . . . (along with *Provincial Freeman* subscriptions) to help defray her travel costs."[35]

That Shadd was attuned to the affordances of the newspaper press for recirculating Black feminist politics should come as little surprise, given she was also the first African American woman we know of to edit a newspaper. In print from March 24, 1853, to the summer of 1860, the *Provincial Freeman* was one of the longest-running self-sustaining Black-owned and Black-edited papers of the nineteenth century.[36] Shadd sought to establish a subscription list of 3,000 readers for the weekly four-page broadsheet of seven columns per page, charging a rate of $1.50 per year, and she secured traveling agents to do so. Jane Rhodes notes that through these agents, the paper reached readers in "Detroit, Philadelphia, Pittsburgh, Cincinnati, and other American cities" as well as readers in its home of Canada West where, as Shirley Logan documents, African American immigrants such as Mary Bibb "formed the Windsor Ladies Club, also referred to as the Mutual Improvement Society, in 1854 . . . the first female literary society in Canada."[37] The *Provincial Freeman* also facilitated the recirculation of Frances Harper's work, publishing her essay "Christianity" in the September 2, 1854, issue along with William Still's letter recommending that essay as part of the soon-to-be published *Poems on Miscellaneous Subjects*.[38] Harper and Shadd had shared the stage when Harper debuted as an abolitionist speaker on August 30, 1853, reading her poetry to an audience at Brick Wesley Church in Philadelphia.[39]

Shadd's editorial work was part of her larger investment in the Black press as both "the power for doing good" and a beacon "stand[ing] on the watch-tower." Her commitment included cofounding the Provincial Union in Toronto with activists such as William P. Newman, Samuel Ringgold Ward, Alexander Hamilton, Levi Foster, Coleman Freeman, Thomas Smallwood, and Samuel Lewis in the late summer of 1854. The Provincial Union wedded "principles of universal freedom" to the "promot[ion of] literature, general intelligence, [and] active benevolence" as literary and benevolent societies in the United States had been doing for decades; named Shadd's paper its organ; and formed a "Ladies' Committee . . .

to devise other measures [than its annual fairs in Toronto, Hamilton, London and Chatham] for promoting . . . the support of the people's organ, the *Provincial Freeman*."[40] In July 1856, *Frederick Douglass' Paper* announced that Hezekiah Ford Douglass was coeditor with Shadd Cary (Shadd had married that year), who received praise from Frederick Douglass for bravely sustaining the *Provincial Freeman* "with very little assistance from others," while "contend[ing] with lukewarmness, false friends, open enemies, ignorance and small pecuniary means. He added that "owing to the hard work to which its editor is subjected . . . it is not very well edited."[41]

Shadd's activism was no doubt informed by that of her father, Abraham Shadd, a colored convention activist and a newspaper agent. By the mid-1850s, she was "one of only a handful of officially recognized women delegates in the convention movement." She participated in or attended conventions along with women who were connected to the Black press in various ways, such as Charlotte Ray, the first wife of *Colored American* editor Charles Ray; and Henrietta Green Regulas Ray, his second wife. Henrietta Ray was the secretary of New York City's African Dorcas Society in 1828, which predated the earliest documented literary society in that state, the African Clarkson Society of New York City, founded in 1829. She went on to lead the New York Female Literary Society in 1834, which raised funds for the *Colored American*. Sydna E. R. Francis, wife of colored convention delegate Abner Francis, was also "president of the Ladies Literary and Progressive Improvement Society of Buffalo and [a] leader in the city's Dorcas society," which also raised funds to support the *Colored American*. Mary Jeffrey, who in 1849 had been treasurer of the Syracuse Provisional Committee, which raised financial support for the *Impartial Citizen*, then edited by Samuel Ringgold Ward, was "begrudging[ly]" seated as a delegate at the 1853 Colored National Convention at Frederick Douglass's urging. She was also president of the Geneva Women's Antislavery Society.[42] Samuel Ward became Shadd's nominal editor of the *Provincial Freeman* from its inception in March 1853 to August 26, 1854, when Shadd finally revealed herself as editor. Like so many of her contemporaries, Shadd was also active in literary societies, including the Bethel Historical and Literary Society in Washington, DC, which she was a member of in the 1880s when she formed the Colored Women's Progressive Franchise Association to promote "women's political and economic rights."[43] Such interconnections between Black female activists, the literary and benevolent societies they led, the colored convention movement where they went unseated and unnamed for decades, and the fledgling Black newspapers their organizing efforts kept in print highlight what Martha Jones identifies as Black public culture's interrelatedness and, following Jones's lead, what P. Gabrielle Foreman calls the overlapping of literary societies and colored conventions in "concerns, methods, and members. . . . for decades."[44]

Shadd also engaged in Black feminist recirculation with a canny use of staged letters to the editor. Scholarship has long acknowledged that she published letters she wrote to herself as the cloaked editor of the *Provincial Freeman* using both her own signature and a variety of pseudonyms.[45] Doing so feigned a feedback loop through which she presented her own political arguments but had them appear as voices within a sustained debate among like-minded readers of the paper. In late May 1855, Shadd wrote as X.Y.Z. to tell her readers in the United States that Chatham, Canada West, had "among all classes and complexions, good mechanics, storekeepers, teachers, and laborers. This is the nucleus for the trade of Kent County, a thriving place, and though once the seat of abominable prejudice, is fast becoming unexceptionable in every sense." In the June 9, 1855, issue, Shadd wrote as Z. H. M. from Lefroy, Canada West to promote that "small village . . . fifty-two miles from Toronto, by railway" that would soon see "the erection of several buildings . . . among which is that of a School-house and place of worship." Emigrants could thrive where "wages are good, and labour greatly in demand." The letter closed with a nod to emigration debates and a flattering address to the "independent" reader: "I shall use this opportunity to say that colored men of a free and independent disposition . . . and who will maintain that disposition at the risk of seeking other quarters for an abode, I think might do well here."[46] Shadd donned these pseudonyms to keep the emigration debate at the forefront of the *Provincial Freeman*'s columns, presenting it as a shared and collective concern as she promoted opportunities for Black self-reliance in Canada West's settlements. The paper's wider public was represented through such letters as surely sharing in the values of independence and self-reliance, as Shadd used what Warner calls reflexivity to create for her readers the sense that "I don't just speak to you; I speak to the public in a way that enters a cross-citational field of many other people speaking to the public."[47]

Shadd also used proxies to recirculate her political views on woman's rights as though they were widely shared, writing letters to herself in the spring and summer of 1854 that contended that women had a divine right to exercise their mental faculties, signing them variously as "Henrietta W—S.," "Dolly Bangs," "Canuck," and "Benjamin."[48] Shadd also wrote articles and offered readers reprints of articles on the reform of married women's property laws in the United States, the United Kingdom, and Canada, where such reform was the focus of woman's rights agitation. In the United States, property included a woman's ability to use her earnings to support and educate her children and to refuse the indenture of her child.[49] Her work had impact; Martha Jones argues that she should be credited with "extending the woman question debate into the realm of publishing while also creating a forum in which women's voices were being heard with unprecedented clarity."[50]

Like Stewart, Shadd was a controversial figure, and she alienated the very readers she needed onside. When she announced that she would remove her name as editor from the masthead of the *Provincial Freeman* in August 1854, she reasoned that the paper would do better with women readers, in particular, without a woman in the editorial chair: "The ladies will be pleased, and assist to sustain [the paper], which they will not do while a *colored* female has the ugly duty to perform; then it is hoped that the childish weakness, seen in some quarters[,] will disappear altogether." Two months later she wrote a letter that began "Dear C" to herself and signed it M. A. S. In it she railed at women for never reading newspapers and, consequently, for being unable to think for themselves. "If there is any one thing that tends to intensify one's contempt for the *muslin multitude*, it is the nothingness the delicate creature displays when invited to aid in a work for the general good," she wrote. "You would be surprised at the pains they take to impress you with their 'feebleness'. . . . Must not think of helping without getting Mr. ___'s consent. . . . Young ladies who have no Mr. ___s to think for them, really do not know,—they never read the newspapers. . . . What a set!" Shadd took her final leave roughly a year later in the June 30, 1855, edition through an article titled "Adieu," notifying her readers that William P. Newman would take over as editor while she became an agent securing subscriptions for the paper. She also threw down a gauntlet: "To colored women, we have a word—we have 'broken the Editorial ice,' whether willing or not, for your class in America; so go to Editing, as many of you as are willing and able, and as soon as you may, if you think you are ready."[51]

When the Black press exploded in the final decades of the nineteenth century (sixty-eight Black-owned newspapers were founded in 1887 alone, and a total of 575 had been established by 1890), and "twenty-three black women in the nation . . . had achieved status as journalists by 1891," similar assertions that Black women could be or already were a force in journalism would be issued by the likes of Gertrude Mossell in the *New York Freeman* (1886), Lucy Wilmot Smith in *The Journalist* (1889), and Carrie Langston in the *Atchison Blade* (1892).[52] Shadd's invitation to Black women to become journalists predated these women by at least thirty years, and though she was no longer an editor after 1855, she continued to be involved in the Black press, working as an agent and contributor for Frederick Douglass's *New National Era* and John W. Cromwell's *People's Advocate* when she returned to the United States.

Because they make such strong use of recirculation, we can regard Mary Ann Shadd's tactics as indebted to those Stewart pioneered for Black feminists in the press. And like Stewart, Sarah Mapps Douglass, Sarah Forten, Amy Matilda Cassey, and Elizabeth Jennings Sr., Shadd worked in a context shaped by literary societies and the political potential they cultivated in and for their members. Even though she experienced Black women in Canada West as highly bound by gender proscriptions, it is clear that by midcentury, literary societies influenced many Black women who sought to be capable in debate, as this 1852 letter to *Frederick Douglass' Paper* indicates: "I am not expecting to be a public speaker; but I should like to be prepared to express myself intelligibly, either before a society of ladies or a mixed assembly, if I should ever be called to do so unexpectedly."[53] And these same women were so integral to literary character as a liberatory political strategy that when the editors of the *Weekly Anglo-African* opened a reading room in November 1859 on Prince Street in New York City, a female reader of the magazine from Hartford, Connecticut, wrote to say "it will be productive of good, especially if the ladies patronize it and enter into discussion upon the merits of the different periodicals on the files. Nothing calls into action and better strengthens one's judgment as this habit of conversing on what we read."[54] Elizabeth McHenry documents that the reading room provided the venue for these types of discussions as well as "a course of popular lectures," linking, as did literary societies, a broad notion of literacy, civic debate, recirculation, and women's educational development for members of New York's African American community.[55]

Black Flow and Making Place

Letters to the editor are community made visible on the page. They facilitate what Michael Warner maintains is "the achievement of this cultural form": the press "allow[s] participants in its discourse to understand themselves as directly and actively belonging to a social entity that exists historically in secular time and has consciousness of itself."[56] By sharing readers' views in a form that offers opportunity for debate, if not also actively courting or staging such debate as Mary Ann Shadd did, letters to the editor are a press form that intensifies the sense of direct and active belonging that Benedict Anderson argued the media form itself created through a "mass ceremony" of "imagined community."[57] They lend a degree of authority to the individual writing them because the form signals a public voice or a voice issuing from a recognizable collective. This press form can also be said to mobilize, even as it manifests, cultures of circulation to performatively shape collectives "through their inscription in specific social practices such as . . . reading," writing or having a letter written, and the democratic or "rational" debate that Jürgen Habermas argued was the hallmark of the public sphere.[58] Understanding the formative effects of literary societies upon Black women's politics and, in turn, Black feminism as co-constitutive with the Black press would mean that we study letters to the editor as evidence of collective civic identity, collective voice, and a collectivist politics that included Black women. In doing so, we would begin to, as Gaonkar and Povinelli put it, "foreground the social life *of* the form rather than [only] reading social life *off* of it."[59] The Black press is more than an archive for the study of Black literature, history, and politics, although it is also this. Press forms must be seen to matter as more than the content they offer to readers or scholars and be further explored as constitutive, as forms that "regimes of recognition demand" within a larger terrain in which power is distributed according to "institutions of intelligibility, livability, viability."[60]

Reading letters to the editor as also indexing nineteenth-century Black women's collective and relational practices of making place requires us to understand the function of this press genre in the early Black press. Nineteenth-century Black newspapers relied on their readers for content. For example, emigrant readers sent editors their local newspapers as reprintable content, as did San Francisco *Elevator* readers in India, Australia, New Zealand, Japan and China.[61] Editors also brokered correspondent roles for readers who could offer "local color" or political insights and views of interest to others, and these roles could grow from letters to the editor that were regarded as useful or of interest to other readers. As Eric Gardner documents, *Christian Recorder* editors "earnestly solicit[ed] correspondence from all parts of the United States" in 1867, and they established broad rules for letter writers: brevity, good writing, no "personal flings and feuds," no anonymous submissions, and the revelation of a pseudonymous correspondent's full name prior to publication.[62] They also very clearly linked the provision of content and subscription to this press form by promising "better terms with the editor and publisher" for contributors who wrote for the paper and convinced others to subscribe while they were at it.[63] Letters to the *Christian Recorder* "regularly filled at least a quarter and often half of the paper's space," and they were a particularly vital form of connection between soldiers and their communities during the Civil War.[64] By 1876, when the reported circulation of the four-page *Elevator* was 866, the circulation of the *Christian Recorder* was 5,000. We know from Eric Gardner's detailed research on *Christian Recorder* subscribers from 1861 to 1867 that they "were both incredibly diverse geographically *and* quite mobile." "Individual identified first-time subscribers" in those years were 37.6 percent female and 62.4 percent male.[65]

Brian Thorton contends that although letters to the editor have not been systematically studied, they are nonetheless "of vital importance in gauging the impact that the African-American press was having at a given time."[66] This seems clear both at a social and economic level, given how *Christian Recorder* editors solicited letters to the editor from readers and subscribers. Letters to the editor are also a significant index of how Black women made place in print and were a constitutive genre for the formation and reach of their political expression. I suggest that geospatial data visualizations can illuminate letters to the editor as a press genre that may appear to register movement in a limited way—by originating in one location and being addressed to another—and to register individual concerns and opinions. Yet it is also a press genre that marks *collective* material and historical geographies. Even though editors cue letters with their choice of newspaper content and their editorials, curate and edit what they publish, and have been known to pen such letters themselves for publication, letters to the editor nonetheless register shared and collective concerns of relation, space, movement, and place making.

As Judith Madera has argued, "print representation was already the work of thinking around dominant geographies" for Black writers in the nineteenth century.[67] Because they could not claim to "own" space and were either traded as possessions or had nominal rather than actual freedom at the time, African Americans tended not to conceive of space or place as fixed or as something to be possessed. Instead, they conceived "of place as flow, place as connectivity," thereby making place "a source of hope," as Madera puts it.[68] It is vital to consider the question of how Black flow may make place and not take space. This requires us to rethink assumptions that tend to render space transparent, as Henri Lefebvre would put it, or that render space somehow natural rather than structured by inequities. One such assumption that requires rethinking when we are reading for Black flow is the alignment of mobility with autonomous movement. The physical or spatial movement that letters to the editor index makes them one way to read African American mobility as a practice of making place. Geospatial data visualizations of letters to the editor can map both social and physical movement, including movement and migration facilitated through the founding occupation and "frontier" extension of white supremacist settler colonialism. And for African Americans, it must be remembered that the ability to exercise autonomy as individual choice has been a matter of collective freedom and rights uninsured in practice, however much they may be written in law.

Visualizing an individual's letters to the editor, such as those of Edmonia Highgate, a northerner who taught freedmen in the South following the Civil War, does not immediately make apparent a Black woman's mobility that complicates dominant scripts of both movement's alignment with freedom and mobility's alignment with individual autonomy (figure 2.1). When Highgate's letters to the *Christian Recorder*, the *New Orleans Tribune*, and the *Colored Tennessean* from February 1865 to November 1867 are mapped in a geospatial data visualization, they appear to evidence an exercise of freedom as autonomous movement.[69] She was highly mobile for an educated Black woman in her social position immediately following the war; she moved from the Northeast to Virginia, Maryland, New Orleans and rural Louisiana, and Mississippi. Yet she was also moving and working on stolen lands, as the visualization and its legend attempts to make clear. She moved from unceded lands stolen by white colonial settlers from Indigenous nations before 1776 to lands that Spain had seized and that the United States acquired through the Louisiana Purchase, and on to lands the Choctaw Nation ceded to the United States under the treaty of Dancing Rabbit Creek in 1830, which instigated their forced removal via the Trail of Tears.

An interscale reading of Highgate's letters that combines both close reading and data visualization will reveal several important factors. Her movements were undertaken in service of education, a political value understood as crucial to collective Black freedom and progress. Yet even before her published letters to the editor appeared, Highgate's movement in service of that collective value was at times forced, such as when racism resulted in her being denied a teaching position in Syracuse, New York (Onondaga and Haudenosaunee territory), which Eric Gardner documents resulted in her move to "Montrose, Pennsylvania [Munsee Lenape] and then to Binghamton, New York [Susquehannock, Haudenosaunee, and Onondaga territory], to teach."[70] Later she applied to the American Missionary Association, which was hiring trained Black teachers to educate the freedpeople. Teaching took Highgate first to Norfolk, Virginia (Lumbee territory), and later to a post in Maryland (Piscataway territory) "by early 1865."[71] Her letters from New Orleans (Choctaw and Chitimacha territory) published in the *Recorder* and the *Colored Tennessean* in the spring, summer, and late fall of 1866 offered accounts of the school she had charge of; what she called a "crisis in

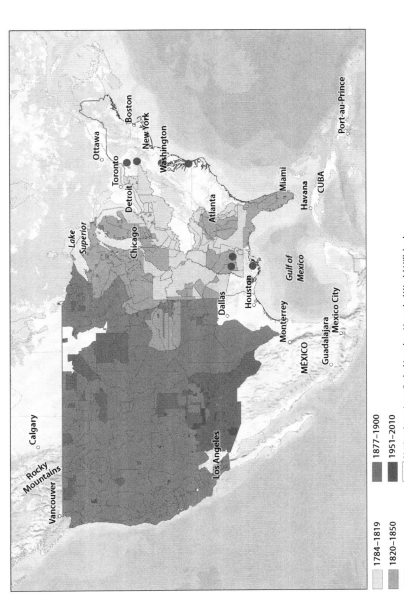

Figure 2.1. Locations from which Edmonia Highgate wrote letters to the editors of the *Christian Recorder* and the *New Orleans Tribune*, February 1865–October 1867. Produced by Teresa Zackodnik in ArcGIS using base layers created by Claudio Saunt, eHistory. *Note:* This legend also applies to figures 2.4–2.7, though it is not reproduced with each figure.

educational affairs" that the city's freedmen and women faced; the New Orleans Massacre of July 30, 1866; and the climate of violent threat African Americans faced in Louisiana.[72] Highgate also wrote to the *Recorder* of her travels up the James River in hope of seeing her brother, who had been wounded on a Civil War battlefield; she did not yet know he had already died from the injuries he sustained.[73]

Highgate's *Recorder* letters additionally detail the threat of violence she taught under while in rural Louisiana, where she was shot at by whites during a horseback ride.[74] Any notion of Black women's movement as an exercise of mobility—autonomous freedom or exercised will—is difficult to maintain alongside a critical awareness that then, as now, spaces of safety for Black women were and are both highly relative and precarious. Further, any notion of African American mobility at this time as freely exercised choice is possible only by ignoring both the context of the Civil War as an event that impacted that mobility and the larger context of African American enslavement in the United States, the future of which that war would decide. In other words, while a data visualization will "read" movement in particular ways, it has a limited ability to attend to the complexity of African American mobility and movement that an interscale reading methodology brings to the surface. In the case of the letters I discuss here, those written by individuals not only index that person's movements but are also vectors of collective African American movement and its political, economic, and material implications. Considering letters such as those Edmonia Highgate wrote to the *Christian Recorder*, the *New Orleans Tribune*, and the *Colored Tennessean* call for a recalibration of mobility to account for the ways its exercise by African Americans exceeded the standard assumption that autonomous movement was the result of autonomously exercised choice or freedom. Such a recalibration becomes all the more necessary when we consider that Black movement continues to be entangled with settler-colonial theft of land. As Judith Madera has argued, "materially and affectively, national spatialities are polyphonous constructions" that both "embed different histories" and "proliferate them."[75] Because the settler colonialism of the US nation-state is still promulgated as a narrative of "free" mobility, accepted notions of mobility as autonomously exercised freedom of movement are critically and ethically inadequate for understanding Black flow.

Black Feminist Place Making

Reading letters to the editor as multiply indexing a collective making of place as flow and connectivity adapts to newspapers Joanna Brooks's "reconce[ption] of books not as objects of exchange and consumption but as *vectors of social movement*."[76] Brooks underscores the importance of "consider[ing] the Black experience of public space in the development of a Black counterpublic print tradition," so that entering the public sphere is understood to be a spatial, collective, material, and political movement for African Americans.[77] In other words, the entry of African Americans into the public sphere and their movement within both public space and political system is indexed by their counterpublic print tradition, including the Black press. That collective entry into and movement within the public sphere fundamentally challenges democratic individualism as much as a historical and ongoing Black collective experience of public space in what is known as the United States has contested the illusion of that space as public in any meaningful way. Consequently, it is possible to read letters to the editor as a key form of Black flow, that "does as it makes" by "feeling out the normative organizational codes that cohere in oppressive power systems, and then finding disruptions in, contradictions to, and corridors through these codes."[78] Making place in print is an act that contests or disrupts who can speak publicly of what and where as well as who can be, and who can move, where. It is a practice and making of Black flow. And making place through letters to the editor is clearly something to attend to when we learn that "a massive amount" of the correspondence addressed to papers like the *Christian Recorder* "focused on questions of mobility."[79]

The letters African American women wrote to newspapers over the first five decades of the life of the Black press are an "archive of movement and spatial representation," what Madera would call a "circulating commons," that indexes a communally grounded Black feminist place making.[80] I take as fundamental the contentions of the leaders of the Black women's club movement that the position of Black women registered a zero limit of Black citizenship, and so Black women's politics constituted the vanguard of a collective Black politics that was both actual and aspirational. This was expressed by Anna Julia Cooper as "Only the Black woman can say 'when and where I enter . . . the whole race . . . enters with me'" in 1892.[81] I read this circulating commons as an African American collective entry into the public sphere and public space.[82] Through letters to the editor, Black women actively made place for themselves and for their communities in a nation that refused to recognize them as citizens with rights and protections. In what follows, I focus on the letters Black women wrote to thirteen Black-owned and Black-edited newspapers in publication from 1827 to the mid-1870s,[83] as well as to William Lloyd Garrison's *The Liberator*, with its 80 percent African American subscription base,[84] and to Hampton Normal and Agricultural Institute's *Southern*

Workman. These papers were based in the Northeast—*Freedom's Journal* (New York, NY; 1827–1829), the *North Star* (Rochester, NY; 1847–1851), *Frederick Douglass' Paper* (Rochester, NY; 1851–1858), *The Liberator* (Boston, MA; 1831–1865), and the *Christian Recorder* (Philadelphia, PA; 1852–); in the South—the *Colored Tennessean* (1865–1866), *The Southern Workman* (1872–1939), the *Missionary Record* (1869–1879), the *New Orleans Daily Creole* (1865–1857), *La Tribune de la New Orleans/The New Orleans Tribune* (1864–1869), and the *Weekly Louisianian* (1872–1882); in the Midwest—*Cleveland Gazette* (Cleveland, OH; 1883–1941); and in the West—the *Pacific Appeal* (San Francisco, CA; 1862–1880) and the San Francisco *Elevator* (1865–1898). Of these papers, the *Christian Recorder*, the San Francisco *Elevator*, and the *Southern Workman* together account for 71 percent of the letters to the editor that form my dataset.[85] Geospatial data visualizations of these letters offer us both a view of Black women's politics across multiple scales—local, regional, and national—and across time, albeit one that was mediated by editors of these papers.

African American women were using the press and letters to the editor to assert their presence and their political views from the year the first Black periodical, *Freedom's Journal*, was published in 1827. Even though the Black press published far more letters penned by men, the intensity of Black women's political assertion through this press genre can be visualized regionally in a heat map, in which color and color intensity index the degree of women's political activity and engagement as registered through the number of letters to the editor women wrote from the locations documented (figure 2.2).[86] A heat map visualizes the intensity of that political assertion regionally: darker color indexes greater political activity and engagement as registered through the number of letters to the editor Black women wrote. A white area encircled by a darker area indicates the highest intensity of Black women's political activity via this press form. Since letters to the editor are cued by newspaper content and register a readership's active engagement with the media form, this visualization documents that African American women were knowledgeable about and participated in the print-based circulation of Black politics.[87] It also tells us that they understood themselves as active participants in a Black public. Disrupting the settled scholarly understanding that antebellum and early postbellum African American politics and its expression in print culture was concentrated primarily in the Northeast corridor, this visualization shows us that Black women's political engagement through the press as readers and writers was more intense in the West than in the Northeast across these five decades. California was a nexus of Black women's political activism that far outstripped its population. Following this press genre also reveals that Louisiana and Mississippi were

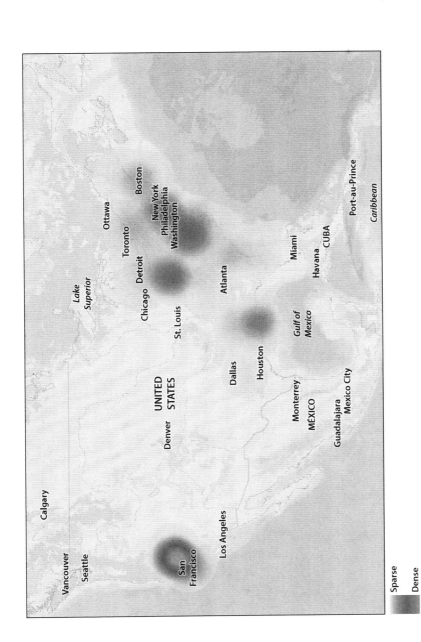

Figure 2.2. Heat map of the origins of African American women's letters to the editor, 1827 to mid-1870s. Produced by Teresa Zackodnik in ArcGIS.

very active locations for Black feminism in these decades.[88] An interscale reading of letters to the editor challenges several operative understandings that have been foundational to how we conceive of the early Black press, of Black readers and their engagement with newspapers as indexed by published correspondence, and of Black politics.

Letters to the editor trace the movement of people, ideas, and politics or a "circulating commons." The circulation of politics can be difficult to document beyond known networks of political leaders, organizations, and political gatherings or associations, yet letters to the editor may offer us further insight into politics on the ground as part of everyday Black life. Generalizing a reading of Black women's politics at the level of the local or the regional, as figure 2.2 does, is complicated by an attention to a letter writer's location alongside the location of the paper to which they wrote. Such attention reveals that Black women's politics are moving across scales and exceeding the fixity of any individual's physical location. For example, Black women living in Philadelphia wrote letters to the editor of the *Pacific Appeal* and the San Francisco *Elevator*. The San Francisco *Elevator* circulated these women's political views internationally through the Pacific and into Asia via Black seamen working on the Pacific Mail Steamship Company and emigrant readers, and the paper had agents in Panama City, Yokohama, Japan (for China and Japan), Honolulu, and British Columbia.[89] Considering Black women's letters to the editor as a circulating commons makes it difficult to generalize or delimit political activism and engagement at any scale once we see how Black women's politics were exceeding the fixity of any individual's physical location through the particular circulation routes of individual newspapers. Through this press form, Black women's political engagement and activism had a national and international reach that developed along with and sustained the fledgling Black press.

Mapping Black Women's Freedom Dreams

As geospatial data visualizations can make clear, nineteenth-century Black women's politics were asserted through the press in different regions simultaneously and were also sustained over time. Their letters to the editor reveal multiple and varied assertions of Black freedom that sought to make place for their communities in a nation hostile to their presence. They also claim Black women's right to be involved in those public political battles. Making political place for African Americans in the public sphere meant a repeated assertion of what Robin Kelley calls "freedom dreams" in the face of realities otherwise. Kelley argues that political and social movements are often evaluated in terms of their success rather than by the visions they fostered and sought to make real, visions that fueled both continued struggle and successive generations of sustained activism.[90] His assertions are as valid today when considering social and political movements such as Black Lives Matter as they are when considering early Black feminisms. In figure 2.3, which visualizes Black women's letters to the editor focused on freedom, the size of the circle indicates the number of letters written. These letters argued for women's contributions to abolitionist politics and asserted their positions in debates on the Fugitive Slave Act of 1850, the Civil War, and the material conditions of soldiers on the battlefields. Following the war, Black women wrote letters to newspapers seeking to reunite families that were fractured by both slavery and the Civil War. They wrote to share their community Jubilee celebrations with readers across the country. And Black women's letters to the editor also drew attention to neo-slave conditions for freedpeople under an ongoing racial capitalism that was leveraged through the prison system and its exploitations of labor, such as the chain gang.

Mapping letters to the editor reveals that they register the movement of politics across physical space as well as time, and in doing so they also register movement into the public sphere collectively and politically even when they appear to be indexing local political concerns. A paper's circulation coupled with African American communal reading practices further complicates and magnifies the mobility of politics registered in this press form. Animated visualizations can help us apprehend that spatial and temporal mobility. Mapping African American women's letters on education and education reform in an animated visualization (see https://youtu.be/mXcfRvnNVH4?si=8ad3OX4DSmdOoL4U) reveals that this political focus was active for Black women in the Midwest by the 1870s, in the West in the early 1860s, and decades earlier for African American women in the East and the South. Clearly, education and education reform were sustained political values for African American women across the nation, and they were registering it in print whenever a Black paper in circulation provided them with a venue.

While they can help us see Black flow and the circulation of Black feminist politics across space and time, data visualizations can also challenge our understandings of the political in very useful ways. As scholarship on Black politics has long argued, any understanding of the political must be recalibrated from a focus on formally organized and national politics to on-the-ground, informal, and infrapolitical forms and political practices.[91] White-dominant frames of what registers as political, particularly within feminist politics, also must be challenged if

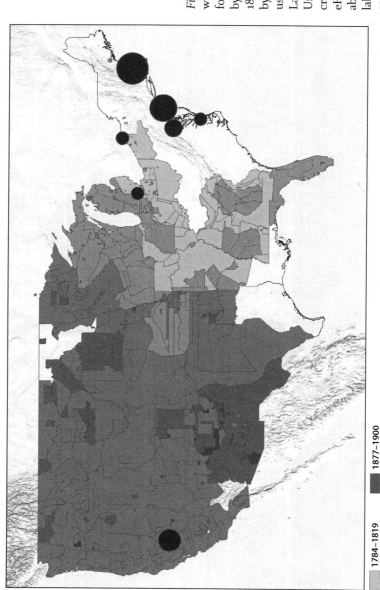

Figure 2.3. African American women's letters to the editor focused on freedom, clustered by location of letter writers, 1827 to mid-1870s. Produced by Teresa Zackodnik in ArcGIS using Native American Ceded Lands and Native American Unceded Lands base layers created by Claudio Saunt, eHistory. Keywords in letters: abolition, Civil War, convict labor, Emancipation, families separated, freedmen, fugitive, Lincoln, post–Civil War, prison, slavery, soldiers.

nineteenth-century Black women's politics are to be more accurately apprehended. Framing Black feminist politics according to the recognized white feminist script of rights for women—women in abolition, woman's place, woman's rights, woman suffrage, and education for women—results in a misapprehension that Black feminist politics were nascent from the 1820s through the mid-1870s (figure 2.4). That such a focus on the pursuit of democratic liberal individualism and women's access to it misconceives the scope, intent, and constituencies of nineteenth-century Black feminisms becomes abundantly clear when set alongside a data visualization of Black feminisms as advocating for the collective rather than exclusively for gender-focused rights (figure 2.5). Broadening keywords to political concerns such as education and education reform, Black civil rights, temperance, sharecropping, wages and employment, conventions, the Black church, and prisons and convict labor reveals significant Black feminist political activity in these decades. Again, in these geospatial data visualizations, circle size is a comparative indicator of number of letters written or political engagement.

Finally, data visualizations of letters to the editor also have the potential to unsettle established understandings of Black politics with an attunement to the particularity of Black women's activism as part of that political terrain. The nineteenth-century Black church has long been established as the Black community's institutional base for the development and organization of its politics and has been understood as the "center of black life, political, social and religious."[92] Richard Newman has argued for an understanding of both the Black church and "community organizations and educational institutions" as sites of "shadow politics." Although "traditionally . . . defined by sociologists as . . . alternate" and "liminal" *spaces* "of political activity," he redefines shadow politics as "parallel black political *practices* that both challenged racialized American political institutions and, at the same time, lay claim to core elements of those institutions."[93] Scholarship has long cited the church's centering of education as a foundational priority in order to argue for the institution's centrality to Black political freedom struggles.[94] Yet only 8 percent of African American women's letters to the editor focused on or mentioned the church from the late 1820s through the mid-1870s, even including in church-based periodicals, such as the *Christian Recorder* (figure 2.6). This is all the more surprising when we know from the work of scholars such as Martha Jones that Black women were pursuing reforms to the institutional structure of Black churches and women's ability to access them. For example, the AME Daughters of Zion advocated the licensing of women as preachers in 1848,

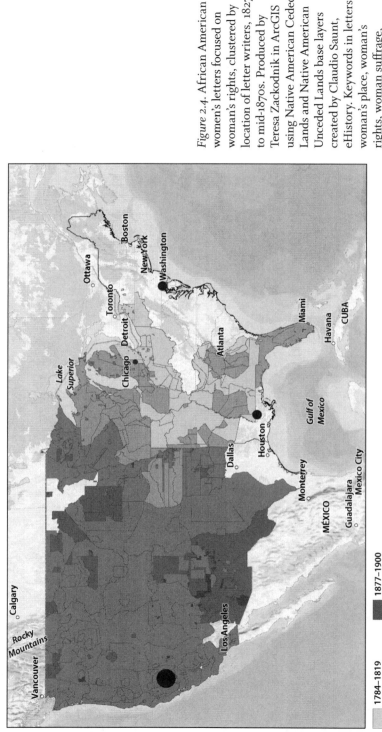

Figure 2.4. African American women's letters focused on woman's rights, clustered by location of letter writers, 1827 to mid-1870s. Produced by Teresa Zackodnik in ArcGIS using Native American Ceded Lands and Native American Unceded Lands base layers created by Claudio Saunt, eHistory. Keywords in letters: woman's place, woman's rights, woman suffrage, women in abolition, women's education.

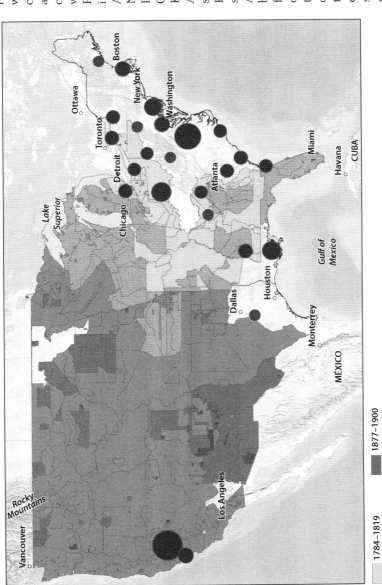

Figure 2.5. African American women's letters focused on collective conditions, rights, and political institutions, clustered by location of letter writers, 1827 to mid-1870s. Produced by Teresa Zackodnik in ArcGIS using Native American Ceded Lands and Native American Unceded Lands base layers created by Claudio Saunt, eHistory. Keywords in letters: Fifteenth Amendment, Black male suffrage, abolition and slavery, Black civil rights, Black suffrage, segregated railway, AME, Baptist, church, benevolent societies, charity, fundraising, child rearing, orphanage, colored conventions, conduct, respectability, convict labor, prison, education, education reform, employment, home ownership, self-reliance, self-support, sharecropping, wages, literary societies, race unity, racial progress, temperance.

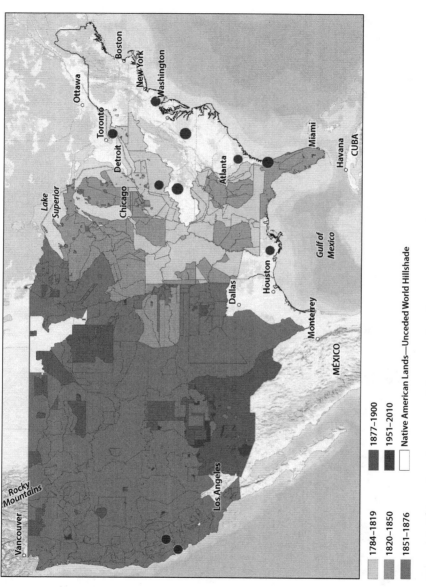

Figure 2.6. African American women's letters to the editor mentioning the church, clustered by location of letter writers, 1827 to mid-1870s. Produced by Teresa Zackodnik in ArcGIS using Native American Ceded Lands and Native American Unceded Lands base layers created by Claudio Saunt, eHistory.

at the same time that the first woman's rights convention was being organized in Seneca Falls.[95] Although 40 percent of Black women's letters to the editor in these decades focus on education and education reform, they say nothing of the church. The primacy of the Black church as a political institution, a made place, or a shadow political practice is not borne out in Black women's use of this press form to register and mobilize their politics from 1827 through the mid-1870s. This suggests an avenue ripe for further study.

The Digital Turn and Reading Black Feminist Futures in the Nineteenth Century

Reading letters to the editor as vectors of social movement has ramifications for how we understand both this press form and Black women's collectivist politics, but it can be difficult to undertake with the sheer number of objects of study made available by the digitization of historical African American newspapers. Our boon is also our challenge. Although the digitization of these newspapers facilitates research, it has not made it possible to depart from traditional reading methods, nor is that necessarily desirable. For example, from the Readex African American Newspapers, Series 1, 1827–1998, which collects 282 newspapers, I read 1,700 letters to the editor published from 1827 to the mid-1870s in order to determine whether their writers were women and they were, consequently, part of my dataset.[96] Reading letters to the editor remains a time-intensive prospect with the digital turn.[97] The accuracy of digitized collections is also affected by the limitation of OCR (optical character recognition) with microfilm of historical papers in varying condition and by the "dirty data" resulting from uncorrected OCR. Digitized collections are also bound by database features, such as search protocols, tagging, and errors. Readex's collection is based on the project that Google Books began and then abandoned to digitize much of the Wisconsin Historical Society's (WHS) collection of historical African American newspapers. Readex is often misunderstood as exhaustive, with the exception of the few titles that are part of Accessible Archives and JSTOR. Yet WHS librarians say that in taking over Google's abandoned project, Readex omitted a significant number of titles from the library's holdings, which, though extensive, also do not capture the entirety of the historical Black press that is scattered across the country in special collections, regional libraries, and microfilm holdings if it is preserved.[98] Many Black newspapers and magazines are also lost to time; titles are mentioned in other newspapers or in writings about the Black press from the late nineteenth century onward but have not yet been located.⁹⁹ Finally, scholars have been vocal about the paywalling of digitized archival materials, a practice that is antithetical to the preservation of such documents for public knowledge. The effects of these delimitations for studying and understanding Black women's lives and their political activism should not be underestimated nor should paywalling history be acceptable, particularly when it is the paywalling of freedom struggles.

Researchers working with digital humanities tools need also to seriously attend to foundational epistemological assumptions. Distinguishing between constructivist and realist models of knowledge, Johanna Drucker advocates for a self-conscious digital humanities that acknowledges its ideological and epistemological investments, which are evident in foundational choices such as terminology. "*Capta* is 'taken' actively," she argues, a terminology choice that reflects a constructivist understanding of what, in contrast, a realist approach calls "*data*[, which] is assumed to be a 'given' able to be recorded and observed."¹⁰⁰ For projects focused on racially minoritized individuals or collectives, assuming that data is a neutral and objective "given" would be highly problematic. Kim Gallon has posed further crucial questions for digital humanities research: "What do we do with forms of humanity excluded from or marginalized in how we study the humanities and practice the digital humanities? What are the implications of using computational approaches to theorize and draw deeper insight into a modern humanity that is *prima facie* arranged and constructed along racial lines?"¹⁰¹ Black Studies has brought such questions to the fore through its deliberations on "the human," and digital humanities researchers must keep these questions active in their work.

The self-consciousness Drucker and Gallon advocate for must, in other words, extend from the way data is imported and "normalized" to the tools used to visually render it for interpretation. Historian R. J. Morris argues that databases and spreadsheets push the researcher strongly "toward a narrative dominated by groups and regularities and away from the particularity of person, place, and event."¹⁰² Anyone working with data visualizations knows their reliance on comma-separated-value (CSV) spreadsheets. Creating datasets on which to base digital visualizations pushes researchers to "normalize data," what Tara McPherson defines as "stripping it of meaningful, idiosyncratic context, creating a system of interchangeable equivalencies" in order to arrive at markers such as keywords that represent how the data will be read and made to mean.¹⁰³ Here, Gallon's insights into the tension foundational to what she calls a "technology of recovery" are urgently needed: "Any connection between humanity and the digital . . .

requires an investigation into how computational processes might reinforce the notion of a humanity developed out of racializing systems, even as they foster efforts to assemble or otherwise build alternative human modalities."[104] Digital tools, what they depend upon, and the results they produce can reinforce anti-Black ontologies rather than alternatives to them.

The tools the digital turn makes available to readers, students, and researchers nonetheless make it possible to reconceive of and read letters to the editor as a political instrument of marginalized collectives rather than a form of public expression primarily available to those individuals privileged enough to have access to and a place within the public sphere. One route to reading the circulating commons that Black women created through these newspapers is to "follow the genre," as Dallas Liddle proposes, and as I have done here—to ask what it reveals about how Black women understood newspapers as a media form with affordances for their political concerns and activism.[105] Geospatial data visualizations of letters to the editor can map letters to the editor as a vector of Black women's political movement across space and, when animated, over time; they show us the ways Black women were making place for both themselves and other African Americans during decades when their freedom and civil rights continued to be unsecured. As a research method and a reading protocol, data visualization can be very useful in at least three ways: it can illuminate a phenomenon or pattern more clearly or for the first time; it can prompt us to ask new questions of our archives and challenge or reanimate settled readings and understandings by helping us see differently; and it can help us to apprehend scope and scale even as it both assists and challenges us to manage both when working with archives that strain yet still call on the abilities of long-established modes of reading.[106] I join others in suggesting that we need also to advance the scholarly tendency to produce broad, generalized descriptions of archives and networks with digital humanities tools by pursuing more finely grained analyses that nonetheless manage to read archives of significant size.[107]

To apprehend Black women's collective and relational practices of making place that refuse settler-colonial practices of taking or possession, we must remain attuned to the scale of the collective in a press genre we are critically predisposed to read at the scale of the individual. I develop this argument further in the next chapter by considering letters that African American and Indigenous female students and graduates wrote to Hampton's *Southern Workman*, an understudied resource that testifies to the entanglements of newly freed African Americans with the early residential school system and ongoing colonization. These letters not only register Black and Indigenous geographies as resisting and refusing colonial thefts and representations of space and place but also offer what Madera calls "nonrepresentational geographies." As such, they are productively read as "deliberations about the ways places get produced rather than the outcomes of that production. Put another way, they are about the relations that come together to make place."[108]

Chapter Three

Geographies of Racialization, Occupation, and Refusal in the *Southern Workman*

> A geographical imperative lies at the heart of every struggle for social justice.
>
> —RUTH WILSON GILMORE

In February of 1871, Sojourner Truth wrote A. M. Powell, editor of the *National Anti-Slavery Standard*, from Florence, Massachusetts, with her "appeal to the people of Rhode Island and Massachusetts . . . to petition Congress to give the Freed People a grant of land so that they can be led to earn their own living, and be taken off the support of the government." She had been traveling through the Northwest, New England, and the Mid-Atlantic gathering petition signatures since August 1870 and wrote that she "hop[ed] some body would print a little of what I am doing, but the papers seem to be content simply in saying how old I am." Seven years earlier, in 1864, Truth had traveled to Washington, DC, to meet President Lincoln, a meeting brokered by Elizabeth Keckley, who "led a local freedpeople's relief society . . . the 1862 Ladies' Contraband Relief Association" and was "dressmaker and personal attendant" to Mary Todd Lincoln.[1] Truth stayed to work at camps in and around Washington for the National Freedmen's Relief Association and the Freedmen's Bureau (the Bureau of Refugees, Freedmen, and Abandoned Lands) from 1864 to 1868. By 1868, in the face of sustained criticism by conservatives, the Freedmen's Bureau had all but shut its doors and congressional support for the freedpeople had waned while their needs increased in a postwar economy.[2] Truth worked to place refugees of the war with employers, but by the late 1860s and early 1870s she had become convinced that allotment of land in the West for refugee resettlement on the "model" of "the Indian reservation" was the solution.[3] In this 1871 letter to the *National Anti-Slavery Standard*, Truth wrote of having "got fifty petitions printed at my own expense" for land for the freedpeople, calling out their suffering in and around Washington, DC, as " a shame, while the government has so much unoccupied land in the West, where they might earn their living." She closed with her plans to go "to Kansas . . . in hopes of finding the land there. . . . I hope you will print all that you can on this subject and so help me in my work, for it will benefit you as well as the rest of the people."[4]

Truth's 1871 petition to Congress is noteworthy, not least for the way it linked freedpeople's capacity to "become useful" self-supporting "citizens" with granting them "a portion of the public land in the West,"[5] land which, of course, was only "public" because it was stolen Indigenous territory. As Nell Irvin Painter documents, Truth's logic prevailed among both Black and white reformers at "antislavery meetings and black labor conventions." In Louisiana and Tennessee, freedpeople were organizing to resettle in Kansas, "the quintessential free state— home of the martyred John Brown and firmly Republican."[6] By 1879, an exodus of tens of thousands to Kansas from Mississippi, Louisiana, Texas, and Tennessee— "Exodusters," who were driven out by violence, voter intimidation, and a Democratic Party retaking state power, had made Truth's plan a reality. Waves of Black migration to Kansas and Western plains states make clear that Black flow cannot be disentangled from settler colonialism's theft and occupation of Indigenous territories even at two centuries' remove from Jamestown.

African Americans were forced through enslavement to "participate" in settler colonialism and were later coerced into such relations to land through white supremacist settler-colonial structures, such as the opening" of the West that drew the Exodusters and initiatives to educate Southern freedpeople in manual and agricultural labor. These structural approaches to racializing labor, space, and movement developed alongside Indigenous contestations and refusals of settler-colonial occupation, racialized constructions of relations to space and land, and the aggressive management of movement within what is now known as the US nation-state. Democratic individualism underlay the larger settler-colonial removal and severalty of sovereign lands and territories that sought to control Indigenous movement and place making by transforming Indigenous peoples' relations to and responsibilities for land into individual possession and settlement.[7] This ongoing reconfiguring of place into space, a reconfiguration that depends upon its incessant racialization as well as the racialization of movement within it, profoundly affected (and continues to affect) both Black and Indigenous peoples. Turning in this chapter to a focus on letters from African American and Indigenous graduates and students published in the Hampton Normal and Agricultural Institute's publication *The Southern Workman* from 1873 to 1898,[8] I suggest that an interscale reading of letters to the editor offers ways to understand Black and Indigenous geographies, the entanglement of Black semi-citizenship with settler colonialism, and press forms as relational tools through which collectives can assert relation and make place in non-possessive and non-extractive ways.[9]

While considering how Black women used press forms for their collectivist politics that aimed to benefit Black communities, I have been arguing for the development of new reading protocols and methods. In this chapter, I explore letters to the editor as not only collectivist rather than individualist in their use but also as relational in their praxis of making place in the print-based public sphere. Letters to the editor in *The Southern Workman* (1872–1939), a monthly periodical produced by Black and Indigenous students at Hampton, suggest such a reading protocol because they foreground at least three important considerations: the entanglement of freedpeople's education with the residential school system, Black and Indigenous approaches to place that refuse settler-colonial notions of both space as possession and mobility as exercised autonomy, and the ways a press form that we take to be the "free" expression of an individual can be used to register the condition, refusals, and political desires of collectives. Letters in the *Workman* call us to examine intersecting investments in democratic liberalism that underwrite how letters to the editor are understood to function as a press form and investments that justified genocidal projects such as land severalty, residential education, and the generation of an underpaid and "nominally free" labor force that would "improve" land as colonial possession. In the orientation of the chapter, I attempt to take seriously that Black feminisms are collectively oriented forms of social justice struggle developed within the US nation-state's foundational and formative exercise of genocide and slavery as what Ruth Wilson Gilmore calls "interrelated fatalities," functioning through what Wendy Cheng and Rashad Shabbaz name as "expansive circuits of power that operate across scale[s]" of the "body, region, nation, world."[10] This would mean that studying Black women's politicized work with the periodical press and its genres or forms would not isolate their intellectual and activist labor from, but would put it in dialogue with, Indigenous peoples' use of the media and its affordances.

Hampton, *The Southern Workman*, and "Civilizing" Emancipation

The early 1870s through the late 1890s were decades when the US nation-state declared Indigenous peoples "wards of the government, a colonized people" (1871) rather than making treaty with them as nations; when reformers were calling for "an end to the reservation system"; and when the Dawes Act of 1887, "hailed by reformers as the 'Indian Emancipation Act,'" was allotting agency or reservation lands to Indigenous "heads of household" provided they renounced their tribal belonging.[11] The federal Bureau of Indian Affairs also began funding boarding schools in the late 1870s, and within ten years virtually every reservation had one in operation. At the same time, the education of African Americans in the South was underfunded despite a 25 percent increase of Black children in the region.[12] Hampton's founder and first principal, General Samuel Armstrong, tapped into this divide in educational priorities and a growing government and philanthropic interest in educating Indigenous peoples by the early 1880s in order to subsidize the education of African Americans at Hampton. Focusing nearly exclusively on Indigenous students rather than African Americans in the *Workman*, even though Indigenous students constituted only 17 percent of the school's enrollment, Armstrong was able to increase both philanthropic support and dollar-for-dollar government funding of Indigenous students that was used for the school as a whole.[13] During Reconstruction and into the 1880s, the Black press was also distinguishing between Native Americans and African Americans in terms of fitness, both civilizational and physical.[14] Hannah Gourgey documents the intensification of this representational politics during the late 1880s and 1890s connected to the prioritization of Indigenous peoples in government funding aimed at "civilization."[15] The Indian School Service had more than tripled in size by 1899, and fully 45 percent of those the service employed were Indigenous graduates of schools such as Hampton as part of a design to accelerate assimilation of Indigenous peoples into white settler-colonial society.[16]

In 1868, Hampton Normal and Agricultural Institute was founded by General Samuel Armstrong in Hampton, Virginia (Powhatan Territory) to educate the freedpeople following the Civil War using half the funds of Virginia's 1862 Morrill Act.[17] The American Missionary Association (AMA) originally financed its operations.[18] Whites had burned the town of Hampton and then abandoned it to Union occupation, making it a "city of refuge for the first mass escape" of enslaved people in the area. These refugees increased the "peninsula's black population . . . from 10,000 to 40,000," and the AMA established its first station for the freedpeople there. Hampton quickly became both "an unusual opportunity for carrying out Radical Reconstruction" and "the scene of deep rifts among [Freedman's] bureau agents, missionaries, and freedmen."[19] In order "to train teachers for the public schools and make industrial leaders for the race," Hampton offered African Americans "education for life" that combined discipline with "productive labor."

Hampton graduates were seen as ideal representatives of the school who would take its ethos, ideology, and training back to their communities, particularly the institution's emphasis on education, the moral value of hard work, self-sufficiency, property ownership, and respectability. The first African American graduating class left Hampton in 1871, and roughly 90 percent of its early graduates became teachers.[20]

On October 31, 1877, Hampton enrolled its first Indigenous student, Peter Johnson (Ute), who spent "twenty months . . . plead[ing] with the Indian Office for permission to return home" because Armstrong had suspended his "rations" when he "refus[ed] to perform manual labor." Johnson's refusal prompted Armstrong to write Commissioner Ezra Hayt (and eventually President Hayes) to ask that he be given the chance "to try Military prisoners like the Nez Perce."[21] By April 1878, Hampton had its first "Indian" class, twenty-two Indigenous warriors who had been taken prisoner in the Red River War of 1874 and moved from Fort Sill, Oklahoma (Comanche territory), to Fort Marion, St. Augustine, Florida (Imucuan territory), where Richard Henry Pratt developed the educational philosophy and practices he would use at Carlisle Indian Industrial School a year later.[22] Armstrong referred to Hampton's program as a "tender violence," and the school has since been critiqued for using a "pacifying" pedagogy to train its students in skills that were already becoming outmoded.[23] At the time Hampton began enrolling Indigenous students, it was being criticized by "radical local blacks," such as "John W. Cromwell, the militant editor of the Richmond *Virginia Star*" (1877–1888), for turning the freedpeople's school into a prison and making African Americans wards of the state.[24] In the early twentieth century, W. E. B. Du Bois called out Hampton for perpetuating the view of African Americans as a docile servant class.[25] Meanwhile, some Hampton students, such as Booker T. Washington, who later founded Tuskegee Institute, viewed their Indigenous peers as "interlopers" in a school "established for the benefit of the Negro."[26]

Anti-black and anti-Indigenous practices at the school further entangled Black semi-citizenship with settler colonialism in the "Indian Program" and the outing system. Hampton's growth plan included a summer outing program that sent Indigenous students to New England farms for summer employment, a form of unremunerated labor that was a source of funding for the school.[27] Curiously, and not a little ironically, the outing system was seen as a way to disrupt any alignment of "the Indian" with "the Negro" and to connect "red and white interests" in the public mind that could eventually lead to the education of Indigenous students in the public system.[28] This was one location of the widely held belief that Indigenous peoples could be integrated into American society whereas African Americans could not, in part based on the notion that 260,000 Indigenous peoples who were "disappearing" were easier to "racially engulf" than eight million African Americans.[29] While Armstrong mirrored Black exploitation in the outing program, he kept African American and Indigenous students segregated at the school for fear of a unified and resistant front.[30]

Armstrong, who was dubbed the "greatest educational salesman" of the nineteenth century, used the *Workman* to sell everything from the school's educational ethos and plan to the services of Hampton's printing press.[31] Hampton students were exposed to periodicals as essential reading and teaching material and African American and Indigenous male students were trained in all aspects of print production. They produced Hampton's print jobs, including the school's periodicals.[32] The *Workman* was presented as "furnish[ing] a variety of choice reading" with news of "what is going on in the world," all in a package that promised to "please and profit both young and old alike."[33] It essentially advertised the school's success at training "races" regarded as less "advanced" than whites and was used to secure ongoing government and philanthropic funding for the school. Because Hampton graduates used the *Workman* in their teaching, its circulation extended the Hampton ethos of education as physical and moral discipline through hard work beyond its classrooms into the African American and Indigenous communities where they lived and worked. The paper began publication in the spring of 1872, and within two months boasted that it had "found its way into over one hundred Northern, and *Five hundred* Southern homes, and is taken in eighteen different states."[34]

The *Workman*'s initial agent listing included Black activist Frances Ellen Watkins Harper, who was living in Philadelphia by 1872.[35] The training and experience in print production that Indigenous students received at Hampton meant that some, like Harry Hand (Crow Creek Sioux), established their own papers upon leaving the school.[36] In the 1870s and 1880s, the *Workman* was publishing the work of Black intellectuals and political figures such as Frederick Douglass and Gertrude Mossell,[37] and at the turn into the twentieth century it published the work of Black feminists who addressed its Hampton Negro Conferences, such as Anna Julia Cooper, Josephine Turpin Washington, Lucey Craft Laney, Victoria Earle Matthews, Fannie Barrier Williams, Mary Church Terrell, Anna E. Murray, Sarah Collins Fernandis, and Janie Porter Barrett.[38] Doing so made the *Southern Workman* an important print space for Black feminist recirculation focused on education, labor, the club movement, and social settlement work. The paper clearly also addressed an African American audience as well as its former students, both Black and Indigenous, and circulated through Black communal reading practices of which it demonstrated cognizance. In a letter published in May 1872, a reader told of receiving the paper from his son—"I liked it so much that I had it read, by a better scholar then myself in Sunday school, and then I loaned it until it was worn out." The *Workman* encouraged "several families subscribing and reading in common" to make taking the paper affordable.[39]

In addition to complex conditions of production and circulation, the *Workman*'s pages were sites for student and graduate expression that ran counter to Hampton's public image. Their letters appeared in regular, serialized columns in the four-page, four-column monthly, entitled Letters from Hampton Graduates, The Indian Department, Letters of Returned Students (Indigenous students "returned" to their reservations), and Scholarship Letters.[40] These serial columns often took up significant space in an edition; Letters from Hampton Graduates typically ran across one or two pages and published ten to fifteen letters.[41] "A confluence of black, white, and Native voices from across nations, with a racially and culturally complex publication history, complicates how we place the *Southern Workman*," observes Sidonia Serafini.[42]

Letters in the *Workman* were cued by Hampton's teachers, who wrote their graduates "a Christmas letter along with an inquiry sheet asking for current positions and activities" and by the other letters published monthly in the periodical.[43] Students took such controlled cuing beyond a yearly report by writing the paper throughout the year. They addressed their letters to Armstrong as the *Workman*'s managing editor or to their "Dear Teacher" or to their "Dear friends," and it is clear that they understood that these letters might be published like others they read in its pages. Although the conditions of the *Workman*'s cuing may have been direct if not coercive, students responded as readers of any periodical might by deviating at times from the cue for an expected response.[44] Students were also selected to write scholarship letters intended to demonstrate the school's government and philanthropic funding at work. Such letters by Indigenous students were presented as evidence of their acquired English and their conversion to Christianity, proof of Hampton's successful "civilizing." But some letters also mention the ongoing debt their writers were attempting to repay the school for their education, and others make clear that remaining in Armstrong's good graces meant connections for employment and philanthropic support for their teaching.[45]

The power dynamics at Hampton and those that followed its students after graduation throw into stark relief the broader limitations of reading letters to the editor for the assumed content of democratic debate, given that all such letters are carefully screened by editors at any periodical, thereby making their writers "contingent contributors."[46] That said, if we want to understand how letters to the editor might be put to work resistantly, looking to highly constrained uses of this press form is necessary. Rather than seeing letters to the *Workman* as exceptions or somehow not letters to the editor at all, I suggest that they foreground the illusions of democratic individualism instead of performing to expectations of either the school or the settler-colonial nation-state.

Black Semi-citizenship in Occupied Territory

Overall, letters from African American graduates in the *Workman* from the 1870s through the 1890s offer an important record of education in Black communities in the Chesapeake region and the Carolinas. They document the value those communities placed on education for both children and adults; the poor salaries and conditions at racially segregated schools; the pedagogies teachers used, including newspaper reading; and the brokering of Northern philanthropy to provide educational materials to these underfunded schools. Letters written by both African American and Indigenous graduates also reflect the centrality of work and temperance in Hampton's values and ideology. Yet graduates parted ways on the topic of the school's colonial and liberal ideology of land and home ownership as foundational to self-sufficiency: Indigenous graduates refused to advocate these values while the letters of African American graduates did so consistently.

Contextualizing that advocacy of Hampton's ownership ethos is crucial. Enslaved African Americans were forced to participate in the colonization and settlement of Indigenous lands while being understood themselves as objects to subdue, own, and possess, as was the land. Consequently, as Judith Madera details, the question of land as territory—"common land ownership for a collective or a people"—became bound up in African American freedom discourses and political imaginings, although that territory was far more often imagined as extranational than as possible within a nation-state practicing slavery. Black political leaders and intellectuals imagined land free from "white territorialization" in Canada, Haiti, and Liberia throughout the 1850s, when the desire for "an altered relation to land" intensified as the US nation-state became an extended site of Black surveillance and capture under the Fugitive Slave Act of 1850.[47] Activists understood a Black deterritorialization effected by Black movement as the "creative destruction of white materialist space-as-production," even as they also saw white settler colonialism as deterritorializing Indigenous peoples who had no legal claim to their land and African Americans who had no legal claim to their labor.[48]

This larger context of an altered Black relation to land complicates any easy understanding of Hampton's self-sufficiency ethic as faithfully enacted by African American graduates in a "meritocratic ownership of land."[49] Rather, letters from Black graduates published in the *Workman* exposed property ownership as a farcical criterion of "racial advancement" or citizenship. An African American graduate wrote from Speedwell, Wythe County, Virginia (Cherokee territory) on January 24, 1873, that "not one colored person in this district owns a house of his own to my knowledge. Again, they have no chance to purchase if they wanted to. . . . The owners of the land won't sell. So you can plainly see they have no chance, especially when they work for fifty cents per day and board themselves." On November 16, 1878, P. wrote from Portsmouth County, Virginia (Powhatan territory) that "the majority of the colored people are *very very* poor; few of them own the land they live on. . . . [They] work in the swamps and in ditch digging; their wages bring forty five cents per day and board, or rations, which consist of five lbs of bacon and a peck of meal a week."[50] A decade later, Black graduates wrote that "the majority of colored people here are poor and very much neglected" and that "men had to leave their wives and children and go off to other States to find work."[51] Such letters critique the school's ethos as out of all keeping with conditions African Americans faced and make clear that liberal democratic individualism, with its roots in land theft and occupation, attempted to usher newly freed African Americans into indebted semi-citizenship and ongoing settler colonialism for decades following the Civil War.

Black graduates' letters in the *Workman* record both their writers' interest in politics and the school's request for reports on local and regional politics of various sorts, including labor, funding for education, Black voter turnout, and vote buying. Here the scholarly conception of Hampton as "pacifying" in its attempts at "civilizing" is challenged by what these letters detail. Of particular concern were the November 1879 elections in Virginia, in which state debt readjustment was at issue. Graduates' letters published in the December 1879 and January 1880 issues of the *Workman* reported that Black Virginians unanimously agreed they should not be required to finance the repayment of state debt. Their unremunerated labor had already underwritten the economy of the state and the nation, and they were refusing any attempt to direct their taxes as free persons to the post–Civil War debt of a former Confederate state. These letters mark debt beyond monetary accounting as what Fred Moten and Stefano Harney call "a prescription of disorder" that "precisely in its unresolvability, in that it can never be repaid or paid off, is . . . an interminable deferral of coming to terms."[52] These graduates were refusing the terms of not coming to terms the state of Virginia proposed and with that also refusing the condition of indebtedness into which they were being ushered as semi-citizens in a nominally post-Emancipation nation-state. Their letters also record that many Black voters were so concerned that their franchise would be manipulated they refused civic participation.[53] Hampton's teachers were evidently concerned about the states of semi-citizenship that graduates experienced because they solicited letters on these very issues.

Many Black graduates' letters also offer a politicized critique of limited labor opportunities in racially discriminatory state school systems or of manual labor conditions in states that were overly reliant on agriculture and the exploitations of tenant farming and sharecropping.[54] These letters are directly critical of conditions on the ground and implicitly critical of Hampton's focus on teaching and on agricultural and manual labor as the predominant forms of training it offered, since these only further entangled graduates in a semi-citizenship that extended the reach of racial capitalism beyond slavery. The *Workman*'s September 1893 issue published Mr. and Mrs. W. J. Claytor's letter from State Normal and Industrial College in Tallahassee, Florida (Apalachee territory): "There is very little money in circulation here. The renters are having a very hard time. Cotton has been as low as three cents a pound. A great many tried raising tobacco this year but there is no one to buy it." A graduate who signed himself only as E. noted that he had never been employed as a teacher after leaving the school, that he was $300 in debt because he had followed Hampton's ethic of home ownership, and that he was working as a waiter in the Eagle Hotel on Staten Island (Lenape territory) to become solvent again. And I. wrote from somewhere in New Jersey (Delaware territory), where she taught children who were unable to attend school for want of clothing in the cold winter: "I can tell you it is hard, hard, and I often think I shall give it up. . . . We are trying to draw them from the street corners."[55]

Some of these letters written by Black graduates also contested racialized space as it was being actively constructed through employment segregation and the separation of families resulting from migration for better work. Sadie C. Collins, who had recently moved to Marshallville, Georgia (Creek territory), for work at an AMA school, wrote in early 1893 of mass migration from the state to Oklahoma, a further entangling of Black semi-citizenship with Indian removal and colonial occupation: "A train carrying five hundred bound of [sic] Oklahoma has been reported to me this week, these from a small town about seven miles from here, and its surrounding plantations. . . . I happened to encounter one of those emigrating companies on my way down here in the station at Atlanta [Muskogee Creek and Cherokee territory]." Collins asked "a young girl . . . where she was going and why," and the girl replied, "'out der whar some o' de Cook county folks' had gone and were 'doin' well.' Dey got 'long so po' up in Cook county.'"[56]

Such letters, together with those that provided information that Hampton had solicited regarding poorhouses, local jails, the convict lease system, and rates of incarceration, paint a dire picture of African American unfreedom, whether during or after Reconstruction. As early as 1879, the *Workman* published a graduate's letter that offered his observations on chain gangs while traveling through North Carolina (Lumbee, Skaruhreh/Tuscarora, Cheraw, and Mánu: Yį Isuwą [Catawba] territories), South Carolina (ᏣᎳᎨᏆᏗ Tsalaguwetiyi [Eastern Cherokee] and Congaree territories), and Georgia (Mvskoke [Muscogee] and Hitchiti territories). In the spring of 1884, the paper published letters focused on counties in Virginia that detailed higher rates of incarceration for African Americans, the vast majority of whom had committed petty offenses, and enforced convict labor to work off fines. According to these reports, Black women who were incarcerated for prostitution formed one-third of Virginia's prison population. Letters describing the conditions of poorhouses indicate they were exclusively populated by African American women and children.[57] One such letter from Staunton, Virginia (Monacan territory), connected the rates of African American incarceration for petty theft and prostitution to limited agricultural employment and whites' perception that African Americans "have come up in *large numbers* from east Virginia and now *swarm* the cities and towns of . . . the 'Garden Spot of Virginia [the Shenandoah Valley].'"[58] The result was a racialization of crime, sentencing, prisons, and poorhouses. His interview with "the jailor" confirmed that "the whites commit the worse crimes, the colored a greater number of small ones," and he documented that in 1883, fully 36 percent of Staunton's African American population was incarcerated, 81 percent of whom had been jailed for "petty larceny."[59] Black graduates' letters document very clearly what scholars such as Elizabeth Cohen, Saidiya Hartman, Stephen Knadler, Joanne Pope Melish, and Michelle Wright frame as an anti-Black semi-citizenship that emerged at transitional moments from slavery to ostensible freedom, not only nationally following the Civil

War but earlier in states that enacted gradual emancipation.[60] Knadler calls our attention to "partial, indebted semi-citizenship" as a state of "excluded inclusion," or what scholars of the contemporary prison-industrial complex term racial capitalism's "surplus life."[61]

That anti-Black semi-citizenship was and is entangled with the ongoing colonization of Indigenous peoples. Jodi Byrd, Alyosha Goldstein, Jodi Melamed, and Chandan Reddy argue for the necessity of understanding this entanglement through "economies of dispossession," or "multiple and intertwined genealogies of racialized property, subjection, and expropriation" in which "dispossession not only presupposes and configures possession itself but also is a relation of taking and violence that works at once to produce and delimit subjectivation, property, and value."[62] Shona Jackson has also argued that "to be anti-black is also to be fundamentally anti-Indigenous. It is a rejection of indigeneity (both in the New World and in Africa) as incompatible with the epistemic terrain of European modernity, its social and political structures, representative frames, and transformative processes."[63] Others refer to the capture of Africans in the transatlantic slave trade as a theft of their natal indigeneity or "natal alienation."[64] As Moten and Harney contend, "Black people are indigenous people, doubly displaced—from the land and the *socius*, in the land and in the *socius*. This displacement placed black people no place," in a "nonlocality of a general diffusion that is, at once, generative and genocidal."[65] These positions connect to those of scholars who dispute the notion that diasporic Africans are or can be settlers in the Indigenous lands they have been forced to labor on as captives.[66] As Byrd, Goldstein, Melamed and Reddy ask, how might it "be possible to think and work for a relationality grounded both in place and in movement, which simultaneously addresses Black geographies, dispossessions, and other racialized proprietary violences as incommensurate to yet not apart from Indigenous land and sovereignty?"[67]

In Transit: Spatial Aggressions and Relational Movement

To read graduate and student letters in the *Workman* as entangled in a settler colonialism that sought to control both Black and Indigenous movement would also be to read for what Jodi Byrd (Cherokee) conceives of as transit. She argues that "to be in transit is to be made to move" but also that "to be in transit is to be active presence in a world of relational movements and countermovements. To be in transit is to exist relationally, multiply."[68] It is no accident that, like the letters from African American graduates, letters from Indigenous graduates attended to labor opportunities as creating and maintaining racialized space. These constructions of space not only actively sought to whiten land as settler-state territory but also continued to marshal the coerced settling labor and presence of African Americans after slavery in the larger and ongoing project of removal and occupation. Indigenous graduates attested to multiple and interlocking technologies of colonization and occupation, such as the coercion to democratic individualism through the land theft effected by severalty and allotment, the reduction of complex relational structures and responsibilities to individual manual labor designed to "improve" land as a possession, and the use of "education" as removal, disruption, and attempted cultural genocide. As Joanne Barker (Lenape) writes, "Indigenous land is not capitalism's land." Rather, land "defines a mode of relationality and related set of ethics and protocols for lived social responsibilities and governance defined within discrete Indigenous epistemologies."[69] Early generations of Indigenous graduates encountered Bureau of Indian Affairs agents who refused to hire them as teachers in reservation schools and offered them poorly paid manual labor instead. "I am not teaching because the Indian Agency here refused to give me employment as a teacher last summer soon after I arrived home. He told me that I was too young to teach school," wrote Michael-Young Man Oshkeneny (Menomonee) in 1833. "The Indians were all expecting me to teach and they were in favor of having me one of the teachers. . . . After this I did not look to the Indian Agent for employment."[70] Oshkeneny had been educated at Carlisle and Hampton before returning to Keshena, Wisconsin (Očhéthi Šakówiŋ and Omāeqnomenew-ahkew [Menominee] territories). While agents clearly worked to undermine Indigenous sovereignty and self-governance, students who were barred from teaching in reservation schools exerted pressure, along with their chiefs, on agencies that eventually resulted in more favorable hiring practices, including "statutory preference for Indian employees on reservations."[71] Scholarship has also documented that in some cases Indigenous youth were sent to Hampton by their chiefs as a strategy for better understanding treaty and governance negotiations and so they could represent their nation in such negotiations.[72]

Even though Hampton consistently presented letters from Indigenous students as evidence of the school's success at "civilizing" them, for example by drawing attention to their command of English, Indigenous graduates refused the school's ethos. A letter written by Ma-ah-chis Soaring Eagle (Cheyenne), one of the "St. Augustine prisoners" brought to Hampton by Pratt on April 13, 1878, was published in the October edition of the *Workman* that year as an example of how "the Indians succeed in writing English."[73] Soaring Eagle wrote that he both wanted to be

Christian and would "try to be a good boy like the white man."[74] Other graduates, like Susette La Flesche (Omaha), who was teaching Omaha in a reservation school, wrote auto-ethnographic letters focused on how "Indians" understood or perceived white people and their need of Christianity.[75] John King (Shawnee) wrote a letter that advocated Hampton's ideology in action as "Indian boys" learned trades such as carpentry, blacksmithing, or farming.[76] Both were cued to provide "proof" of Hampton's success: La Flesche wrote Hampton's "Northern friends" and King's was a scholarship letter. Although Hampton published a number of letters from Black graduates who endorsed the school's program of self-reliance, including home and land ownership,[77] it is extremely rare to see any Indigenous graduates writing of holding land in severalty or advocating ownership of any kind.[78] Rather, they refused the school's "civilizing work" through their silence in the very act—writing a letter—designed to prove its success. As Carol Batker suggests of Indigenous writers during "the Era of Assimilation (1879–1934)" we can also see in the *Workman* an "intense struggle over individualism and community" in which writers "oscillat[ed] between individualistic models and communal models, showing us that these came to be markers with distinct political uses."[79] What we think we know of Hampton's intentions and results, then, is challenged by students and graduates who wrote letters to the paper, and this is particularly evident if we are reading more holistically for how their letters circulated and were read as interconnected.

Reading letters to the editor for content tells us something of how Hampton entangled anti-Black and anti-Indigenous agendas and of how students managed its ideology and practices and their combined results. This protocol of reading also reveals how letters were clearly selected to fortify and further circulate Hampton's public image. Yet such an approach is also foundationally contradictory because it assumes that democratic individualism predicated on notions of "the human" provides access to the print public sphere when, in fact, both "the human" and democratic individualism are unexamined technologies of settler-colonial racialization within a deeply stratified nation-state. We cannot say Indigenous- and Black-authored letters to the editor in the *Workman* are simply mouthpieces for the school without first presuming they could be expressions of a liberal democratic subject with access to unfettered expression if we encountered them in another paper that appeared to be less overt in its politics. It should come as little surprise, then, that content-based reading can at times risk misperceiving what student and graduate letters in the *Workman* register, particularly so because that type of reading reduces the voice of collectives to the level of the individual or reduces to the level of a single school and its ideology what is the nation-state's broader project of intertwined racial capitalism, genocide, and land occupation. Established ways of reading and understanding letters to the editor as a press form risk maintaining or cooperating with ongoing white supremacist settler-colonial technologies by obscuring larger racializing processes in their attention to the scale of the individual, whether that individual is the letter writer or the periodical editor.[80]

Geospatial data visualizations of Indigenous students' letters to the editor published in the *Workman* from the late 1870s through the late 1890s that plot where those Hampton students came from registers the wars of "Indian Removal" and the imprisonment of Hampton's first Indigenous students at St. Augustine, Florida (figure 3.1). Such a visualization can foreground the effects of settler colonization on Indigenous peoples ensnared in Hampton's "tender violence." Most Indigenous graduates and students were highly circumscribed in their movement: they "returned" to their agencies after time in the summer "living out" program; they were employed to teach the Hampton ethos at other agencies; or they moved on to further residential schooling at institutions such as Carlisle Indian Industrial School; Saint Joseph's Indian Industrial School at Keshena, Wisconsin; White's Indiana Manual Labor Institute in Wabash; The Lincoln Institute of Philadelphia; or Hope Indian School on the Santee Agency in South Dakota.[81] This visualization's plot points register what spaces Hampton was actively representing as those that Indigenous peoples could occupy, when they could do so, and why, in what was a repeated inscribing of occupied and highly racialized space. Maps as a representation of space are inflected by and serve the power interested in the *production* of space they represent, and this visualization starkly presents settler colonialism's claim to space and territory at the expense of Indigenous relations to, Indigenous understandings of, and Indigenous responsibilities for place and land.

Yet a close reading of Indigenous students' letters published in the *Workman* during these decades reveals that they register these larger spatial aggressions of removal only obliquely through rare and passing mention of severalty and allotment, which are cast as reflecting the school's ethos of self-sufficiency through land and home ownership and so appear to be much more benign than they were. Nonetheless, the collision of Indigenous geographies with the "transit of empire"[82] is recorded in letters to the *Workman* through signature and can be elaborated with further research in Hampton's records and publications to create data visualizations that help a reader see what is otherwise silent in the letters' content: colonial occupation that constructs reservation lands as racialized "Indian" and

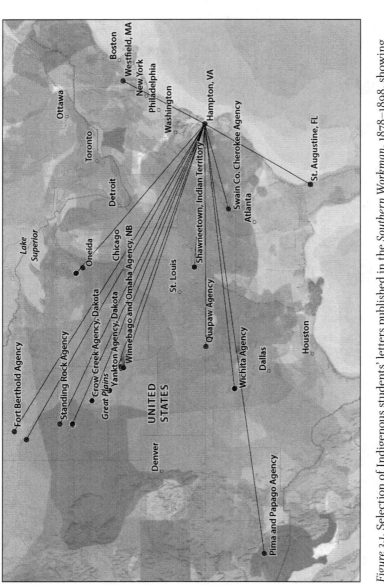

Figure 3.1. Selection of Indigenous students' letters published in the *Southern Workman*, 1878–1898, showing letter origin locations. Produced by Teresa Zackodnik using a base layer from Native Land Digital, Creative Commons. *Note*: To interact with the territory-, language-, and treaty-specific maps the project has built, go to Native Land Digital at https://native-land.ca/. Colors and shapes represent different First Nations' lands. To interact with the ArcGIS map I have produced, go to https://arcg.is/1aenmCo. I refer to the data represented here as a selection of student and graduate letters from the *Southern Workman* because only those that noted the student's origin are included in my dataset.

the removal of Indigenous peoples to them. This research process also reveals the conscription and control of Indigenous movement through space outside those lands, which then actively racializes that space as white settler colonial because Indigenous peoples are presumed to no longer be present in or in relation to it. Putting movement and space in the foreground with a geospatial data visualization helps us begin to read what the letters mark yet do not seem to mention in their content at all: Hampton's work within a multifaceted settler-colonial racialization of space that shuttled Indigenous students and graduates between residential school(s) and reservation(s) in a national "experiment" to "civilize the Indian." "Boarding schools were . . . deeply concerned with disciplining bodies," writes Mishuana Goeman (Tonawanda Band of Seneca), "distancing indigenous people from land, and destroying the cultural ways that nurtured relationship to land and their communities."[83] Indigenous students were rarely expected to do anything but return to the reservation and serve as models of Hampton's "civilizing" after their education, a conscription that preserved a racialization of space and served the interests of a settler-colonial nation.

A geospatial visualization of African American students' letters from the same decades suggests at least three things to consider: (1) more graduates wrote from the Chesapeake region and the Carolinas than anywhere else; (2) movement beyond these areas appeared to open up in the 1880s; (3) yet this movement farther afield remained relatively rare (figure 3.2). Pausing to consider what such movement or the relative lack thereof might tell us is critical, since the letters of Indigenous and Black Hampton students remind us that movement indicates neither freedom nor an exercise of individual autonomy in any straightforward or uncomplicated way. Rather, consideration of the entanglements of Black semi-citizenship with settler-colonial occupation requires us to reanimate settled critical understandings of mobility as questions rather than assertions.

Timothy Creswell has defined mobility as "a fragile entanglement of physical movement, representations, and practices" that include how movement is understood and the conventions that arise around it.[84] Louis Everuss would unpack this as "a combination of: (1) material elements, as even those purely imagined are still embodied in the imaginer; (2) symbolic elements, as movements cannot be understood separately from their representation; and (3) social practices, as the way mobilities occur and are interpreted is influenced by the social settings and historical contexts in which they exist."[85] As Euan Hague notes, and as anyone living these realities already knows all too well, "at all levels of government in the United States, legislation has determined the manner in which non-white individuals can

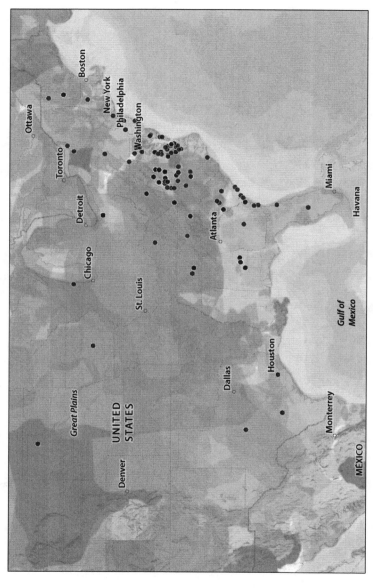

Figure 3.2. Selection of African American students' letters published in the *Southern Workman*, 1873–1896, showing letter origin locations. Produced by Teresa Zackodnik in ArcGIS using a base layer from Native Land Digital, Creative Commons. *Note*: To interact with the ArcGIS map I have produced, go to https://arcg.is /1Ogz18. I refer to the data represented here as a selection of student and graduate letters from the *Southern Workman* because only those that noted the student's origin are included in my dataset.

move, which spaces they can access, and where they can live." For some time, African American mobility has been read as "the most pervasive form of resistance" to the "spatial practices of white Supremacy," given that Black movement has been and continues to be both (en)forced and highly constrained. Such an assertion appears to acknowledge that while African American mobility is material, responses to its exercise have arisen from its symbolic meanings. Both the spaces African Americans can move into and that movement itself are represented as measures of freedom and citizenship as well as threat, creating both constraining legislation and collective Black praxis.

Yet a resistance-constraint dichotomy underwritten by a notion of autonomy as individual choice is inadequate for understanding Black mobility that was shaped by conditions of semi-citizenship in the late nineteenth century.[86] Attending to letters Black women wrote to the *Workman*, I return to the question of Black women's mobility. As indexed by their letters to the paper and supplemented by published Hampton records, African American women students and graduates were the most mobile from the early 1870s through the mid-1880s. Eight of the 136 Black women in my dataset relocated as many as five to ten times to pursue their education and seek employment as teachers (figure 3.3). The eight women whose letters this visualization are based on wrote letters to the editor focused on education, their teaching experiences, and the poverty of the communities where they worked.[87] Only two reflected back the Hampton ethos of home or land ownership, and one of these two used that ethos to advocate for mothers as educators in their homes, writing from the perspective of giving up teaching upon marriage. One of these eight women was born enslaved and another is identified in Hampton publications as the daughter of a formerly enslaved parent. These women traveled to Hampton for their education from Virginia; from Charleston, South Carolina; and from Baltimore, Maryland during Reconstruction or very shortly after its end, indicating their commitment to their communities.

As Gerda Lerner documented some fifty years ago in her editorial comments on Caroline Smith's 1871 excerpted testimony to the Joint Select Committee to Inquire into the Condition of Affairs in the Late Insurrectionary States of the US Congress, "the violence which marked the overthrow of the Reconstruction governments fell with particular fury on teachers and supporters of black schools."[88] Smith recounted being "whipped" by "Ku-Klux" numbering "twenty-five or thirty, perhaps more" for continuing to teach African American students in Atlanta, Georgia.[89] Yet two of these eight Hampton graduates—Sarah Collins and Ann Anderson—wrote of traveling as far afield as Florida and Texas, respectively, to

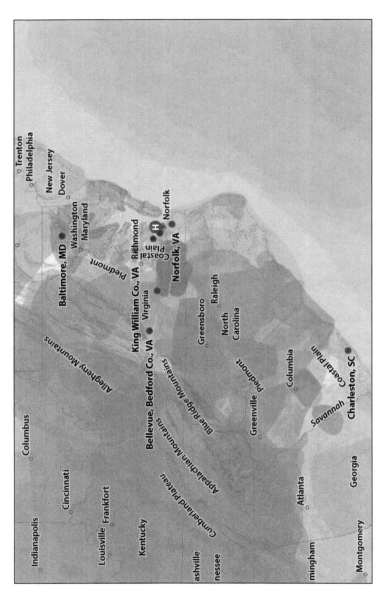

Figure 3.3. Origin location of most mobile African American women graduates of Hampton Normal and Agricultural Institute (circled "H"), classes of 1872–1885. Produced by Teresa Zackodnik in ArcGIS using a base layer from Native Land Digital (Creative Commons license). *Note:* To interact with this map, go to https://arcg.is/10niLb.

pursue teaching in Black communities following the failure of Reconstruction in 1877.[90] As Lerner notes, schools became resegregated in the South at this time. Many schools for Black children were operational for only "a few months of the year" and "expenditures for buildings and supplies and teacher's salaries [were] a fraction of that spent for the white schools."[91] Time and time again, these conditions are recounted in letters to the *Workman* from Hampton graduates, but they did not blight these women's achievements. Collins later became known for her Black feminist and social work under her married name, Sarah Collins Fernandis. She was active in the social settlement movement and established a public library branch in 1903 near the Colored Social Settlement of Washington, DC. In 1904, she established a daycare center, a kindergarten, and a school that offered afternoon classes in domestic skills for African American girls. Fernandis also founded and led the Colored Cooperative League in 1913 and lectured in the northeastern states on Black women workers' conditions. The *Workman* published her letters, her lectures at the Hampton Negro Conferences, and her poetry.[92]

Although Fernandis may be the most famous of this highly mobile group of Hampton graduates, Lucy E. Smith (class of 1879) moved ten times to be educated at Hampton and then to teach in small schools in Chesterfield County, Virginia, from 1879 to 1881; in Drury's (Drewry's) Bluff, Virginia, in 1881; in Berlin, Virginia, from 1881 to 1882; and in Tuskegee, Alabama in 1882 (figure 3.4). She became a student at Saint Augustine's Collegiate Institute in Raleigh, North Carolina, in 1883, where Anna Julia Cooper had been a student in the late 1860s and then an instructor from 1884 to 1887. Smith went on from Saint Augustine's to teach summer school at Haywood, Beaufort, and Asheville, North Carolina, from 1884 to 1885. As many graduates did, she wrote her former Hampton teacher Miss Cleveland in March of 1893 from her home in Chesterfield, Virginia. Smith had returned to the first community she had taught in, married, and had ceased teaching. After her marriage, her focus was on mothering, which she referred to as an educator role. Yet despite her unusual degree of movement, Smith, like most Hampton graduates, did not range far afield of the Chesapeake region and the Carolinas, areas most of the women in my dataset hailed from.

Lucy Boulding (class of 1881) was born enslaved in Burkeville, Virginia. She relocated six times, including her move to Hampton, yet she never left Virginia until the early 1920s, when she moved to New York City, where she died in 1924. Her feminist activism included organizing the Slater Lyceum and raising funds for a library associated with it in Staunton, Virginia, in the mid-1880s and membership in the Lynchburg Women's League in the 1890s, one of six Black women's

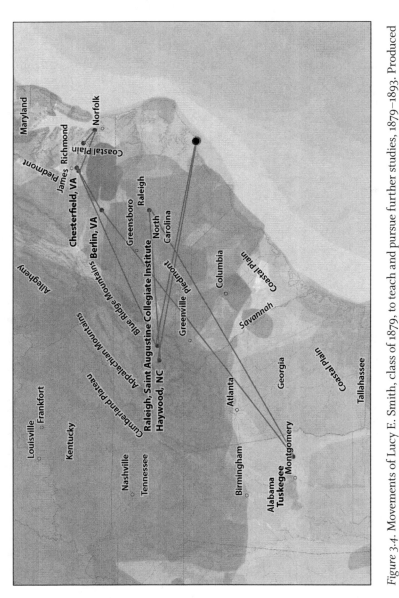

Figure 3.4. Movements of Lucy E. Smith, class of 1879, to teach and pursue further studies, 1879–1893. Produced by Teresa Zackodnik in ArcGIS using a base layer from Native Land Digital (Creative Commons license). *Note:* To interact with this map, go to https://arcg.is/nTPSX.

clubs in the state. Boulding was also a teacher and a matron at the Virginia Collegiate and Industrial Institute (founded 1893), which offered African Americans industrial education, teacher training, and college preparation. She wrote the *Workman* about her activist and organizing endeavors and was one of the first three African American women to vote in Lynchburg, Virginia, following the ratification of the Nineteenth Amendment.[93]

How might we read the mobility of Black women graduates of Hampton, such as Lucy E. Smith, whose movement beyond the Chesapeake and Carolinas is limited even as the dataset indicates that these women exercised a high degree of mobility compared to their Hampton peers? Would we read it through a resistance-constraint dichotomy and say their mobility was constrained in decades during which we know that post-Reconstruction racialized violence was on the rise? Would we read their movements as indications of their individual choices to remain closer to where their relations lived, the (re)unification of family being a priority following the disruption of the Civil War? Do their movements demonstrate the limited employment opportunities Hampton brokered for its graduates? Can we reasonably apply generalizations about movement to Black women at this time when we consider that their mobility as migrants was being pathologized? By the late 1890s, Victoria Earle Matthews had written about that pathologizing in the *Workman* and in a speech at a Hampton Negro Conference that the *Workman* recirculated.[94]

The tendency to assume that autonomy asserted as individual choice underwrites mobility has led to suggestions that "new mobilities" studies risks uncritically "celebrat[ing] . . . the mobile" by "privileg[ing] contemporary analyses" over "historical examinations" of movement and by centering "the notion of autonomous, free-floating individuals."[95] Instead, reminders that "it is problematic to assume that enhanced mobility is self-evidently positive or equally shared" are necessary, as is historicization of movement.[96] As Mimi Sheller has argued, "Mobilities have always been the precondition for the emergence of different kinds of subjects, spaces, and scales."[97] By indexing spatial movement and movement into the public sphere—making place in print—as *collective* for African Americans, the letter to the editor as a press form requires us to think critically about the degree to which reading both the lack of and the exercise of movement is premised on an unquestioned liberal assumption that autonomously chosen/privileged movement *is* mobility.

The mobility and movement of Indigenous and African American is highly complex, and letters to the *Workman* written by individuals not only index that person's movements but are vectors of collective movement. Together this means that we need to recalibrate an understanding of mobility as exceeding the standard equation of movement as autonomously exercised choice or freedom. Putting the collectivizing of datasets in dialogue with school records and the content of individuals' letters illustrates the dialectical relation between collective and individual mobile ontologies. Structural and systemic forces operate on collectives that are targeted for control and elimination. As Judith Madera has argued, "Materially and affectively, national spatialities are polyphonous constructions. They do more than embed different histories; they proliferate them."[98] The nation-state promotes settler colonialism as the exercise of "free" mobility, rendering any notion of mobility as freedom of movement critically and ethically inadequate for understanding what both place and movement mean for African Americans and Indigenous peoples. What assumptions must we set aside and what questions might we ask when using data visualization tools to understand letters such as those Hampton's Black and Indigenous students and graduates wrote?

Black and Indigenous Geographies in Letters to the Editor of the *Southern Workman*

By identifying the racialization of space that "naturalizes both identity and place," the letters of Hampton students and graduates contested the spatial project of colonization and domination.[99] That contestation is perhaps uniquely revealed in these letters to the editor not only because this press form can trace space, movement, and their control but also because the letters constitute a serial press form that the *Workman* collected into recurring columns that dominated the publication in these decades. By confronting a repetitive racializing of space and movement through a serial form that, as Carey Snyder and Leif Sorensen argue, signals an ongoing and open dialogue, these letters repeatedly counter and expose the larger social work to naturalize and present as fixed or closed what is, in fact, a highly contrived and anxiously reasserted equation of race and space.[100] Translating Katherine McKittrick's work on Black geographies to how this press form can be used, we might say that letters written by Black and Indigenous students "expose domination as a visible spatial project that organizes, names, and sees social differences and determines *where* social order happens."[101] Their letters document a complex mobility and spatiality in a mix of collective movement and relative stasis, whether forced, coerced, or circumscribed through the racialization of space. The complexity of mobility recorded by both movement and stasis asks that we unsettle and question contemporary scholarly assumptions about mobility, public space, racialization, and acts of taking space and making place, both physically and in print.

In September 1902, the *Workman* published a letter from Juanita (Espinosa) Ketosh (Piegan Blackfoot), who wrote from the Crow Agency at Pryor, Montana (Cayuse, Umatilla, Walla Walla, Apsáalooke [Crow], Tséstho'e [Cheyenne], and Očhéthi Šakówiŋ territories) (figure 3.5).[102] Ketosh, whose name was White Buffalo, had been taken to Hampton in August 1890 from the Blackfoot Agency in Montana (Cayuse, Umatilla, Walla Walla, Ktunaxa ʔamakʔis, Niitsítpiis-stahkoii ᐊᒢᒪᑯ ᓴᒃᒃ [Blackfoot/Niitsítapi ᐊᒢᒢᑐ], and Michif Piyii [Métis] territories). She left the school in July 1893, and in 1894 the *Workman* reported that she was a student at Grant Institute in Genoa, Nebraska (Pâri [Pawnee] and Očhéthi Šakówiŋ territories). She eventually became an "assistant matron" there and, at some point, was also a student at Haskell Institute in Lawrence, Kansas (Washtáge Moⁿzháⁿ [Kaw/Kansa], ᏌᏃᎳᏃᎠ ᏦᎣᎴᏅ ᏣᎴᎠ ᎶᎡᏍᎠ^ [Osage], Očhéthi Šakówiŋ, and Kiikaapoi [Kickapoo] territories).[103] Ketosh observed that the Crow were "way behind the Sioux. They still have their dances, call on their own medicine men, and dress as they did twenty years ago." In Pryor, there were "a few Carlisle girls and a lot from other schools that can talk as good English as I can . . . but if you should ask them questions they would be 'too ashamed' to answer." While these "school girls often come in to talk" with Ketosh "about the happy school days," they also revealed that residential schooling had disconnected from their community. They didn't "dress as they did" while at Carlisle because "the Indians laugh and make so much fun of us." They had no sewing machines to make the dresses they were taught to sew and "cannot sit around in a white woman's dress with comfort in a camp" anyway, and they "have no house we can fix up like our rooms at school." Ketosh might appear to have been criticizing these girls along with her own Blackfeet of the Crow Reservation, but she ended her letter with an indictment of the naïve beliefs that fueled residential schools such as Hampton and Carlisle. "I feel so sorry for a girl when she comes home from school. She looks as if she had not a friend on earth. It is so easy for Indian school-boys and girls to say 'I am going back to help my people and teach them the right way to live,'" she writes. "But what a different thing to do it!"[104]

Kate Henderson's (Sioux) letter is even more complicated by her history and the geographies central to it (figure 3.6). On October 1, 1892, Henderson wrote the *Workman* from Puyallup Agency, Tacoma, Washington (Puyallup, Cayuse, Umatilla, and Walla Walla territories): "I applied for a transfer from the Belknap Indian School [at Fort Belknap in Montana] to this school, and my request was granted. . . .

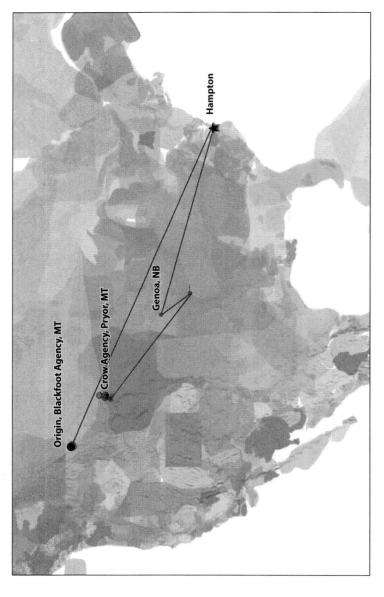

Figure 3.5. Removals of Juanita (Espinosa) Ketosh, 1890–1902. First known location: Blackfoot Agency, Montana; last known location: Crow Agency, Pryor, Montana. Produced by Teresa Zackodnik in ArcGIS using a base layer from Native Land Digital (Creative Commons license). *Note:* To interact with this map, go to https://arcg.is/1H9mmP1.

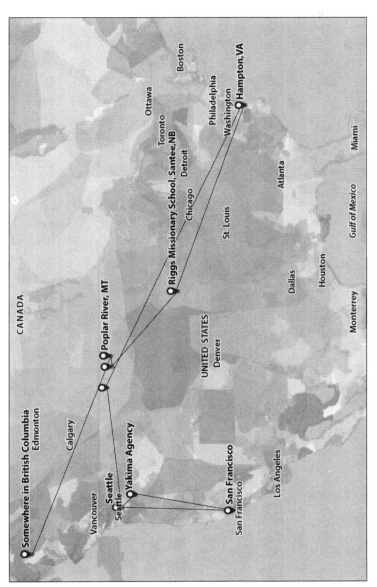

Figure 3.6. Removals of Kate Henderson, 1880s–1963. First known location somewhere in British Columbia; last known location, Seattle, Washington. Produced by Teresa Zackodnik in ArcGIS using a base layer from Native Land Digital (Creative Commons license). *Note:* To interact with this map, go to https://arcg.is/1nC4KD.

I am a stranger here and feel a little bit lonesome but will feel at home in a few days" She continued, "I want to subscribe for the *Southern Workman* for a year. . . . I don't want to miss this month's number. . . . I am just hungry for Hampton news."[105] In his account of working as a superintendent in the boarding school system, Edwin Chalcraft detailed what he had learned of Kate Henderson's life. He described her as part of a "wandering band of Sioux Indians" who had returned "mid-winter" to Poplar River, Montana (Cayuse, Umatilla, Walla Walla, Očhéthi Šakówiŋ, Niitsítpiis-stahkoii ᑯᒡᒐ·ᐟᑦ· ᓱᵇᑿᑉ [Blackfoot/Niitsítapi ᑯᒡᒐᔆ], Assiniboine, and Michif Piyii [Métis] territories) from somewhere in British Columbia (Dakełh Keyoh [ᑕᐯᑊ ᗸᑫᕁ], Yekooche, Takla, Dënéndeh territories). Thomas Henderson, who was running a "trader's store" on the Fort Peck reservation (Cayuse, Umatilla, Walla Walla, Apsáalooke [Crow], Očhéthi Šakówiŋ, Niitsítpiis-stahkoii ᑯᒡᒐ·ᐟᑦ· ᓱᵇᑿᑉ [Blackfoot/Niitsítapi ᑯᒡᒐᔆ], and Michif Piyii [Métis] territories) that he had established shortly after the Custer Massacre of 1876, "bought the child from her grandmother for a few dollars," later "took her to the Riggs Missionary School at Santee, Nebraska" (Očhéthi Šakówiŋ, Pánka tónde uk^{h}éthi^n [Ponca], and Yankton territories), and then on to Hampton on July 9, 1888.[106]

Kate Henderson graduated in 1891 from Hampton and was given a teaching position by the commissioner of Indian Affairs at Fort Belknap reservation in Montana (Cayuse, Umatilla, Walla Walla, Očhéthi Šakówiŋ, Niitsítpiis-stahkoii ᑯᒡᒐ·ᐟᑦ· ᓱᵇᑿᑉ [Blackfoot/Niitsítapi ᑯᒡᒐᔆ], and Michif Piyii [Métis] territories), where she taught for three years.[107] In September 1892, she was "transferred" to the Puyallup Agency school (Cayuse, Umatilla, Walla Walla, spuyaləpabš [Puyallup] territories) a mile outside Tacoma, Washington. After she married Samuel McCaw in October 1893, the couple left their positions at the Puyallup school and moved to Yakima (Cayuse, Umatilla, Walla Walla, Yakama, and Ichishkiin territories), where Samuel was eventually employed as a bookkeeper. After his death, Kate Henderson returned to teaching at the Yakima reservation school. Chalcraft visited Standing Rock reservation (Sihásapa, Tséstho'e [Cheyenne], Očhéthi Šakówiŋ, and Itazipco territories) as supervisor of Indian Schools and began inquiring about Kate Henderson's grandmother, who lived there, and her mother, "The Woman with the Pretty Hand," who lived 275 miles south of Standing Rock on the Devil's Lake Reservation (Anishinabewaki ᐊᓂᔑᓈᐯᐗᑭ, Očhéthi Šakówiŋ, Michif Piyii [Métis], and Yanktonai territories). He eventually met Kate's mother and learned that Kate had been sending her money and letters every three months through the Devil's Lake agent, who read the letters and wrote her mother's replies. Chalcraft documents that Kate Henderson remarried, to a white Tacoma Post Office employee who was transferred to San Francisco (Ohlone, Ramaytush, and Muwekma territories). By 1936, she was living in Seattle (Cayuse, Umatilla, Walla Walla, dxʷsəq̓ʷəbš [Suquamish], dxʷdəwʔabš [Duwamish], bəqəlšuł [Muckleshoot]), widowed again and trying to prove her relation to her mother as heir to both her mother's allotment at Devil's Lake and her grandmother's allotment at Standing Rock. She was successful in both claims but continued to live in Seattle.[108]

Given such social, political, economic, and material realities, it is significant that the spatial complexity of letters to the *Workman* also includes the affective and imaginative. Whether they were teaching and living in small, isolated communities or had returned to reservations, graduates wrote repeatedly that these letters and the paper itself offered them a sense of affective connection and the validation of shared or similar experiences. Numerous letters from African American graduates mention teaching near one another yet distant enough that regular contact is impossible.[109] Instead, that sense of connection is facilitated by letters to the paper, all of which share the common experience of working hard to establish a school with little funding in poor, remote communities. Occasionally, letters refer to Hampton as "home," as Georgina Washington's did.[110] Attending to the spaces and movement these letters register also means reading them for the imagined place made through the connection and affinity they were actively creating. McKittrick argues that we must read Black geographies for the "philosophical, material, imaginary, and representational trajectories" and the spaces they comprise.[111] Hampton's Black graduates wrote letters that both represented historical Black geographies and actively created Black geographies of imaginative and affective connection by making specific mention of other Hampton graduates by name. As Serafini observes, in the *Workman*'s pages, both Black and Indigenous students and graduates interrogated "the myriad ways in which people of color must negotiate the notion of 'home' within a society that organizes humanity by a binary racial system and on terms of second- or third-class citizenship."[112] That binary racializing system was also a settler-colonial one that positioned Indigenous students and graduates as both "disappearing" and assimilable and served to racialize Black students and graduates in the ways Serafini notes.

The letters Indigenous graduates wrote further complicate reading for affective desire, both because the affective is often unclear in its object when they reference Hampton and the people there and because what often accompanies an expression of affective connection to people they had known at Hampton is also testimony of the school's attempts to rupture and remake relations to place and people.¹¹³ Carrie (Half) Paypay (Cheyenne) wrote the *Workman* in February 1893 from the Cheyenne River Agency, South Dakota (Sihásapa, Tséstho'e (Cheyenne), Očhéthi Šakówiŋ, and Mnicoujou territories), which she had been returned to in 1889. She had been brought to Hampton with five other Cheyenne on November 29, 1886, by Rev. J. J. Gravatt, and upon her return was working as a field matron.¹¹⁴ "I think of Hampton all the time, and would like to see you all dear Hampton friends," she wrote. "When I was over there at the school I always have a good time and I try not to make any troubles for the teachers."¹¹⁵ She also wrote to *Talks and Thoughts of the Hampton Indian Students* about her work as a laundress for "$25 a month and . . . rations" for the Boys Boarding School at Fort Bennett, South Dakota (Sihásapa, Tséstho'e (Cheyenne), Očhéthi Šakówiŋ, and Mnicoujou territories). "My friends in the East may have forgotten me, but I don't forget you. I remember all the same. . . . Now please, please don't forget your dear friend Carrie PayPay [sic], who thinks of Hampton as her own home."¹¹⁶ She had married George Paypay (Isanti Sioux), also a Hampton student, who became an Episcopal preacher and was ordained as a deacon in 1888 at Fort Bennett, which the US Army had established on the Cheyenne River Agency in 1870 to control the Sioux.¹¹⁷ That agency, the fourth largest in the United States at 5,000 square miles, was created in 1889 from lands that, like the Crow Creek reserve, were once part of the territory of the Great Sioux Nation, which means that Carrie (Half) Paypay was "returned" in 1889 to an agency she had not left in 1886 because it did not yet exist. By 1891, the Cheyenne River Agency had been moved 56 miles up the Missouri River. What was "home" to her when she wrote to *Talks and Thoughts* in 1893?¹¹⁸

Mishuana Goeman (Tonawanda Band of Seneca) helps us understand that what we might call Indigenous geographies are literal and material, personal and collective, discursive and figurative, epistemological and ontological: "Indigenous peoples make place by relating both personal and communal experiences and histories to certain locations and landscapes—maintaining these spatial relationships is one of the most important components of politics and our identity. Indigenous Nations claim land through a discursive communal sharing," she continues, "and land is not only given meaning through consensus of claiming territory but also through narrative practices. Indigenous conceptions of land are literally and figuratively the placeholder that moves through time and situates indigenous knowledges." They are a powerful way that Indigenous peoples, in making place, "[resist] imperial geographies that order time and space in hierarchies that erase and bury indigenous connections to place and anesthetize settler-colonial histories."[119] When Indigenous graduates' letters refer to Hampton as a place they wish to return to, as "home," they register both affective connections made while there and the twinned tools of removal and a coercion to attend residential school designed to fracture connection to land and one's people. It is difficult to parse the affective bonds these letters may register from the violences that made their conditions possible. This is arguably the point; letters attesting to affective connection also surface Indigenous connections to place and thus can be read as rupturing "anesthetic" settler-colonial histories.

The mobility of Indigenous women who were taken to Hampton from the mid- to late 1880s differs radically from the school's representation of "returned" students, however much they were still referred to as such in Hampton publications. Their letters and the geographies we can research reveal that Indigenous students were often entangled in colonizing residential education prior to and following their time at Hampton, and they record the complex coerced mobility and displacement from traditional territory that was the result of that entanglement. Reading for making place that Hampton graduates' letters often center, even when they are limited materially in their movement, requires attention to the spatial and relational violences they also register. Such reading is urgently needed in the face of the school's attempt to determine and represent their movements otherwise.

It is also important to bear in mind that both African American and Indigenous students and graduates were reading these letters in the *Workman* and that they often subscribed to or asked for more copies of the paper to be sent to them so they could stay in connection through them, however brokered that connection had always been by Hampton's "tender violence." Several graduates who wrote to the paper commented on an ongoing series of letters from African American graduate Ackrel A. White that were published in the *Workman* from January 1878 through May 1881 detailing his movements and missionary work in Sierra Leone.[120] The Mendi Mission in southern Sierra Leone at Kaw Mendi had been established by the AMA; its genesis lay in abolitionist efforts in 1839 to legally free and resettle the captives of Sierra Leone who had seized the ship *La Amistad* (on which they were being trafficked to Cuba), sailed it up the eastern US coast, and landed in New York (Munsee Lenape territory), where they faced trial. The Amistad Committee, which operated the Mendi Mission, was also central to the establishment of schools for freedmen, the Port Charles experiment in the South Carolina Sea Islands (Yamasee, Kusso, and Guale territories), and later the Black historical colleges and universities of Fisk (ᏣᎳᎩᏱ Tsalaguwetiyi [Cherokee, East], S'atsoyaha [Yuchi], and Shawandasse Tula [Shawanwaki/Shawnee] territories), Howard (Piscataway and Nacotchtank [Anacostan] territories), Atlanta (Mvskoke [Muscogee] territory) and Berea (ᏣᎳᎩᎯ Tsalaguwetiyi [Cherokee, East], S'atsoyaha [Yuchi], and Shawandasse Tula [Shawanwaki/Shawnee] territories).[121] The Mendi Mission was in operation from 1842 to 1882; Joseph Yannielli refers to it as "a transatlantic branch of the Underground Railroad and a key frontier of action and imagination in the global contest over slavery." Its "most visible symbol . . . the *John Brown* steamship," constructed in the 1880s when memory of Brown's insurrectionary efforts "began to be supplanted in the United States by the defeat of Reconstruction and the culture of reconciliation," also marked the mission's earlier efforts to develop an "export economy in free labor cotton and sugar" that had intensified with the outbreak of the Civil War.[122] Donal Lindsey documents that "in 1883, the AMA exchanged its Mendi mission . . . for the ABCFM's [American Board of Commissioners for Foreign Missions] Indian missions in Nebraska and Dakota."[123]

Mention of the Mendi Mission in the *Workman* encoded these Black geographies of natal alienation and theft, revolt, "return," and internationally networked abolitionist efforts entangled in missionary work on the western coast of the African continent. African American graduate readers who shared White's experiences at Hampton seemed to eagerly look forward to his next installment and to traveling imaginatively with him, even if physically they remained in that narrower orbit of Virginia and the Carolinas. The degree to which they knew the fullness of the geographies they were imagining themselves into is not clear, nor is it clear whether they understood them to be aspirational, emancipatory, or as entangling freedom with unfreedom via the routes and movement of people and the products of their labor.

It is even less clear whether African American and Indigenous students and graduates understood their experiences to be as entangled as they were. For Indigenous graduates and students, reading of Kate Henderson as a much-lauded example of Hampton's success would have meant being confronted with the realities, not the imagined possibilities, of mobility in occupied territories that racialized those lands within the larger settler-colonial project. The degree to which their African American peers understood this, however, is hard to know beyond documented bonds built between Black and Indigenous students who studied at Hampton together. Such ties include those between teachers and students: Hampton's Black female teachers tried to learn Indigenous languages and bonded with their students, who saw them as "surrogate parents," while Indigenous students rejected the school hierarchy that positioned their African American teachers below their white teachers.¹²⁴ When Hampton graduates requested copies of the *Workman* in order to stay connected to one another, we see the failure of the school's attempts to segregate both the students and their histories from one another.

A reading protocol for letters to the editor that challenges the print-capitalism thesis and its possessive liberal individualism by moving beyond an attention to the individual's economic and cultural capital, whether editor or reader, offers us the opportunity to think about how press forms can and did serve the politics of collectives. I have suggested that an interscale reading of this press form can show us restraint of movement, racialization of space, and the Black and Indigenous geographies that refused and resisted these settler-colonial processes. Geospatial data visualizations can enable a focus on collective mobility and movement as well as a focus on racializing occupied space, both of which can help us apprehend what solely reading the content of such letters for individual democratic debate will either miss or minimize. Yet as tools, data visualizations are also "embedded in often obscured ideologies swirling around researchers as well as their data, all of which influence both our interpretations and arguments."¹²⁵ We must remember that for projects focused on racialization, assuming that data is neutral would be highly problematic, as are foundational assumptions about "the human," which Black studies critiques foreground as do elaborations of recognition and its refusal within Indigenous studies.¹²⁶ Working with a periodical such as the *Workman* makes such questions difficult for researchers to ignore. This chapter's geospatial visualizations are based on a dataset of selective and situated letters to the editor published in the *Workman* from 1873 to 1898.¹²⁷ It has been limited by the ability to identify a writer, their location, or the date of their letter. The data visualizations I have produced are thus offered as suggestive rather than representative. And while this chapter has focused on reading letters to the editor as indexing the production of racialized space, including how movement and constraints upon it as well as making place or remaining in place can register and refuse such racialization, that work with collectives has come at the expense of visualizing a nation-specific reading of Indigenous students' letters collectively that I have nonetheless tried to account for through individual histories as far as I could research them. Here, Kim Gallon's call for our attention to "how computational processes," including our rendering of data for use, "might reinforce the notion of a humanity developed out of racializing systems" is vital.¹²⁸ Digital tools, what those tools depend upon, and the results they produce can reinforce both anti-Black and anti-Indigenous ontologies instead of offering or supporting alternatives to them, and researchers working with them must be aware of those risks and be transparent about where they lie.

My interest in a collective level of analysis over (and at times in dialogue with) an individual level produced visualizations of occupied and racialized space, constraint of movement, and challenges to those processes, but at times it also risks replicating at least one aspect of what I seek to study by reducing Indigenous groups to a pan-Indigenous collective. I sought to counter that with attention to specific nations and their territories as well as to students and their geographies of removal and resistance. And yet, because the goal of settler colonialism at the time the letters in my dataset were written was to "disappear" the sovereignty of Indigenous groups through allotment and coercing Indigenous people to adapt to democratic individualism, a focus on the collective scale seems necessary in order to think beyond those colonizing projects. Still, such a "normalizing" of data, to recall Tara McPherson's insights, risks reaffirming the settler-Indigenous binary that, in turn, keeps active a racializing binary of "white" versus "racialized."[129] This is of particular concern given the situatedness of the *Workman* in Powhatan Confederacy territory and Hampton's history as the first arrival point of captive Africans in 1619.[130] Despite early uses of indenture and slavery to control white, Black, and Indigenous peoples within the Virginia colony that initially mobilized a nonbinary settler colonialism, the larger project of "Indian removal . . . helped solidify a biracial South and reinforce white power," even as Indigenous "resistance to dispossession and segregation helped loosen the hold of Jim Crow in the region."[131] In other words, the clarity and starkness of data visualizations may also sacrifice the complexity of entangled anti-Blackness and anti-Indigeneity as well as refusals of, or resistance to, these technologies of theft and violence specific to each Indigenous nation.

A further and significant consideration is the availability of base layers for tools that visualize geospatial data: those that are free and easiest to use often tend to be limited to contemporary and thus settler-colonial mapping and satellite topography. Historical maps are a building project for makers, and while projects are "georeferenc[ing] and digitiz[ing]" historical maps "as vector layers" so that they might be used by researchers who are not makers, "the process of converting historical maps into GIS-compatible formats is time-consuming, resource intensive, and expensive."[132] Digitized maps such as those built by the Whose Land and Native Land Digital partnership, an Indigenous-led nonprofit based in what is now known as Canada, are sophisticated, interactive maps of the world's Indigenous territories but were not available as overlays or base layers until February 2023.[133] The founder of Native Land Digital, settler Victor Temprano, also acknowledges the temporal considerations of working with his site, which is both open to community updating and constantly under revision. Thus far, Native Land Digital has been unable to "specify different time periods, separate existing and historical nations, and highlight the movement of nations across time." Developing this capacity "would be a huge logistical challenge . . . requiring time, sources, and resources not currently available to" this project as a largely volunteer nonprofit.[134]

The stakes of geospatial data visualizing capabilities and limitations for research on white supremacist settler colonialism and Indigenous and African American refusal and resistance are crucial for researchers to consider. As Richard White argues of spatial history more broadly, "Visualization and spatial history are not about producing illustrations or maps to communicate things that you have discovered by other means. *It is a means of doing research*; it generates questions that might otherwise go unasked, it reveals historical relations that might otherwise go unnoticed, and it undermines, or substantiates, stories upon which we build our own versions of the past.'"[135] For example, what questions are we as researchers not asking if we are working with settler-colonial renderings of land in our geospatial data visualization work? These considerations indicate significant limits to the "big tent," or mainstreaming, of digital humanities tools and to their "neutral" use in any research project. I draw attention to these limits as a self-conscious part of research projects like this one that do not take as given the "humanity" produced by a racializing system. We must acknowledge that racializing colonial processes are not confined to the temporal past or surpassed by technological development, but rather continue to underwrite the production of both the situated data and the technology with which we work. Although data visualizations are central tools in the digital humanities, they should not be mistaken for analysis itself, and the data they are based on should not be mistaken for "transparent" or "self-evident" information, as Lisa Gitelman and Virginia Jackson caution about data generally. Rather, data visualizations may help us ask new questions about our material, thereby making new readings and interpretations possible.[136] This is but one reason why this chapter does not exchange data visualization for close reading, instead exploring what can result when both are active.[137] The reading protocols and tools we use are firmly embedded in racializing and settler-colonial processes even as they may reveal their intertwined operation as a spatial project.

For African Americans and Indigenous peoples during the rise of the residential school system and during Reconstruction and its dismantling, making place refused and countered settler attempts to make land a possession devoid of histories, attachments, experiences, and ways of knowing as well as attempts to racialize space to control Black and Indigenous movement through and presence in it. Black and Indigenous peoples mobilized letters to the editor to make place in the public sphere through a publication they were imagined only to labor to produce, not to use. And as the geospatial data visualizations offered in this chapter render starkly, this press form indexes collective Black political mobilizing locally, regionally, and across the nation, even as it also marks the complex ways Black people were managed spatially by the nation-state. Letters to the editor enable such readings of power and counters to it when we work to read across scales. Combining readings of movement and space as material and seemingly transparent facts with readings of the place making that memory, history, imagination and feeling achieve fundamentally challenges what we conceive mobility, movement, space, and place to entail and mean. It is especially acute for those who study Black and Indigenous print cultures to prioritize attention to movement and making place as material, affective, and imaginative and as acts that produced and preserved knowledge, given that for these collectives, movement and space have been wielded as technologies of domination.

Chapter Four

Feminist Black Internationalism in *The Crisis* and *Negro World*

Black geographies are central to understanding how Black women used periodicals and press forms politically. They exceed scales of community, region, and nation even as they are entangled with and work to make place in them. As Katherine McKittrick argues, Black geographies and histories present a rupture to the teleological given that the very symbols of "modern technological progression," such as the ship, are often the fraught locations of "Black subjectivity and human terror, Black resistance, and in some cases, Black possession."[1] Black geographies also employ "a distinct spatial imaginary to oppose the land use philosophy that privileges profits over people," as George Lipsitz observes.[2] In turning to focus on columns as offering affordances to Black feminisms in newspapers and magazines, I consider not only what Black women published in this press form but how they bent it to their purposes to make global affiliations imaginatively available to readers. Black feminisms have both a long history that is foundational to the development and sustainability of the Black press and a practice of using the affordances of this media form and its genres to imagine other futures. Considerations of claims to progress, modernization, and improvements on "the past" and its technologies that circulated at the turn of the twentieth century in discourses on American democracy and media change are also vital to considering the ways Black feminisms were brokering greater internationalist affiliations.

The early twentieth century has been hailed as a pivotal moment for Black internationalism, Black feminisms, and the Black press. Its markers include the

National Association of Colored Women (NACW), founded in 1896, and the emergence of 344 new Black papers in the period from 1900 to 1909, a print culture explosion.[3] The forty-six Black women who were established as journalists and/or editors in the Black press by 1905 have been described as "more dramatically political [and] more varied in their activities" than any others who preceded them.[4] Scholarship on the most prominent Black feminists, journalists, and editors frequently highlights their internationalist politics. Examples include Anna Julia Cooper's critique of internal and external colonization, US imperialism, and racism, which first appeared in the monthly *The Southland* (1891) and later in her manifesto *A Voice from the South* (1892); Pauline Hopkins's indictment of US imperialism in the Philippines and her call for Black uplift "in all quarters of the globe" in *The Colored American Magazine* (1900–1904); Jessie Fauset's pan-Africanism in *The Crisis* (1918–1926); and Amy Jacques Garvey's editorials and column Our Women and What they Think (1924–1927) in *Negro World*, which aligned peoples of the African diaspora with emergent movements for equal rights in nations worldwide.

Considerations of gender and the geographical and temporal reach of Black politics are also central to current scholarship on Black internationalisms.[5] While there are important exceptions, historiographies of Black internationalism tend to be strongly gendered and to focus on the achievement of men such as Cyril Briggs, Martin Delaney, W. E. B. Du Bois, C. L. R. James, Marcus Garvey, and Claude McKay.[6] Women are frequently positioned in a secondary and supportive role if their work is examined at all.[7] Current scholarship on cultures of Black internationalism also debates whether it emerged during and after World War I or during the interwar years, when "the imperatives of what Edward Said has called 'adversarial internationalizations' (attempts at organizing alliances to challenge the prevailing discourses of Western universalism)" shaped Black transnational print culture and intellectual exchange. Scholars also debate whether conditions at the turn of the century further developed an already-existing Black radicalization and internationalism.[8] Those who argue that Black internationalism predates the early twentieth century contend that even though its "various forms and expressions" were developed "in opposition to new formations of empire following from World War I," nonetheless, "the desire for racial freedom and unity stemmed from a prior radicalization." Here, the distinction is not temporal but one of degree: "Black subjects found themselves asking deeper structural questions of capital and the political world around them" that aimed to contest "the very forces that produced the differences that divided them."[9] Early twentieth-century

Black internationalism was neither emergent nor new, they argue, but rather took on a particular focus and force in the wake of World War I, when the ravages of empire were understood to be concomitant with the exploitative and disenfranchising effects of capital and the metropolitan nationalisms that emerged from the League of Nations. Both sides of this debate agree that Black internationalisms turned on a "tension between the use of the nation-state system to achieve statehood, territorial sovereignty, and recognition in the international political system, and the call for an internationalism that could subvert the nation-state system and related forms of national and international governance."[10]

Given the tendencies to gender Black internationalisms masculine and throw much of the scholarly light on the early to mid-twentieth century, we would do well to remember that early African American feminists also pursued critiques of capital, empire, and nation and sought adversarial affiliations that included and went beyond Black diasporic solidarities. In other words, a progressivist and masculinist teleology of Black internationalisms requires a Black feminist corrective to its chronopolitics, much as narratives of the Black press and its development do. For example, during the 1850s, abolitionists Ellen Craft and Sarah Parker Remond linked the conditions and interests of the British working class, Irish tenant farmers, and enslaved African Americans under the forces of empire and capital. Mary Ann Shadd Cary's feminist Black nationalism in the *Provincial Freeman* and in her 1852 pamphlet *Notes on Canada West* promoted a settler colony of empire rather than the United States as the site for a Black transnation, enacting a tension between nation, empire, and transnation that became a driver of Garveyism nearly a century later.[11] To understand the interplay between Black feminisms (including Black feminist internationalisms) and the Black press we need a longer view that captures the historical use of particular press forms by Black women and their distinctive mobilization of established journalistic practices. We also need to consider more fully women's work in Black internationalist politics, including their feminist disidentifications with and critiques of such movements.

In focusing on how Jessie Fauset and Amy Jacques Garvey innovated on the press form of the column to pursue adversarial internationalisms through their use of recirculation, collage, and collaboration with readers, this chapter underscores their practices as developing from a much longer history of Black feminisms in the periodical press. As Michael West, William Martin, and Fanon Che Wilkins remind us, Black internationalism's "ideal of universal emancipation unbounded by national, imperial, continental, or oceanic boundaries—or even by racial ones" has taken the form of "successive waves of Black international struggles [that] have countered, shaped, and at times destroyed central pillars of capital and empire, racial as well as political."[12] They argue the Great Awakening of the 1730s and 1740s created the "intellectual scaffolding for the Black international" during its first wave, giving that politics a "biblical accent" that we see nearly a century later in early Black feminists' work to open the Black church further to women, in the revivals of the Second Great Awakening, and in the early nineteenth-century international evangelical work of Black women.[13] Black feminist internationalizing also took the forms of abolition, emigration, and anti-lynching that was pursued, in part, through the abolitionist and Black press. Fauset's use of reprinting and Jacques Garvey's collage column are part of a Black feminist practice of recirculation and collaboration that consistently engaged in making place for Black communities in the print public sphere. However much Fauset and Jacques Garvey continue to be aligned primarily with pan-Africanism and Garveyism in scholarship, they pursued an adversarial internationalism in their columns that articulated a multiple and complex solidarity with oppressed peoples regardless of race, even as they also fostered a uniting of the Black diaspora.[14]

Jessie Fauset's Textual Dissonance in *The Crisis*

Jessie Fauset continues to be primarily remembered as the "midwife" of the Harlem Renaissance. As the literary editor of *The Crisis* from 1918 to 1926, she brought African American writers such as Claude McKay and Langston Hughes to the attention of readers and arts patrons. Although she has been dismissed as one of the less talented writers of the Harlem Renaissance for producing what has been called accommodationist fiction, her work as literary editor of *The Crisis* was anything but that.[15] Fauset was also the acting editor of *The Crisis* from 1919 to 1926 in W. E. B. Du Bois's absence.[16] The final issue fully under Fauset's direction—the June 1919 issue—was the best-selling issue in the history of *The Crisis* at over 104,000 copies (figure 4.1).[17]

The Crisis: A Record of the Darker Races (Baltimore, MD: 1910–), the official organ of the National Association for the Advancement of Colored People (NAACP), "sought to be not only a beacon to Black folk but the conscience of the nation."[18] Selling for ten cents a copy or $1.00 for a yearly subscription, *The Crisis* was initially a twenty-page monthly in 1910 that had grown to fifty pages by its April 1912 issue. It had become self-sustaining by 1916 because it successfully attracted advertisers and increased its circulation. In that April 1912 issue, for example, *The Crisis* ran three pages of front advertisements and nine pages of back advertisements. This volume of advertising remained stable as its circulation

Figure 4.1. Cover of *The Crisis*, June 1919. Courtesy of The Modernist Journals Project.

exploded from a print run of 1,000 in November 1910 to "6,000 copies a month" by spring of that year. "By February 1912, circulation had risen to 16,000; by April 1912, to 22,500. By 1919, circulation had risen to around 100,000."[19] While its African American readership was sizeable—in 1916, 80 percent of *Crisis* readers were African American—Michael Fultz notes that after 1919, "circulation dropped precipitously, averaging only 62,000 in 1920. . . . By 1924 it had dropped to 35,000 and by 1930 to 30,000."[20] Notably, Fauset not only edited its best-selling issue, selling 4,000 more copies than *The Crisis* ever sold in its history, but was in charge of the periodical for several months at its peak circulation in 1919.

There is debate over whether *The Crisis* was a "middlebrow" publication, whose "early circulation figures and advertising policies register . . . an interest in reaching broader, less exclusive, and far more socially heterogeneous audiences," a "patrician" periodical "marketed . . . to a more upscale readership," or a Black radical periodical.[21] While *The Crisis* is understood to have been a "militant integrationist" publication, its brand of racial integration for the New Negro "entailed the 'Blackening' of the national culture" as an element in its pan-Africanism and Black internationalism that argued for solidarity of "the darker races" around the globe.[22] *The Crisis* threatened the racial imaginary of the nation, registered most forcefully in physical threats to its Southern agents and the 1919 demand of Arkansas governor Charles H. Brough "that the U.S. postmaster general keep the *Crisis* out of his state."[23]

From December 1918 to that record June 1919 number and in her Looking Glass column, Jessie Fauset pursued a Black internationalism that went beyond pan-Africanism and positioned the condition of Black Americans under US racism as linked to oppression and exploitation around the world. The Looking Glass opened with a literature section that focused on publications by or about "the Negro" and then reprinted, under separate headings, coverage in selected periodicals of lynching, labor, education, African Americans in the war effort, and debates regarding the rights of "the Negro."[24] In columns such as Opinion and The Looking Glass, *The Crisis* made use of reprinting to such a degree that the *Washington Bee* accused it of "wait[ing] for news to come to" it, as though it were a nineteenth-century publication.[25]

Reprinting as Fauset employed it was hardly retrograde and was not used as a labor- or cost-saving device, as the *Bee*'s criticism implied. Rather, this established journalistic practice was highly politicized in *The Crisis*, arguably developing under Fauset's hand from Black feminist recirculation, Black communal reading practices, and the circulatory nexus of the Black press and literary societies examined in chapter 1. Fauset offered spare editorializing comment, if any, on the pieces she chose to reprint in the column, making The Looking Glass a multivoiced collage that could effectively produce politicized, critical, and conscious readers of the press.[26] Anne Carroll has argued that *The Crisis* offered "composite texts" that juxtaposed discordant elements in ways "characteristic of the montage or collage." Similarly, Russ Castronovo has said its "geography of beauty . . . invites dissonance" through assemblage and confrontation enabled by the interplay between visual and written text.[27] Ann Ardis underscores that this dissonant juxtaposition was textual and not exclusively visual.[28]

Fauset's reprinting choices in The Looking Glass were deliberately dissonant: the column consistently offered detailed coverage of lynching—both its supposed justifications and arguments against it—alongside the accomplishments of African Americans or discrimination against Black workers alongside Black soldiers' accomplishments in the war and the contributions of Black women to war industries. This crafted dissonance was geared toward enabling critical connections across pieces in the column that would facilitate her readers' formation of an internationalized, adversarial political consciousness. Fauset's politicized textual assemblage called readers to understand that the condition of the American "Negro" was not only similar to but also linked to the condition of the South African "kaffir," and to Africans under the "soulless capitalism" of the Belgian Congo and Portuguese Africa. But Fauset went beyond pan-Africanist politics when she also underscored the linked conditions of the American "Negro," the European Jew, and "natives" of US imperial conquest in the Philippines, Hawai'i, and Puerto Rico.[29] The pan-African and internationalist politics that emerged in Fauset's column can be understood as a "third something," a concept Anne Carroll has adapted from Sergei Eisenstein, who saw montage as enabling "a maximum degree of affectiveness" by "allow[ing], even forc[ing], the reader of the visual or verbal text to synthesize meaning from its disparate pieces."[30] The product of that "third something"—meaning arrived at not through explicit statement but suggested by conjunction—was active at a textual level both in each Looking Glass column and across issues.

In the October 1918 issue of *The Crisis*, Fauset recirculated coverage of the heroism of African American soldiers along with a piece from the *San Antonio Express* detailing a fund that had been established to reward anyone "directly responsible for the arrest and conviction of those who incite riots and mob outbreaks that result in lynchings, and of those who perpetrate the lynching crime itself." Near the end of that piece, an interesting qualifier is offered: "The system of rewards will apply to any and every crime of lynching committed in the bounds of [the] Continental United States—that is exclusive of the American possessions of Porto Rico [sic], Hawaii, the Philippine Islands, the Panama Canal Zone etc." Without comment, Fauset encouraged her readers to be critically aware of a democracy that not only condoned the lynching of African Americans, forcing groups such as the Express Publishing Company to devise a system of reward to sanction this national shame, but one that also went to war to defend democracy even as it expanded its empire in the Pacific and the Caribbean. Fauset's column also included the heading "Migration Justified," under which she recirculated an excerpt from I. K. Friedman's series on Black migration and democracy in the *Chicago Daily News*. Friedman argued that "democracy working hand in hand with the growth of industry" in the North would redress the prejudices and inequities under which African Americans had labored despite Emancipation: "This same [factory-based] industry . . . tore down the walls of the ghetto for the Jew in Europe and threw wide open in these very recent years the doors of all professions and trades to American, French and English women. There is no denying it! This colored migration is part and parcel of the same movement—a movement that advances with accelerated speed to . . . make the world safe for democracy and glorious for the future."[31] Readers might wonder at the democratic possibilities of capitalist industry, particularly if they had knowledge of the capitalist interests that were driving American imperial expansion masquerading as a civilizing mission. By recirculating such stories without comment in her column, Fauset left readers to interpret their juxtaposition. This would arguably have a democratizing, if not also politically open-ended, effect that Fauset could neither predict nor account for. In other words, by recirculating such stories without comment in her column Fauset opened a space for this "third something," a critique of US imperialism abroad and its links to American capitalism at home through an attention to how the rights of minoritized and racialized peoples fared under both.

In the October and November 1918 issues of *The Crisis*, Fauset's use of recirculation to promote pan-African politics also marked her Black internationalist politics as looking beyond a national color line. In the November 1918 issue, Fauset opened her column with Claude McKay's account of racism in the United States as consciousness-raising: "Looking about me with bigger and clearer eyes, I saw that this cruelty in different ways was going on all over the world. Whites were exploiting and oppressing whites even as they exploited and oppressed the yellows and Blacks. And the oppressed, groaning under the lash, evinced the same despicable hate and harshness towards their weaker fellows."[32] The heading "Race Superiority" then called readers to reconsider capitalism's democratic possibilities: Fauset recirculated a piece from *The Independent* that critiqued the claims of "the Teutonic super-race" with its discussion of Germany's bureaucratic "soulless capitalism" in the "Belgian Congo" as outstripping the "excessively cruel" practices of "private plantation owners in Belgian and Portuguese Africa, and even in a few parts of French Africa."[33] Fauset offered no editorializing to assist her readers in making the connections needed across the October and November issues to see that neither private nor state capitalism operated independently of exploitation of and violence to "the Negro," but those connections are clear enough.

W. E. B. Du Bois is remembered as a pan-Africanist for what Alys Weinbaum has called "racial globality," his "robustly revolutionary and internationalist goal of Black belonging in the world."[34] Jodi Melamed credits his thinking in the 1940s through the early 1960s with a "race radical analysis" that "reveal[ed] continuities between prewar colonial capitalism and postwar U.S. global ascendancy and expanding transnational capitalism," that "deploy[ed] race to mark the continued unevenness of capitalist development," that "suture[d] a global political economic critique of race and racism to a call for socialism," and that understood "black culture as a vehicle for a historically transmitted consciousness" that resisted nationalist ideology by "using race as a hermeneutics to expand the domain of democratic accountability to include such matters as economic governance."[35] However, Fauset's work in *The Crisis* decades earlier demonstrates that she shared with Du Bois a recognition of the "problem of the color line" as global in scale rather than national and a recognition of "the Color Problem and the Labor Problem" as " two sides of the same human tangle."[36] Through recirculation, she offered a "race radical analysis" that aligned Black Americans both with "the darker races" around the globe and with all oppressed and exploited peoples.

In issues of *The Crisis* from January through June of 1919, Fauset's column pursued that "tangle" of the color problem and the labor problem through a critique of empire. In the January 1919 issue, under the heading "Colored Laborers," Fauset juxtaposed discussions of African American labor with Black labor in South Africa. Drawing on a letter by "Mr. Van Gelder, of the Empire Mattress Company, which manufactures mattresses for Sears-Roebuck & Company," that was published in the *Literary Digest*, Fauset quoted his views about hiring Russian-American and Polish-American workers: "They were an ignorant lot, cringing in their servility and totally unaccustomed to being treated decently. However, as they were taught the work and received good treatment they assumed an insolent air of independence and became unreasonable in their demands." Van Gelder's solution to his "insolent" Eastern European immigrant workers and their wage demands was to go South, where he found an African American labor force—some skilled machinists—that he could hire "at a much higher salary, of course, than [they were] getting South" but for no more than his discontented white workers received. When he found he could no longer compete for the labor of boys—Black or white—as tufters, he turned to migrant African American women because they "are limited in their choice of occupations." The overall result was a "pleasant and appreciat[ive]" workforce and "increased production at the same outlay."[37] Fauset sets this narrative of exploited migrant Black women alongside reprinted coverage of a debate in South Africa that ran in the New York *Evening Post*: "The Transvaal is now discussing whether unskilled labor shall be the exclusive property of Kaffir natives, or whether white men shall be employed for such work. . . . Although certain interests oppose the employment of white men at comparatively high wages, several newspapers and organizations are strongly in favor of educating white men to perform all the important work of the country." In a rare editorializing comment, Fauset added: "This would bar the Kaffir from employment of any kind. After all this horror and bloodshed, still the world does not realize the inevitable relationship between economic oppression and disaster."[38] Highlighting similarities between the British empire's policies in South Africa and US labor practices in the South and North as exemplified, not coincidentally, by the *Empire Mattress Company*, Fauset exposed the color line as a tool for pitting one labor force against another in the pursuit of production "efficiencies" around the globe.[39]

Fauset again foregrounded the exploitation of Black women in the US labor market in the June 1919 issue of *The Crisis*, both in a section of her column titled Colored Women in Industry and with excerpts from Walter White's exposé of Southern work-or-fight laws in the *New Republic*. Colored Women in Industry recirculated articles from the *Public Ledger* (Philadelphia) and the *Springfield Republican* of Massachusetts. The *Public Ledger* argued that African American women were not given "fair play" in the labor market; trained stenographers were forced to accept factory work and professionals, such as a West Indian schoolteacher, were forced to take janitorial work at a department store. Without comment Fauset moved to the *Springfield Republican*, which detailed the employment opportunities and working conditions of 2,185 African American women in 217 factories in

New York City, who "enter[ed] 'industry' without trade training, or previous 'industrial' experience after five or six years of domestic service." These were the conditions facing most working Black women in industry and certainly the vast majority of those who had left the South for the North. "Most of the women were employed on the simpler and rougher processes and in most cases worked under less desirable conditions and for less pay than white women, even when doing the same work. Seventy-six per cent . . . were paid from $8 to $12 a week—now regarded as below the necessary minimum—while a few received as little as $5 a week and a few as much as $20," detailed the *Republican*. "Where white and Negro women worked together the Negroes generally fared better than when they were employed separately. It was not so easy to exploit them." Only 1 percent of Black women in industry considered in this study belonged to a union. The study's recommendations focused on training Black women transitioning from domestic to factory work, on unionization, and on Black female leadership: "The committee's suggestions seem to get to the heart of the matter. They are that greater emphasis be placed upon the training of the colored girl[;] . . . that every effort be made to stimulate trade organization among colored women; that industrial leaders be developed among them; and that the colored woman be generally accepted in industry by the American employer and the public at large." Significantly, the author of the article understood that "woman's place in industry," regardless of race, was a factor in "woman's place . . . in citizenship" that "cuts across race lines."[40]

Three pages later, Fauset reprinted excerpts of Walter White's accounts of work-or-fight laws in the South that offered evidence he had gathered for the NAACP in October 1918.[41] Following US Army Provost Marshal Enoch Crowder's May 24, 1918, order that "all able-bodied men must be employed in an essential job if they were not part of the military," work-or-fight laws were adopted in Southern states to stem the tide of the Great Migration and keep African American women in domestic work and Black men working for lower wages than they could earn in Northern war industries.[42] As Tera Hunter notes, white southerners "deliberately designed" these laws "to break the will of Black workers."[43] In some states, they applied to "men through the age of 55, ten years past the draft age." These laws were also applied to women and were "enforced with extreme prejudice."[44] The excerpts Fauset chose to reprint revealed that Alabama's work-or-fight law empowered employers to confiscate the employment card of any disgruntled worker who left the job as a form of protest, which prevented them from obtaining other employment, and alerting officials to a violation of the law. In the first excerpt she reprinted, a Black cook demanding higher wages from the mayor, her employer, quit and was subsequently arrested and fined. The mayor had confiscated her employment card, so that when the "deputy sheriff appeared at her door and demanded that she show her work card," she could not provide it and was arrested and . . . brought up for trial . . . before the mayor himself." The judgment was a $14 fine, which "was paid by the Mayor, who then said to her, 'Go on up to my house, work out the fine and stop your foolishness.'" In another example, a Black woman peeling potatoes on her front porch was charged with vagrancy, arrested, and imprisoned when she told "an officer, . . [who] asked her if she was working, . . that her duties at home required all of her time and that her husband earned enough to allow her to stay at home." The article added that "no record could be found of any able-bodied white woman being molested" under Alabama's work-or-fight law.[45] By including excerpts from White's report in The Looking Glass with Colored Women in Industry, Fauset brought into focus the impact of the war effort on racialized labor markets both North and South; the justice system's role in preventing labor- and community-based solidarities; and the ways Black women's work could be exploited as surplus labor by denying them the markers of womanhood, such as working at home as a reprieve from the public and the market, or by casting them as inherently inferior workers. Fauset's recirculation aimed to heighten critical consciousness of the social and economic climate that pitted the North against the South in competition for the labor of Black men and women.

In the March 1919 "Overseas Number" of *The Crisis*, Fauset made clear that the exploitation of Black labor and responses to Black labor unrest were no different in South Africa. Under the heading "The Restless South African," Fauset's reprinting choices highlighted the role of the market in political unrest. An article by a Rev. Balmsworth for the London *Enquirer* opened with this copy: "In South Africa the native question is always with us. . . . But of late years an uneasy feeling has been steadily growing in the minds of thoughtful observers that South Africa is unconsciously drifting towards grave racial conflict." Balmsworth continued: "A new spirit and new ideas are in the air, and the native demands more and better education, greater opportunities of development, more freedom, more land, a less restricted franchise, more self-government—and so on." The similarities between the demands of Black South Africans and those of Black Americans are unmistakable here. In South Africa, that new spirit extended to white government officials when a Black labor strike in Johannesburg, during "which the natives concerned were so unjustly treated" that "protests [were issued] from every [political] party in South Africa" in response and a commission to investigate was established.

The commission's report proposed greater representation in Parliament for Black South Africans, but that was answered with a call for "real democracy" by Sidney Percival Bunting, a founder of the International Socialist League (which became the Communist Party of South Africa). Bunting proposed that in addition to political representation, "there must be some form of industrial organization, some guild or industrial union through which the native, along with all other workers, white or colored, can exercise a voice in the control, the ordering, and the development of his life and work and of the conditions under which he labors." He was subsequently prosecuted for "inciting to public violence," a prosecution that Balmsworth likened to "the dark days of industrial slavery, of the early nineteenth century, with its suppression of trade unionism and the rights of combination."[46]

From her recirculation of labor conditions in the Transvaal in the January 1919 issue to the outcome of Black labor strikes in Johannesburg in the March issue and Colored Women in Industry in combination with White's exposé of Southern work-or-fight labor laws in June, Fauset's column explored the possibilities of racial and labor solidarity in the context of laws, social conditions, and labor practices. Readers learned that the possibilities for such solidarities in a democratic nation-state were no greater than they were in a colony of the British Empire. Fauset's juxtaposition of these three columns also highlighted how Black women were too rarely the focus of analysis, even when they were particularly targeted through both gender and racial ideologies. Even when Black woman's labor conditions were discussed, readers were left with the clear impression that committee recommendations would have little impact in the market and that the need for work and wages would continue to mean that Black women would have little choice between domestic service and poorly paid factory work. Fauset's efforts to mobilize a pan-Africanist and Black internationalist consciousness in her readers as well as her incisive attention both to the "color line" as global and to the "color problem" as inter-implicated with the "labor problem" make a strong case for placing Fauset in a context that includes Amy Jacques Garvey, someone who is understood as more radical in her politics.

Textual Assemblage in Amy Jacques Garvey's Column Our Women and What They Think

"The Negro papers I read out here [are] *The Crisis*, the *Brownies Book*, *Crusader*, *Journal of Negro History*, *Negro World*, the *Emancipator*," wrote A. Goldsmith of Port Melbourne, Australia to Carter J. Woodson, editor of the *Journal of Negro History*, in 1920.[47] Amy Jacques Garvey and Jessie Fauset evidently shared readers. In Our Women and What They Think, which ran in *Negro World* from February 1924 to the end of April 1927, Jacques Garvey created an assemblage or collage column that addressed women readers as part of a Black internationalist politics that was affiliated with but reached beyond Garveyism. Composed of one or two editorials penned by Jacques Garvey, articles written by readers and UNIA women, readers' letters to Our Letterbox, household tips and recipes, and advertisements for such products as the Madame Bess Corset Company's Reducing Girdle and Madame C. J. Walker's hair products, Our Women also recirculated news stories on such topics as Filipino women in public life, Egyptian civilization, the 1924 Emigrant Laborer's Act in the West Indies, and women's rights in Estonia, Japan, Turkey, Russia, Poland, and China. Like Fauset, Jacques Garvey was not only pan-Africanist but also internationalist in her political outlook. Recirculation in Our Women functioned to create a public that understood Garveyism as one movement among many around the world for independence and equal rights and women as essential to Black nationalist and internationalist politics.

Marcus Garvey and Amy Ashwood Garvey, Garvey's first wife, founded the United Negro Improvement Association (UNIA) in Jamaica in August 1914 to unite "all the Negro peoples of the world into one great body and to establish a country and government absolutely their own" in Africa by "expel[ling] European imperialists" from "the rightful homeland of all people of African descent."[48] As Robert Hill and Barbara Bair write, "Garvey offered a doctrine of collective self-help and racial independence through competitive economic development" and promoted "'a universal business consciousness' among Blacks in all parts of the world."[49] Scholars of Garveyism frequently call it a pro-capitalist movement, but Black capital as the route to economic independence sat alongside political organization and the development of race consciousness and race pride as the foundational elements of a movement that also critiqued the exploitative effects of capitalism for "the Negro." As Mary Rolinson and others have noted, "Garvey's ideology . . . derived from a masterful intertwining of the most important strands of Black thought in the nineteenth century."[50]

The UNIA was initially unpopular in Jamaica, and the association migrated with the Garveys to the United States in July 1918. Increased migration to the United States from the Caribbean coincided with the UNIA's operation from its Harlem base. In 1924, 12,243 Afro-Caribbean migrants arrived in the United States, the majority of whom "headed to . . . New York City. By 1930, almost a quarter of Black Harlem was of Caribbean origin." Caribbean migrants to the

United States shared with African Americans the broad radicalizing experiences of World War I and racist treatment in the military or upon return home after the war as well as the 1919 race riots in major US cities and uprisings in the Caribbean.[51] These migrants arrived with "an internationalist, Pan-Africanist perspective" developed from their migratory movement and labors in the Panama Canal zone, "on banana plantations . . . in Central America, . . [and] on sugar plantations in Cuba, Puerto Rico, and the Dominican Republic." In search of work, some of these migrants had traveled as far as India and China. Others had sought work in West Africa and the Middle East. A large number had lived in Europe or had fought for the British army during the world war in Europe, Egypt, Iraq, or Palestine.[52] Eventually, UNIA branches were established in the United States, Canada, Britain, the circum-Caribbean, South America, Africa, Europe, and Australia. UNIA news and copies of *Negro World* were taken to far-flung ports by Black seamen. While an accurate count does not exist, the organization is estimated to have had some four to six million members worldwide, "approximately half of whom were in the United States."[53]

In addition to its radicalized, internationalist and pan-Africanist Caribbean migrant members, the UNIA claimed its strongest support from African Americans. In 1921 and 1922, UNIA membership peaked at "1,176 divisions," of which "close to 80 percent . . . were in the United States." Scholarship has focused on UNIA strength in coastal cities and its popularity in the South.[54] By 1926, the UNIA had "423 divisions" in the South alone "and almost 500 in the rest of the United States." According to information in 1920 census schedules, the majority of American Garveyites were "married, literate, Black Belt tenant farmers and sharecroppers with wives and daughters in their households."[55] Garvey's Black nationalism was aspirational in its envisioning of a restored Black empire on the African continent, imaginative in its address to Blacks around the world as united in cause and politics despite being fragmented by the diaspora spatially, and pragmatic in its program of supporting Black-owned businesses. In its iconography, particularly the UNIA-owned Black Star Line shipping corporation, Garveyism combined the aspirational, the imaginative, and the pragmatic; UNIA members could buy shares in the fleet and imagine their triumphant "return" to Africa aboard its ocean liners.

Given that the average US Garveyite was literate and the average Caribbean Garveyite, including those who formed one-quarter of Black Harlem's population, was "highly literate," it should come as no surprise that the UNIA's *Negro World* was a highly successful weekly from August 1918 through 1933. With a love of oratory and books and a "voracious appetite for knowledge, including subversive knowledge," a high percentage of Caribbean migrants to the United States were professionals and skilled tradespeople.[56] Many would have already been reading papers such as the *Pittsburgh Courier* (1907–1966), A. Philip Randolph and Chandler Owen's magazine the *Messenger* (1917–1928), and fellow migrant Cyril Briggs's magazine the *Crusader* (1918–1922) before they arrived in the United States.

Negro World became part of the movement's multifaceted approach to envisioning and realizing an empowered Black space and mobility and was recognized as part of the Caribbean vanguard in radical periodical publication in the United States in the 1920s. Censored and banned as seditious in Nigeria, the Belgian Congo, French West Africa and through much of the circum-Caribbean, *Negro World* circulated covertly via Black seamen who smuggled the paper into these areas and to South Africa, Canada, Australia, and the South Pacific. *Negro World* had an inaugural run of 3,000 copies, but "after six months of publication, its circulation reached near 50,000." Even though it was suppressed in 1919 and 1920,[57] the periodical achieved a "wide circulation of . . . as much as 75,000 in 1921"[58] and ran more advertisements than other Black radical periodicals, evidence of its large readership. *Negro World* is regarded by scholars as forcing the Black press to expand its international coverage.[59] As with the Black press generally, estimates of *Negro World*'s readership far outstrip its circulation figures. Amy Jacques Garvey claimed the paper had 11 million readers in the February 20, 1926, issue.[60] The political anxiety that motivated the suppression of *Negro World* in the circum-Caribbean is evident in the US investigation of Garvey that the FBI began in November 1919, propelled by J. Edgar Hoover's identification of Garvey as a Communist sympathizer and a dangerous radical.[61] Garvey was brought to trial for using the mails to defraud UNIA shareholders in the Black Star Line on May 18, 1923. The trial ended on June 21 with his conviction. He was imprisoned on February 8, 1925, in the federal penitentiary in Atlanta, Georgia, following a failed appeal. Two years later, President Calvin Coolidge commuted Garvey's sentence and he was deported to Jamaica.

From February 2, 1924, through the end of April 1927, Amy Jacques Garvey edited the woman's page of the paper perceived to be the most radical Black periodical of its day, capable of marshaling millions of supporters to a Black nationalist program that was seen as threatening the balance of power between whites and Blacks around the globe.[62] Her column Our Women and What They Think pursued a radical politics, as did *Negro World* as a whole, but Jacques Garvey's column also agitated for a shift in power in the Garvey organization itself. Women's representation as delegates in the UNIA increased as the movement declined, as Winston James notes: "When the movement was but a shadow of its former self, 39.5 percent of the delegates [to UNIA conventions] were women, rising to 49.1 percent in 1938. The women of the UNIA were . . . the most faithful and loyal Garveyites."[63] By the time Jacques Garvey's column appeared in *Negro World*, Garveyite women had already agitated for greater representation in the leadership of the UNIA. Yet, as James documents, while three of the UNIA's six directors were women when the organization's headquarters were first established in Harlem in 1918, "the role of women within the UNIA declined in inverse proportion to the size of the movement. Thus, at its height, the UNIA had only one woman, Henrietta Vinton Davis, among its top leaders."[64] Nonetheless, women understood themselves as central to "putting the program over," as the rallying cry went, whether as members of UNIA divisions, as delegates, as members of women's auxiliaries, or in organizational roles such as lady presidents of local branches. Their participation in the UNIA included its all-female auxiliaries: the Black Cross Nurses, which developed from the ladies division organized by Amy Ashwood Garvey and undertook "social welfare and organizational functions," and the Universal African Motor Corps, a "paramilitary auxiliary for women."[65] Honor Ford-Smith has argued that "the UNIA placed far more emphasis on women's organizing in their own groupings than any other nationalist organization at the time."[66] In the pages of *Negro World*, women contributed letters to The People's Forum column and wrote division reports for the News and Views of the UNIA Divisions section.

However, at the 1922 UNIA convention, Victoria Turner, a member from St. Louis, made five recommendations on behalf of "the women of the U.N.I.A. and the A.C.L. [who] know that no race can rise higher than its women." Those recommendations included "that a woman be head of the Black Cross Nurses and Motor Corps," that women have membership "on every committee. . . . [and] in the important offices and field work of the association," and that "Lady Henrietta Vinton Davis be empowered to formulate plans with the sanction of the President-General so that the Negro Women all over the world can function without restriction from the men."[67] Women from Chicago, Detroit, New Orleans, New York, Florida, Maryland, Indiana, and Ohio rose to speak in favor of these recommendations, but Garvey responded by saying "he did not see any reasons for the resolutions, as the women already had the power they were asking for under the constitution."[68] Two years later, Amy Jacques Garvey wrote that she had established her Our Women column to answer "the repeated requests by our women to express themselves on all matters relating to humanity at large, and our race in particular." She saw the page as "unique, in that it seeks to give out the thoughts of our women on the subjects affecting them in particular and others in general. This pleases the modern Negro woman, who believes that God Almighty has not limited her intellect because of her sex."[69]

Amy Jacques Garvey was born in Kingston, Jamaica, on December 31, 1896, into a "comfortably middle class" family. Her father, George Jacques, had lived in Cuba and spent some time in Baltimore. Together, Amy and her father read "foreign newspapers and periodicals on Sundays." She worked for a while as a clerk-typist in her father's law office, but she left for the United States in 1917, staying "with relatives in New York" upon her arrival. After Amy Jacques heard Marcus Garvey speak, she made an appointment to see him. She became his private secretary, and in 1922 she married him. She was "an ardent supporter of the UNIA, and a radical Black nationalist up to her death in Kingston in 1973."[70] Amy Jacques Garvey served as an associate editor of *Negro World* from 1924 through 1927 and edited Our Women until April 30, 1927. After the column closed, she remained a contributing editor to the paper. In her time with *Negro World*, Jacques Garvey wrote over "two hundred editorials," Ula Taylor notes, and her Our Women column "coincided with the most turbulent period of the UNIA," including Marcus Garvey's indictment in 1923 and conviction and imprisonment in 1925.[71] While she was editor of the woman's page, Jacques Garvey was also "the premier propagandist of Garveyism," as Barbara Bair puts it, "traveling to division meetings throughout the country, lobbying for Garvey's release in Washington, and publishing the two-volume *Philosophy and Opinions* in 1923 and 1925."[72]

Like Fauset's Looking Glass column, Jacques Garvey's Our Women used juxtaposition to make politicized connections without editorial comment. For example, in the September 13, 1924, issue, Jacques Garvey reprinted a story from the *Nation* on the occupation of Haiti as an example of US economic imperialism in the Caribbean alongside a story from the *Cape Argus* on segregation in Cape Town and another from *Current History* on the demand for self-government in the US-occupied Philippines. She juxtaposed these pieces with her own editorial, "Work of the Oppressors in North Africa." Often her recirculation choices focused on women's rights, such as the article "Activities of Filipino Women in Public Life Are Potent Forces in the Progress of Nation" from the *Filipino Independent*, which argued that professional opportunities in the Philippines were as good for women as they were for men. It urged women to read the daily paper to be in touch with the needs of their people and documented the over 300 women's clubs in the Philippines that were associated with social settlements, were working to improve health conditions and decrease the infant mortality rate, and had established a women's employment agency, a day nursery, a mother's league, and free legal aid.[73] Our Women also recirculated articles on labor, the League of Nations, nationalism and empire, the rise of "the Orient" in world politics, industry and "surplus women" in Britain, divorce law in Moscow, dress reform in Turkey, and unionism in China, to name only a few of the reprints that offered readers of Our Women an international perspective on women, labor, and world politics.

Jacques Garvey's recirculation choices came from a diverse selection of papers around the world, including the Egyptian paper the *Bishara Nahas*; Caribbean papers such as the Belize *Independent*, the Dominica *Chronicle*, and the St. Kitts *Union Messenger*; South African papers such as the Johannesburg *Star*; and the *Daily Worker*, the *New Republic*, and papers from across the United States, particularly those from New York City. The page offered syndicated news from the Associated Press, the Lincoln News Service, and the World's Bureau. Jacques Garvey also encouraged readers to save the papers they were reading. "Put a wrapper on it and mail it to others," she wrote, including to her at *Negro World*. Because of her access to the international press through her readers, she was able to recirculate articles that may not have been available through syndicated news services.[74]

Jacques Garvey's reprinting choices mobilized recirculation in order to deliberately constitute a politics of global solidarity among all peoples involved in liberation and empowerment struggles. Reprints in Our Women represented by a data visualization capture the internationalism she was working to construct by presenting press coverage of such struggles, including feminist agitation in Turkey, Russia, England, and the Philippines, as linked to those of Black women in the United States (figure 4.2). The column represented Garveyite women as active in a Black internationalist politics affiliated with but reaching beyond Garveyism, and it was also where women took space in *Negro World* beyond The People's Forum column or in division reports. In other words, Garveyite women took space in the paper in ways that contested their roles in the organization, and they extended the reach of the organization's politics through the connections they elaborated along with Amy Jacques Garvey.

Our Women was unique not only for its textual assemblage and recirculation but also because unlike other columns in the Black press, it was designed to be collaborative as the co-creation of its editor and *Negro World*'s women readers.

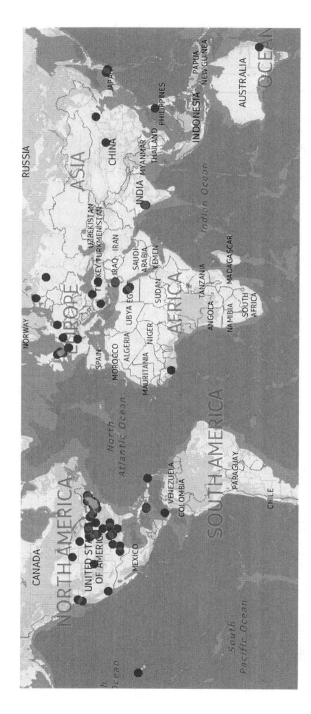

Figure 4.2. Origin location of reprinted content in Our Women and What They Think, *Negro World*, 1924–1927. Produced by Nicholas Van Orden in CartoDB.

Jacques Garvey first called women to contribute to the column in its second issue on February 9, 1924, in blocked text in the center of the page above the fold:

WOMEN OF THE NEGRO RACE!
Let the World know
What you are
thinking and doing
Send in your articles, poems and essays to
Mrs. Amy Jacques Garvey, care of Negro World,
55 West 135th street, New York City.

She envisioned a column that women readers would contribute to. In August, Jacques Garvey stepped up her calls with an editorial titled "Have a Heart" that ran a full half-column, the space she typically took to offer her standard two editorials. She wrote: "Our appeal is not only made to members of the Universal Negro Improvement Association but to all Negro women of all climes. You have an opportunity of airing your views in English, French and Spanish. By your expressions and opinions you will be able to help the race materially." She urged educated women to "help your less informed sisters. Mix among them a little more; hear their woes and sufferings." Yet she did not privilege formal education or limit her call for contributions to educated women; rather, she encouraged collaborative effort so that all voices could be heard in the paper: "Those of us, who, unfortunately, cannot express ourselves on paper, can get someone who is better equipped to clothe our sentiments in proper language and send same into our office. . . . It is common knowledge that some of the most beautiful sentiments and lofty ideas emanate from the brains of women who have had very little education."[75]

Women from across the United States and as far away as Liberia, South Africa, Panama, Jamaica, Haiti, Cuba, and Australia wrote articles, poetry, and letters for the page. Several were regular contributors. Hannah Nicholas submitted articles from August 23, 1924, through September 12, 1925.[76] Theodora Holly contributed articles on the condition of Haitian women in February and March of 1925 and became the French editor of *Negro World* in February of that year.[77] Amelia Sayers Alexander began as a letter writer and later submitted articles to the page in 1924 and 1925.[78] In all, thirty-three women published articles throughout the life of Our Women from February 1924 to April 1927. They wrote on topics that ranged in focus from women as educators to "right living."[79] Yet Jacques Garvey repeatedly reissued her call for contributions, and was clearly frustrated that women who read the paper did not more fully take up the opportunity to voice their views in

Our Women.[80] By February 12, 1927, her editorial "Our Page Is Three Years Old" revealed that Jacques Garvey was ready to throw in the towel: "The writer has had to produce this page under great strain, especially within the last two years, and if our women readers do not care to contribute to its columns, then we think it best to discontinue same, or pass it over to another lady, who will write on fashions and housewife's topics only." Jacques Garvey's frustration was no longer even thinly veiled: "This last resort will be a reflection on the intelligence of our women readers, who should endeavor to use this opportunity to impress their opinions on the rest of us and also on the men. In this way we will be able to command a respectful hearing before the world, and prove that Negro women are great thinkers as well as doers."[81] Her health had suffered while she edited the column and organized agitation for Garvey's release, and others on *Negro World* staff, including T. Thomas Fortune, had edited Our Women in that period. By 1926, Madame de Mena's letter calling this silence "an awful calamity" was the only one to appear on the page, and there are no letters at all in the column in 1927.[82] All of the five signed pieces in the January 29, 1927, edition of the column were written by men.

While Jacques Garvey aspired to more for Our Women, her column was unprecedented for its multivocality and for the geographical reach it conveyed to readers through both her reprinting choices and women's contributions. That sense of many voices issuing from around the globe was central to the politics the UNIA was working to achieve, a politics Jacques Garvey attempted to broaden further by calling women beyond the membership of the UNIA to contribute to her page. Our Women calls us as readers now to press on our understanding of texts and their circulation as not only communicating political arguments but also as shaping a politics. Here, again, it is worth reflecting on Benjamin Lee and Edward LiPuma's characterization of "circulation and exchange . . . as constitutive acts in themselves."[83] Through recirculation and reader contributions, Our Women took up the self-conscious and deliberate work of constituting a politics of global solidarity that included not only UNIA women but also all peoples involved in liberation and empowerment struggles. Both "local" and singular arguments as well as events covered in papers throughout the world took on a greater significance in Our Women, but perhaps even more important, readers were encouraged to see their own condition in national and international frames. At a time when the League of Nations was redefining what nation-states were and which entities could claim that status, Jacques Garvey and the women who contributed to her column were defining collectives through the affective and imaginary connections of shared experience and political interest and were creating a Black internationalist space that was not wholly dependent on where a person was located or where they might have come from, but on how the reader connected to those multiple collectives, some that were diasporic but many that were not. The page was an international and transpolitical space in which mobility and spatiality of people and political concerns were conveyed through the act of recirculation as well as through the content and signatures of reader's letters and articles.

Our Women is a remarkable example of how self-reflexive address can shape readers as conscious of their position in a much wider whole. Every week, the page repeated the act of gathering voices that appeared to issue from multiple places and across varied press forms and formats—editorials, letters, signed pieces, syndicated news articles, and reprints from city dailies and weeklies, monthly specialized periodicals, organization publications, and national papers. Through such recirculation, Our Women readers encountered the page's Black internationalist and feminist politics as having critical mass that brought them into relationship with a unity of purpose, howevermuch they were heterogeneous in their views and were dispersed geographically. As Ula Taylor has argued, Jacques Garvey understood "the sharing of ideas—theorizing—as a form of activism."[84]

One marker of Jacques Garvey's editorial work as constitutive rather than simply transmissive is *Negro World*'s role in shaping Aboriginal politics in Australia. The first organized Aboriginal political group in Australia was the Australian Aboriginal Progressive Association (AAPA), founded in 1924. It was preceded by the Sydney Coloured Progressive Association in 1903. Most members of that group were African Americans and West Indians who came through Sydney as seamen and formed allegiances with Aboriginal wharf laborers working on Sydney's docks.[85] Black nationalist movements, particularly Garveyism, which had a Sydney branch in the early 1920s, informed the "political directives and rhetoric of the 1920s Aboriginal leadership." At times, the AAPA and the UNIA in Australia overlapped in membership and leadership. In August 1924, Jacques Garvey received a letter from the Sydney UNIA branch organizer, L. Lacey, noting that 10,0000 Aboriginals had been organized in New South Wales. Lacey estimated that a further 60,000 could be organized in the rest of the country if they could be reached on reservation land, but he noted that interference from missionaries and the government's Aboriginal Board would be potential obstacles. John Maynard documents that Lacey later became the treasurer of the AAPA. Lacey's letter was not reprinted on the woman's page; instead, it was given a more prominent position on page 3 of *Negro World* under the headline "Australia Sends Greetings to the Fourth International." Lacey also wrote in this letter that his sister,

Mrs. Hassen, was treasurer of the Sydney branch and that she planned to send Jacques Garvey some Australian newspapers, a response to her solicitation of papers from readers. Lacey was interested in receiving American newspapers in turn, especially *Negro World*, so that he might circulate them among "our people" and "enlighten them a bit." Although John Maynard has identified Lacey as Aboriginal,[86] he closed his letter with a pan-Africanist identification with Africa as the motherland: "I hope that God will hasten the day when we will be back in our mother country again."[87] Maynard notes that "only months after this correspondence, news of the establishment of the AAPA was announced in Sydney." Garveyism's influence on the AAPA is evident in their shared motto of "One God! One Aim! One Destiny!" and the APPA logo "Africa for the Africans—Australia for Australians."[88]

Just as Amy Jacques Garvey's influence is evident in *Negro World* beyond its women's column, Our Women was not the only page in the paper where women's voices were heard. Women were regular reporters for The News and Views of the U.N.I.A. Divisions page, they wrote letters for The People's Forum, and they contributed articles for the paper beyond Our Women. But Garvey's column conveyed the sense that women were speaking to women about issues vital to them rather than to the UNIA or to *Negro World*'s readership as a whole. Our Women mixed politicized contributions and reprints with the standard fare of women's pages, running regular "Smile," and "Suggestions to Housewives" sections and carrying advertisements for beauty preparations, clothing, and treatments for "female troubles." Most turn-of-the-century Black periodicals offered either a woman's page devoted to fashion or social events or a woman's column focused on politics and women's issues.[89] Although both are, of course, political, the Black press rarely offered them together to their readers in the same column.[90] That Jacques Garvey did so speaks to more than her page's appeal to a diverse group of readers with varying interests. The mix of the political and the seemingly mundane in Our Women enabled the column to actively shape a Black feminist internationalism grounded in a domestic dailiness through its circulation.

The page's particular brand of Black feminist, Black nationalist, and internationalist politics was presented as just as "natural" an interest for women as household tips, regular pieces on health and hygiene by the Black Cross Nurses, and ads for fabric remnant sales (figure 4.3). In the January 23, 1926, issue, an article by the Black Cross Nurses of New York City hailed mothers as shaping their children and, by extension, the race even in utero: "Educate your children at the

Figure 4.3. Our Women and What They Think page, *Negro World*, January 23, 1926.

beginning and through the entire months of pregnancy, because maternal study is most promotive of talents. . . . Pre-natal influences may do as much in the formation of character as all the education that can come after."[91]

Alongside this article ran reprints titled "Woman Suffrage," noting the nations that had extended the vote to women in the period from 1893 to 1922; "White Man's Misrule Devastating to Africa," originally published in the *African World*; and "To the Poor Colored Worker," on coal mining in "India, Africa and China . . . labor that toils underground for less than two cents an hour" written by Shapurji Saklatvala, one of the earliest members of the Communist Party of Great Britain to serve as a Member of Parliament. The page also ran a letter from Madame Maymie Turpeau de Mena with the title "Part Women Must Play in the Organization." De Mena's letter encouraged Garveyite women to stop limiting their vision of female roles in the movement to the Black Cross Nurses or division secretaries and instead to "line up for women's rights in this great organization." De Mena, who was born in Nicaragua, had the title assistant international organizer by 1926. The next year, she was appointed fourth assistant president general of the UNIA, and in 1931 she reorganized the Port Limón branch of the UNIA in Costa Rica, where the movement remained active throughout the 1930s.[92] The collage form of the column and Jacques Garvey's combination of reprints, original contributions, her own editorials, and advertising, enabled the page to politicize the everyday and thereby make motherhood as important to Black nationalism as a piercing critique of colonization in Africa.

While Jacques Garvey's "everyday" politics is evident at the macrolevel of Our Women, readers' letters to the editor mark the microlevel work of that press form. In a more explicit way than recirculation, perhaps, letters to the editor make evident the self-reflexivity that creates a public by addressing it. It is also the press form through which African American women first entered the press and through which we consistently hear their voices across nineteenth- and early twentieth-century Black periodicals. Recirculation and the letter to the editor are productively understood as related practices and forms for Black women's politics. At least two aspects of epistolarity in the nineteenth-century United States link letter writing to newspapers in a connective history at the same time that literary societies and the recirculation Black women practiced through them were most popular and active in Black communities. First, the informal exchange of newspapers between individuals through the mail, what postal authorities called "transient" newspapers, was an epistolary practice that predated the widespread exchange of personal correspondence until "Congress's Acts in 1845 and 1851 . . .

lowered the cost of sending a letter," granting "access to the mails for vast numbers of ordinary Americans."[93] Until that time, as David Henkin documents, the postal service functioned to "circulate printed newspapers and subsidize political communication," and "the discrete and deliberate posting of individual transient papers . . . constituted or approximated letter writing."[94] That newspapers, their informal exchange between individuals, and letter writing are linked in a broader American history of political communication circulated through the post seems particularly salient to consider when reading letters to *Negro World*, since that paper's success was dependent on informal circulation practices. The paper achieved the geographical reach it did because it was transported, often smuggled, to ports around the world in an informal network of distribution. Second, Eve Tavor Bannet has established orality as integral to trans-Atlantic epistolarity in ways that remind us of the workings of Black literary societies: "Letter writers were advised to imagine they were speaking to their correspondents as they wrote, to write as they would speak, and to listen to the sounds of their words and sentences as they put them down on the page." The receipt of a letter inaugurated a similarly performative act: "Reading a letter aloud in company acted as a vocalizing of the absent writer's speech act in the conversation that it stimulated among the company who heard it." As a result, letters "participated in ritual and collective aspects of social life."[95] Similarly, the activities of any African American literary society included not only writing but also listening to texts read aloud. These aspects of an American and trans-Atlantic epistolary history connect to Black feminist activism and its sites in ways that make it far from coincidental that the letter to the editor was a central, constituting press form for Black feminisms.

Jacques Garvey's column illustrates that reprinting and letters to the editor operated as intersecting elements of recirculation that co-constituted Black feminist political praxis. Letters to Our Women began appearing on the page in April 1924, about nine weeks after Jacques Garvey invited readers to contribute. Over the course of women's activity in "Our Letter Box" from April 1924 to January 1926, the majority of the letters to Jacques Garvey came from the UNIA's base in New York City, the South, and the circum-Caribbean.[96] Letters also arrived from Seattle, Kansas City, Montreal, and the state of Utah, indicating the UNIA's reach into the Pacific Northwest, the Midwest, Canada, and the western United States. Our Women published twice as many letters from women, and those letters came from farther afield than appeared in The People's Forum, including letters from Australia and Liberia.

Formally addressed to Jacques Garvey as editor of "the Woman's Page," these letters frequently inscribed a "we" to whom their writers spoke. Women reflected back Garveyite ideology, from advocating self-help in the form of Black capitalism to calling for a Black empire in Africa and self-identifying as "we Ethiopians" in an echo of the African fundamentalism Garvey promoted. Several letters were written by girls, highlighting that women's roles in the organization included pedagogical ones in its juvenile divisions. Women urged change in the UNIA even as they wholeheartedly supported the organization and adopted its political rhetoric. Some letters even controversially referred to the "Negro woman" as the New Negro, a figure of African American modernity that was being defined by male editors in the Black periodical press in masculinist terms.[97]

Reading "Our Letterbox" gives one a sense of the range of Jacques Garvey's readers, including fifteen-year-old Lillie McReeves, who wrote from Columbus, Ohio, to say she prayed that "our flag, the red, Black and green, will float over a mighty nation in Africa."[98] That Jacques Garvey chose to print this letter was in keeping with her purpose. Jacques Garvey made it clear in her editorial in mid-September 1924 that while she was anxious to receive contributions, she did not print everything that arrived in her mailbox: "We find that the few contributions we receive are not of sufficient literary merit to warrant their publication, and, although many highly educated women write expressing their appreciation of this page, yet they make no effort to maintain it by weekly contributions of articles, news items, poems, etc."[99] Jacques Garvey's curation of readers' letters accomplished a particular kind of work on their own as well as in concert with the reprints she chose, the editorials she wrote, and the reader contributions she solicited.

In some issues, the letters Jacques Garvey published clearly presented the available political positions readers had adopted. For example, one finds letters that urge women to take up leadership roles in the UNIA alongside those that argue for conservative roles for women. Asia Leeds helps us further understand that mix as UNIA women's "definitions of redemption" that connected "the social reproduction of Garveyism and the making of a home life conducive to racial solidarity and race pride" to a break from "restrict[ing] women to the domestic and private sphere."[100] Eunice Lewis wrote from the UNIA stronghold of Chicago on Black women's role in race leadership in a letter published in the April 19, 1924, edition of the paper. Arguing that Garveyite women were not only called to practice the basic tenets of the movement but were "to work on par with men in the office as well as on the platform," she insisted that the true New Negro woman knew that to "help her race, it is necessary to learn all the essentials of leadership."[101] Lewis signed her letter from her home address of 3223 Indiana Avenue, where she had lived from at least 1920. Born in Birmingham, Alabama on April 19, 1895, Lewis migrated to Chicago with her husband, James Lewis (b. 1890 in Montgomery, Alabama) sometime between the birth of their son James Lewis Jr. in 1911 and the 1920 census. All were literate.[102] They joined Black southerners migrating to the industrial North in what is often characterized as an explosion in Chicago's Black population. In 1910, the Black population of the city was 44,103. By 1920, it had more than doubled to 109,458. By 1930, it had more than doubled again, to 233,903.[103]

In this same edition of the column, following a letter from Elizabeth Johnson of Marianna, Arkansas, crediting the paper for raising her race consciousness, Jacques Garvey included a letter from Mrs. P. A. Langhorn from Beggs, Oklahoma. Mrs. Langhorn argued that "mothers of the race . . . are committing crimes if they do not teach their daughters to cook, sew and keep house economically." She attributed divorces to household inefficiency.[104] Scholarship on Black domestic feminism has helped us understand that women's appeals to caring for the home and family were forms of feminist Black nationalism that positioned the home as nation under the guardianship of women. However conservative Langhorn's letter might appear to us now—the only one of the three she wrote that is signed "Mrs." and with what are quite likely her husband's initials rather than her own—it was resolutely Black nationalist in its politics. These letters also captured the nature of Jacques Garvey's column, which could seem at first glance rather conservative in its gender politics. Even though Our Women included suggestions to housewives, recipes, and ads for hair treatments and waist and hip reduction, Jacques Garvey was also cleverly having readers represent back to themselves the contours of the feminist Black nationalist public they were helping to create through "Our Letter Box." Ula Taylor calls her strategy of "allow[ing] conflicting perspectives on the woman's page" an attempt to "foster agitation" that would "encourage women to develop analytically . . . and inspire men to . . . respect their ideas."[105]

By August of 1924, "Our Letter Box" was offering space to women from Honduras and Australia, letters that invoked key elements of Garveyism's political imaginary as well as particular histories and trajectories of the Black diaspora. In the August 2, 1924, edition, Matilda Ingleton wrote from Tela in Honduras to offer her four-point definition of "Negro Womanhood." "The women of every race are makers of nations. If we as Negroes are to establish a nation second to none, we must first of all be intelligent in order to produce to the world intelligence,"

Ingleton opened. "2nd We must be pure in heart, for as we nestle to our bosoms our little ones, what we give them is what they receive . . . 3rd We must learn to respect ourselves, copy the good qualities from the women of other races and give them to our girls especially." Ingleton closed with "4th and lastly. . . . let us, whose hands are full, lend to those that are scanty, and by doing so we will help to further this noble cause . . . of becoming a nation second to none in the world."[106] Ingleton's definition of "Negro Womanhood" was not that different from Langhorn's; it positioned Black women as race mothers who were responsible "to our girls especially" and drew together Black women, racial respectability, and Black nationalism as mutually dependent. For Ingleton and others pursuing a feminist Black nationalism, one version of which could be a domestic and maternal feminism, the Garveyite goal of an independent Black transnation was not possible without women as moral agents.

Another letter from Matilda Ingleton was published in the August 23, 1924, edition, where she called on "every Negro" to "make up his and her mind to dedicate their lives to African redemption and Negro nationalism." She argued that "the Negro forms one of the important cogs in the wheel of world mechanism; without him the machine stops and can go no further." She urged her fellow Garveyites to "realize our position in the affairs of men, and stand out as a race independently, realizing that the world cannot right itself without our contribution of progress and achievement."[107] Ingleton's letter brought together labor, world industry and capital, and Black nationalism under an African fundamentalism that was mobile and translatable to disparate situations and settings because it is not particularized to a specific locale. That mobility was central to Garveyism not only because it drew members from around the world but also because, as Michelle Stephens notes, Garveyism was a "global vision of the race that drew on transatlantic histories of movement, the movements of fugitive slaves and imperial civilizations, the colonized and colonizers, and Black colonial subjects and the agents of empire."[108] Black freedom of movement was central to the UNIA's political platform, from the dissemination of its ideology and newspaper to its iconographic markers, such as images of the Black Star Line. Stephens also notes that Garvey's African fundamentalism was "essentially a philosophy of Black empire that looked consciously to a past imperial paradise, rather than a future socialist utopia, for its model of diasporic Blackness."[109] When Ingleton invoked "African redemption" twinned with "Negro nationalism" as the causes to which Garveyites must dedicate themselves, she was using a rhetoric of African fundamentalism that posited the imagined possibility of resurrecting a "premodern and preimperial past" as the foundation for a "*Black* imperial" future, thereby "eras[ing] the disempowering history of European imperialism and its role in the formation of Black subjectivity."[110]

Yet the fact that Ingleton was writing from Tela, Honduras, raises a particular context for Black labor and Black movement. Hers was a Black geography of restricted mobility serving the needs of capital. In her history of Caribbean migrants in Costa Rica, Lara Putnam documents the movement of eastern Caribbean migrant laborers throughout the western Caribbean. In 1912 and 1913, if these workers were Jamaican, for example, they could be pulled from their labors in the Panama Canal Zone to Costa Rica and Honduras to work on banana plantations for the United Fruit Company. The US Isthmian Canal Commission determined in those years that it preferred Barbadian labor because their government was easiest to contract with. Yet when the volume of banana exports crashed in 1917 and 1918, the United Fruit Company cut wages and fired workers, and migrant workers sought jobs in Cuba's sugar industry. In 1920 and 1921, many returned to Costa Rica when the price of bananas in the United States increased by 50 percent and United Fruit judged it profitable to again cultivate land they had "abandoned a decade earlier."[111] Identifying herself with "the scattered sons and daughters of Ethiopia," Ingleton very likely was one of those Caribbean migrants who traveled to Honduras for work or to accompany a family member.[112] To be a "cog" in this particular "world mechanism" drawing people throughout the Caribbean was to be a cog in the development of the US empire, a descendant of peoples who were cogs in the world mechanism of British empire. It was no small matter for Ingleton to urge Jacques Garvey's readers to understand their labor as a power that could work for them instead of putting them at the whims of market fluctuations in banana prices or the availability of cheaper migrant labor, since that also meant arguing for the development of the self-sufficient and economically independent Black empire that Marcus Garvey promised. Here we see the ways that "Our Letter Box" tapped into the experiences and political imaginings of Garveyite women to further the UNIA program and its larger aim of uniting Black people scattered around the world in spirit, if not in body.

Ingleton's letter in the August 2, 1924, edition of Our Women was followed by one from Sydney, Australia, by Sister E. Nyberg (figure 4.4). Ingleton and Nyberg shared references to "African redemption" or "the cause of African Redemption." Nyberg's letter not only reflected a Garveyite African fundamentalism back to its readers, it also gave Jacques Garvey the opportunity to show her newspaper exchange in action. Nyberg sent Jacques Garvey "a bundle of newspapers in which you will find accounts of the brutal treatment of our people in New Guinea.

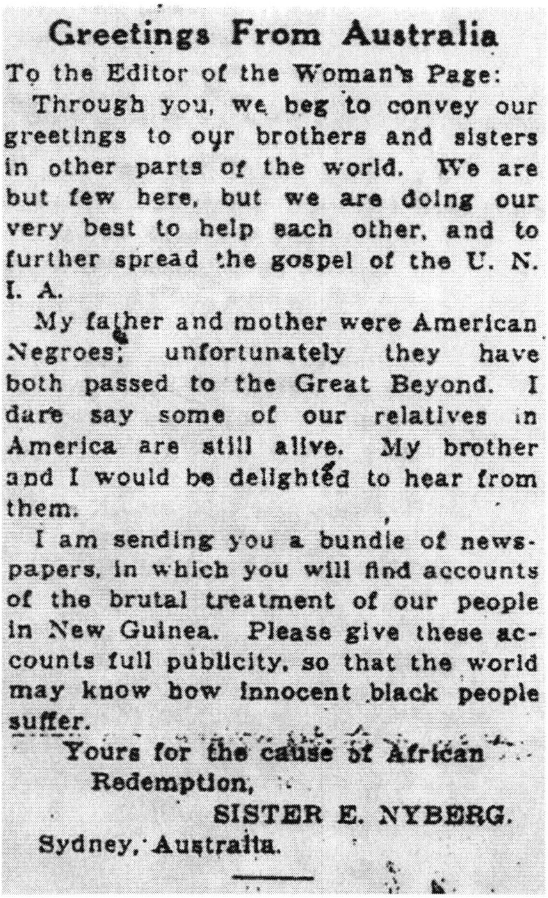

> **Greetings From Australia**
>
> To the Editor of the Woman's Page:
>
> Through you, we beg to convey our greetings to our brothers and sisters in other parts of the world. We are but few here, but we are doing our very best to help each other, and to further spread the gospel of the U. N. I. A.
>
> My father and mother were American Negroes; unfortunately they have both passed to the Great Beyond. I dare say some of our relatives in America are still alive. My brother and I would be delighted to hear from them.
>
> I am sending you a bundle of newspapers, in which you will find accounts of the brutal treatment of our people in New Guinea. Please give these accounts full publicity, so that the world may know how innocent black people suffer.
>
> Yours for the cause of African Redemption,
>
>   SISTER E. NYBERG.
> Sydney, Australia.

Figure 4.4. Letter from Sister E. Nyberg in "Our Letter Box," *Negro World*, August 2, 1924.

Please give these accounts full publicity, so that the world may know how innocent Black people suffer."[113] Now Papua New Guinea, this island is part of what some scholars argue is the "Black Pacific," a region that includes Black communities in Australia, along the Pacific coasts of North, Central, and South America and on islands such as Vanuatu and Fiji, which had no ties to Africa but whose Black residents adopted pan-Africanist identifications with Black people around the world.[114]

Nyberg's letter registers that Black Pacific identification when she claimed solidarity with "our people," Melanesians in New Guinea. She was likely referring to the conditions of Melanesians under the Australian administration, which gained New Guinea as a colony from Germany as an outcome of the 1919 Treaty of Versailles. The Australian government's presence in the island resulted in neo-slave labor for Melanesians on coastal copra plantations. These laborers, who worked under exploitative labor contracts without adequate food or medical attention, died in "great numbers" in the 1920s. It was not uncommon for Melanesians to be kidnapped into this labor force. The practice of district officers instructing "native police to capture Melanesians," whom the officers then "sold to plantations for commissions [,] . . . continued unchanged" as New Guinea transitioned from a German to a British colony after World War I.[115] Readers worked to raise a pan-African and Black internationalist consciousness via Jacques Garvey's recirculation, whether that was through letters like Nyberg's or by sending Jacques Garvey newspapers from which she could choose reprints. Both endeavors established further international sites for the examination of conditions that Black people faced around the world and their need for self-emancipation.

Ethel A. Augustin wrote four months later from Camagüey, Cuba, to alert readers to the conditions of Black domestic workers in that nation. Jacques Garvey ran her letter under the headline "Economic Pressure Put upon the Negro" and placed it top and center on the page. Augustin argued "that Negroes must not be dormant when conditions of late seem to be so critical or that economic pressure is so great and is becoming worse. In Cuba, it is affecting us greatly, and I believe it is so with all Negroes the world over."[116] Augustin was referring to worsening conditions for Afro-Cubans in the labor market. She quoted the Havana *Post*: "Dr. Alfredo Gonzales, consul for the Central Castellan petitioned Secretary Betancourt, of the Agricultural Department, asking authorization for the Spanish association to enter a strong contingent of Spanish maids and cooks into this country." Augustin followed this information with her interpretation: "The motive can easily be perceived. In spite of the fact that our men are steadily thrown out of employment we, the women, will soon have a bitter time. . . . Soon, Spanish women will be taking our places before the stoves and washpans." She placed her concern about Black female wage labor in Cuba in the wider context of "stagnant conditions" in the "West Indies" and "the immigration restriction of the United States" as part of "the economic conditions . . . troubling the Negro more the world over." Calling readers to "rise to a sense of duty," Augustin asked, "Where will we go? What will we do?" if immigration acts, immigrant laborer acts, and agreements between Spain and Cuba meant there was little to no work for Caribbean migrant laborers in the circum-Caribbean region.[117]

The UNIA presence in Cuba was strong. Marc McLeod documents that by 1927 at least fifty divisions were registered there, "more than any other country except for the U.S." Garveyism in Cuba captured the imagination and loyalty of British West Indian migrants, while the UNIA assisted "unemployed and destitute Afro-Caribbean immigrants" during the crash of 1921 and continued through that decade to "pressure the British government to provide better support for its West Indian subjects in Cuba."[118] Coincident with the UNIA's support for West Indian and Afro-Cubans was the rapid rise of the Cuban sugar industry dominated by US capital, particularly the United Fruit Company, which drew on Black Caribbean migrant labor in the region. Acknowledging the inaccuracies of immigration statistics, which can count seasonal migrant laborers more than once or not at all, McLeod documents that "in the first three decades of the twentieth century, as many as 600,000 Afro-Caribbean *braceros* (laborers)" entered the country. By 1931, "77,575 Haitians and 28,206 British West Indians had settled on the island." The size of the Afro-Caribbean settler population was quite likely larger. For example, "the Jamaican Secretary for Immigration in Santiago . . . reported that 'approximately 60,000' British West Indians alone resided in Cuba in 1930."[119] One of every five of these immigrants was a woman. The vast majority of British West Indian migrants were adult workers, a population that was more than 90 percent literate. Ethel Augustin was one of these immigrants to Cuba, writing from the eastern province of Camagüey where agricultural *braceros* worked and settled.[120] Camagüey had its own UNIA school for children and adults, the Antonio Maceo school, named for the Cuban War of Independence hero.

With letters such as Augustin's joining others from the United States, Honduras, and Australia in "Our Letter Box," it is clear that readers were connecting a feminist Black nationalism to an internationalist politics just as Jacques Garvey did in her editorials, her reprinting choices, and the contributor essays she selected for publication. While scholars have cast Jacques Garvey's internationalism as a defense of her pan-Africanism and feminism, I would argue that like Fauset in *The Crisis*, Jacques Garvey worked to place the conditions of "the Negro" in an international frame in order to heighten her readers' political consciousness and the possibility for their action beyond the local and the national.[121] Here, the insights of Gaul and Harris are helpful; they note that "because letters as material objects traversed national borders, the genre offers particularly potent opportunities to dismantle nationalist paradigms."[122] Letters to the editor in Our Women call for us to consider how this press form worked to constitute both a Garveyite Black globality and an internationalist Black feminism. They made real the Garveyite call for a Black transnation that spanned the globe by invoking disparate labor and migratory histories from the Caribbean, the South Pacific, and the United States. David Gerber's consideration of immigrants' letters is pertinent here, particularly his contention that the letter itself is a "singular transnational space."[123] It is important to recognize, however, that these letters to the editor not only constituted Garvey's Black transnation, making real that political ethos that the Black Star Line symbolized, they also serve a necessary function for the writer herself, in the consolidation of identity under the pressures of often-repeated physical dislocation. Gerber reminds us that for immigrants, letter writing maintained a link to "home" and letters themselves were "acts of authorship [as] acts of self-building, at once individual but also deeply social." They were "devices for . . . confirming identities."[124] The need to build and confirm identity were undoubtedly even greater for Black migrants in the United States and those who migrated throughout the circum-Caribbean, whose claim on the societies in which they were living and working was tenuous and provisional and whose claim on "home" was undermined by the controls on labor that sought to delimit their mobility and choice. For example, the US Immigration Act of 1924 denied Afro-West Indian migrants entry, and that same year the West Indies Emigrant Laborers Act offered them little opportunity at "home," a situation Jacques Garvey centered in her January 10, 1925, editorial "How to Help Better the Economic Condition of the West Indies."[125]

Despite the pan-Africanist and Black internationalist politics Fauset and Jacques Garvey worked to develop in their columns, scholarship on Black internationalisms in print culture is only recently turning to focus on women, on multiple sites in the United States, and on nodes in Africa, the Caribbean, Eastern Europe, East Asia and the Black Pacific. Fauset and Jacques Garvey were part of a Black feminist context that included contemporaries such as Margaret Murray Washington, Nannie Helen Burroughs, Mary Church Terrell, and Mary McLeod Bethune, all members of the International Council of Women of the Darker Races, which was founded in 1922 to "create a trans-national, cross-ethnic racial identity for women" and is credited with "import[ing] pan-Africanist critiques about the relationship between racism and imperialism into the US-based Black women's reform movement."[126] Critically engaging with their columns challenges us to broaden our understandings of Black feminisms, Black internationalisms, and Black women's distinctive use of press forms. These women facilitated their readers' reimagining of what it meant to be Black, female, and a worker in a world in which affiliations with other oppressed peoples could bring about a future different from the one being created through the consolidation of nationalisms following World War I. This imagining of a Black geography included and extended beyond Black diasporic spaces. That Fauset and Jacques Garvey worked to do so by bending press forms and journalistic practices such as the column, reprinting, and letters to the editor to their political ends speaks to how Black feminisms have long used what is socially recognizable in their work to imagine life otherwise.

Chapter Five

Intermedial Fugitivity and the "New Negro" Woman in *The Colored American Magazine*

Black women using the press to make place in the public sphere and alliances in and beyond the diaspora rendered and circulated the futures they imagined in a media form made possible by trafficking in Black captivity and exploitation. The advent of print capitalism, or the commercial press, and slavery in the Atlantic world were inextricable, complicating an African American use of newspapers or magazines for liberatory purposes.[1] Fueling the rise and sustainability of periodicals in what is now known as the United States, slave advertisements tend to be studied for their content as historical record, not as "a print genre . . . [and] an essential part" of the media form they "subsidize[d]," as David Waldstreicher observes.[2] Scholarship in the field of slavery studies makes clear that Black captivity and exploitation was fundamental to the economic sustainability of the newspaper as an emergent media form, yet periodical studies has thus far not much acknowledged or grappled with this fact, even though many working in the field have thought carefully about the ways newspapers and magazines can be used to articulate, shape, and mobilize radical, leftist or Black politics and imaginings in varied locations and time periods. This is a pressing issue for periodical studies, all the more so at a time when the field is attending to the digital turn and its effects and to finding a common methodology that might enable a deeper theorization of its objects of study.[3] Calls to remediate periodical studies by shifting its tendency to focus on description toward explanation bear the mark of the digital turn in their focus on the "conceptual language of information technology," such as "thinking of periodicals as systems or networks"[4] or referring to their "action possibilities" as "affordances."[5] The field risks occluding the racial capitalism that was foundational to digital technology in its investment in the explanatory power of new media metaphors to suggest a common methodology; it pays little attention to the foundational role of racial capitalism in the genesis of the media form it studies.[6] This particular consequence of the digital turn has largely not been attended to even while the field discusses vital issues such as paywalls and the "racially discriminatory nature of the archives and databases" that are open to public use;[7] interfaces and degrees of searchability; the replication of older curatorial decisions in what is digitized or available to be digitized;[8] and the narrowing of scholarship to primarily digitized materials.[9]

What are some of the consequences of the mutually dependent relation between slavery and the periodical in the United States, not only for how we understand African American periodicals, particularly but also for future-oriented thinking in the field of periodical studies generally? How are distinctions between old and new less definite and perhaps less productive than they might appear to be for the field?[10] And how does the inflection of old versus new distinctions ignore precisely the ruptures that Black geographies and Black temporality pose to liberal and neoliberal possessive and extractive logics and epistemologies?[11] In this chapter, I suggest that turning back to consider the early use of imagery and language in US newspapers can be one mode of future-oriented thinking about the periodical as a media form. Such a consideration of the media form's past not only connects to the work Black feminists were doing with and in periodicals but also attends to the ways in which Black life, both historical and ongoing, challenges the teleological fantasy of progress on which the US nation-state depends. I work to pursue the double rendition of "economies of representation" and "economies of trafficking"[12] that made newspapers viable as a media form in the United States by first tracing the textual and visual logics of slave advertising[13] before turning to an African American remediation of those racializing commodity logics. Such a "media ecology" is useful for considering illustration in Black periodicals, where the complexities of representing Black life and subjectivities continued to be bound up with those of representing the Black body well after slavery ended.[14] Or, as Jonathan Senchyne has argued, "technologies of racialization emerge in conjunction with technologies of printed words and images," such that "producing oneself as a free subject in print and in life" must necessarily be understood as "embedded within a set of material textual practices . . . [that are] also constitutive in processes of racialization."[15]

Pauline Hopkins's tenure at *The Colored American Magazine* is a salient case study in Black periodical remediation. Her work there deliberately questioned the politics of arriving at the new by ignoring the persistence and force of older visual logics. In turn, her work also helps us consider what might be at stake in the appeal to new media metaphors in scholarly discussions of the future of periodical studies. Calls for a methodology or theorization of periodical study that will move us beyond its "dominat[ion] by discrete analyses of individual case studies" risk dismissing the disruptive particularities such studies can present.[16] Asking how press genres script social understandings that facilitate and proliferate projects of domination can help us better appreciate the possibilities, complexities, and stakes of remediation and show us that much work remains to be done if we are to grapple with the periodical as object of study embedded within particular moments and sets of conditions. Hopkins's use of illustration in the *The Colored American Magazine* to present "the New Negro" at the turn into the twentieth century focalizes the challenges that a racializing press iconography presents to Black feminist work with photographic illustration.

Disappearing Acts: Advertising, Slavery, and Racialization

In "The Matter with Media," James Mussell urges an attention to "the way media mediate," particularly to the disappearing act of the repetitive and generic structures and print forms that "reading sorts . . . from content . . . and then marks as supplementary."[17] Even as the repeated structures, genres, and forms in periodicals are designed to be forgotten, they work constitutively, he contends, "mediating between a specific utterance and the social situation in which it occurs" so that both writers and readers are able to connect the new to the "already known" or "existing social formations."[18] What readers understand and the links they make between what they know and what is new, in other words, is constituted not simply by content or *what* is communicated to them, but by *how* it is communicated. The familiarity of that form or structure, established through repetition, is essential to the mediating work of periodicals. For American periodical studies generally and Black periodical studies particularly, it is crucial to "follow the genre" or to confront the amnesiac effect of advertising related to enslaved people.[19] Repositioning the supplementary as constitutive helps us understand not only how the periodical worked as a racializing medium but also that using periodical illustration to resist such racialization, as African American editors did, necessarily carries with it the disappearing act that is foundational to the media form.

Early American periodicals were simultaneously dependent on the skill, craft, and labor of enslaved people for their production and on representing enslaved people in advertising for sustainability and profit. As Clint Wilson documents, colonial-era print shops "utiliz[ed] the labor of indentured servants or slaves," a practice that continued into the nineteenth century.[20] For example, Rogers and Fowle of Boston, who published *The American Magazine* (1743–1746) and *The Independent Advertiser* (1748–1750), relied on at least one enslaved pressman, Primus, who at the time of his death in 1791 at "more than ninety years of age" had spent fifty years "work[ing] at press." Primus was also pressman on *The New-Hampshire Gazette, and Historical Chronicle*, which was founded in Portsmouth in 1756 by Daniel Fowle and is still in production today as *The New Hampshire Gazette*.[21] As Jonathan Senchyne notes, during Primus Fowle's career as a pressman, he "creat[ed] thousands of copies of newspapers, books, broadsides, and other materials that remain in archives and special collections libraries" today.[22] Peter Fleet, whom Thomas Fleet of Boston enslaved, not only "set type, carved woodcuts," and ran the Fleet press, he also delivered its products, such as *The Boston Evening-Post* (1735–1775).[23] Peter's enslaved sons, Pompey and Caesar, worked alongside him at Fleet's press.[24] Printer Peter Timothy of Charleston, South Carolina, who published *The South-Carolina Gazette* following his father Lewis's death, wrote Benjamin Franklin in 1754 of running the press alone, "excepting a Negro boy, whom I'm training to serve me at the Press."[25] What "serve" meant precisely is not clear; we do not know whether Timothy was training this person to apprentice as a typesetter or to operate the press. By 1815, Philadelphia counted at least one "negro pressman named Andrew Cain," who was then "ninety-four years old."[26] The famous African American ceramic artist and poet David Drake, known as Dave the Potter, also worked as a typesetter on Abner Landrum's newspapers *The South-Carolina Republican* (1824–1827) and *The Edgefield Hive* (1827–1829), while he was enslaved by Landrum in the Edgefield district of South Carolina.[27] In addition to documenting enslaved people as integral to the operation of paper mills in North Carolina, Tennessee, and Kentucky, Beth Barton Schweiger quotes a 1937 interview with Patsy Mitchner that attested to a division of labor in Alex Gorman's printing office, which printed Raleigh's The *The Spirit of the Age* (1849–1865), a temperance paper with the largest circulation of any North Carolina newspaper during its publication: "He had a lot of printers both black and white. The slaves turned the wheels . . . and the white mens done the printing."[28] Schweiger also points out that "slave labor in printing offices was common enough to be mentioned in anti-literacy legislation" in states such as Georgia during the 1830s that "prohibited any person who owned a printing press or type to allow slaves to set type or perform any task that required a knowledge of reading."[29] Notwithstanding this important research, Eric Gardner's observation holds: "The scholarly silence on enslaved people's work for printers and in printing has often been deafening."[30]

Emergent and developing American periodicals were not only dependent on enslaved people's craft and skilled labor—whether in the production of paper, ink, and woodcuts; the setting of type; the operation of the printing press; or the delivery of printed products—they were also financially subsidized by the most profitable form of advertising they carried: slave advertisements. Colonial-era papers devoted roughly one-quarter of their space to advertising that included what Patricia Bradley calls a "slave marketplace," a fact that implicates the development of periodicals with slavery and its growth.[31] Robert Desrochers documents that since knowledge of an impending sale could be spread by enslaved pressmen and typesetters, resulting in escapes, such ads were placed anonymously, thereby positioning printers to "directly broker sales." The result was that printers were "by proxy the most active slave traders . . . [and] the printing office the busiest slave market in town." Slave traders, "more than any other advertisers," used printers to facilitate the exchange of their "goods." Printers were also known to charge fees for holding recaptured runaways for their advertising patrons.[32] Patricia Bradley, David Waldstreicher, and Robert Desrochers offer insight into such advertising in the New England colonies where, although slavery never approached the extent to which it was practiced in Southern colonies, slavery fueled from one-fifth to one-fourth of New England newspaper advertising in the early eighteenth century.[33] By comparison, digitized collections of Maryland and Virginia newspapers document "more than 40,000 advertisements for runaway slaves" alone from 1736 to 1803, a figure that does not include advertisements of slave auctions or enslaved people for sale or hiring out.[34] As Rachel Hall argues, "Southern whites . . . relied heavily on the surveillance function of print culture to control" enslaved people. "The regular publication and posting of runaway and pickup notices called into being a network of interested onlookers beyond the borders of the plantation, linking one plantation to the next, the city to the country, all in the name of protecting the private property of wealthy white Southerners."[35]

From their inception, American periodicals constituted racial difference for their readers through this advertising. White readers were taught that Africans in the colonies were criminal, "untrustworthy, demonic, and violent" as runaways and akin to the animals or goods for sale alongside which they were advertised, and these readers became part of the slavery system, however unconsciously, whether they enslaved Africans or not.[36] Patricia Bradley calls the tone of such advertisements "confident, even confidential . . . , as of one person sharing information with another of similar temperament." The similar assumptions and expectations these ads presumed and addressed turned on the familiar and shared understanding of "blackness" and "whiteness" that periodicals were simultaneously scripting at the microlevel of where the ads were placed—amid advertising for animals and goods and not near advertising for white indentured colonial servants—and at the macrolevel of their "colonywide commonality" as typologizing.[37] Bradley argues that "typographical displays of slave advertisements" were repetitive in their "use of running figures for notices of escaped slaves" and "slave descriptions" that derived "from a narrow band of choices" and used the "all-purpose" term "likely" to describe enslaved people. Such language was never used to describe white indentured servants. Likewise, enslaved people alone were identified "by their talents" in newspaper advertising.[38] The particular was confined in these ads to a generic embodiment: the strength or skill of the person's working body, their physical or temperamental impediments, and the physical marks of slavery's violences on their body. Eighteenth-century America produced "no other compilation of physiological and psychological distortions comparable to these notices," argues Jonathan Prude.[39] Readers sorted enslaved persons from indentured servants through the familiarly repetitive ad content, form, and placement, which scripted a sorting of white from Black unfree labor, loyal servant from criminal runaway, and ultimately whiteness as individualized from blackness as type. As we learn from Mussell's thinking on generic repetition, white readers would have come quickly to make these distinctions half-consciously by discarding from attention the familiar or repeated. In fact, colonial readers could quite literally discard this press genre because "by the mid-1750s, many of the advertisements were published on an extra half-sheet."[40] The typologizing work of these ads—how they constituted blackness and whiteness—became forgotten, so naturalized that it just was.

Yet instead of considering slave advertisements as a print genre that was financially foundational to the periodical as media form in the United States, scholars have analyzed them as documents that augment the historical record of slavery through their accounting of both system and individual. Slave advertisements have been used to document details of plantation life and economy; Black culture, consciousness and communities; material culture and textile history; enslavers' perceptions of enslaved people and their world; and, not least, Black resistance to slavery, including the characteristics of enslaved people who would attempt or effect escape (their literacy levels, their labor skills, their gender), as well as their psychology, motivation, social and familial connection, movement, and destination. Pre-eminent historians of slavery, such as John Hope Franklin, refer to these advertisements as the "most reliable and objective sources" of enslaved people's "discontent" and resistance that we have at our disposal, even though, as he and his co-author Lauren Schweninger take care to acknowledge, they were written by whites.[41] Advertisements for "runaways" are frequently analyzed as a form of biography that offers details of individuals and their self-determined acts that would be otherwise lost to the historical record. Initially, this historical scholarship was built on archival work and produced not only historiography but also the print publication of volumes of transcribed advertisements; it is now based in digital databases.[42] Methods may differ with the advent of digitization, but the explanatory power ascribed to slave advertising has not. Recent distance-reading studies of slave advertising position this press form as documenting "the courageous choices" of enslaved men and women, concluding that "the ultimate value of the runaway ads lies chiefly in what they can tell us about the life stories of individual slaves."[43] In other words, distance reading enabled by the digital turn differs little in its interpretations and conclusions from scholarship based in print sources, dating from at least the 1940s, with their shared and continued investment in the ads' capacity to reveal "an otherwise unobtainable picture of the slave personality."[44] Methods may differ but the explanatory power ascribed to slave advertising has not.

The fundamental paradox of claiming to discern "the slave personality" or "the slave as a person" in these ads—evident in "the slave" as denoting a general case rather than the specificity of a person or personality—or in acknowledging that these advertisements were repeated formulas that nonetheless provide access to "a real person, not an abstraction,"[45] points to the incomplete and necessarily indirect knowledge we have of the psyches and experiences of enslaved individuals and to the importance of acknowledging such documents as "generative resources that enslaved black people adapted to pursue freedom from the very beginning of print-culture traditions in colonial North America."[46] The paradoxes that are foundational to how slavery advertising has been read also point to how much this repetitive and constitutive genre continues to disappear from view as scholars work to study it. Readers and scholars continue to sift content from form, disappearing the slave advertisement's repetitive generic characteristics from its meaning in the process.

Visual Vocabularies: Trade Cuts and the Runaway Icon

Taking seriously the mediating and amnesiac function of slave advertising as a press form would mean keeping in sight the fact that "the circulation of newspapers was itself inseparable from the expansion of internal and imperial trade," that slave "advertisements attempted to use print to bolster confidence in slavery" in "the mid-Atlantic labor system,"[47] and that "slavery and the newspaper grew up together . . . in a close and synergistic relationship."[48] Both image and text became standardized when, as early as the 1760s, slavery broadsides and newspaper advertisements were accompanied by trade woodcuts, wood engravings, and later by metal-cast type. In colonial broadsides that advertised enslaved people for sale, relief woodcuts of partially clothed and muscular male and female Africans and African Americans with feathered skirt, loincloth, spear, or headdress framed text that announced "cargo" or "parcels" of men, women, and children for sale. Marking newly arrived Africans as foreign through excess—depicting them as physically strong and exotic to the point of barbarism—colonial iconography often retained the loincloth, skirt, and spear in runaway ads (figures 5.1 and 5.2). Icons, from which nineteenth-century runaway cuts developed, circulated at the same time: figures with staffs, walking sticks, and cloths around hips, and an icon in which the spear has become the stick on which a bundle of clothing or food is carried, or what Joycelyn Moody calls "the liberty-pole trope" (figure 5.3).[49] These generic illustrations came into increasing use in the early and mid-nineteenth century, circulating in broadsides and newspapers.[50]

The synergistic relationship between the press and the newspaper slave trade was so successful that by the early nineteenth century, "the significance of advertising for the print culture of America" would "be difficult to overestimate," according to Marcus Wood.[51] The racializing typology of cuts and engravings of enslaved people and those who were self-emancipating became central to the "development of a mass advertising industry in America" through the print specimen books that Northern printing firms sent South from the 1830s to Emancipation. Mid-century broadsides depict what Wood has documented as the most common male and female icons (figures 5.4 and 5.5).[52] Just as one enslaved person is rendered the same as any other in the generic text of slave ads—strong laboring and abused body, criminal and deceitful—these ads are generic in their visual iconography, where even "the act of running away always takes the same literal form."[53] Since runaway cuts and types headed advertisements of enslaved

Intermedial Fugitivity and the "New Negro" Woman   163

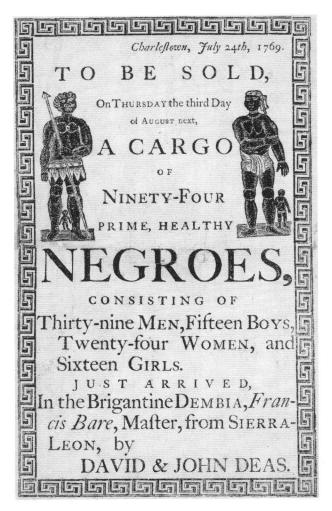

Figure 5.1. Slave auction notice, Charleston, South Carolina, 1769. Courtesy American Antiquarian Society, 01609-1.

people for sale, presumed criminality was also central to their larger typology. As text and image reaffirmed the claims each made about what constituted "blackness," they tempered the threat of an autonomously thinking and acting enslaved person. Depicting walking sticks rather than spears was part of a pacifying semiotics in which the runaway's crime became the theft of self, clothing, and food

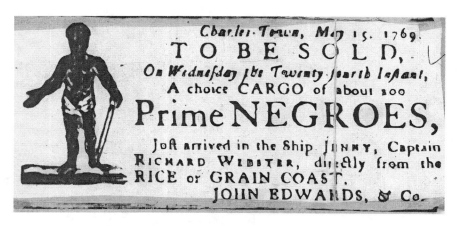

Figures 5.2 and 5.3. Slave auction advertisements, *South Carolina and American General Gazette* (Charleston), January 12, 1769. Courtesy Accessible Archives.

rather than a direct threat of violence as a challenge to power. The icon, reassuring in its presentation of a figure frozen and starkly visible in black ink on white background, came to represent even a potentially threatening criminality as unvaried and completely knowable and to enlist the reader in securing this human trade. The power of these associations for white readers—"the slave" was known, criminal though pacific—is starkly different from a reading of the iconography of such advertising as registering the liberty-pole trope that encodes self-emancipation and self-authoring.[54]

Figure 5.4. Advertisement for a runaway, Bardstown, Kentucky, 1838. Printed Ephemera: Three Centuries of Broadsides and Other Printed Ephemera, Library of Congress, https://www.loc.gov/item/2021767324/.

Photography and "Fugitive Vision"

The power of slavery advertising as a technology of racialization undoubtedly underwrote, along with racist caricature in American print culture broadly, what Sarah Blackwood identifies as a debate in the periodical press "over photographic and pictorial representation . . . at mid-century."[55] With headers such as "Ambrotypes.—This beautiful discovery is a new era in the art of taking a 'counterfeit presentment,'"[56] Black-edited newspapers such as the *New Orleans Daily Creole* (1856–1857) ran articles on photographic technologies that highlighted both fascination with them and an ambivalent investment in their evidentiary capacities. Invented in 1836 and broadly commercialized through the production of cartes de visite and cabinet cards by the 1860s, daguerreotypy and the ability to make multiple copies of an exposure it enabled was received as revolutionary.[57]

166 Great Thinkers and Doers

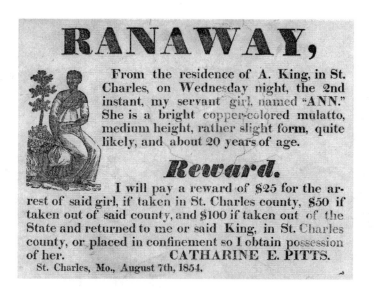

Figure 5.5. Broadside advertisement regarding an escaped slave, August 7, 1854. Catharine E. Pitts, D02488, Mullanphy Family Papers, 1780–1951. Courtesy of the Missouri Historical Society, http://collections.mohistory.org/resource/164245.

First introduced by the French photographer A. A. Disdéri in 1854, cartes de visite appeared in the United States in the summer of 1859 and in one year became a "major fashion." Measuring 2 1/8 by 3 1/2 inches and mounted inexpensively, the carte de visite quickly became collectible; people purchased cartes de visites of celebrities, notable Americans (statesmen and military leaders), and so-called oddities (Siamese twins, thin men, dwarfs) as "cartomania" spread. Prices ranged from $1.50 to $3.00 per dozen; the average price was under twenty cents per card.[58] Because of its popularity and accessibility, the carte de visite was hailed as the democratization of photography through an inexpensive form of studio portraiture. Cabinet cards, which followed in 1866, were prized for their "greater facial detail" made possible by their larger size at 4 1/2 by 6 1/2 inches, or roughly double that of cartes de visite.[59] As Marcy Dinius documents, daguerreotype studios were augmented by itinerant daguerreotypists who "traveled with their equipment from town to town," indicating both a high demand for and the affordability of daguerreotype portraits.[60]

Photographic technologies such as daguerreotypy were used to produce many of the author portraits of slave narratives, and the author-activists Frederick Douglass and Sojourner Truth are famous for their use of that technology.[61] Douglass sat for at least 168 separate portraits from 1841, when he was in his twenties and still a "fugitive," through to the end of his life in 1895.[62] Truth copyrighted her portraits in 1864 but asserted her authorship of them well before then, selling them along with her 1878 *Narrative of Sojourner Truth; a bondswoman of olden time, emancipated by the New York Legislature in the early part of the present century; with a history of her labors and correspondence drawn from her "Book of life"* at her lectures and promoting them in the press through letters to the editor from 1863 to her death in 1883. She sat for at least twenty-eight different portraits.[63] In their photographic praxis, both Douglass and Truth foregrounded the centrality of ontological concerns to photographic technology and the capacity of that technology to document or represent Black life. Truth reportedly said she "used to be sold for other people's benefit, but now she sold herself for her own."[64] She asserted her ownership and authorship of her images by including the phrase "I sell the shadow to support the substance" on her cartes de visite and cabinet cards. Her portraits include a number in which she is posed in studio settings that read as domestic, often ornately so, with vases of flowers, books, knitting, columns, carved chairs, and mantles as props.[65] In one, she holds what is said to be a daguerreotype of her grandson, James Caldwell, in her lap, marking their affective relation. In these ways, Truth used studio props to animate the visual codes of socially recognizable womanhood through which she asserted self-possession and authority. Similarly, Douglass's portraits repeat what Ginger Hill argues is "rapt attention" to "stylish, somber" and "well-pressed" clothing that imaged "order, esteem and propriety." Both Douglass and Truth negotiated the display of "citizen-subject status"[66] via the logic of possessive individualism, which for African Americans animated a tension between self-representation and commodification, given the racializing work of the visual codes that had for a century scripted "blackness" as a commodity to be bought, sold, or recaptured for reward.

In 1864, when Truth commanded an audience with President Lincoln, Douglass was lecturing on photography's potential. From 1861 to 1865, he gave at least four lectures that cast photography as a social leveler, claiming that "what was once the exclusive luxury of the rich and great is now within reach of all."[67] He referred to photography as a uniquely human practice ("man is everywhere a picture making animal") and a stimulant to social and political progress through its ability to both enable critical self-reflection and highlight the gap between the real and the ideal. Douglass rhetorically linked photography as an achievement of technological progress with the Civil War as also promising progress that "cannot but dispel prejudice, dissolve the granite barriers of arbitrary power, bring the world into peace and unity, and at last crown the world with just [sic], Liberty, and brotherly kindness."[68] As a newspaper editor, he ran "news about daguerreotypy," reprinted articles on African American daguerreotypists Augustus Washington of Hartford and J. P. Ball of Cincinnati,[69] and featured advertisements for "local Rochester daguerreotypists" in *Frederick Douglass' Paper* (1851–1858)[70] He also wrote about the economics of American periodicals in a *North Star* (1847–1851) editorial. In the February 22, 1850, issue, Douglass copied the text of fugitive slave ads from the *St. Louis Republican* and noted that as a newspaper editor he had not purchased a fugitive slave icon cast type: "To each of the advertisements . . . is prefixed the figure of a human being, as if in the act of running. We have no such figures nor prints in our office, to enable us to follow copy; but the reader must supply them for himself."[71] Truth and Douglass were attuned for decades to a wider visual culture that any African American liberatory or self-referential use of photography necessarily intervened in. As Douglass put it, "This picture making faculty is flung out into the world—like all others—subject to a wild scramble between contending interests and forces."[72]

When formerly enslaved African American authors utilized print technologies to include an author frontispiece with their codex publications, they worked in a highly complex visual culture fraught with contradictory logics that both typified and individualized in the course of simultaneously serving ensnaring, commodifying, and liberatory aims. The print illustration techniques and image technologies that made the mass reproduction of such frontispieces possible had been used in, or derived from, a century of slavery advertising that racialized African Americans in its work to "promote and protect human bondage" by quite literally typing them visually even while describing their unique identifying features textually.[73] As Joycelyn Moody documents, "frontispiece portraits were a commonplace in books written in English by 1773—when [Phillis] Wheatley's *Poems on Various Subjects* was first published in London" and when colonial-era broadsides and newspaper advertisements were achieving their racializing work. Through the slave narrative's imbrication in visual culture, as Marcus Wood documents, "the personal portrait became irrevocably connected with authorship and ownership."[74] Both the slave narrative genre and the frontispiece portraits of the African Americans who produced them were framed by self-commodifying visual logics and as acts of self-representation by self-possessed liberal subjects according to the visual and political terms available at the time. The old underwrote the new in both the politics and illustration of slave narratives, in other words. Michael Chaney argues that such frontispieces corroborated their subjects' "transformation from slavery to freedom" with the "bourgeois hieroglyphics of commodity objects . . . suits, books, drawing room backdrops," a hieroglyphics that Ginger Hill suggests both conveys the precarity of the formerly enslaved individual's claim to self-possession and critiques that logic of selfhood as a "system of accumulation."[75] Together, "repletion and accumulation expose the limits of a freedom conceived as possession."[76] As acts of African American self-representation, frontispieces necessarily rework and critique rather than move beyond extant visual logics.

The print illustration of slave narratives intermediated photographic and prephotographic image technologies rather than leaving the old behind for the new. Some narratives were illustrated with stock woodcuts that were used in a range of abolitionist publications and scripted understandings of slavery, abolition, and the figure of "the slave" through repeated scenes.[77] With the advent of daguerreotypy, older plate illustration techniques such as stipple engraving and mezzotint were revived to mass reproduce author portrait frontispieces in print texts. The tonal range of photography as a new technology was reproduced by the older technology of stippling that an engraver would incise in the surface of a metal plate, a process in which the "size and darkness of each printed dot" was determined by the force applied to the stipple tool.[78] As Helena Wright documents, mass reproduction of photographic images was initially limited to relief printing from type, engravings, and cuts; to intaglio printing from etched surfaces such as mezzotint, steel and copper engraving, and aquatint; and to planographic printing from flat surfaces, such as lithographs. These were all secondary processes of photographic reproduction or printing that the primary photochemical processes of direct-positive (daguerreotype and ambrotype, which permitted the production of a single image) and negative-positive (wet-plate negatives in the 1850s and dry-plate negatives in the 1880s) followed. By the 1870s and 1880s, collotype provided the best tonal reproduction of a photograph before the development of relief half-tone printing and its use in periodicals and newspapers. Helena Wright details the development of photographic reproduction as anti-teleological: older methods and processes not only persisted but were returned to for their superiority: "Among the earlier processes, collotype and photogravure remained in use through the twentieth century. . . . Their superb reproductive qualities inspired the refinement and ultimate success of the cross-line screen for three- and four-color halftone relief (sometimes called 'process' printing), for rotary photogravure (called rotogravure), and for offset lithography, now the dominant process."[79] In other words, these older print illustration techniques were the necessary partners to the new technology of photography in mass print reproduction.

Even though photography necessarily partnered with older print illustration techniques, accounts of the history of photography in America frequently cast it as transformative, particularly socially transformative as a "social leveler."[80] The press at the time praised its capacities while investing it with national values of "progress, industry, and democracy."[81] Yet photography also inaugurated what Allan Sekula has termed a "shadow archive" that constructed and simultaneously documented so-called racial, class, and ethnic difference in "a social and moral hierarchy" of "public looks: a look up, at one's 'betters,' and a look down at one's 'inferiors.'" As Sekula notes, "especially in the United States, the proliferation of photography and that of phrenology were quite coincident."[82] Bodies were typed through the use of photographic portraiture in ethnographic and anthropometric photography, including the rogues' gallery of criminology. Individuals were also socially disciplined through a medium that offered images of "the 'representative man and woman' through public exhibitions, mass publications, or copies displayed" in the home that were thought to inspire and teach individuals "how to present themselves as good Americans."[83]

Consequently, when African Americans both debated and used photography's complex affordances for Black representational politics as they negotiated "the Negro question" in the early twentieth century, they did so with a technology that was also used to document "the Negro problem."[84] W. E. B. Du Bois's gold medal–winning photographic gallery of African Americans for the Paris Exposition of 1900, the *Exhibit of American Negros*, is a significant touchstone in this history.[85] Composed of three albums totaling 363 images, the exhibit included photographs of "the black poor" and factory workers but was hailed by the Black press for its bourgeois portraits of "representative Negroes" that offered the world evidence of Black modernity and progress.[86] "That the Afro-American is rising cannot be doubted by the most Negro hating pessimist," claimed the *Colored American* in the nation's capital.[87] Du Bois pointedly described the exhibit as "several volumes of photographs of typical Negro faces, which hardly square with conventional American ideals."[88] Du Bois's "representative Negro" was both typical and exceptional and his exhibit turned on, yet also challenged, that familiar distinction between type and exception that has governed racialization in the American visual field since at least the advent of the periodical and slave advertisements in it. Du Bois's portraits, most of which were exhibited mounted in a cameo oval matting, offer both frontal and profile views of subjects in an unmistakable invocation of the "shadow archive" of American ethnography resituated in middle-class portraiture conventions (figures 5.6 and 5.7). In fact, many of these studio portraits were

Figure 5.6. African American Woman, Head-and-Shoulders Portrait, Facing Front, Wearing Coat, Georgia, 1899. Collected by W. E. B. Du Bois, in album Types of American Negroes, vol. 2. African American Photographs Assembled for 1900 Paris Exposition, Library of Congress, https://www.loc.gov/item/99472195/.

the work of African American photographer Thomas E. Askew of Atlanta, although they were not attributed to him.[89] Shawn Michelle Smith argues that Du Bois created a "counter-archive" that engaged the color line "as a nexus of competing gazes in which racialization is understood as the effect of both intense scrutiny and obfuscation."[90]

Visualizing the New Negro Woman: Portraits of "The Race"

Reaching an international stage with Du Bois's *Exhibit of American Negros*, race work with photographic portraiture was also central to African American illustrated magazines at the turn of the twentieth century, including the NAACP's

172 Great Thinkers and Doers

Figure 5.7. African American Woman, Half-Length Portrait, Facing Slightly Right, Georgia, 1899. Collected by W. E. B. Du Bois, in album Types of American Negroes, vol. 3. African American Photographs Assembled for 1900 Paris Exposition, Library of Congress, https://www.loc.gov/item/99472197/.

The Crisis, the *Voice of the Negro* (Atlanta, GA; Chicago, IL; 1904–1907), and *The Colored American Magazine*. With "halftone technology drastically reduc[ing] the cost of illustrations in the 1890s" and its technique of setting photograph and print text on the same page firmly established by 1900, illustrated magazines became more affordable to produce and purchase. This enabled Black periodicals to create what P. Gabrielle Foreman calls an "immediate legibility" for their readership at a time when 45 percent of African Americans were not alphabetically literate.[91] All of these monthlies offered readers highly stylized covers and photographs, which were understood as the mark of their modernity, and a mix of incisive political critique, reviews of art and culture, original literary offerings, and essays. Although their politics ranged not only from magazine to magazine but in the life of each publication, illustrated Black monthlies were important venues for African American women. Josephine St. Pierre Ruffin's *Woman's Era*, the first monthly published by and for African American women, made use of what P. Gabrielle Foreman has called "photographic bylines," portraits that accompanied articles or reports from leading race women and female journalists or appeared on the cover.[92] A host of feminist activists, several of whom were also journalists, including Mary Church Terrell, Fannie Barrier Williams, Nannie Helen Burroughs, Addie Hunton, Margaret Murray Washington, Josephine Bruce, Alice Dunbar Nelson, Mary Talbert, Coralie Franklin Cook, Carrie Clifford, Maria Baldwin and Anna Holland Jones, appeared in the pages of *Voice of the Negro* and *The Crisis* in their "Our Woman's Number" and "Votes for Women" special issues of 1905 and 1915, respectively.[93]

One of the earliest in a growing field of illustrated magazines, *The Colored American Magazine* offered its readers lush, tinted covers and a generous array of photographic illustrations. During her tenure as editor at *The Colored American Magazine* from 1900 to 1904, Pauline Hopkins interwove photographs with race biography in what might be likened to a Du Boisian "Negro Exhibit" or New Negro archive of her own making. Born in Portland, Maine, Hopkins performed with her family's Hopkins Colored Troubadours in the 1880s, was a recognized orator in the 1890s, and was active in the Black women's club movement.[94] In 1899, at the age of forty, Hopkins cofounded *The Colored American Magazine* with four young men in their twenties who had migrated from Virginia to Boston: Walter Wallace, Harper Fortune, Walter Johnson, and Jessie W. Watkins.[95] Hopkins became a well-regarded writer through her short fiction, her novel *Contending Forces* (1900), and her serialized novels *Hagar's Daughter* (1902), *Winona, a Tale of Negro Life in the South and Southwest* (1902), and *Of One Blood, or the Hidden Self* (1903), which appeared in and coincided with her editorship of *The Colored American Magazine*. The magazine also published her fiction and articles under the pseudonyms Sarah A. Allen and J. Shirley Shadrach.[96]

While Hopkins was editor at the magazine from 1900 to 1904, she made print space for Black feminist recirculation, such as Albreta Smith's coverage of Anna Julia Cooper's address "Organized Charity," for Chicago's Phyllis Wheatley Club and Hopkins's own coverage of the National Federation of Women's Clubs' refusal to permit fellow editor Josephine St. Pierre Ruffin to address their meeting in

Milwaukee as a delegate of the Massachusetts Federation of Women's Clubs and a representative of the New England Women's Press Association in June 1900.[97] In the spring of 1904, ownership of the magazine shifted to Fred Moore, who had co-purchased it with Booker T. Washington. This brought the *The Colored American Magazine* under Washington's control, and he moved it from Boston to New York. Hopkins left the magazine at that point, and many scholars speculate she was pushed out by Washington.[98] As Eurie Dahn and Brian Sweeney, directors of the Digital Colored American Magazine project put it, "It is as though the *Colored American* became a different magazine after Hopkins left," becoming "more politically middle-of-the-road and, as a consequence, less focused on women's issues and less concerned with literature as a vehicle for political engagement."[99] After leaving the magazine, Hopkins was immediately hired by *Voice of the Negro*, which she wrote for in 1904 and 1905, and in 1916 she founded the *New Era Magazine* (Boston, MA; 1916) with Walter Wallace, a publication that ran for two issues.

The Colored American Magazine was enabled by African American migration and emerged with "the New Negro," whose self-representation and subjectivity the magazine articulated and shaped with the photographic portraits, race biographies, advertising, and regular departments it offered. As Hazel Carby puts it, the magazine was "an attempt to define as well as create the boundaries of a black magazine-reading public."[100] More recently, Sigrid Anderson Cordell has argued that its identity as a "race magazine" was mediated with its "pragmatic editorial policy of appealing to white middle-class audiences for economic, social, and political support."[101] Yet that pragmatism did not temper its "pan-Africanist agenda" or its insistence on justice at a time when African Americans were the targets of racialized violence through lynching and urban race riots.[102] "What we desire, what we require, what we demand to aid in the onward march of progress and advancement is justice," read its publisher's announcement in May 1900. "Not a justice tempered with policy, or trammeled with prejudice, neither a justice semi-hoodwinked, that discriminates invidiously or with unequal balances . . . but justice, simple, pure, unbiased, unabridged, unadulterated, and undefiled."[103]

The Colored American Magazine was published by the Colored Co-operative Publishing Company, which Wallace, Fortune, Johnson and Watkins also established, and its first issue was available in May 1900. It had a national base of agents, an initial "twenty-four agents for twenty cities in sixteen states" and "eight branch offices" in seven states, two of which were in the South. Just a year later, the magazine had nearly four times as many agents, "eighty-three agents in thirty-three states," and claimed 100,000 readers in its May 1901 issue.[104] As Alisha Knight documents, its agent roster eventually grew to ninety-five.[105] The magazine soon developed an international reach; by 1902, its second year of publication, it had an agent in Liberia, and by 1903 it had "correspondents and patrons in 'China, Hawaii, Manila, West Indies and Africa.'" In 1904 it achieved a circulation high of 17,840.[106] Readers could buy an issue for fifteen cents or subscribe for a year for $1.50. The magazine was made viable by its advertising; it carried "six half-page advertisements" at the back of its second issue and had secured regular advertisers by the end of its first year.[107] Additional capital came from the memberships sold to readers who were able and willing to invest over $5.00 in the Colored Co-operative Publishing Company, which entitled them to "full membership" and dividends "payable quarterly."[108] Readers were invited to collaborate in the magazine through the Here and There department, which offered "short articles or locals" on the "social movements among the colored race. . . . *All are invited to contribute items* of general news and interest."[109] The magazine's cover photographs were frequently cued to sections of this department; Deborah March speculates that readers may have submitted photographic portraits along with their contributions.[110]

The stylized art nouveau covers of *The Colored American Magazine* from May 1901 to February 1904 were the work of J. Alexandre Skeete. Skeete had emigrated from British Guiana in 1888 and was illustrating the *Boston Herald* (1846–1917), one of the nation's oldest dailies, before he joined the magazine's staff in December 1900, when the cover design was first altered (figures 5.8 and 5.9). By the May 1901 issue, Skeete was head of artistic staff and had altered the magazine's cover design again by changing the framing floral motif from lotuses to lilies, adding cameos of Frederick Douglass and Phillis Wheatley, making the design clean and less cluttered with a bold and more prominent masthead, and moving the Colored Co-operative Publishing Company credit to bottom center (figure 5.10).[111]

The tenures of Skeete and Hopkins at the magazine roughly coincided with one another, suggesting that Hopkins's influence and political vision are evident in the Wheatley and Douglass cameos, which together with the magazine's sustained feature of women on its cover from September 1900 to February 1904 proclaimed the race's "fitness" for inclusion in the nation.[112] Across forty issues, with a handful of exceptions, *The Colored American Magazine* gave readers a series of "race women" portraits as their introduction to "a monthly magazine of merit . . . [for] every Negro family" that offered "contributions . . . from the most learned writers,

Figure 5.8. Existing cover design before J. Alexandre Skeete joined the staff of the *Colored American Magazine*, June 1900, vol. 1, no. 2. Reproduced from *The Digital Colored American Magazine*, coloredamerican.org. Original held at the James Weldon Johnson Memorial Collection in the Yale Collection of American Literature, Beinecke Rare Book and Manuscript Library.

Figure 5.9. New cover design by J. Alexandre Skeete of the *Colored American Magazine*, January 1901, vol. 2, no. 3, with lily floral motif and more prominent masthead and Colored Co-operative Publishing Company credit. Reproduced from *The Digital Colored American Magazine*, coloredamerican.org. Original held at the James Weldon Johnson Memorial Collection in the Yale Collection of American Literature, Beinecke Rare Book and Manuscript Library.

Figure 5.10. New cover design by J. Alexandre Skeete of the *Colored American Magazine*, May 1901, vol. 3, no. 1, with lotus motif and cameos of Frederick Douglass and Phillis Wheatley. Reproduced from *The Digital Colored American Magazine*, coloredamerican.org. Original held at the James Weldon Johnson Memorial Collection in the Yale Collection of American Literature, Beinecke Rare Book and Manuscript Library.

novelists and scientists" and documented "all phases . . . of the Negro . . . [in] cuts and photographs."[113] Both these cameos and the use of Black women's portraits pointedly countered New Negro politics and investments. Although who the New Negro would be was hotly debated from 1895 into the mid-1920s, the figure was consistently imagined as male and defined in ways that sought to manage external and self-perceptions of "the Negro" that accompanied the demographic shifts of the first Great Migration.[114] The New Negro was understood to have left behind "the Old Negro's" southern slave past, his enforced servility to whites, and his agrarian labor in order to take on a self-determining future in an industrialized North, where his intelligence, accomplishments, and skills, particularly in the arts, would prove the advancement of the race. Unlike her male contemporaries, Hopkins made an enslaved past central to her notion of the New Negro through her journalism and serialized fiction at the magazine and in her intermediation of photography and illustration with race biography, including the series "Famous Men of the Negro Race" (November 1900–October 1901) and "Famous Women of the Negro Race" (November 1901–October 1902). She intervened in serial repetition in US periodicals as both racializing and potentially liberating by instantiating a Black chronopolitics that ruptured a teleological progression from past to present to future.

Although New Negro politics was deliberately amnesiac about an enslaved past, Hopkins kept it firmly in view—visually, with the cameos of Wheatley and Douglass on every cover and, textually, in the magazine's race biography series that centered first the radical overthrow of slavery in the New World by Toussaint L'Ouverture and the Haitian Revolution and then turned to assaults on the slavery system in the United States with biographies of Wheatley, Douglass, Sojourner Truth, William Wells Brown, Harriet Tubman, Frances Harper, Charles Lenox Remond, and Mary Ann Shadd Cary. The magazine included either portrait engravings or portrait photographs of nearly all of these figures, but it also resisted a rhetoric of exceptionalism and extended Black resistance and activism to a New Negro present by integrating these biographies with composite portraits of contemporary African Americans and their achievements. *The Colored American Magazine* recast the fight to end slavery as not past but necessarily active in the New Negro's future-oriented representation of the race. Such a position is consistent with Hopkins's neo-abolitionist orations delivered at centenary celebrations of William Lloyd Garrison (in 1905) and Charles Sumner (in 1911) in Boston. In these speeches, she linked abolition to the political struggles of the New Negro, indicting the nation for its "broken promises of freedom" and a political "conservatism . . . that has ushered in the twentieth century."[115] The repetition of the logics of slavery in the new century was too clear to ignore, she maintained, for "the influence of an unconquered South, and the acquiescence of an ease-loving North that winks at abuses where commercial relations and manufactures flourish and put money in the purse, have neutralized the effects of the stern policy of these giants of an earlier age. Great indeed was the battle for the abolition of slavery, but far greater will be the battle for manhood rights."[116] Hopkins insisted that national progress could be achieved only through reviving abolition as a political force, and *The Colored American Magazine*'s covers during her tenure at the magazine made the bold claim that "black daughters of the Revolution" were central to the nation's past struggle, present claims, and future possibilities.[117]

While these covers are evidence that the New Negro had already arrived in the form of the New Negro woman, who, Hopkins argued, "holds a unique position in the economy of the world's advancement in 1902," there was deliberately something of the Old Negro in them, further marking her intervention in New Negro debates.[118] The rhetoric the covers articulated turned on social position and accumulation and made a claim in that register: the women's clothing marked their class status and signaled self-possession through commodity possession, much as the frontispiece portraits of formerly enslaved authors have been critically read to do. Instead of imitating and thereby ironizing the frontal and profile views of evidentiary photography, as did many portraits in Du Bois's *Exhibit of American Negros* for the Paris Exposition, the portraits in *The Colored American Magazine* all use a classed and raced asymmetry that was defined by the exclusion of their African American subjects. These portraits were presented in a highly stylized frame, whereas Hopkins and Skeete reserved the clean oval for the cameo etchings of Wheatley and Douglass, positioning two of the most famous (formerly enslaved) men and women of Black print culture as frames for the New Negro woman.

The Colored American Magazine's New Negro women do not gaze at the camera head on but instead follow the conventions of bourgeois portraiture (figures 5.9–5.12). Front-facing poses were read as signifying "the bluntness and 'naturalness' of a culturally unsophisticated class," as John Tagg puts it, in contrast to the "cultivated asymmetries of aristocratic posture. . . . passed on down the social hierarchy, as the middle classes secured their cultural hegemony."[119] Yet the new in these African American uses of bourgeois portraiture has a touch of the old if we accept Suren Lalvani's contention that early photographic portraiture was not simply coincident with physiognomy and phrenology but united with these sci-

Figure 5.11. Cover of the *Colored American Magazine*, September 1902, vol. 5, no. 5, with portrait subject glancing down not at the camera. Reproduced from *The Digital Colored American Magazine*, coloredamerican.org. Original held at the James Weldon Johnson Memorial Collection in the Yale Collection of American Literature, Beinecke Rare Book and Manuscript Library.

Figure 5.12. Cover of the *Colored American Magazine*, March 1903, vol. 6, no. 5, with asymmetric posing of subject. Reproduced from *The Digital Colored American Magazine*, coloredamerican.org. Original held at the James Weldon Johnson Memorial Collection in the Yale Collection of American Literature, Beinecke Rare Book and Manuscript Library.

ences in a common paradigm that took "the arrangements of heads, shoulders, and hands—'as if those parts of our body were our truth.'"[120] Taking the body as the sign of *who one is* was central to both evidentiary and bourgeois portrait photography, which relied on physiognomy's claim that the body was the sign of essence, either of inner character and moral depth or of deviance. Lalvani contends that photographers "operat[ed] within discourses of physiognomy, which gave them a set of typologies by which to orchestrate and adjust posture, expression and lighting."[121] Bourgeois portraiture sought to claim interiority for the middle classes in opposition to its photographically documented lack in the "racial other" and the "lower classes" of evidentiary photography, doing so through codes established originally for the surveillance of these "lower" types, as Sekula has noted. In other words, these uses of photography were co-constitutive.

Shawn Michelle Smith cautions that "visual archives" should be read "against one another to find photographic meaning in the interstices between them, in the challenges they pose to one another, and in the competing claims they make on cultural import."[122] Hopkins's and Skeete's covers enabled and could be said to perform a double rendition by presenting ethnography's Old Negro evidentiary portraits in the magazine's bourgeois portraits of middle-class New Negroes. What neither bourgeois nor evidentiary photography accounted for were the competing claims African Americans could make for how their photographic portraits of "the race" or of "representative Negroes" would be read. Hopkins can be understood to be reactivating Douglass's 1849 affirmation that African Americans were both their own best viewers and the only possible architects of their adequate representation: "Negroes can never have impartial portraits at the hands of white artists. It seems to us next to impossible . . . without most grossly exaggerating their distinctive features. And the reason is obvious. Artists, like all other white persons, have developed a theory dissecting the distinctive features of Negro physiognomy."[123]

These covers can be read as what Leigh Raiford calls photographic sites of Black freedom struggle "through and for the black body, the black eye, and black memory."[124] *The Colored American Magazine*'s covers claimed New Negro progress and modernity paradoxically by mobilizing a future-oriented race politics through the Old Negro with their repeated invocation of the body as evidence of who one is. The covers are also acts of "fugitive vision," working in rather than beyond commodity logics by partaking of mediums—photography and the periodical—that are "so closely aligned to the circulation and distribution of commodities" that they have the "potential to reify the black body (in pain or triumph) as commodity."[125] Quite literally, it was hoped that both black and white Americans would buy the narrative of race advancement cultivated in the New Negro woman, that they would purchase the magazine.[126] Hopkins did not use periodical illustration and bourgeois portraiture despite their fraught history or because she had little choice given the rise of the illustrated magazine. She used these modes of visuality because that history, in which "blackness," unfreedom, and commodity distribution were inter-implicated, needed to be understood as still active in the present, rather than disappearing from view and memory. Hopkins demanded that a politics to redress such conditions, to redress racial capitalism and accumulation, be revived and reimagined. She did so by repeatedly asserting reminding readers of slavery, abolition, and the continued unfreedom of African Americans in a new century and by using the logics of type and exception active in both the slave ad and the photographic archive. In their serial repetition, *The Colored American Magazine* portrait covers recast the disappearing slave or Old Negro in the New Negro woman through an intermedial fugitivity that insisted the historical past was very much alive in both the present and in the futures her readers could imagine.

By taking seriously both the work of generic forms and structures in the periodical as having an amnesiac mediating function achieved through repetition and African American women's work with periodical illustration, I seek to foreground the political potential and stakes of visuality and memory both for a Black feminist liberatory politics in the periodical and for a productive querying of methodological turns in periodical study. Following the genre—including its racializing work—and how Black feminists used or bent it to their purposes is essential for understanding how newspapers and magazines co-constituted, while disseminating, Black women's politics. Following the genre is also central to unpacking how periodicals mediate understandings of the new through familiar forms and structures. This methodology emerges from established practices of reading periodicals not from the digital turn, although that turn has much to offer us and is unquestionably part of an ongoing theorization of how periodicals work. Integrated, multiple, and intermedial approaches to periodicals, or what Ann Ardis has called media ecology, entail "scrupulous attention to both the materiality of print and its intermedial relationships with other communication technologies— even when, especially when, we allow historical data to 'disrupt and reconfigure' longstanding historical generalizations and conceptual or theoretical or genre paradigms."[127] The particularity of Black periodicals, in their situatedness and the distinctive work they undertake as a result, calls for a media ecology approach that reads through broader paradigms or methods while also asking how and why they are challenged, disrupted, or reworked. But they also call us back to the fundamental entanglement of slavery and periodicals in the United States, to the double rendition of economies of representation and trafficking that made newspapers and illustrated magazines viable. Manifesting and grappling with the disruptions such a history poses to an amnesiac and teleological fantasy invested in the new supplanting the old was at the center of Pauline Hopkins's work to imagine and depict a New Negro present and future in *The Colored American Magazine*.

Coda

The New Underground Railway

In October 1952, Charlotta Spears Bass addressed an American Labor Party rally at Madison Square Garden with calls to action that continue to resonate today. "We want a government that acts for people, not for profits. We want the wealth of our land used for life—not death. We want a government that will enforce the constitutional rights of people, not destroy them."[1] Nominated by Paul Robeson and W. E. B. Du Bois on the Progressive Party ticket, she was the first Black woman to run for the vice presidency of the United States.[2] It would take another sixty-nine years for a Black woman to be elected to that office. Bass had run for Congress in 1944, for Los Angeles City Council in 1945, and again for Congress in 1950, the same year that Du Bois ran for the New York Senate on the Labor Party ticket; both ran on peace and colonial independence platforms.

Bass's activism and her work as a newspaperwoman constitute significant contributions to Los Angeles and California politics. But they were also the reason federal authorities targeted her for surveillance. From 1912 to 1951, Bass edited the *California Eagle* (Los Angeles, CA; 1879–1966), a five-cent Friday weekly that was the largest Black weekly on the West Coast. In the mid-1920s, the *Eagle* employed twelve staff, ran at twenty pages, and had a circulation of 60,000, or nearly four times the Black population of Los Angeles, the city where it was published.[3] By the 1940s, the FBI and the House Un-American Activities Committee had accused her of being a Communist, the Office of the Secretary of War had identified the *Eagle* as a threat to national security, the US Department of Justice had claimed that the paper was funded by Japan and Germany, and the US Post Office had recommended that the Department of Justice revoke Bass's mailing permit, which enabled her to do mass mailings at a lower cost than first-class mail.[4] In the midst of these accusations, the *Eagle*'s circulation dipped to 17,600, equivalent to a quarter the size of the Black population of Los Angeles.[5] Bass refused to bend to government pressure, declaring, "When a person, an organization, even a newspaper gets the courage and fortitude that it is going to require to put this old world in such condition that it will be a fit and happy abode for all the people, they must first be prepared to have their heads cracked, their hopes frustrated, and their financial strength weakened."[6]

Bass's fortitude is clear throughout her journey to become editor of the *Eagle* and raise it to the stature it had in the 1920s. She had worked her way up from the $5.00 per week she earned selling subscriptions to the paper to being asked by its editor and owner, John Neimore, on his deathbed to assume the role of editor in 1912. Two months later, Bass bought the debt-saddled paper at auction for $50.00.[7] At the time, the *Eagle* "had financial assets amounting to $10.00 in cash and not more than $150.00 in overdue bills," Bass recalls.[8] Within a year she had hired Joseph Bass, who had recently migrated to Los Angeles. He had been an editor and longtime reporter for papers such as the *Topeka Call* (Topeka, KS; 1893–1898), the *Topeka Plaindealer*, and the *Montana Plain Dealer* (1906–1911) of Helena, Montana. Together they edited and managed the *Eagle* while also taking on print jobs from Black churches and fraternal orders.[9] In her memoir, Bass referred to the *Eagle* under Neimore's editorship "as a new Underground Railway, an agency to attract Negroes to California, where they would enjoy a greater portion of freedom and human rights than in their former slave environs."[10] Bass had migrated to Los Angeles in 1910. Born in South Carolina,[11] she had moved first to Rhode Island, where, at the age of twenty, she worked as an office clerk and solicitor of advertisements for the *Providence Watchman*, and at thirty years old she moved west to Los Angeles for health reasons.[12]

Active in the Double V campaign following World War II, Charlotta Bass was a Garveyite, a pan-Africanist, and a leader in the NAACP. In the 1920s, she served as lady president of the UNIA's Los Angeles division, the largest in the West.[13] In 1919, she attended Pan-African conference and promoted both the UNIA and the NAACP in the *Eagle*'s pages.[14] This was, to put it mildly, an unusual political combination, but Bass was far from the expected. During her tenure as *California Eagle* editor, she withstood "physical and verbal abuse, libel suits, unlawful arrests, and death threats,"[15] some of these from the Ku Klux Klan, as she battled against the racism facing African Americans who, like herself, had migrated to California and Los Angeles and formed coalitions with Latinx Angelenos and agricultural laborers in the state.

African Americans were drawn to the garden city in the early twentieth century as an alternative to industrial cities in the North and Midwest. Black-owned newspapers such as Jefferson Edmonds's *Liberator* (Los Angeles, CA; 1900–1941), the *Colored American* (Washington, DC; 1893–1904), and the *New Age* (Butte, MT; 1902–1903) promoted Southern California as a migration destination to readers. In the midst of a population boom and after his first visit in 1913 on a membership drive for the NAACP, W. E. B. Du Bois said of Los Angeles in *The Crisis*: "Nowhere in the United States is the Negro so well and beautifully housed, nor the average efficiency and intelligence in the colored population so high. Here is an aggressive, hopeful group—with some wealth, large industrial opportunity and a buoyant spirit."[16] At the time of Du Bois's visit, Los Angeles was "replac[ing] San Francisco and Oakland as the center of African American life in California."[17] Hopeful though they may have been, Black migrants such as Bass knew that Du Bois's "matchless Southern California" oversold the reality and that African Americans faced unemployment, segregation in schools and neighborhoods, and refusals of service in stores and restaurants, as they did elsewhere in the nation.

Through her political coalitions, Bass organized direct action campaigns out of the offices of the *Eagle* that ranged from attempting to halt the production and later the screening of D. W. Griffith's *Birth of a Nation* (1915),[18] to publicizing employment segregation on the Boulder Dam project, in the Southern California Telephone Company, at the Los Angeles County Hospital, and in other Los Angeles businesses.[19] As she recalls, "the slogan 'Don't spend your money where you can't work,' adopted by the *California Eagle* and the Industrial Council, was . . . on everyone's tongues" in 1934 when she brought that boycott to the city. Bass founded the Industrial Council of Los Angeles, which fought job discrimination, and collaborated with Leon Washington, the *Eagle*'s advertising manager, in borrowing the slogan from the *Chicago Whip* (1919–193?).[20] As a result of direct-action campaigns in the Black labor movement, African American customers in Los Angeles withdrew their purchasing power to boycott employment segregation at white-owned buisnesses, and her editorials in the On the Sidewalk column were instrumental in desegregating the Los Angeles Fire Department and exposing employment segregation within the Los Angeles Police Department (LAPD). These actions made Bass a sought-after speaker in the Black labor movement across the country, and she used her speeches to promote her newspaper, linking direct action to the *Eagle*.

After a 1925 *Eagle* editorial in which Bass exposed a Ku Klux Klan plan to "control the Negro vote" in Watts, she was "threatened by members of the Klan who came to the Eagle Print Shop late at night, when she was alone." She ran them off with a gun. The KKK did not stop there; it sued her for libel (unsuccessfully).[21] Bass was undeterred, and went on to cover lynching in the *Eagle*, linking that violence to the paper's campaign to support the Scottsboro boys in 1933.[22] She was highly visible for her editorial column From the Sidewalk, which she used to call out extrajudicial police violence against African Americans and organize mass protests that demanded reforms in the LAPD, such as racial sensitivity training and hiring African American officers. None of those demands were heeded.[23]

During the early 1940s, Bass worked in Black-Chicano/a coalitional politics through the Sleepy Lagoon Defense Committee, which "an interracial coalition of labor leaders, journalists, and community activists" formed in 1943. The committee was co-chaired by Luisa Moreno, Bert Corona, and Cary McWilliams (figure C.1).[24] The Sleepy Lagoon case was the largest mass conviction in California history. Six hundred Latinx youth were arrested by the LAPD on suspicion of the murder of José Diaz, a farmworker in his early twenties whose body was found in the Sleepy Lagoon reservoir. In all, seventeen defendants were convicted on charges ranging from assault to first-degree murder. The committee worked for two years on the release of Chicano men wrongly convicted of murder, drawing attention to "the racial brutalities inflicted upon Mexican American zoot suiters during the summer of 1943."[25] *Eagle* reporter Al Waxman reframed salacious mainstream coverage of the Sleepy Lagoon trial by reminding readers of Black and Chicano/a rights and the "national rhetoric" that supported their "self-determination."[26] Their activist work resulted in Waxman and Bass being named, along with twenty other members of the Citizens' Committee for the Defense of Mexican-American Youth, in the 1943 report of the California Senate Factfinding Subcommittee on Un-American Activities (CUAC).[27] Bass continued to be named in subsequent reports for her membership on the Los Angeles Committee for Protection of the Foreign Born, founded in September 1950 in response to growing anti-immigrant sentiments.

Bass's activism, her close association with Black leftists such as W. E. B. Du Bois and Paul Robeson, and her politicized editorship of the *Eagle* made her a target of the federal government, which was surveilling the Black press as part of the Red

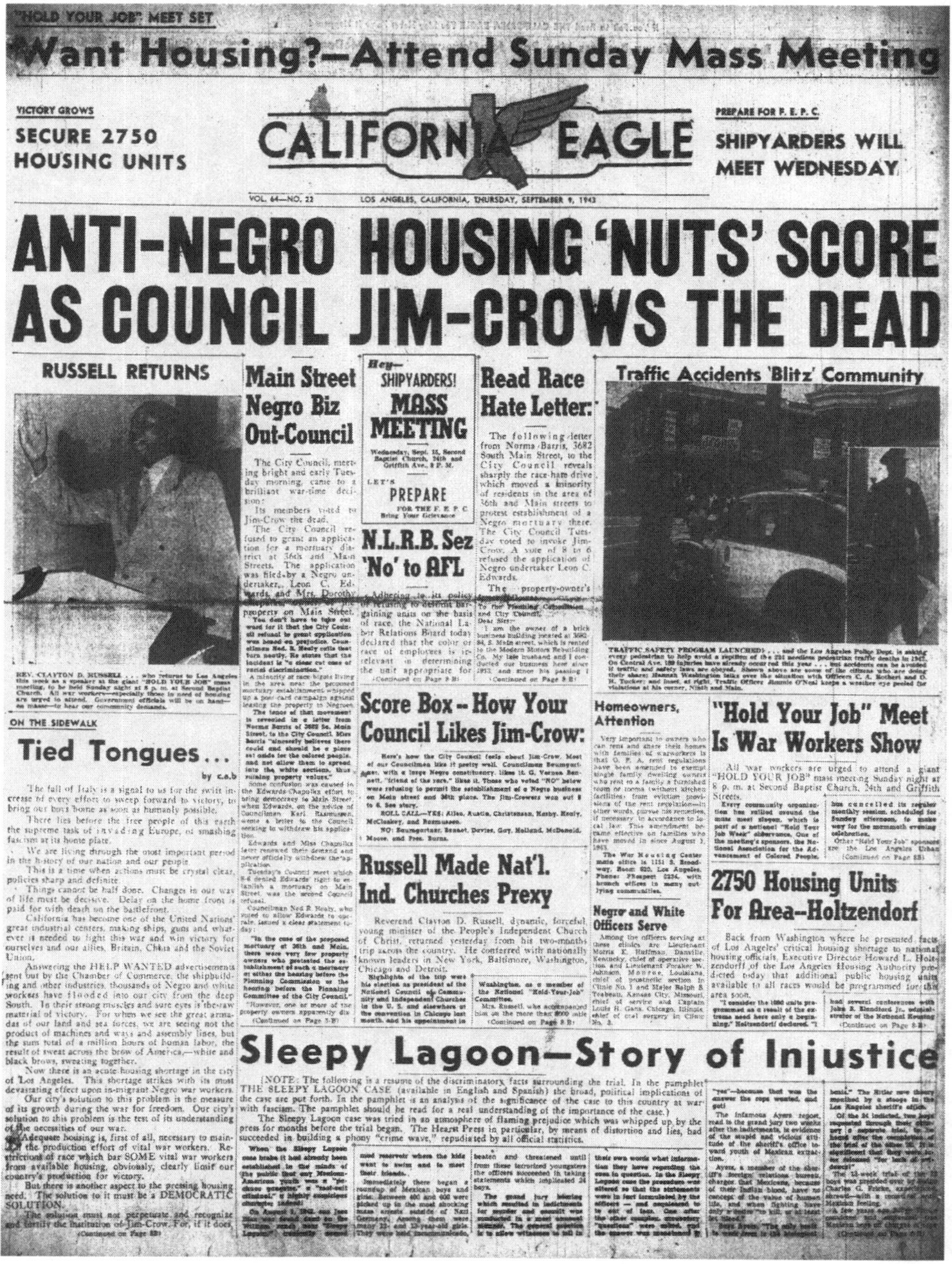

"HOLD YOUR JOB" MEET SET

Want Housing?—Attend Sunday Mass Meeting

VICTORY GROWS

SECURE 2750 HOUSING UNITS

CALIFORNIA EAGLE

PREPARE FOR F. E. P. C.

SHIPYARDERS WILL MEET WEDNESDAY

VOL. 64—NO. 22 LOS ANGELES, CALIFORNIA, THURSDAY, SEPTEMBER 9, 1943

ANTI-NEGRO HOUSING 'NUTS' SCORE AS COUNCIL JIM-CROWS THE DEAD

RUSSELL RETURNS

REV. CLAYTON D. RUSSELL . . . who returns to Los Angeles this week as a speaker at the giant "HOLD YOUR JOB" mass meeting, to be held Sunday night at 8 p. m. at Second Baptist Church. All war workers—especially those in need of housing are urged to attend. Government officials will be on hand—en masse—to hear our community demands.

Main Street Negro Biz Out-Council

The City Council, meeting bright and early Tuesday morning, came to a brilliant war-time decision:

Its members voted to Jim-Crow the dead.

The City Council refused to grant an application for a mortuary district at 36th and Main Streets. The application was filed by a Negro undertaker, Leon C. Edwards, and Mrs. Dorothy ...

Hey—SHIPYARDERS! MASS MEETING

Wednesday, Sept. 15, Second Baptist Church, 24th and Griffith Ave., 8 P. M.

LET'S PREPARE FOR THE F. E. P. C. Bring Your Grievance

N.L.R.B. Sez 'No' to AFL

Read Race Hate Letter:

The following letter from Norma Barris, 3682 South Main Street, to the City Council reveals sharply the race-hate drive which moved a minority of residents in the area of 36th and Main streets to protest establishment of a Negro mortuary there. The City Council Tuesday voted to invoke Jim-Crow. A vote of 8 to 6 refused the application of Negro undertaker Leon C. Edwards.

The property-owner's ...

(Continued on Page 8-B)

Traffic Accidents 'Blitz' Community

TRAFFIC SAFETY PROGRAM LAUNCHED . . . and the Los Angeles Police Dept. is asking every pedestrian to help avoid a repetition of the 251 needless pedestrian traffic deaths in 1942.

ON THE SIDEWALK

Tied Tongues...

by c.a.b

The fall of Italy is a signal to us for the swift increase of every effort to sweep forward to victory, to bring our boys home as soon as humanly possible.

There lies before the free people of this earth the supreme task of invading Europe, of smashing fascism at its home plate.

We are living through the most important period in the history of our nation and our people.

This is a time when actions must be crystal clear, policies sharp and definite.

Things cannot be half done. Changes in our way of life must be decisive. Delay on the home front is paid for with death on the battlefront.

California has become one of the United Nations' great industrial centers, making ships, guns and whatever it needed to fight this war and win victory for ourselves and our allies, Britain, China and the Soviet Union.

Answering the HELP WANTED advertisements sent out by the Chamber of Commerce, the shipbuilding and other industries, thousands of Negro and white workers have flooded into our city from the deep South. In their strong muscles and sure eyes is the raw material of victory. For when we see the great armadas of our land and sea forces, we are seeing not the product of machines and ways and assembly lines, but the sum total of a million hours of human labor, the result of sweat across the brow of America,—white and black brows, sweating together.

Now there is an acute housing shortage in the city of Los Angeles. This shortage strikes with its most devastating effect upon in-migrant Negro war workers.

Our city's solution to this problem is the measure of its growth during the war for freedom. Our city's solution to this problem is the test of its understanding of the necessities of our war.

Adequate housing is, first of all, necessary to maintain the production effort of vital war workers. Restrictions of race which bar SOME vital war workers from available housing, obviously, clearly limit our country's production for victory.

But there is another aspect to the pressing housing need. The solution to it must be a DEMOCRATIC SOLUTION.

The solution must not perpetuate and recognize and fortify the institution of Jim-Crow. For, if it does, ...

(Continued on Page 8B)

Score Box—How Your Council Likes Jim-Crow:

Russell Made Nat'l. Ind. Churches Prexy

Reverend Clayton D. Russell, dynamic, forceful young minister of the People's Independent Church of Christ, returned yesterday from his two-months trip across the country. He conferred with nationally known leaders in New York, Baltimore, Washington, Chicago and Detroit.

Homeowners, Attention

Negro and White Officers Serve

"Hold Your Job" Meet Is War Workers Show

All war workers are urged to attend a giant "HOLD YOUR JOB" mass meeting Sunday night at 8 p. m. at Second Baptist Church, 24th and Griffith Streets.

2750 Housing Units For Area—Holtzendorf

Back from Washington where he presented facts of Los Angeles' critical housing shortage to national housing officials, Executive Director Howard L. Holtzendorff of the Los Angeles Housing Authority predicted today that additional public housing units available to all races would be programmed for the area soon.

Sleepy Lagoon—Story of Injustice

(NOTE: The following is a resume of the discriminatory facts surrounding the trial. In the pamphlet THE SLEEPY LAGOON CASE (available in English and Spanish) the broad, political implications of the case are put forth. In the pamphlet is an analysis of the significance of the case to this country at war with fascism. The pamphlet should be read for a real understanding of the importance of the case.)

The Sleepy Lagoon case was tried in an atmosphere of flaming prejudice which was whipped up by the press for months before the trial began. The Hearst Press in particular, by means of distortion and lies, had succeeded in building a phony "crime wave," repudiated by all official statistics.

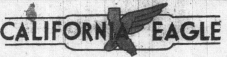

Figure C.1. Front page of the *California Eagle*, September 9, 1943, showing the types of political issues Charlotta Bass highlighted in her paper. Internet Archive.

Scare. The FBI kept an active file on Bass, and in 1943, the same year she was first named in a CUAC report, the US Post Office requested that the Justice Department revoke her mailing permit, claiming that the *Eagle* was subversive. Some of these tactics were similar to those used against Marcus Garvey's *Negro World* in the 1920s, and Bass argued successfully against them. The CUAC also accused her of being a Communist and regarded the Progressive Party as "a creature of the Communist Party."[28] Bass denied this allegation in 1948, although she did work closely with members of the Communist Party USA who, like her, had primary roles in the Civil Rights Congress.[29] She also worked that year as co-chair of Women for Wallace on the Progressive Party's campaign to elect Henry A. Wallace to the presidency. The damage was difficult to contain, however, and these public accusations cost the *Eagle* many readers.[30] Despite these challenges, Bass agitated against racially restrictive housing covenants, the activism she became most well known for. She formed the Los Angeles Home Owners Protective Association, which was an ally to several homeowner defendants in cases enforcing racially restrictive covenants through eviction and arrest, in 1945. As Bass writes in her memoir, such cases were part of achieving the 1948 ruling by the US Supreme Court that deemed such covenants unconstitutional.[31] She also continued to advocate for the Black press in California and was one of twelve founding directors of the Negro Press Foundation of California, which formed on February 15, 1949, two years before she sold the *Eagle*.[32]

Government campaigns against Black activists such as Bass continued throughout the 1950s. Following her travels to the Soviet Union in 1950, the State Department attempted to revoke her passport in 1951, although Bass refused to relinquish it.[33] In this she kept good Black feminist company with the likes of women such as Claudia Jones, who was first arrested in 1948 under the 1918 Immigration Act and was arrested again in 1951 and charged under the Smith Act with other Communist Party members. The Smith Act "made it illegal to advocate or be a member of an organization that advocated the violent overthrow of the United States government." Jones was "found guilty in January 1953 and sentenced to one year and one day in jail and a $2000 fine."[34] Bass cofounded the Sojourners for Truth and Justice and served as its national chairperson in 1951 and 1952. The Sojourners for Truth and Justice, a 132-member Black feminist pacifist organization and the only group on the Communist Left led by Black women, was critical of US foreign and domestic policies and the state's role in violence against Black women. Jacquline Castledine refers to the Sojourners, whose members such as Claudia Jones, Louise Thompson Patterson, Shirley Graham

Du Bois, Eslanda Goode Robeson, Alice Childress, Mary Church Terrell, and Lorraine Hansberry were known for their Communist and Black nationalist politics, as "the most militant black feminist organization of the postwar era."[35] Surveilled as dangerous, Bass was also dismissed by *Time* magazine as "dumpy, domineering . . . childless . . . [and] bitterly radical" in 1952.[36]

Bass retired from editing and public political life shortly thereafter and moved to Lake Elsinore, but she continued her activism undeterred, protesting apartheid in South Africa at the age of 85 and advocating for prisoners' rights in California through the mid-1960s. In the fall of 1964, she converted her garage in Lake Elsinore into "a community reading room . . . [and] voter registration site."[37] As Anne Rapp documents, Bass's garage reading room "sponsored discussion forums, contained a small library, and fostered interracial communication and understanding." It was also a site for organizing direct action, such as fundraising to support the voter registration drive in Mississippi during the summer of 1965.[38] In 1967, at the age of ninety-one, a stroke survivor living in a nursing home, Charlotta Bass was still considered a "potentially dangerous" security threat by the FBI.[39]

Keeping the *Eagle* Aloft

Scholarship on Bass focuses much more on her political activism, some of which I have recounted, than on the workings of the *California Eagle*. More recently, she has been analyzed as an important figure in both Black political life and Black-Chicano/a coalitional politics in Los Angeles. Recent scholarship sees her as an important precursor to "coalitions of the 1970s such as that between the Black Panthers and the Brown Berets."[40] The result is that her activism and resulting government surveillance tend to explain her sale of the *Eagle* in 1951 as necessary to her Progressive Party bid for the vice presidency, but the *Eagle*'s financial records complicate that narrative.[41] They give us a rare look at how hard it was to keep a Black newspaper viable during the 1930s and 1940s, even one like the *Eagle* with a strong subscription base in the state. If we are to consider the Black press as co-constitutive of Black feminist politics—both the futures Black feminists imagined and those they could make possible—then the *Eagle*'s economic sustainability and the challenges it faced are crucial factors we cannot ignore.

Bass produced the *Eagle* in house until 1934. In 1929, Bass had moved from 814 South Central Avenue, which she continued to maintain as the paper's business offices in what the *Eagle* dubbed the city's Black Belt, to 1607 East 103 Street in Watts and expanded the *Eagle*'s printing plant. The new plant had a multilith, chief offset, kluge, power cutter, double-exposure linotype, a printing frame for plate burning, and a proof press.⁴² At the time the production plant opened, the paper had reduced in size from twenty pages per week to twelve pages of seven columns each. Starting in the spring of 1929, the paper ran the equivalent of four pages of ads (a third of its print space) and included a four-page magazine section. On March 5, 1930, the *Eagle* announced a contest to garner new subscriptions for the paper that ran for forty days beginning on March 7 and offered eight prizes, including a 1930 Essex Sedan worth $1,050, gold, furs, sport coats, and a radio; in all, the prizes totaled $2,266. The winnings were soon converted to a single $500 cash grand prize and 25 percent commission for "all non-winners," citing a survey of contest candidates that had revealed that they preferred cash,⁴³ and the contest was extended from April 26 to May 21 (figure C.2). The *Eagle* announced eleven winners on May 23. True to Black women's long history of support for the Black press, nine of the winners were women. Ethelyn Hunter of Pasadena led the winners with 710,000 "votes." Though it is impossible to know how many subscriptions the posted votes tallying 3,117,000 across these eleven winners amounted to, this was likely the point, since advertising could be better secured with the sense that the *Eagle* had dramatically transformed its subscription base through this contest.⁴⁴ Within a month of the contest closing, the *Eagle* was running the equivalent of two pages of ads in an eight-page publication (down from four of

Figure C.2. Advertisement for the 1930 subscription contest, *California Eagle*, May 9, 1930. Internet Archive.

twelve pages), an advertising proportion that was consistent with the 2.5 pages of ads it ran in 1929, when production moved to Watts.[45]

As was the case for most Black newspapers, advertising was never a revenue mainstay for the paper.[46] *Eagle* account entries for May 1930 indicate that the paper's account balance opened that month at $35.32 and never rose above $374 as debits depleted deposits in short order. That month's balance forward to June was $10.59, or half of what most *Eagle* employees earned in a week. Records from the Charlotta Bass Collection indicate that from 1929 through 1933, she paid her secretary, Adele Ashford, $20 weekly and her compositor, Jesus Cano, an average of $21 weekly. John Prowd, Samuel Hamilton, and Max Williams, the *Eagle*'s linotype operators, earned an average of $20 to $30 weekly, and her "all-around printer," William Solomon, earned $17 a week.[47] As advertising manager, Leon Washington was paid an average of $20 a week; and in the spring of 1933, Loren Miller, a civil rights attorney and the city editor, was paid $15 to $30 a week. Bass also paid $10 per week in postal fees to distribute the paper to its subscribers, while shouldering the costs of keeping the *Eagle*'s equipment in good repair, maintaining an insurance policy, and, of course, paying telephone and utility bills. The paper's records indicate that from 1929 to 1933 Bass dealt with Morrell Ink and with General Paper, a subsidiary of the Zellerbach Corporation, a company that would dominate print production in the West.[48]

In other words, the paper's operations were tight. The Black population of Los Angeles at this time was 38,894 or 3.1 percent of the city's total population, and even with a statewide or cross-racial appeal, the *Eagle* would probably never have been able to stay in the red with its $2 yearly subscription fees.[49] James Jeter notes that correspondence with the Associated Negro Press News Service reveals that the Basses were "chronically slow or behind on paying [the *Eagle*'s] bill." Bass's nephew, John Kinloch, wondered "where the money came from to pay the bills."[50] Despite the expansion to a larger printing plant in Watts, the effects of the Depression are clear: the *Eagle*'s bank statements reveal that these were very lean years. In April and March 1933, the paper incurred no fewer than sixteen bounced checks.[51]

Despite these financial strains, Bass diversified, understanding that radio competed with print news media. In 1938, the *Eagle* began producing a fifteen-minute "newspaper-of-the-air" broadcast on a local radio station six nights a week.[52] Bass's nephew, John Kinloch, who had recently moved from Harlem to Los Angeles to study at the University of California at Los Angeles, was on-air announcer.[53] The show went into hiatus at some point but was revived around 1940, when the

California Eagle Hour began to air every Sunday on KFVD. The program provided "information about news, sports, social events and other activities in Los Angeles' African-American community."[54] Bass also made Kinloch managing editor of the *Eagle*, but he enlisted in the country's first integrated infantry unit in World War II and was killed during the war.

By the late 1940s, the California Senate Factfinding Subcommittee on Un-American Activities's investigation of Bass was costing the *Eagle* both advertisers and readers. Its circulation dropped to 17,600, or roughly a third of its high in the 1920s.[55] As subscription and circulation were declining, the paper was also losing staff. Ann Rapp notes that "writers and printers left for military service, for higher paying jobs in war industries, and for positions at rival newspapers." Bass tried to increase subscriptions with what the paper called "victory drives," but the *Eagle* was often on the brink of bankruptcy.[56] In 1947, Bass shifted from printing the *Eagle* in house to outsourcing its production to the Compton Printing Company at prices ranging from $476 to $649 per weekly issue.[57] Compton Printing Company boasted on its letterhead that it was the "largest independent rotary pressroom in the West." It worked a virtually nonstop schedule, "operating night and day serving the Southwest with newspapers and circulars," as its invoices announced.[58]

By May of 1948, Bass was facing a new set of problems. She received notice from the Los Angeles Newspaper Guild of violations, including complaints that she was underpaying some staff and that she had failed to notify the guild of staff vacancies, a requirement to ensure that editors staffed their publications with unionized employees. The notice focused on the paper's employment practices in 1947; according to complaints, the *Eagle* owed $2,123.75 in unpaid wages and vacation pay to nine employees, both salaried employees and those who were paid per column. One employee so owed was Cyril Briggs, the radical founder of the African Blood Brotherhood (1917) and *The Crusader Magazine* (New York, NY; 1918–1922).[59] For an activist and editor who had consistently championed the rights of African American workers and was a leader in the West Coast Black labor movement, coping with financial pressure and an employee labor dispute must have been extraordinarily difficult.

Bass responded within two weeks of receiving the notice from the guild with a very short letter on May 19, 1948. "My financial status is in a state of bankruptcy, which matter I am now discussing with my lawyers," she wrote. "However, while I am in a state of financial collapse just now, does not mean that I intend to dodge any obligations." She said that the *Eagle* was "in the process of being incorporated," which she anticipated would be "completed and active within about two weeks," and that following incorporation she anticipated that the *Eagle*'s new Board of Directors would be "glad to discuss and renew a contract with the Guild."[60] In August, Bass's lawyer, Ben Margolis, a well-known civil rights attorney she had worked with on the Los Angeles Committee for Protection of the Foreign Born, was also retained by the guild. He attempted to act as an intermediary and to advocate for arbitration of the dispute that would avoid a formal complaint about Bass and the *Eagle* to the California Labor Commission. Bass defended her 1947 employment practices in a letter to the guild dated October 4, 1948. She noted that "Eugene and June Hilyard have never been salaried employees of the *California Eagle* in charge of circulation. But they did circulate the paper on a 'pay and take it' basis." Bass also said that while Cyril Briggs was employed by the paper, he waived his vacation "of his own free will" in the year in question and that Briggs had entered into a side agreement with a "Mr. [Edward] Banbridge . . . a very unsatisfactory employee," in which Banbridge worked part time in the *Eagle* office "and used the other time soliciting advertisements on a commission basis. I can produce evidence, also, to show that Mr. Banbridge used this as a medium to appropriate monies gathered in the name of the *Eagle* for his own use." Bass provided the guild with affidavits from two other employees that attested to their acceptable employment conditions and salaries. She closed her letter by saying that she was "willing to abide by the direction of the Guild, and to meet whatever demands the Guild may see fit to make in these matters."[61]

On October 12, 1948, Margolis wrote the guild to document his failure to resolve this dispute "without undue publicity and without any public attack on the paper." He had attempted to pursue that course, he said, because Bass had operated the *Eagle* "a pro-labor Negro newspaper, one of the two or three such newspapers in the United States." The guild chose not to informally arbitrate the dispute and instead sent Bass a telegram, "stating that her attitude on labor relations was to be judged solely upon the basis of her conduct . . . and that the matter was going to be turned over to the Labor Commission."[62] Having been accused of being wholly under Communist Party control in 1943 by the California Senate Factfinding Subcommittee on Un-American Activities, when the Subcommittee was also investigating Bass for her politics and activism, may have been relevant to the Guild's decision.[63] As she had said she would, Bass incorporated the *Eagle*, filing papers with the Negro Press Foundation on February 19, 1949; she was listed, along with Margolis, as one of its twelve directors.

Under these financial and labor difficulties, Bass sold the *Eagle* to Loren Miller in 1951. Before long, he was drowning in the costs of its production. Miller was a lawyer and activist. He had been city editor at the *Eagle* in 1929 and had worked with Bass to represent complainants in racially restrictive housing covenant suits, such as the famous Sugar Hill case in 1945.[64] In 1950, just before the sale, the paper had a documented circulation of only 10,000.[65] As early as 1956, only five years after he purchased it, the *Eagle* was unable to pay invoices from the Compton Printing Company for the paper's weekly production. Compton threatened several times to sue Miller for failure to pay on the *Eagle*'s outstanding balance, which ran as high as $4,127.47 plus interest in the period from 1956 to 1962. Miller negotiated several times in this six-year period to pay interest only. Compton Printing continued to produce the paper, but it repeatedly threatened legal action.[66]

In 1964, Miller was appointed as a municipal judge, and he sold his majority stock ownership in the *Eagle* to fourteen investors, each of whom contributed between $1,000 and $3,000.[67] A. S. "Doc" Young, then a writer for the *Los Angeles Sentinel*, became the editor; Joseph Bingham became managing editor; and James Tolbert of the Hollywood-Beverly Hills NAACP became managing publisher. Together they took the *Eagle*'s circulation from 3,000 to 21,000 within their first six months. They altered the paper to a tabloid format of fifty-eight pages and resurrected its radio presence with a twice-daily newscast on K-DAY AM.[68] Within months, the paper's operating costs were running "$4,100 a week." Although advertising revenue paid roughly half those costs, this group "ran up unpaid bills of $25,000" in their first four months of operation. The paper closed on January 7, 1965, due to mismanagement, just five months and one week after its first issue under Young, Bingham, and Tolbert.[69] Charlotta Bass had sustained the *California Eagle* for thirty-nine years through both the Depression and the Red Scare, weathering competition from two papers she had made possible by employing their founding staff—the *Los Angeles Sentinel* (1934–) and the *Los Angeles Tribune* (1940–1960).[70]

The work Bass faced to keep the *California Eagle* in operation was not unlike what Beatrice Cannady shouldered while editing the Portland *Advocate* (1903–1936) from 1912 to 1933. At a youthful twenty-three years old, Cannady took over producing the four-page weekly soon after she married Edward Daniel Cannady, the sole remaining member of the *Advocate*'s ten founders by 1912. Kimberly Mangun documents that Cannady "worked as the *Advocate*'s business manager, associate editor, linotype operator, and editorial and news writer" as the paper reached a "peak ... [of] some three thousand" subscribers.[71] The paper was sustained for over twenty years by advertising, by subscribers beyond Portland's relatively small African American community of 1,500, and by both white and Black readers within and beyond the state of Oregon. It sold for five cents per copy and promoted Portland and the Pacific Northwest as a veritable garden for Black migrants, much as Los Angeles had been promoted by the *Eagle*. Cannady, an attorney, quipped that she dressed "to vamp the judge" because "men enjoy beauty. The judge and jury are impressed by it."[72] While traveling East in September 1927 as a delegate to the Pan-African Conference in New York City, Beatrice Cannady told the *New York Amsterdam News* (1943–) that "the door is open for us. Much of the state is yet unoccupied. The land is wonderfully fertile and will grow almost anything. The state would welcome good farmers." She promoted Oregon as idyllic in the *Chicago Defender*: "Out there we have solved the Race problem to the satisfaction of everyone."[73] However, evidence suggests that such statements were hyperbolic. Cannady lobbied Portland, as Bass had done in Los Angeles, to ban D. W. Griffith's *Birth of a Nation* from its theaters, leading NAACP protests in the summer of 1915 as the Portland branch's secretary and spokesperson. The film was screened in the spring of 1918, the spring of 1922, and the winter of 1923, and the "talking" version was scheduled to come to Portland in 1931. Each time Cannady led a protest. Only the 1931 protest was successful.[74]

During these decades, Beatrice Cannady used the *Advocate* and her speaking engagements to draw attention to employment segregation and housing discrimination as Oregon became new territory for the Ku Klux Klan when it moved north from California in the spring of 1921. Kimberly Mangun documents that she was "a popular speaker, often giving as many as a hundred talks a year" as an "unofficial spokesperson for the city's African American population."[75] And just as Bass was both a Garveyite and a member of the NAACP, Cannady combined her NAACP work with the *Advocate*'s front page headlines on Marcus Garvey's illness and incarceration.[76] In addition to their leadership work in the NAACP on the West Coast, Bass and Cannady also shared a commitment to pan-Africanist politics; Cannady attended the Fourth Pan-African Congress in New York City in 1927. In 1932, Cannady ran for a seat in the Oregon legislature, the first African American to do so.

Both editors opened reading rooms or libraries. Bass's garage reading room was established in 1964 after she sold the *Eagle* and left politics, and Cannady amassed what some called "the most complete public library this side of Chicago," which she opened to all races. She also made her living room public, a place where people could either read or "interview her on matters pertaining to race relations and the history and development of the Negro race."[77] She published columns written by African American women, such as Kit Reid's Arrow Tips and suffragist Emma Lue Sayers's Los Angeles Social Circle, in the *Advocate* through the late 1920s. Sayers held leadership positions in both the Los Angeles branch of the NAACP and the California League of Women Voters.[78] Sayers's column brought Bass into the pages of the *Advocate* when she reported on an event Bass hosted as president of the Los Angeles Press Club to honor Nick Chiles. Chiles had edited the *Topeka Plaindealer*, which he had purchased from Bass's husband in 1898.[79] Cannady also promoted Black women's clubs, Black fraternal orders, and Black church organizations in the *Advocate*, as the Black press had done through its first newspapers in the early nineteenth century. She founded Portland's Tuesday Morning Esperanto Club, whose meetings included her weekly lectures on Black history. The club hosted events such as "Mable Byrd discuss[ing] 'the economic problem as it affected the Negro in America.'"[80]

And, like Bass's expansion of the *Eagle* in 1929, Beatrice Cannady chose to purchase additional equipment in 1931, the *Advocate*'s twenty-eighth anniversary, when she touted her paper as the "only Negro newspaper . . . in the state of Oregon and the only one owning its own plant North of Frisco."[81] As was the case for the *Eagle*, the move did not go as well as planned, and in 1931, the *Advocate* shut down one of its two offices and moved to twice monthly publication in the summer months.[82] Cannady, like Black press editors often were forced to do, devoted considerable print space to reminding her readers to renew subscriptions and encouraging them to secure subscriptions from friends, families, neighbors, and businesses they patronized: "Pay your subscription to *The Advocate* so you can meet old St. Peter with a clear conscience."[83] She ran an elaborate subscription contest in 1931 that, like the contest Bass ran in 1930, offered a car and gold as prizes. "Advertisements, notices about the rules and regulations, extra 'opportunity coupons,' and front-page articles ran week after week" in the *Advocate* to promote it. Three of the five contest winners were Black women, a majority as in Bass's contest, but it is unlikely that Cannady raised the subscriptions she would have needed to pay for the major prizes offered, although she kept the *Advocate* running for another two years.[84] Beatrice Cannady was a crucial part of the longevity of the *Advocate* for twenty years. She left Portland in 1936, settling in Perris, seventy miles southeast of Los Angeles. There, she wrote for the Perris *Precinct Reporter* and held interracial "fireside meetings" at the ranch she lived on with her third husband. She died at age 85 in 1974.[85]

One cannot examine Charlotta Bass and Beatrice Cannady as newspaper editors in the West and Pacific Northwest without looking at their political commitments. Together they reveal an ongoing pattern of Black women's dual commitments to fostering and sustaining publications that they used to disseminate and realize their politics. Bass's garage reading room and Cannady's library and the Tuesday Morning Esperanto Club echo the Black feminist work undertaken through literary societies and lyceums as political training grounds and sites of reading and writing that sustained the Black press economically and Black communities politically. Like other early twentieth-century editors such as Jessie Fauset, Amy Jacques Garvey, and Pauline Hopkins, Cannady and Bass were attuned to the connections between American imperialism abroad and American colonialism and race politics at home. And like many Black feminists before and since their time, they shared an informed cynicism about US government policies and operations as obstacles to rather than potential fulfillments of freedom struggles. Bass and Cannady worked creatively and hard to keep their newspapers afloat as they pursued the Black feminist practice of using the press to amplify, disseminate, and cultivate publics for their politics. Under their editorship, the *California Eagle* and the Portland *Advocate* made California and the Pacific Northwest home for imagined Black futures.

Appendix: *African American Literary Societies and Lyceums*

This chronological listing of African American literary societies and lyceums includes those founded by women and by men, and those that were female in membership, male in membership, and had members of all genders. Where a year is included in parentheses following the name of a society, this is the known founded-by date. This listing is largely derived from digitized historical African American newspapers. It is limited by OCR searching, which creates "dirty data" through incomplete character recognition and, as a result, yields far from complete or exhaustive results. Consequently, although this list significantly extends our knowledge of African American literary societies and lyceums, it is not a complete record.

Abbreviations

A	*The Appeal: A National Afro-American Newspaper*, Washington, DC (1885–1923)
AA	*The Afro-American Advance*, Minneapolis and St. Paul, MN (1899–1905)
AAA	*Afro-American Advocate*, Coffeyville, KS (1891–1893)
AAP	*Africo-American Presbyterian*, Charlotte, NC (1879–1939)
AAS	*The Afro-American Sentinel*, Omaha, NE (1893–1899)
AB	*The Atchison Blade*, Atchison, KS (1892–1898)
AC	*The American Citizen*, Kansas City, KS (1888–1909)
AE	*Amherstburg Echo*, Amherstberg, ON, Canada (1874–2012)
AP	*The Advocate*, Portland, OR (1923–1933)
AR	*The African Repository, and Colonial Journal*, Washington, DC (1825–1892)
ASP	*Arkansas State Press*, Little Rock, AR (1941–1959)
BA	*The Broad Ax*, Salt Lake City, UT (1895–1899); Chicago, IL (1899–1931)
BAA	*The Afro-American*, Baltimore, MD (1892–1900)
BC	*The Commonwealth*, Baltimore, MD (1915)
BNA	*Northern Advance*, Barrie, ON, Canada (1852–1938)
CA	*The Colored American*, New York, NY (1837–1842)
CAW	*The Colored American*, Washington, DC (1893–1904)
CC	*The Colored Citizen*, Cincinnati, OH (1863–1873)
CDN	*Chatham Daily News*, Chatham, ON, Canada (1914–1991)
CG	*The Cleveland Gazette*, Cleveland, OH (1883–1945)
CP	*The Capitol Plaindealer*, Topeka, KS (1936–1938)
CR	*The Christian Recorder*, Philadelphia, PA; Nashville, TN (1852–)

DE	*The Dallas Express*, Dallas, TX (1893–1970)
E	*The Elevator A Weekly Journal of Progress*, San Francisco, CA (1865–1904)
EFA	*The Emancipator and Free American*, New York, NY (1841–1844)
EFP	*The Essex Free Press*, Windsor, ON, Canada (1895–1968)
EJPM	*The Emancipator and Journal of Public Morals*, Boston, MA (1834–1835)
ER	*Essex Record*, Windsor, ON, Canada (1861–1888)
FDP	*Frederick Douglass' Paper*, Rochester, NY (1851–1860)
FJ	*Freedom's Journal*, New York, NY (1827–1829)
FP	*The Fair Play*, Fort Scott, KS (1898–1899)
G	*The New York Globe*, New York, NY (1880–1884)
HG	*Huntsville Gazette*, Huntsville, AL (1879–1894)
HI	*The Independent*, Houston, TX (1898–1905)
HK	*Herald of Kansas*, Topeka, KS (1880)
HSJ	*The State Journal*, Harrisburg, PA (1882–1885)
IF	*The Freeman*, Indianapolis, IN (1884–1927)
IO	*The Inter Ocean*, Chicago IL (1872–1914)
IR	*The Indianapolis Recorder*, Indianapolis, IN (1897–)
ISB	*Iowa State Bystander*, Des Moines, IA (1894–1916)
KCA	*Kansas City Advocate*, Kansas City, KS (1914–1926)
KCP	*The Plaindealer*, Kansas City, KS (1932–1958); published as *The Kansas City and Topeka Plaindealer* (May 20, 1932–November 3, 1933)
KE	*The Kansas Elevator*, Kansas City, KS (1916)
KW	*The Kansas Whip*, Topeka, KS (1933?–1956)
L	*The Leader*, Washington, DC (1888–1894)
LA	*Leavenworth Advocate* Leavenworth, KS (1888–1891)
LCH	*The Langston City Herald*, Langston City, Oklahoma Territory (1891–1902)
LF	*The Leavenworth Herald*, Leavenworth, KS (1894–1899)
LS	*The Lexington Standard*, Lexington, KY (1892–1912)
MDA	*The Memphis Daily Appeal*, Memphis, TN (1847–1886)
NA	*The New Age*, Portland, OR (1896–1905)
NBW	*National Baptist World*, Wichita, KS (1893–1894)
NE	*Nicodemus Enterprise*, Nicodemus, KS (August 17–December 23, 1887)
NECA	*National Enquirer, and Constitutional Advocate of Universal Liberty*, Philadelphia, PA (1836–1838)
NODC	*New Orleans Daily Creole*, New Orleans, LA (1856–1857)
NOT	*New Orleans Tribune/La Tribune de la Nouvelle-Orleans*, New Orleans, LA (1864–1869)
NR	*The National Reflector*, Wichita, KS (1895–1897)
NS	*The Negro Star*, Wichita, KS (1908–1953)

NSFA	*The Northern Star and Freeman's Advocate*, Albany, NY (1842–1843)
NSR	*The North Star*, Rochester, NY (1847–1851)
NYA	*The New York Age*, New York, NY (1887–1953)
NYF	*The New York Freeman*, New York, NY (1884–1887)
NYG	*The New York Globe*, New York, NY (1880–1884)
OE	*The Enterprise*, Omaha, NE (1893–1914)
OS	*Oakland Sunshine*, Oakland, CA (1897–1922)
P	*The Plaindealer*, Detroit, MI (1883–1895); published as *The Plaindealer: An Inter-State Weekly Journal* (April 15, 1892–1895)
PA	*The People's Advocate*, Washington, DC (1876–1886?)
PF	*The Pennsylvania Freeman*, Philadelphia, PA (1836–1854)
PFWA	*The Provincial Freeman*, Windsor, Canada West (1853–1854); Toronto, Canada West (1854–1855); *The Provincial Freeman and Weekly Advertiser*, Chatham, Canada West (1855–1857)
PQW	*Paul Quinn Weekly*, Waco, TX (1900–1916)
PWB	*The Parsons Weekly Blade*, Parsons, KS (1892–1901)
RG	*The Gazette*, Raleigh, NC (1893–1898)
RS	*The Rising Son*, Kansas City, MO (1896–1918)
SA	*The Southern Argus*, Fort Scott, KS (1891–1892)
SC	*The State Capital*, Springfield, IL (1886–1910)
SE	*The Salina Enterprise*, Salina, KS (1908–1909)
SLC	*St. Louis Clarion*, St. Louis, MO (192?-19?)
SLP	*St. Louis Palladium*, St. Louis, MO (1884–1911)
ST	*The Savannah Tribune*, Savannah, GA (1875–1960; 1973–)
TA	*Torchlight Appeal*, Fort Worth, TX (1886–1893)
TC	*The Topeka Call*, Topeka, KS (1891–1893
TG	*The Grit*, Williamsport, PA (1882–1993)
TL	*The Liberator*, Boston, MA (1831–1865)
TO	*The Times-Observer*, Topeka, KS (1891–1892)
TP	*The Topeka Plaindealer*, Topeka, KS (1900–1932)
TS	*The Sentinel*, Trenton, NJ (1880–1882)
TSL	*The Kansas State Ledger*, Topeka, KS (1892–1894); *The State Ledger* (1894–1906)
V	*The Vindicator*, Coffeyville, KS (1904–1906)
WA	*Western Appeal*, St. Paul, MN (1885–1888)
WAA	*The Weekly Anglo-African*, New York, NY (1859–1861)
WB	*The Washington Bee*, Washington, D.C. (1882–1922)
WCR	*Western Christian Recorder*, Kansas City, KS (1892–1952)
WER	*The Evening Record*, Windsor, ON, Canada (1893–1917)
WL	*The Weekly Louisianan*, New Orleans, LA (1870–1882)
WLA	*The Wisconsin Labor Advocate*, La Crosse, WS (1886–1887)

WO   *The Western Outlook*, San Francisco, CA; Oakland, CA (1894–1928)
WP   *The Weekly Pelican*, New Orleans, LA (1886–1889)
WR   *The Western Recorder*, Lawrence, KS (1883–June 20, 1884); Atchison, KS (June 27–November 6, 1884)
WS   *The Wichita Searchlight*, Wichita, KS (1900–1912)
WWA   *The Wisconsin Weekly Advocate*, Milwaukee, WI (1898–1915)

Alabama

Frederick Douglass Literary Society, Mobile (*WB*, April 9, 1887, 2)
Excelsior Literary Club, Mobile (*WB*, June 4, 1887, 2)
Literary Club, Birmingham (*L*, December 8, 1888, 2)
Triana Literary Society, Triana (*HG*, June 5, 1889, 3)
Hartsell Literary Society, Huntsville (*HG*, March 11, 1890, 3)
Second C. P. [Cumberland Presbyterian] Church Literary Society, Huntsville (*HG*, December 3, 1892, 3)
Peabody Literary Society, Normal (*IF*, April 29, 1893, 1; January 4, 1896, 1)
Tennysonian Literary Society, Tuscumbia (*HG*, October 7, 1893, 2)
Normal Literary Society, Normal (*HG*, February 10, 1894, 2)
Young Progressive Literary Association, Huntsville (*HG*, July 21, 1894, 3)
Mobile Lyceum, Mobile (*IF*, October 15, 1910, 2)

Arkansas

Desney Lyceum, Hot Springs (*IF*, March 22, 1890, 4)
Helena Literary Society, Helena (*IF*, November 29, 1890, 6)
St. James Lyceum (1891), Helena (*IF*, February 7, 1891, 1)
Hot Springs Literary Society, Hot Springs (*NYA*, March 21, 1891, 4)
Disney Literary Society, Brinkley (*P*, June 24, 1892, 6)
Brinkley Lyceum, Brinkley (*P*, June 24, 1892, 6)
Whittier-Stowe Debating Lyceum, Fort Smith (*IF*, August 13, 1892, 2)
St. John's Lyceum, Fordyce (*IF*, April 15, 1893, 8)
AME Church Lyceum, Helena (*IF*, May 20, 1893, 5)
Arnett Lyceum, Hot Springs (*IF*, December 23, 1893, 5)
Young Ladies and Gents Occidental Literary Club, Arkadelphia (*IF*, 27 January 1894; see also Logan, *Liberating Language*, 91)
Grey Lyceum, Arkadelphia (*IF*, February 2, 1895, 6)
Philosophian Literary Society, Hot Springs (*IF*, December 30, 1899, 9)
Wableaseka Lyceum, Wableaseka (*IF*, April 4, 1908, 6)
Childress Junior High School Literary Society, Childress (*ASP*, December 5, 1941, 2)
Upchurch Training School Literary Society, Prescott (*ASP*, December 18, 1942, 8)
Wilmar Literary Society, Wilmar (*ASP*, February 5, 1943, 2)
Sanders Literary Society, Sanders (*ASP*, March 12, 1943, 4)
Newport High School Literary Society, Newport (*ASP*, December 24, 1943, 6)
Booker T. Washington Literary Society, Lonoke (*ASP*, March 15, 1946, 4)

Searcy Literary Society, Searcy (*ASP*, November 1, 1946, 2)
Carver High Literary Society, Augusta (*ASP*, September 5, 1947, 2)
Douglass High School Literary Society, Dardanelle (*ASP*, September 26, 1947, 2)
Sweet Home Junior High School Literary Society, Willisville (*ASP*, December 3, 1948, 6)
Booker T. Washington High School Literary Society, Jonesboro (*ASP*, November 11, 1949, 6)
Richard B. Harris Literary Society, Augusta (*ASP*, January 19, 1951, 3)
Fargo Training School Literary Society, Fargo (*ASP*, October 5, 1951, 1)

California
San Francisco Athenaeum (1853), San Francisco (*FDP*, September 22, 1854, 4)
Sacramento Musical and Literary Society, Sacramento (*FDP*, May 18, 1855)
Progressive Lyceum (1869), San Francisco (*E*, February 5, 1869)[1]
Eliott Literary Institute, San Francisco (*E*, December 5, 1874, 3)
Oakland Literary and Aid Society, Oakland (*G*, July 7, 1883, 4; *WO*, October 22, 1921, 3)
San Francisco Lyceum, San Francisco (*E*, September 8, 1888, 3)
Bethel Lyceum, Oakland (*OE*, August 24, 1895, 4)
T. M. D. Ward Lyceum, San Francisco (*OE*, May 2, 1896, 4)
West Oakland Lyceum (1907), Oakland (*IF*, June 15, 1907, 1)
New Era Debating and Literary Association, Oakland (*IF*, June 15, 1907, 1)
Dunbar Literary Society, Oakland (*OS*, March 20, 1915, 3)
Washington-Douglass Literary Society, San Francisco (*WO*, April 24, 1915, 3)
Bethel Literary Society, Oakland (*WO*, August 14, 1915, 2)
Athenian Literary and Art Club, San Diego (*Minutes of the Eleventh*, 59)
Zion Literary Society, Oakland (*WO*, December 18, 1926, 1)
Phys-Art-Lit-Mo Club, Los Angeles (*PNYA*, July 2, 1927, 3)
The Rho Club, Ro, Psi, Phi Medical Sorority, Los Angeles (*PNYA*, July 30, 1927, 4)
J. C. Price Literary Society, San Francisco (*WO*, February 25, 1928, 8)

Colorado
Colorado Springs Literary Society (*LNYA*, October 5, 1889, 3)
Church Aid Literary Society, Colorado Springs (*LNYA*, November 30, 1889, 3)
Pueblo Literary Society, Pueblo (*IF*, November 22, 1890, 2)
Ida B. Wells Literary Society, Leadville (*LH*, December 4, 1895, 2)
Twentieth Century Dramatic and Literary Club, Pueblo (*TP*, December 1, 1905, 2)
Colorado Springs Lyceum, Colorado Springs (*TP*, October 16, 1908, 3)
Eureka Literary Society, Denver (*TP*, January 7, 1910, 6)
Handy Chapel Literary Society, Grand Junction (*TP*, November 26, 1915, 8)
Dahlie Art and Literary Club, Colorado Springs (*Minutes of the Eleventh*, 59)
DuBois Reading Circle, Colorado Springs (*Minutes of the Eleventh*, 59)
Olympia Art and Literary Club, Colorado Springs (*Minutes of the Eleventh*, 59)
Delphian Literary Society, Denver (*KCP*, June 9, 1933, 3)

Connecticut

Literary and Religious Institution (1834), Hartford (Porter, "Organized Educational Activities," 558)
New Haven Literary and Debating Society (1841), New Haven (*CA*, February 27, 1841; *FDP*, September 28, 1855, 3; Ripley, *The Black Abolitionist Papers*, 168)
New London Lyceum, New London (*G*, April 21, 1883, 4)
Literary and Historical Association, New Haven (*G*, July 28, 1883, 4)
AME Zion Literary Society, New Haven (*G*, March 8, 1884, 1)
Langston Lyceum, New Haven (*G*, September 6, 1884, 4)
Young Men's Literary Society, Masonic Temple, New Haven (*NYF*, February 27, 1886, 4)
Norwich Literary Society, Norwich (*NYF*, May 1, 1886, 1)
New London Literary Society, New London (*NYF*, May 1, 1886, 1)
Philip A. Bell Literary and Aid Society, New Haven (*NYF*, July 24, 1886, 4)
Newport Historical Literary Society, Newport (*NYA*, January 11, 1890, 2)
Zion Literary Society, Hartford (*NYA*, March 29, 1890, 1)
Hamilton Literary Society, New London (*NYA*, May 31, 1890, 4)
St. John's Literary Society, New London (*NYA*, June 21, 1890, 4)
Ladies Lyceum, Hartford (*NYA*, June 21, 1890, 4)
Ocean House Literary, Newport (*NYA*, September 6, 1890, 4)
Newport Lyceum, Newport (*NYA*, September 6, 1890, 4)
YMCA Lyceum, New Haven (*IF*, March 14, 1891, 1)
Young People's Lyceum, South Norwalk (*IF*, March 28, 1891, 1)
AME Church Lyceum, Norwalk (*IF*, August 6, 1892, 1)
Calvary Lyceum, Norwalk (*IF*, August 6, 1892, 1)
Frederick Literary Society, New Haven (*CAW*, November 18, 1899, 5)

Delaware

Literary Society, Wilmington (*CA*, September 25, 1841, 117)
Garnet Literary Society, Wilmington (*G*, March 1, 1884, 1)
Ezion M. E. Church Lyceum (1890), Wilmington (*NYA*, June 28, 1890, 4)
Murray Lyceum, Wilmington (*NYA*, September 20, 1890, 1)
Bethel AME Literary Society, Wilmington (*NYA*, October 18, 1890, 1)
Payne Literary Society, Wilmington (*NYA*, October 25, 1890, 1)
Hopkin Lyceum, Gilbert Presbyterian Church, Wilmington (*NYA*, December 13, 1890, 3)
Zion M. E. Church Lyceum, Wilmington (*IF*, December 9, 1893, 5)

Florida

Young Men's Literary Society, Pensacola (*NYF*, February 5, 1887, 2)
Emerald Lyceum, Jacksonville (*IF*, December 12, 1891, 4)
Emerald Lyceum, Pensacola (*IF*, July 2, 1892, 5)

Georgia

Augusta Lyceum, Augusta (*G*, April 7, 1883, 2)
Athens Lyceum, Athens (*G*, May 12, 1883, 2)
Bruce Literary, Macon (*WB*, July 31, 1886, 1)
Atlanta Literary Society, Atlanta (*ST*, June 1, 1889, 2)
Gateway Literary Society, Decatur (*HG*, July 27, 1889, 3)[2]
E. A. Ware Lyceum, Savannah (*ST*, November 23, 1889, 3)
Baptist Church Lyceum, Decatur (*SC*, May 9, 1891, 4)
Philosophian Literary Society, Georgia State Industrial College, Savannah (*ST*, June 3, 1893, 3)
Ware Lyceum, Atlanta University, Atlanta (Logan, *Liberating Language*, 92)
Phyllis Wheatley Literary Club, Atlanta University, Atlanta (Little, "The Extra-Curricular Activities of Black College Students," 43)
Athene Literary Club, Atlanta University, Atlanta (Little, "The Extra-Curricular Activities of Black College Students," 43)
Douglass Literary Club, Atlanta University, Atlanta (Little, "The Extra-Curricular Activities of Black College Students," 43)
Henry Highland Garnet Literary Society, Savannah (*ST*, October 14, 1893, 2)
Columbus Literary Society, Columbus (*ST*, December 2, 1893, 3)
First Congressional Church Lyceum (1895), Savannah (*ST*, January 26, 1895, 3)
Young People's Lyceum of the First African Baptist Church, Savannah (*ST*, August 31, 1895, 3)
Young Men's Lyceum Club, Savannah (*ST*, November 2, 1895, 3)
Phi Kappa Literary Society, Savannah (*ST*, February 22, 1896, 2)
Washburn Lyceum, Beach Institute, Savannah (*ST*, March 13, 1897, 3)
Frederick Douglass Lyceum, Savannah (*ST*, May 29, 1897, 3)
Douglass Literary and Debating Society, Augusta (*CAW*, May 13, 1899, 5)
Ashburn Literary Society, Ashburn (*ST*, July 28, 1900, 2)
Savannah Literary Society, Savannah (*ST*, August 11, 1900, 2)
Phyllis Wheatley Literary Society, Georgia State Industrial College, Savannah (*ST*, December 8, 1900, 2)
Acme Literary Society, Georgia State Industrial College, Savannah (*ST*, February 23, 1901, 2)
Montezuma Literary Society, Montezuma (*ST*, December 16, 1902, 2)
Frederick Douglass Literary Society, Georgia State Industrial College, Savannah (*ST*, January 31, 1903, 2)
Frances E. W. Harper Literary Club, Savannah (*ST*, July 29, 1905, 5)
J. B. Ford Literary Society, Sengstacke Academy, Savannah (*ST*, March 24, 1906, 4)
Dunbar Memorial and Literary Society, Waycross (*ST*, April 23, 1910, 5)
Negro Historical and Literary Society, Atlanta (*ST*, February 3, 1912, 2)
Douglass Literary Society, Atlanta University, Atlanta (*ST*, April 24, 1915, 1)
Pi Gamma Literary Society, Morehouse College, Atlanta (*ST*, November 27, 1915, 6)
Waycross Literary Society, Waycross (*ST*, February 24, 1917, 5)
Frederick Douglass Literary Society, Waycross (*TP*, May 18, 1918, 6)
Progressive Boys' Literary Society, Savannah (*ST*, November 2, 1922, 5)

Idaho
Paul Lawrence Dunbar Lyceum (1907), Boise (*IF*, September 14, 1907, 4)

Illinois
Philosophy Literary Society, Chicago (*CG*, October 6, 1883, 4)
Acme Club, Chicago (*NYG*, April 12, 1884, 4)
Eastern Literary Society, Chicago (*NYG*, October 11, 1884, 4)
Prudence Crandall Club, Chicago (*NYF*, April 10, 1886, 4; *IF*, August 30, 1890, 8)
Metropolitan Club, Bethel AME (1890), Chicago (*IF*, April 26, 1890, 5)
Garden City Lyceum, Chicago (*IF*, January 4, 1890, 1)
Dumas Literary Circle, Chicago (*IF*, August 30, 1890, 8)
Bethel Literary Society (1891), Chicago (*IF*, December 26, 1891, 1; *ST*, January 28, 1911, 2)
Evanston Lyceum, Evanston (*IF*, January 3, 1891, 12)
Parlor Social Lyceum (1892), Cairo (*SC*, August 13, 1892, 1)
Quinn Chapel Lyceum, Chicago (*CG*, February 25, 1893, 2)
Fern Leaf Literary Society, Cairo (*IF*, June 10, 1893, 7)
Payne Literary Society, Chicago (*IF*, August 5, 1893, 1)
Chicago Woman's Club, Chicago (*CG*, February 9, 1895, 1; Knupfer, *Toward a Tenderer Humanity*, 115)
Phyllis Wheatley Club, Chicago (*IF*, December 12, 1896, 7; Knupfer, *Toward a Tenderer Humanity*, 115)
Neighborhood and Literary Society, Chicago (Knupfer, *Toward a Tenderer Humanity*, 114)
Grace Presbyterian Church Youth Lyceum (1899), Chicago (*BA*, October 14, 1899, 4)
Ideal Woman's Club, Chicago (*A*, August 19, 1899)
West End Woman's Club, Chicago (*WWA*, November 8, 1900, 5; Knupfer, *Toward a Tenderer Humanity*, 115)
Men's Sunday Lyceum, Chicago (*CAW*, April 6, 1901, 2)
Hyde Park Literary Society, Chicago (*IF*, January 25, 1902, 2)
St. John Lyceum, Springfield (*IF*, March 15, 1902, 4)
St. Mark's Sunday Lyceum, Chicago (*BA*, July 19, 1902, 1)
Woman's Club of Irving Park, Chicago (*IO*, November 8, 1903, 47; Knupfer, *Toward a Tenderer Humanity*, 115)
R. L. H. Literary Society, Riverside (*TP*, March 24, 1905, 3)
Frederick Douglass Center's Woman's Club, Chicago (*BA*, November 11, 1905, 4)
Frederick Douglass Center's Young People's Lyceum, Chicago (*BA*, November 11, 1905, 4)
Standard Literary Society, Chicago (*BA*, December 3, 1910, 3; *TP*, December 18, 1914, 7)
Englewood Lyceum, Chicago (*BA*, March 29, 1913, 2; see also Knupfer, *Toward a Tenderer Humanity*, 111)
St. Mark's Lyceum, Chicago (*BA*, September 13, 1913, 2)[3]
University Society Club, Chicago (*BA*, July 31, 1915, 4; Knupfer, *Toward a Tenderer Humanity*, 114)

Indiana

George W. Williams Literary Society, Jeffersonville (*NYG*, September 15, 1883, 2)
Independent Literary Society, Jeffersonville (*NYF*, October 1, 1887, 1)
Shorter Lyceum, Muncie (*CG*, January 14, 1888, 1)
Council Bluffs Lyceum, Council Bluffs (*IF*, January 17, 1891, 1)
Bethel Literary Circle, Indianapolis (*IF*, December 8, 1894, 4)
Trinity Mission Lyceum, Indianapolis (*IF*, November 30, 1895, 8)
Bethel Mite Lyceum, Indianapolis (*IF*, January 11, 1896, 8)
Walter's Chapel Lyceum, Indianapolis (*IF*, April 3, 1897, 1)
Wabash Literary Society, Wabash (*IF*, March 4, 1899, 7)
Olivet Literary Lyceum (1900), Indianapolis (*IR*, March 3, 1900, 3)
Sunday Afternoon Lyceum, Vincennes (*IR*, February 17, 1900, 1)
Olivet Church Young People's Literary Society, Indianapolis (*IR*, September 29, 1900, 4)
Allen Lyceum, Allen Chapel (1901), Indianapolis (*IF*, October 26, 1901, 8)
Matthew Simpson Epworth League, Indianapolis (*IF*, June 18, 1904, 8)

Iowa

Lyceum Educational Literary Society, Sioux City (*IF*, November 11, 1893, 4)
Douglass Lyceum (1897), Keokuk (*IF*, April 24, 1897, 1)
High Cynthians Lyceum, Keokuk (*IF*, April 24, 1897, 1)
Albia Literary Society (1898), Albia (*ISB*, November 18, 1898, 4)
Ne Plus Ultra Pardon Lyceum, Oskaloosa (*ISB*, January 21, 1898, 1)
Old Folks Lyceum, Des Moines (*ISB*, April 15, 1898, 1)
Paul L. Dunbar Lyceum, Des Moines (*ISB*, April 7, 1899, 1)
Young People's Lyceum, Mount Pleasant (*ISB*, July 29, 1899, 4)
Des Moines Negro Lyceum Society, Des Moines (*IF*, November 20, 1909, 4)

Kansas

Sumner Literary Society, Topeka (*HK*, March 12, 1880, 3)
Lawrence Literary Society, Lawrence (*WR*, September 14, 1883, 3)
Union Literary Society, Lawrence (*WR*, December 7, 1883, 3)
Olathe Literary Society, Olathe (*WR*, February 15, 1884, 3)
Wichita Literary Society, Wichita (*WR*, April 11, 1884, 3)
Union Literary-Lecture Association of Douglass Co., Lawrence (*WR*, April 11, 1884, 3)
Willing Workers Literary Society, Atchison (*WR*, May 9, 1884, 3)
Atchison Literary Society, Atchison (*WR*, June 27, 1884, 3)
Young Folks Literary Society, Lawrence (*WR*, August 15, 1884, 2)
Nicodemus Lyceum (1887), Nicodemus (*NE*, October 12, 1887, 4)
Fort Scott Lyceum, Fort Scott (*AC*, April 5, 1889, 4)[4]
East Creek Lyceum, Topeka (*AC*, April 26, 1889, 4)
Oxford Literary Society, Oxford (*LA*, November 16, 1889, 1)
Parlor Lyceum (1891), Atchison (*TO*, October 24, 1891, 2)
Columbian Literary Society, Kansas City (*LA*, June 27, 1891, 4)

John R. Lynch Lyceum, Baxter Springs (*SA*, July 23, 1891, 1)
Whittier Literary Society, Lawrence (*TO*, October 3, 1891, 2)
Tennesseetown Literary Society, Tennesseetown (*TC*, October 4, 1891, 1)
Shaungalunga Literary Society, Shaungalunga (*TC*, October 4, 1891, 1)
C. M. E. [Colored Methodist Episcopal] Literary Society, Topeka (*TO*, October 24, 1891, 3)
Langston Literary Society, Lawrence (*TO*, October 31, 1891, 3)
A. M. E. Church Literary Society, North Lawrence (*TO*, October 31, 1891, 3)
North Lawrence Baptist Literary Society, North Lawrence (*TC*, November 1, 1891, 1)
St. Mark's A. M. E. North Topeka Literary Society, North Topeka (*TC*, November 1, 1891, 1)
A. M. E. Literary Society, Kansas City (*TO*, November 7, 1891, 2)
American Progressive Literary Society, Topeka (*TC*, November 8, 1891, 1)
Pleasant Hour Reading and Literary Circle, Topeka (*TC*, November 8, 1891, 1)
Brown's Chapel A. M. E. Literary Society, Topeka[5]
C. M. E. Church Lyceum (1891), Topeka (*TC*, November 8, 1891, 1)
Garnett Literary Society, Garnett (*SA*, November 12, 1891, 4)
N. B. Alamode Literary Society, Baxter Springs (*SA*, November 12, 1891, 4)
Progressive Club, Lawrence (*TO*, December 5, 1891, 1)
Athenian Literary Society, Kansas City (*TO*, December 12, 1891, 3)
West Side Literary Society, Baxter Springs (*SA*, December 17, 1891, 4)
Coffeyville Literary Society, Coffeyville (*AAA*, March 4, 1892, 1)
Progressive Literary Society, Tennesseetown (*TO*, March 19, 1892, 3)
Evening Zephyr Literary Society, East Topeka (*TSL*, October 21, 1892, 1)
American Literary Society, Atchison (*AB*, October 29, 1892, 4)
Washington Street Lyceum, Topeka (*TC*, November 21, 1892, 3)
Platonian Literary Society (1893), Leavenworth (*LH*, March 24, 1894, 3)
8th Street Church Literary Society, Atchison (*AB*, January 28, 1893, 4)
Baptist Church Literary Society, Topeka (*TC*, March 19, 1893, 3)
Turner's Lyceum, Parsons (*PWB*, April 8, 1893, 3)
St. James A. M. E. Literary Society, Lawrence (*PWB*, April 22, 1893, 3)
Cherokee Literary Society, Cherokee (*PWB*, September 2, 1893, 3)
Platonian Literary Society, Hobson Normal Institute, Parsons (*PWB*, October 28, 1893, 3)
John Brown Lyceum, Wathena (*AB*, November 25, 1893, 3)
B. Y. P. U. [Baptist Young People's Union] Literary Society, Leavenworth (*LH*, April 14, 1894, 2)
Chanute Literary Society, Chanute (*PWB*, April 28, 1894, 4)
Girard Literary Society, Girard (*PWB*, May 5, 1894, 4)
Inter-State Literary Society, Atchison (*TSL*, October 26, 1894, 1)
Second Baptist Literary Society, Wichita (*NBW*, November 2, 1894, 8)
Tecumseh Literary Society, Tecumseh (*TSL*, November 2, 1894, 1)
Progressive Literary Association, Columbus (*PWB*, December 8, 1894, 3)
Kansas City Literary Society, Kansas City (*LH*, December 15, 1894, 3)

Vesper Literary Society, Kansas City (*LH*, December 15, 1894, 3)
Ida B. Wells Lyceum, Parsons (*PWB*, April 27, 1895, 4)
Wheatley Literary Society, Atchison (*LH*, June 15, 1895, 2)
Young Men's Progressive Club Literary Society, Parsons (*PWB*, August 24, 1895, 1)
Brilliant Literary Lights Society, Leavenworth (*LH*, August 31, 1895, 3)
B. P. Y. U. Literary Society, Topeka (*TSL*, April 24, 1896, 1)
Eden Literary Society, Topeka (*TSL*, April 24, 1896, 1)
Oswego Literary Society, Oswego (*PWB*, January 2, 1897, 1)
A. M. E. Literary Society, Coffeyville (*PWB*, January 23, 1897, 1)
M. E. Literary Society, Chetopa (*PWB*, February 27, 1897, 1)
Second Baptist Young People's Literary Club, Hutchinson (*NR*, October 23, 1897, 5)
A. M. E. Literary Society, Hutchinson (*NR*, October 23, 1897, 5)
Home Mission and Literary Society, Winfield (*PWB*, October 30, 1897, 1)
A. M. E. Literary Society, Winfield (*PWB*, November 13, 1897, 2)
James A. Handy Literary Society, Kansas City (*WCR*, February 5, 1898, 2)
Mound City Lyceum, Mound City (*FP*, April 22, 1898, 4)
Paola Literary Society, Paola (*FP*, November 4, 1898, 1, and March 10, 1899, 3)[6]
Paul Dunbar Literary Society, Emporia (*TP*, February 10, 1899, 4)
AME Church Literary Society, Wamego (*TP*, February 10, 1899, 2)
Wilberforce Literary Society, Emporia (*TP*, March 3, 1899, 2)
Bannaca Literary Society, Lawrence (*TP*, November 17, 1899, 4)[7]
Church Aid Literary Society, Topeka (*TP*, November 17, 1899, 3)
Valley Falls Literary Society, Valley Falls (*TP*, November 24, 1899, 3)
James A. Handy Literary Society, Western University, Kansas City (*TP*, February 2, 1900, 3)
Douglass Literary Society, Nicodemus (*TP*, February 23, 1900, 3)
Tabernacle Baptist Literary Society, Hutchinson (*TP*, March 2, 1900, 2)
Brown's Chapel A. M. E. Literary Society, Parsons (*PWB*, April 6, 1900, 1)
Baptist Lyceum, Junction City (*TP*, April 6, 1900, 2)
AME Literary Society, Ottawa (*TP*, April 6, 1900, 2)
Oak Leaf Art and Literary Society, Topeka (*TP*, April 13, 1900, 3)
Junction City Lyceum, Junction City (*TP*, June 1, 1900, 1)
Frederick Douglass Literary Society, Newton (*TP*, June 22, 1900, 4)
Vinita Literary Society, Vinita (*PWB*, September 21, 1900, 3)
St. James Baptist Literary Society, Emporia (*TP*, September 28, 1900, 3)
Lancaster Literary Society, Lancaster (*AC*, October 12, 1900, 3)
F. M. B. [First Missionary Baptist] Church Literary Society, Oskaloosa (*TP*, November 9, 1900, 4)
Educational Literary Society, Emporia (*TP*, December 7, 1900, 2)
Scicnerona Literary Society, Abilene (*TP*, January 25, 1901, 4)
Young Ladies' Lyceum of Warren St. Baptist Church, Lawrence (*TP*, May 10, 1901, 1)
Topeka Literary Society, Topeka (*TP*, September 27, 1901, 3)
Sterling Literary Society, Sterling (*TP*, November 22, 1901, 4)

Adelphia Art and Literary Club, Quindaro (*TP*, December 6, 1901, 4)
Booker T. Washington Literary Society, State Industrial College, Manhattan (*TP*, December 6, 1901, 4)
Daughters of the King Literary Society, Topeka (*TP*, December 6, 1901, 3)
Attucks Literary Society, Topeka (*TP*, December 6, 1901, 3)
Blossom Art and Literary Club, Wichita (*TP*, December 31, 1901, 4)
Up-to-Date Literary Society, Mount Olive Baptist Church, Paola (*TP*, December 31, 1901, 4)
Banneke Literary Society, Paola (*TP*, December 31, 1901, 4)[8]
Eureka Club, Lawrence (*TP*, December 31, 1901, 4)
Edward W. Blyden Lyceum Society, Kansas City (*AC*, January 17, 1902, 1)
Frederick Douglass Literary Society, Parsons (*TP*, February 7, 1902, 4)
Mission Church Literary Society, Kansas City (*AC*, March 7, 1902, 1)
The Forum, Lawrence (*TP*, May 2, 1902, 4)
Second Baptist Literary Society, Perry (*TP*, May 16, 1902, 4)
St. John Literary Society, Salina (*TP*, July 11, 1902, 4)
Marion Literary Society, Marion (*TP*, January 16, 1903, 4)
Progressive Literary Society, Baxter Springs (*TP*, February 13, 1903, 4)
Booker T. Washington Literary Society, State Industrial School for Boys, Topeka (*TP*, March 6, 1903, 3)
Central High School Lyceum, Club, Kansas City (*RS*, May 22, 1903, 5)
Galena Literary Society, Galena (*TP*, May 29, 1903, 4)
Tabernacle Baptist Church Literary Society, Wichita (*CC*, September 5, 1903, 2)
B Street Baptist Church Literary Society, Atchison (*TP*, November 20, 1903, 4)
Athenian Lyceum, Western University, Quindaro (*TP*, November 20, 1903, 3)
Lane Chapel C. M. E. Literary Society, Topeka (*TP*, December 4, 1903, 3)
Normal School Lyceum, Emporia (*WS*, January 2, 1904, 5)
Literati Society, Emporia (*WS*, January 2, 1904, 5)
Union Literary Society, Gate City (*TP*, January 22, 1904, 4)
Occidental Literary Society, Kansas City (*TP*, February 26, 1904, 3)
Winfield Literary Society, Winfield (*TP*, April 8, 1904, 4)
Washington Literary Society, Kansas City (*TP*, November 11, 1904, 3)
New Hope Literary Society, Topeka (*TP*, November 18, 1904, 3)
Pallacean Girls League, Lawrence (*TP*, January 6, 1905, 1)
The Coterie, Topeka (*TP*, January 6, 1905, 1)
Afternoon Circle, Atchison (*TP*, January 6, 1905, 1)
Du Bois Literary Society, Kansas City (*TP*, January 6, 1905, 1)
K. and L. of Protection Literary Society, Edwardsville (*TP*, January 6, 1905, 1)
Sunday Forum, Kansas City (*TP*, January 6, 1905, 1)
Eta Epsilon Delta Club, Topeka (*TP*, January 6, 1905, 1)
N. U. G. literary society, Salina (*TP*, June 23, 1905, 2)[9]
Toussant La Overture Literary Society, Wichita (*WS*, September 2, 1905, 2)
Treble Clef Literary Society, Kansas City (*TP*, November 24, 1905, 6)
Payne Literary Society, Iola (*TP*, November 24, 1905, 6)
St. John Baptist Church Lyceum, Weir City (*TP*, November 24, 1905, 8)

People's Literary, Parsons (*TP*, December 1, 1905, 2)
Musical Literary Society, Independence (*V*, December 1, 1905, 7)
Green Leaf Literary Society, Chanute (*V*, December 15, 1905, 1)
Evolution Literary Club, Evolution (*V*, December 22, 1905, 6)
Pratt Literary Society, Pratt (*WS*, November 10, 1906, 5)
Lehunt Literary Society, Lehunt (*TP*, January 25, 1907, 5)
Allen Chapel Literary Society, Salina (*SE*, January 14, 1909, 1)
St. Paul AME Church Literary Society, Wichita (*WS*, May 22, 1909, 5)
People's Literary Society, Lawrence (*TP*, November 19, 1909, 3)
Weir Literary Society, Weir (*TP*, November 26, 1909, 3)
AME Church Literary Society, Ellsworth (*TP*, January 7, 1910, 4)
AME Church Literary Society, Wellington (*WS*, March 12, 1910, 1)
John Brown Literary Society, Wichita (*WS*, November 12, 1910, 5)
AME Church Literary Society, Pittsburg (*TP*, December 16, 1910, 3)
Mt. Hebron Baptist Church Literary Society, Pittsburg (*TP*, December 16, 1910, 3)
Fairview Literary Society, Fairview (*TP*, November 10, 1911, 1)
Orient Literary Society, Kansas City (*TP*, February 9, 1912, 1)
Dunbar Literary Society, Topeka (*TP*, July 12, 1912, 5)
AME Literary Society, Independence (*TP*, September 13, 1912, 2)
AME Literary Society, Junction City (*TP*, October 4, 1912, 3)
Handy Literary Society, Hutchinson (*TP*, October 11, 1912, 2)
ME Literary Society, Manhattan (*TP*, December 6, 1912, 7)
Western Searchlight Literary Society, Stockton (*TP*, January 3, 1913, 5)
Silone Yates Literary Society, Olathe (*TP*, December 26, 1913, 2)
Hiawatha Literary Society, Hiawatha (*TP*, February 20, 1914, 7)
Union Literary Society, Kinsley (*TP*, May 1, 1914, 1)
Autumn Leaf Art Club and Literary Society, Fort Scott (*TP*, July 17, 1914, 2)
AME Church Literary Society, Paola (*TP*, October 23, 1914, 8; *TP*, October 27, 1922, 4)
Mutual Literary Society, El Dorado (*TP*, January 1, 1915, 1; *TP*, January 15, 1915, 7)
Senior Literary Society of Calvary Presbyterian, Topeka (*TP*, March 12, 1915, 5)
Progressive Literary Society, Manhattan (*TP*, April 2, 1915, 7)
AME Church Literary Society, Chanute (*TP*, July 30, 1915, 1)
Du Bois Literary Society, Newton (*TP*, January 7, 1916, 4)
East Side Literary Society of the Third Baptist Church, Topeka (*TP*, January 21, 1916, 5; *TP*, February 4, 1916, 5)
White Cloud Literary Society, White Cloud (*TP*, March 31, 1916, 6)
Pierian Literary Club, Kansas City (*KE*, April 22, 1916, 4)
Mount Olive Literary Society, Quindaro (*KCA*, July 14, 1916, 4)[10]
Grant Literary Society, Emporia (*TP*, December 14, 1917, 3)
Beacon Light Literary Society, Ottawa (*TP*, June 22, 1917, 2)
Frankfort Teachers' Reading Circle, Clinton School, Frankfort (*Minutes of the Eleventh Biennial Convention of the National Association of Colored Women*, 62)
Excelsior Literary Society, Weir (*TP*, April 4, 1919, 3)

Pierian Literary Society, Topeka (*TP*, February 27, 1920, 3)
N. C. Cleaves Literary Society, Wichita (*NS*, January 28, 1921, 4)
W. T. Vernon Literary Society, Arkansas City (*NS*, February 25, 1921, 4)
Yale Literary Society, Yale (*TP*, October 14, 1921, 1)
Alpha Literary Society, Parsons (*NS*, April 4, 1924, 4)
Cherryvale Literary Society, Cherryvale (*NS*, April 10, 1925, 4)
Mt. Zion Baptist Literary Society, Wichita (*NS*, December 10, 1926, 4)
Athenian Literary Society, Wichita (*NS*, December 10, 1926, 4)
Deborah Art and Literary Society, Shiloh Baptist Church, Topeka (*TP*, August 26, 1927, 1)
Garden City Literary Society, Garden City (*NS*, December 7, 1928, 1)
Dorcas Art and Literary Society, Topeka (*NS*, July 26, 1929, 1)
Literary Society, Kansas Vocational School, Topeka (*NS*, October 11, 1929, 3; *TP*, October 11, 1929, 2)
Excel Literary Society, Cherryvale (*NS*, February 19, 1932, 2)
Standard Literary Society, Metropolitan Baptist Church, Kansas City (*KCP*, January 13, 1933, 8)
Junior Literary Society, Metropolitan Baptist Church, Kansas City (*KCP*, September 8, 1933, 3)
Young People's Historical and Literary Society, Wichita (*NS*, November 10, 1933, 4)
Junior Missionary and Young People's Literary Society, Wichita (*KCP*, February 23, 1934, 5)
Negro Historical and Literary Society, Topeka (*KW*, October 23, 1937, 4)
AME Literary Society, Oskaloosa (*CP*, January 7, 1938, 7)
Second Baptist Literary Society, Wellington (*NS*, February 3, 1939, 2)

Kentucky
Literary and Musical Aid Society, Louisville (*NYF*, April 2, 1887, 4)
Paris Lyceum, Paris (*CG*, April 30, 1887, 1)
Wayman Lyceum, Harrodsburgh (*IF*, March 12, 1892, 4)
Whittier Lyceum, Frankfort (*P*, March 24, 1893, 2)
Y. G. and L. Reading Circle, Bowling Green (*IF*, January 6, 1894, 8)
Bowling Green Lyceum, Bowling Green (*IF*, January 6, 1894, 8)
Epsworth League, Bowling Green (*IF*, June 16, 1894, 1)
Pleasant Green Baptist Church Literary Society, Lexington (*LS*, January 27, 1900, 4)
Citizens' Lyceum (1905), Louisville (*IF*, November 25, 1905)[11]
Bacon Literary Society, Louisville (*ST*, December 10, 1910, 6)

Louisiana
Southern Literary Society, New Orleans (*NODC*, November 10, 1856, 2)
Langston Literary Association, New Orleans (*NOT*, May 11, 1865, 2)
Progressive Literary Society (1871), New Orleans (*WL*, March 5, 1871, 5)
Amelicus Club, New Orleans (*WL*, August 28, 1875, 2)
New Orleans University Literary Society, New Orleans (*WL*, May 15, 1880, 3)

Rose Bud Literary Society, New Orleans (*WL*, February 5, 1881, 3)
Literary and Debating Society, New Orleans (*WL*, May 21, 1881, 3)
Hespurian Literary Society, New Orleans (*WL*, May 28, 1881, 3)
St. James Literary Society, New Orleans (*WL*, July 16, 1881, 3)
Rose Bud Literary Society, Shreveport (*WL*, October 22, 1881, 3)
Cooperators Benevolent and Literary Association (1884), New Orleans (*WP*, June 29, 1889, 3)
Frederick Douglass Literary Society (1887), St. Helena (*WP*, July 23, 1887, 2)
Sumner Literary Society, Straight University, New Orleans (*WP*, January 29, 1887, 1)
Philomathean Literary Society, Straight University, New Orleans (*WP*, January 29, 1887, 1)
Acanthus Literary Society, New Orleans (*WP*, January 29, 1887, 3)
Mareschal Neil Literary Circle, New Orleans (*WP*, February 5, 1887, 3)
Leland Lyceum, Leland University, New Orleans (*WP*, February 5, 1887, 1)
Iolanthe Literary Circle, New Orleans (*WP*, March 5, 1887, 3)
Calanthe Literary Circle, New Orleans (*WP*, April 9, 1887, 3)
Dew Drop Social and Literary Circle, New Orleans (*WP*, April 16, 1887, 3)
Mallalièu Literary Society, New Orleans (*WP*, May 21, 1887, 2)
Sumner Social and Literary Circle, Shreveport (*WP*, July 2, 1887, 2)
St. John the Baptist Literary and Benevolent Society, Algiers (*WP*, July 16, 1887, 4)
Opelousa Literary Society, Opelousa (*WP*, July 30, 1887, 2)[12]
Philomathean Literary and Social Circle, New Iberia (*WP*, July 30, 1887, 2)
Camellia-Japonica Literary Circle, New Orleans (*WP*, October 1, 1887, 3)
Philomathean Literary Club, New Orleans (*WP*, April 20, 1889, 3)
Golden Leaf Social and Literary Club, New Orleans (*WP*, August 31, 1889, 3)
Platonic Lyceum, New Orleans (*IF*, November 29, 1890, 6)
Tulane Avenue Baptist Church Lyceum, New Orleans (*IF*, October 10, 1891, 1)

Maine

Gardiner Lyceum (by 1827), Gardiner (*FJ*, November 30, 1827, 3)

Maryland

Young Men's Mental Improvement Society for the Discussion of Moral and Philosophical Questions of All Kinds (before 1835), Baltimore (Porter, "Organized Educational Activities," 558)
Phoenix Society (before 1835), Baltimore (Porter, "Organized Educational Activities," 558)
East Baltimore Mental Improvement Society (1837 or 1838), Baltimore (Douglass, *The Life and Times of Frederick Douglass*, 15)
Galbreth Lyceum (by 1859), Baltimore (*WAA*, September 7, 1859, 2; *WB*, April 11, 1885, 2)[13]
Baltimore Lyceum (1860), Baltimore (*WAA*, June 2, 1860, 3)
Lone Star Lyceum, Baltimore (*WAA*, March 10, 1860, 3)
King Solomon Lyceum, Baltimore (*WAA*, June 2, 1860, 3)

216   Appendix

Clinton Lyceum, Baltimore (*WAA*, June 2, 1860, 3)
Bethel Moral and Mental Improvement Society, Baltimore (*WAA*, June 2, 1860, 3)
Ebenezer Church Lyceum, Baltimore (*WAA*, June 2, 1860, 3)
Nazarite Lyceum (1879), Baltimore (*AC*, April 19, 1879, 3)
St. Paul's Lyceum, Baltimore (*PA*, October 30, 1880, 1)
Roxana Literary Association, Baltimore (*G*, May 26, 1883, 4)
Bethesda Literary Society, Georgetown (*PA*, September 6, 1883, 6)
Junior Assembly Literary Circle, Baltimore (*G*, June 28, 1884, 1)
Wendell Phillips Literary Society, Baltimore (*NYF*, April 24, 1886, 4)
Charles Sumner Lyceum, Baltimore (*NYF*, April 24, 1886, 4)
Benjamin Brown, Sr. Literary Society, Baltimore (*NYF*, April 24, 1886, 4)
Nonpareil Musical and Literary Society, Baltimore (*NYF*, May 15, 1886, 4)
Lincoln Literary Club, Baltimore (*NYF*, May 29, 1886, 4)
Monumental Literary Club, Baltimore (*WB*, June 5, 1886, 2)
Young Ladies' Christian Lyceum, Baltimore (*WB*, June 12, 1886, 4)
St. John's Lyceum (1887), Still Pond (*NYF*, April 2, 1887, 4)
St. John's Lyceum, Stanley (*NYF*, April 2, 1887, 4)
Wesley Literary Society, Baltimore (*IF*, November 22, 1890, 2)
Monumental Literary and Scientific Association, Baltimore (*IF*, February 27, 1892, 3)
Dickersons Lyceum, Harvredegrace (*IF*, May 14, 1892, 6)
Xavier Lyceum, Baltimore (*BAA*, October 26, 1895, 3)
St. Mary's Lyceum, Baltimore (*IF*, February 8, 1896, 5)
Young Men's Literary Society, Ocean City (*CAW*, July 21, 1900, 9)
Ocean City Lyceum, Ocean City (*CAW*, August 18, 1900, 5)
Eliza Smith's Lyceum, Princess Anne (*CAW*, February 28, 1903, 9)
B. O. Byrd Lyceum, Princess Anne Academy, Princess Anne (*CAW*, November 21, 1903, 13)
Pikesville Literary Society, Pikesville (*BC*, July 24, 1915, 3)[14]

Massachusetts
Young Ladies Literary Society (1827), Lynn (*FJ*, August 24, 1827, 3)
Literary Institution of Topsfield, Topsfield (*FJ*, August 8, 1828, 1)
Afric-American Female Intelligence Society (1832), Boston (Porter, "Organized Educational Activities," 558)
Young Men's Debating Society (1834), Boston (*TL*, October 10, 1835, 162)
Thompson Literary and Debating Society (before 1835), Boston (Porter, "Organized Educational Activities," 558)
Boston Philomathean Society (1836), Boston (*TL*, April 2, 1836; *EFA*, September 29, 1842; Lamontagne, "A Study of Black Intellectual and Literary Societies")
Adelphic Union for the Promotion of Literature and Science (1836), Boston (*EFA*, September 29, 1842, 87; Lamontagne, "A Study of Black Intellectual and Literary Societies"; Porter, "Organized Educational Activities," 558)
Wilberforce Debating Society of New Bedford, New Bedford (*CA*, March 7, 1840)
Young Men's Literary Society (1845), Boston (Muhammad, "Literacy Development and Practices," 7; Porter, "Organized Educational Activities," 558)

New Bedford Lyceum, New Bedford (*FDP*, March 23, 1849, 2)
Worcester Lyceum, Worcester (*WAA*, January 28, 1860, 1)
Ladies' Sewing Society Literary Club, Great Barrington (*G*, May 26, 1883, 4)
Banneker Club, Boston (*G*, March 29, 1884, 4; *NYF*, June 4, 1887, 1)
Garrison Lyceum, Boston (*G*, September 27, 1884, 4)[15]
Clinton Literary Society, Boston (*G*, October 11, 1884, 4)
Young People's Literary Society, Worcester (*NYF*, February 6, 1886, 4)
Young People's Industrial, Social, and Literary Union, New Bedford (*NYF*, March 13, 1886, 4)
Tawawa Literary Society, New Bedford (*NYF*, March 5, 1887, 1)
Literary Union, New Bedford (*NYF*, March 5, 1887, 1)
Sumner Literary Society, Lynn (*NYF*, March 5, 1887, 4)
Garnett Literary Society, 12th Baptist Church, Boston (*NYF*, May 21, 1887, 1, and May 28, 1887, 1)
Central Labor Lyceum, Boston (*NYF*, June 4, 1887, 1)
Cambridge Lyceum, Boston (*IF*, November 14, 1891, 5)
Smith Lyceum, New Bedford (*NYA*, January 9, 1892, 1)
Young Men's Lyceum, Springfield (*IF*, March 12, 1892, 2)
Springfield Lyceum (1893), Springfield (*IF*, February 25, 1893, 8)
Boston Literary and Historical Association (1901), Boston (*W*, December 8, 1906, 1)
Lincoln Musical and Literary Club, Boston (*Minutes of the Eleventh Biennial Convention of the National Association of Colored Women*, 64)

Michigan
Young Men's Lyceum and Debating Society (before 1846), Detroit (Porter, "Organized Educational Activities," 558)
Oak and Ivy Literary Club, Detroit (*G*, April 17, 1883, 1)
St. Matthews Lyceum, Detroit (*IF*, January 5, 1889, 5)[16]
Bethel Church Lyceum, Detroit (*P*, October 4, 1889, 5)
Second Baptist Church Lyceum, Detroit (*P*, November 1, 1889, 6)
Second Baptist Church Lyceum, Ann Arbor (*P*, August 15, 1890, 2)
Adrian Lyceum, Adrian (*P*, October 31, 1890, 2)
Ladies' Lyceum, Ypsilanti (*P*, March 20, 1891, 4)[17]
Arnett Chapel Lyceum, Grand Rapids (*IF*, November 4, 1899, 2)

Minnesota
Robert Banks Literary Society, St. Paul-Minneapolis (*WL*, August 28, 1875, 2)
AME Church Mite Literary Society, St. Paul (*G*, December 22, 1883, 1)
Shorter Lyceum, Minneapolis (*WA*, February 4, 1888, 4)
Labor Lyceum for Women, St. Paul (*IF*, July 20, 1889, 7)
Entre Nous Literary Society, St. Paul (*BA*, August 11, 1895, 8)
Young Men's Christian Association, St. Paul-Minneapolis (*WWA*, April 18, 1901, 8)
Bethesda Lyceum, Minneapolis (*A*, May 2, 1903, 3)
Baptist Church Literary Society, St. Paul (*A*, May 27, 1911, 3)

Social and Literary Society, St. Paul (*A*, May 31, 1913, 3)
Zion Presbyterian Literary Society, St. Paul (*A*, October 24, 1914, 4)
Adelphia Club, St. Paul (*Minutes of the Eleventh Biennial Convention of the National Association of Colored Women*, 65)

Mississippi

Rust Literary Society, Holly Springs (*HG*, February 16, 1884, 3)
Golden Leaf Lyceum, Aberdeen (*IF*, August 1, 1891, 5)
Lyceum, Alcorn University, Rodney (*IF*, November 12, 1892, 6)
Literary Gem Society, Alcorn University, Rodney (*IF*, November 12, 1892, 6)
AME Church Lyceum (1893), Grenada (*IF*, February 11, 1893, 8)
Young Men's Lyceum, Jackson College, Jackson (*TSL*, February 17, 1893, 2)
Douglass Lyceum, Shannon (*IF*, February 16, 1895, 1)
Young People's Lyceum, Water Valley (*IF*, September 14, 1895, 2)
Fisk Literary Society, Haven Institute, Meridian (*ST*, December 18, 1897, 3)[18]

Missouri

Excelsior Literary Society, Lincoln Institute, Jefferson City (*G*, June 23, 1883, 4)
Mt. Zion Lyceum (1890), Trenton (*NYA*, November 15, 1890, 4)
Willing Workers Lyceum (1890), St. Joseph (*LA*, December 6, 1890, 3)
Ciceronian Literary Society, Kansas City (*TO*, September 4, 1891, 3)
Frances Street Baptist Church Lyceum, St. Joseph (*TO*, November 28, 1891, 1)
New Hope Baptist Lyceum, St. Joseph (*TO*, December 26, 1891, 3)
AME Church Lyceum, St. Joseph (*TO*, December 26, 1891, 3)
Joplin Literary Society, Joplin (*SA*, January 21, 1892, 4)
Benevolence Literary Society, Sedalia (*TO*, February 27, 1892, 3)
Athenian Literary Society, Sedalia (*TO*, March 12, 1892, 3)[19]
Mt. Hope Lyceum, St. Joseph (*AB*, February 11, 1893, 4)
Elite Lyceum, St. Louis (*P*, May 12, 1893, 6)
Brunswick High School Literary Society, Brunswick (*LH*, October 5, 1895, 2)
Unity Baptist Literary Society, Joplin (*PWB*, September 25, 1897, 1)
St. John's Baptist Literary Society, Joplin (*PWB*, September 25, 1897, 1)
St. Paul Baptist Literary Society, Kansas City (*AC*, May 6, 1898, 1)
Alumni of the St. Joseph Colored High School Literary Society, St. Joseph (*TP*, December 22, 1899, 3)
Athenian Literary Society, George R. Smith College, Sedalia (*TP*, December 6, 1901, 4)
Masonian Literary Society, George R. Smith College, Sedalia (*TP*, December 6, 1901, 4)
Lyceum Sketch Club, St. Louise (1904) (*SLP*, January 16, 1904, 1)
Book Lovers Club, Kansas City (1904) (*TP*, April 15, 1910, 4; *Minutes of the Eleventh Biennial Convention of the National Association of Colored Women*, 651; Davis, *Lifting as They Climb*, 414)
AME Church Literary Society, Liberty (*TP*, February 3, 1905, 8)

Douglass Lyceum, St. Joseph (*IF*, April 8, 1905, 1)
Douor Club, Kansas City (*TP*, November 24, 1905, 1)
Pandora Circle, Kansas City (*TP*, November 24, 1905, 1)
Second Baptist Church B.Y.P.U. Literary Society, Kansas City (*TP*, November 24, 1905, 6)
The Square Deal Literary Society, Kansas City (*TP*, November 24, 1905, 6)
Burn's Lyceum, Kansas City (*TP*, November 24, 1905, 6)
Y.M.C.A. Literary Society, Kansas City (*TP*, November 24, 1905, 6)
M. E. Church Literary Society, Joplin (*TP*, December 1, 1905, 2)
Zion AME Church Literary Society, Lexington (*TP*, March 27, 1908, 3)
Trenton Literary Society, Trenton (*TP*, July 30, 1915, 3)
Mount Olive Literary Society, Gallatin (*TP*, August 6, 1915, 4)
Dunbar Literary Society, Fayette (*TP*, April 21, 1916, 1)
Twilight Literary Society, Kinsley (*TP*, June 16, 1916, 7)
Harmony Art and Literary Club, Kansas City (*Minutes of the Eleventh Biennial Convention of the National Association of Colored Women*, 65)
The Woman's Musical and Literary Club, Springfield (*TP*, July 5, 1918, 4)
Pierian Literary Society, Lincoln Institute, Jefferson City (*TP*, May 28, 1920, 1)
Biblical Literary Society, Vandalia (*TP*, April 8, 1938, 8)

Montana
St. James Literary Society, Helena (*IF*, February 3, 1894, 6)
Wordsworth Lyceum, Helena (*OE*, December 7, 1895, 4)
AME Church Literary Society (1907), Butte (*CG*, December 14, 1907, 2)

Nebraska
Progressive Age Literary Club (1871), Omaha (*OE*, April 4, 1896, 3)[20]
Do All Things Well Club, Omaha (*NYF*, September 24, 1887, 2)
Solan Literary Society, Council Bluffs (*IF*, November 22, 1890, 2)
Bishop Worthington Lyceum, Omaha (*PWB*, December 9, 1893, 2)
Mt. Zion Baptist Church Literary Society, Lincoln (*OE*, February 1, 1896, 4)
Mt. Pisgah Baptist Church Literary Society, Omaha (*OE*, March 14, 1896, 3)
Baptist Literary Society, Nebraska City (*OE*, May 23, 1896, 4)
Nebraska City Literary Society, Nebraska City (*OE*, July 11, 1896, 4)
St. John's AME Church Literary Society, Omaha (*AAS*, September 4, 1897, 2)
Newman M. E. Church Literary Society, Lincoln (*IR*, March 24, 1900, 1)
Progressive Literary Society, Omaha (*TP*, November 19, 1909, 6)

New Jersey
Tyro and Literary Association (1832), Newark (Porter, "Organized Educational Activities," 558)
Literary Society, Newark (*WAA*, November 12, 1859, 1)
Langston Musical and Literary Lyceum, Jersey City (*NYF*, February 6, 1886, 3)

Sunday School Literary Association, Newark (*NYF*, October 9, 1886, 4)
Newark Literary Society, Newark (*NYF*, February 12, 1887, 1)
Bethel AME Church Literary Society, Newark (*NYF*, October 1, 1887, 1)
Young Ladies' Literary Society, Sommerville (*NYA*, January 11, 1890, 1)
Palmer Lyceum, Newark (*NYA*, February 8, 1890, 4)
Young People's Literary Association of the 4th Baptist Church, Elizabeth (*NYA*, March 8, 1890, 4)
Whittier Literary Society, Orange (*NYA*, April 5, 1890, 4)
Ariston Literary Society, Jersey City (*NYA*, April 19, 1890, 4)
Zion Lyceum, Paterson (*NYA*, May 3, 1890, 4)[21]
Wilson Union Lyceum, Newark (*NYA*, August 9, 1890, 1)
Star Lyceum, Newark (*NYA*, August 16, 1890, 4)
Zion Lyceum, Jersey City (*NYA*, August 16, 1890, 4)
Douglass Lyceum, Paterson (*NYA*, September 27, 1890, 4)
J. P. Sampson Literary Society, Asbury Park, (*NYA*, September 26, 1891, 4)
Presbyterian Church Young People's Literary Association, Newark (*NYA*, November 19, 1892, 1)
Zion Literary Society, Atlantic City (*IF*, July 15, 1893, 5)
Memorial Literary Society, Atlantic City (*IF*, July 15, 1893, 5)
Asbury Lyceum, Atlantic City (*IF*, July 15, 1893, 5)
Franklin ME Church Summer Literary and Debating Society, Cape May (*CAW*, July 22, 1899, 2)
Labor Lyceum, Paterson (*AA*, October 20, 1900, 4)
J. C. Price Lyceum, Asbury Park (*CAW*, July 20, 1901, 12)

New Mexico
AME Lyceum, East Las Vegas (*TP*, June 3, 1910, 8)
Phyllis Wheatley Literary Club, Las Vegas (*TP*, August 14, 1914, 4)

New York
Philomathean Literary Society (1826), New York City (*CA*, April 29, 1837; *PA*, February 19, 1881, 2)
African Clarkson Society (1829), New York City (Porter, "Organized Educational Activities," 557)[22]
Female Lundy Society (1833), Albany (*NYA*, May 30, 1891, 4)[23]
Phoenix Society (1833–1839), New York City (*TL*, June 29, 1833; *CA*, July 7, 1838, and February 16, 1839)
Troy Female Benevolent Society (1833), Troy (*CA*, April 1, 1837, 1)
Phoenixonian Literary Society (1833), New York City (*CA*, July 8, 1837, 1, September 4, 1839, February 6, 1841, and July 3, 1841)
Ladies Literary and Dorcas Society (1833), Rochester (Porter, "Organized Educational Activities," 558)
Garrison Literary and Benevolent Association (1834), New York City (*TL*, April 19, 1834, 63; Porter, "Organized Educational Activities," 558)

Ladies' Literary Society (1834), New York City (*CA*, September 23, 1837; *FDP*, March 24, 1854, 4; *PA*, February 21, 1880, 3; Porter, "Organized Educational Activities")
Literary Society (1835), Poughkeepsie (Porter, "Organized Educational Activities," 558; *CA*, September 19, 1839)
New York Juvenile Literary Society, New York City (*AR*, May 1, 1835, 146)
Mental and Moral Improvement Society (before 1837), Troy (Porter, "Organized Educational Activities," 558; *CA*, October 14, 1837)
Debating Society (before 1837), Buffalo (*CA*, November 4, 1837; Porter, "Organized Educational Activities," 558)
Young Ladies Literary Society (before 1837), Buffalo (*CA*, November 4, 1837; *CA*, February 3, 1838; Porter, "Organized Educational Activities," 558)
Female Dorcas Society (before 1837), Buffalo (*CA*, November 4, 1837)
Troy Literary Society (before 1837), Troy (Porter, "Organized Educational Activities," 558; *TP*, December 12, 1902, 2)
Debating Society, (before 1837) Troy (Porter, "Organized Educational Activities," 558)
Union Society of Albany (1837), Troy and Vicinity for the Improvement of the Colored People in Morals, Education and the Mechanic Arts, Albany (*CA*, April 15, 1837)
Men's Literary Society, Buffalo (*CA*, November 4, 1837)
Juvenile Literary Society, Buffalo (*CA*, November 4, 1837)
Phoenixonian Library and Debating Society (1839), Poughkeepsie (*CA*, September 19, 1839)
Union Lyceum (1839), New York City (*CA*, November 23, 1839)
Eclectic Fraternity, New York City (*CA*, October 5, 1839)
Franklin Forum, New York City (*CA*, October 5, 1839)
Tyro Association, New York City (*CA*, October 5, 1839)
Literary and Library Union (1841), New York City (*CA*, March 6, 1841, 2)
Hamilton Lyceum (1841), New York City (*CA*, December 25, 1841, 151)[24]
Albany Literary and Debating Society, Albany (*NSFA*, March 10, 1842, 31)
Debating Society (before 1843), Rochester (Porter, "Organized Educational Activities," 558)
Debating Society (before 1843), Schenectady (Porter, "Organized Educational Activities," 558)
Ladies' Literary and Progressive Association, Buffalo (*NSR*, May 11, 1849, 3; Francis, "To a Charitable Public"; Francis, "Buffalo")[25]
Young Men's Debating and Mental Improvement Society, Rochester (*FDP*, December 3, 1852)
Young Men's Literary Productive Society No. 1, New York City (*FDP*, October 27, 1854, 2)
New York Literary and Productive Union, New York City (*FDP*, February 9, 1855, 3)[26]
New York Library Association, New York City (*FDP*, March 2, 1855, 3)
Youth's Literary Society (1857), New York City (*WAA*, November 12, 1859, 1)[27]
Williamsburg Lyceum (1857), Williamsburg (*WAA*, February 4, 1860, 2)
Utica Literary Society (1859), Utica (*WAA*, February 25, 1860, 2)
Ladies' Literary Society, Troy (*WAA*, November 5, 1859, 1)
Empire Club, Brooklyn (*WAA*, November 12, 1859, 1)

Ariel Club, New York City (*WAA*, November 12, 1859, 1)
Young Men's Literary Association, New York City (*WAA*, November 26, 1859, 3)
Hudson Lyceum, Hudson (*WAA*, December 31, 1859, 3)
Niagara Literary Association (1860), Niagara (*WAA*, June 30, 1860, 1)
Welsey Methodist Literary Association (1860), Saratoga Springs (*WAA*, July 14, 1860, 3)
Young Men's Union Christian Association Literary and Debating Society, New York City (*PA*, June 7, 1879, 2)
AME Zion Sunday School Clintonian Lyceum (1883), New York City (*G*, March 17, 1883, 3)
Bethel Literary Association, New York City (*G*, January 20, 1883, 3)
Lincoln Literary and Musical Association, New York City (*G*, January 20, 1883, 3)
Brooklyn Labor Lyceum, Brooklyn (*G*, March 3, 1883, 3)
St. Mark's Lyceum, New York City (*G*, March 10, 1883, 3)
Madison Avenue Congregational Church Literary Society, New York City (*WB*, June 2, 1883, 4)
Saratoga Literary and Historical Association, Saratoga Springs (*G*, August 11, 1883, 1)
Young Ladies' Literary Society, Utica (*G*, November 17, 1883, 4)
Douglass Lyceum, Norwich (*G*, December 8, 1883, 4)
Liberty Literary Society, Troy (*G*, December 15, 1883, 4)
Oneida Literary Society, Oneida (*G*, January 19, 1884, 1)
Excelsior Lyceum, Syracuse (*G*, January 19, 1884, 4)
15th Street Union Church Lyceum, New York City (*G*, February 23, 1884, 3)
Young Men's Literary Society, Kingston (*G*, March 1, 1884, 4)
AME Church Mutual Aid Literary Society, Albany (*G*, July 26, 1884, 1)
Lincoln Literary Lyceum, New York City (*G*, August 9, 1884, 3)
Goldey Literary Society, New York City (*G*, September 27, 1884, 3)
Brooklyn Literary Union (1886), Brooklyn (*NYF*, April 24, 1886, 3)
Carleton Junior Literary Society, Albany (*NYF*, January 2, 1886, 4)
Shiloh Lyceum, New York City (*NYF*, January 16, 1886, 3)
Sumner Literary Society, Ithaca (*NYF*, January 23, 1886, 4)
Literary and Sinking Fund Society, St. Augustine Protestant Episcopal Church, Brooklyn (*NYF*, February 27, 1886, 3)
Mignonette Social and Literary Club, New York City (*NYF*, February 27, 1886, 3)
Wendell Phillips Literary Society, Troy (*NYF*, March 6, 1886, 1)[28]
Tuesday Night Lenten Club, New York City (*NYF*, April 10, 1886, 3)
Third Baptist Church Progressive Society, Springfield (*NYF*, April 17, 1886, 1)
Lansingburgh Literary Society, Lansingburgh (*NYF*, May 1, 1886, 1)
Bridge Street Lyceum, New York City (*NYF*, May 1, 1886, 3)
James Morris Williams Lyceum, Brooklyn (*NYF*, May 22, 1886, 3)
AME Bethel Church Literary Society, Brooklyn (*NYF*, July 24, 1886, 3)
Presbyterian Literary Society, Troy (*NYF*, November 27, 1886, 4)
Metropolitan Literary Society, Buffalo (*NYF*, January 15, 1887, 4)

Lockport Literary Society, Lockport (*NYF*, February 5, 1887, 1)
Mignonette Social and Literary League, New York City (*NYF*, February 12, 1887, 3)
AME Lyceum, Jamaica (*NYF*, June 11, 1887, 4)
Waiters' Literary Society, Ithaca (*NYF*, July 9, 1887, 4)
Zion Lyceum, Ithaca (*NYF*, July 9, 1887, 4)
Mt. Olivet Literary Society, New York City (*NYF*, August 6, 1887, 3)
Abyssinia Baptist Church Lyceum, New York City (*NYF*, August 6, 1887, 3)
Jamaica Literary Society, Jamaica (*NYF*, September 17, 1887, 4)
Poughkeepsie Lyceum, Poughkeepsie (*WB*, January 14, 1888, 1)
Fort William Henry Literary Society, Lake George (*WB*, July 28, 1888, 3)
Christian Mission Lyceum, New York City (*NYA*, November 2, 1889, 1)
Stitt Lyceum, Newburgh (*NYA*, November 16, 1889, 4)
Eastern District Lyceum, New York City (*NYA*, November 23, 1889, 3)
Church Aid and Literary Society of St. Augustine's P. E. Mission, Brooklyn (*NYF*, November 30, 1889, 3)
AME Zion Lyceum, Tarrytown (*NYA*, December 7, 1889, 4)
Zion Lyceum, Kingston (*NYA*, December 28, 1889, 4)
Zion Lyceum (1890), Saratoga Springs (*NYA*, October 25, 1890, 1)
Baptist Church Lyceum (1890), Flushing (*NYA*, December 13, 1890, 3)
Buffalo Lyceum, Buffalo (*P*, January 10, 1890, 2)
Zion Church Lyceum, Buffalo (*NYA*, January 11, 1890, 3)
Shiloh Lyceum, Newburgh (*NYF*, January 18, 1890, 5)[29]
West Indian Literary and Mutual Society, New York City (*NYA*, January 25, 1890, 3)
Union Lyceum, New York City (*NYA*, January 25, 1890, 3)
AME Zion Lyceum, Peekskill (*NYA*, February 22, 1890, 4)
Bradley Lyceum, Portchester (*NYA*, March 22, 1890, 4)
Ladies' Literary Society, Peekskill (*NYA*, June 7, 1890, 4)
St, John's Lyceum, Orange (*NYA*, June 14, 1890, 4)
Literary Society of St. Benedict's, New York City (*NYA*, October 4, 1890, 3)
St. John's Literary, Brooklyn (*NYA*, October 18, 1890, 3)
AME Zion Church Literary Society, Derby (*A*, November 8, 1890, 4)
Rochester Lyceum, Rochester (1891) (*NYA*, December 26, 1891, 4)
AME Zion Church Lyceum, Sag Harbor (*NYA*, January 17, 1891, 4)
AME Zion Lyceum, Elmira (*NYA*, April 11, 1891, 4)
J. G. W. Musical and Literary Society, Rochester (*NYA*, April 18, 1891, 1)
Concord Literary Circle, Brooklyn (*A*, May 2, 1891, 2)
Silver Key Literary Society, Rochester (*NYA*, July 18, 1891, 2)
United Literary Society, Saratoga Springs (*NYA*, August 8, 1891, 4)
Baptist Mission Literary Society, New York City (*NYA*, August 15, 1891, 3)
Turner Lyceum, Brooklyn (*NYA*, August 22, 1891, 3)
Golden Censer Literary Society of the Nazarene Congregational Church, Brooklyn (*NYA*, September 26, 1891, 3)
AME Zion Church Young People's Lyceum, Elmira (*A*, December 5, 1891, 2)
Smith Lyceum, Harlem (*A*, December 5, 1891, 2)

Salem Mission Baptist Church Lyceum, Brooklyn (*NYA*, January 9, 1892, 3)
Star Lyceum, Brooklyn (*NYA*, January 30, 1892, 1)
Zion Lyceum, Harlem (*NYA*, January 30, 1892, 1)
Seidel Musical and Literary Society, Brooklyn (*NYA*, February 6, 1892, 1)
S. L. C. Lyceum of the Douglass Memorial Church, Elmira (*IF*, December 3, 1898, 3)
Frederick Douglass Literary Society, Saratoga Springs (*AC*, August 10, 1899, 1)
Trinity Lyceum, Brooklyn (*IF*, October 13, 1900, 4)
T. O. C. Club, Buffalo (*IF*, August 3, 1901, 1)
Frederick Douglass Lyceum, Buffalo (*CAW*, August 17, 1901, 11)
F. M. D. Ward Literary Society, New York City (*TP*, November 22, 1901, 3)
Young People's Lyceum, Hamilton Street AME Church, Albany (*CAW*, May 2, 1903, 10)
Yonkers Lyceum, Yonkers (*CAW*, June 13, 1903, 3)

North Carolina
Oak City Lyceum, Raleigh (*G*, January 27, 1883, 1)
Congregational Church Lyceum, Raleigh (*NYF*, March 5, 1887, 1)
Elm City Lyceum (1890), New Berne (*IF*, November 1, 1890, 6)
Warrenton Lyceum, Warrenton (*NYA*, May 17, 1890, 5)
Lincoln Lyceum (1893), Washington (*IF*, May 13, 1893, 4)
Lincoln Lyceum, Wilmington (*IF*, June 3, 1893, 4)[30]
Hickory Literary Society, Hickory (*RG*, May 1, 1897, 4)
Atheneum Literary Society, Newton (*RG*, May 1, 1897, 4)
Daniel Webster Literary Society, Shaw University (*RG*, May 15, 1897, 3)
Shiloh Institute Literary Society, Warrenton (*RG*, May 15, 1897, 2)
Fayetteville Keystone Lyceum, Fayetteville (*IF*, August 28, 1897, 3)
Clayton Preparatory Lyceum, Clayton (*RG*, January 22, 1898, 3)
Clarisophic Literary Society, Charlotte (*AAP*, December 21, 1899, 2)
Mattoon Literary Society, Charlotte (*AAP*, December 21, 1899, 2)
Douglass Literary Society, Charlotte (*AAP*, December 21, 1899, 2)
Literary and Musical Society, Raleigh (*CAW*, September 15, 1900, 12)
Grace AME Zion Church Lyceum, Charlotte (*WB*, August 31, 1901, 6)
Hood Literary Society, Livingston College, Salisbury (*CAW*, May 17, 1902, 7)
Garrison Literary Society, Livingston College, Salisbury (*CAW*, May 17, 1902, 7)
Agricultural Literary Society, A & M College, Greensboro (*ST*, July 15, 1911, 7)

Ohio
Literary Society (before 1843), Cincinnati (Porter, "Organized Educational Activities," 558)
Literary Society (before 1843), Columbus (Porter, "Organized Educational Activities," 558)
Young Ladies' Literary Society (1846), Oberlin College, Oberlin (*FDP*, September 1, 1854, 3)
Literary Society, Ripley (*NSR*, June 16, 1848)

Aeolian Literary Society (1852), Oberlin College, Oberlin (Logan, *Liberating Language*, 86)[31]
Literary Societies of Western Reserve College, Hudson (*FDP*, July 14, 1854, 2)
Union Literary Society, Oberlin College, Oberlin (*FDP*, September 1, 1854, 3)
E. L. Lyceum, Cincinnati (*CC*, May 19, 1866, 2)
Wilberforce University Literary Society, Wilberforce (*PA*, August 21, 1880, 1)
Cleveland Benevolent and Literary Society, Cleveland (*G*, April 21, 1883, 4)
Wilson Lyceum, Wheeling (*CG*, October 13, 1883, 2)
Walnut Hills Lyceum, Cincinnati (*CG*, April 26, 1884, 3)
Quinn Chapel Lyceum, Ironton (*CG*, May 17, 1884, 1)
Ideal Literary Society, Cleveland (*CG*, May 24, 1884, 3)
High School Literary Society, Ironton (*CG*, April 11, 1885, 4)
Mt. Zion Congregational Church Lyceum, Cleveland (*CG*, October 3, 1885, 4)
Literary Aid Society, Wheeling (*CG*, October 31, 1885, 1)
Douglass Lyceum and Literary Circle, Springfield (*CG*, November 21, 1885, 1)
Steubenville Lyceum, Steubenville (*CG*, December 19, 1885, 1)
St. James Lyceum, Steubenville (*CG*, March 27, 1886, 2)
Eaker Street Lyceum, Dayton (*CG*, December 18, 1886, 1)
Baptist Literary Society, Sandusky (*CG*, January 1, 1887, 1)
Rust Church Lyceum, Oberlin (*CG*, May 21, 1887, 2)
Cory Chapel Lyceum, Cleveland (*CG*, December 10, 1887, 3)
Young People's Lyceum (1888), Akron (*CG*, January 21, 1888, 1)
Cary Lyceum, Cleveland (*CG*, February 4, 1888, 3)
Warren Lyceum, Toledo (*P*, October 25, 1889, 2)
Juvenile Lyceum, Ravenna (*CG*, November 9, 1889, 2)
Warren Church Lyceum, Toledo (*IF*, November 22, 1890, 1)
Third Baptist Church Lyceum, Toledo (*IF*, November 22, 1890, 1)
Union Baptist Church Lyceum (1892), Cincinnati (*P*, October 28, 1892, 3)
Young People's Lyceum, Wellsville (*CG*, March 5, 1892, 2)
Findlay Lyceum, Findlay (*P*, April 22, 1892, 7)
Baptist Lyceum, Chillicothe (*IF*, June 18, 1892, 1)
Wendell Phillips Literary, Chillicothe (*IF*, June 18, 1892, 1)
Energetic Workers Literary Society, Union Baptist Church, Youngstown (*CG*, January 21, 1893, 1)
Banneker Lyceum, Oberlin (*P*, April 21, 1893, 6)
Phyllis Wheatley Lyceum, Cleveland (*CG*, March 10, 1894, 3)
Young Men's Lyceum League, Springfield (*CG*, June 16, 1894, 1)
Tawawa Lyceum, Springfield (*CG*, March 7, 1896, 1)
Baptist Church Literary Society, Troy (*CG*, November 14, 1896, 1)
Literary Society, Marysville (*CG*, November 28, 1896, 1)
East End Lyceum, Columbus (*IF*, February 13, 1897, 4)
Paul L. Dunbar Society, Toledo (*CG*, May 8, 1897, 1)
Elysian Literary Society, Cincinnati (*CAW*, April 9, 1898, 7)
Zion Baptist Literary Society, Cincinnati (*CAW*, May 14, 1898, 7)

East Side Lyceum, Columbus (*CG*, November 12, 1898, 1)
Minerva Reading Club, Cleveland (*CAW*, August 26, 1899, 5, and November 7, 1903, 3)[32]
Silver Leaf Literary Society, Salem (*CG*, October 14, 1899, 1)
Payne's Second Historia Literary Society, Youngstown (*CG*, May 5, 1900, 1)
Reveille Lyceum, Columbus (*CG*, November 15, 1902, 1)
Young People's Lyceum, Salem (*CG*, November 21, 1903, 1)
Ohio Lodge Lyceum, Cleveland (*CG*, December 5, 1903, 3)
Lincoln Literary Society (1904), Mt. Zion Church, Cleveland (*CG*, February 20, 1904, 5)
Queen Esther Literary Society, East Liverpool (*CG*, June 11, 1904, 1)
Trefoil Literary Society (1905), Cleveland (*CG*, June 10, 1905, 1)[33]
Zion Church Lyceum (1906), Akron (*CG*, August 11, 1906, 1)
Wheel of Progress Reading Circle, Akron (*CG*, August 11, 1906, 1)
Dunbar Club Lyceum, Cincinnati (*IF*, November 19, 1910, 2)
Fortnightly Reading Club, Columbus (*Minutes of the Eleventh Biennial Convention of the National Association of Colored Women*, 67)
Alston Reading Circle, Mechanicsburg (*Minutes of the Eleventh Biennial Convention of the National Association of Colored Women*, 67)

Oklahoma

Young Men's Philosophical and Literary Society, Guthrie (*IF*, August 23, 1890, 5)
Langston High School Literary Society, Langston (*LCH*, March 26, 1892, 3–4)
Young Men's Literary Society, Langston (*LCH*, April 23, 1892, 4)
Atoka Literary Society, Atoka (*PWB*, January 19, 1895, 3)
Methodist Church Literary Society, Enid (*TP*, March 9, 1906, 6)
Union Literary Society, Vinita (*TP*, June 19, 1908, 4)
Dunbar Literary Society, Bartlesville (*WS*, August 12, 1912, 4)
First Baptist Literary Society, Vinita (*TP*, January 15, 1915, 3)
Pleasant Hour Literary Club, Guthrie (*TP*, March 3, 1916, 6)
First Baptist Church Literary Society, Guthrie (*TP*, March 10, 1916, 7)
AME Church Literary Society, Enid (*TP*, April 7, 1916, 4)
Art, Literary and Social Club, McAlister (*Minutes of the Eleventh Biennial Convention of the National Association of Colored Women*, 67)

Oregon

Paul Lawrence Dunbar Literary Society, Portland (*NA*, January 27, 1900, 2)[34]
Zion Literary Society, Portland (*NA*, January 20, 1906, 5)

Pennsylvania

The Reading Room Society for Men of Color (May 28, 1828), Philadelphia (Muhammad, "The Literacy Development and Practices within African American Literary Societies," 6)
Colored Reading Society of Philadelphia for Mental Improvement, Philadelphia (*FJ*, December 26, 1828, 3)

Philadelphia Female Literary Society (1831) (*TL*, December 3, 1831, 196; *TL*, October 13, 1832, 163; *TL*, November 29, 1834, 190; Porter, "Organized Educational Activities," 559)[35]

Theban Literary Society (1831), Pittsburgh (Porter, "Organized Educational Activities," 573; Rollin, *Life and Public Services of Martin R. Delany*, 39)

Library Company of Colored Persons (1833), Philadelphia (*TL*, April 18, 1835; *CA*, December 2, 1837; *WAA*, August 20, 1859, 3; Porter, "Organized Educational Activities," 557)

Minerva Literary Association (1834), Philadelphia (*CA*, September 15, 1838; Porter, "Organized Educational Activities," 557)

Philadelphia Association for Moral and Mental Improvement of the People of Color (1835), Philadelphia (*NECA*, January 21, 1837, 78; Porter, "Organized Educational Activities," 557)[36]

Rush Library and Debating Society (1836), Philadelphia (*PF*, May 21, 1840; Porter, "Organized Educational Activities," 557)

Edgeworth Society (before 1837), Philadelphia (Porter, "Organized Educational Activities," 557; Winch, *The Elite of Our People*, 117)

Young Men's Literary and Moral Reform Society of Pittsburgh and Vicinity (1837), Pittsburgh (*CA*, September 2, 1837; Porter, "Organized Educational Activities," 557)

Archer's Literary Club (before 1838), Philadelphia (*CA*, September 2, 1837)

Demosthenian Institute (1838), Philadelphia (*CA*, April 24, 1841, 30; *CA*, July 24, 1841, 82; Logan, *Liberating Language*, 62; Porter, "Organized Educational Activities," 557)[37]

Young Men's Philadelphia Library Association (before 1839), Philadelphia (*PF*, September 26, 1839; *CA*, October 5, 1839)

Young Men's Union Literary Association (1839), Philadelphia (*CA*, February 2, 1839)

Gilbert Lyceum (1841), Philadelphia (Porter, "Organized Educational Activities," 557; Winch, *The Elite of Our People*, 117)

Women's Association of Philadelphia (1849), Philadelphia (*NSR*, March 9, 1849, 1, June 15, 1849, July 13, 1849)[38]

Banneker Institute (1854), Philadelphia (*WAA*, August 20, 1859, 3; *WB*, November 8, 1884, 2)

Histrionic Club (1857), Philadelphia (*TL*, April 2, 1858, 55)

Sarah M. Douglass Literary Circle (1859), Philadelphia (*WAA*, April 14, 1860, 2)

Philomathesian Literary Society, Alleghany (*WAA*, September 3, 1859, 3)

Wesleyan Literary Society, Pittsburgh (*WAA*, September 3, 1859, 3)

Young Men's Literary Association, Reading (*WAA*, September 24, 1859, 3)

Progressive Workingman's Club Lyceum (1878), Philadelphia (*TS*, March 26, 1881, 2)[39]

Bethel Historical and Literary Association, Philadelphia (*PA*, September 25, 1880, 1)

Tassonian Literary Association, Philadelphia (*TS*, September 17, 1881, 3)

Young People's Musical and Literary Society, Philadelphia (*G*, January 6, 1883, 1)

Blyden Literary Association, Wilkes-Barre (*G*, March 3, 1883, 4)

Tasseniary Literary Society, Philadelphia (*WB*, March 17, 1883, 3)

Hamilton Literary Society, Philadelphia (*WB*, March 17, 1883, 3)

AME Historical Literary Association, Philadelphia (*WB*, March 17, 1883, 3)
Garnet Literary Association, Lincoln University, Oxford (*G*, May 26, 1883, 4)
Berian Literary Society, Philadelphia (*WB*, June 9, 1883, 2)
Hannibal Literary Society, Philadelphia (*WB*, June 9, 1883, 2)[40]
Macedonian Literary Society, Camden (*WB*, June 9, 1883, 2)
Echo Literary Society, Philadelphia (*G*, October 27, 1883, 1)
Young People's Association Lyceum, Philadelphia (*G*, November 10, 1883, 1)
Philomathean Club, Harrisburg (*HSJ*, December 13, 1883, 3)
Wesley Sabbath School Literary Association, Harrisburg (*HSJ*, December 13, 1883, 3)
Bethel Literary Society, Middletown (*HSJ*, January 5, 1884, 4)
Erie Literary Society, Erie (*HSJ*, January 19, 1884, 1)
Oak Lyceum Society, Williamsport (*HSJ*, February 2, 1884, 1)
Baptist Literary Society, Philadelphia (*HSJ*, February 9, 1884, 4)
Wylie Avenue Literary Society, Philadelphia (*HSJ*, February 9, 1884, 4)
Garnett Literary Society, York (*HSJ*, March 8, 1884, 4)
Reading Literary Society, Reading (*HSJ*, April 19, 1884, 4)
St. Paul Literary Society, Bellefonte (*HSJ*, April 19, 1884, 4)
Young People's Literary and Musical Society, Reading (*HSJ*, May 3, 1884, 4)
AME Bethel Literary Society, Wilkes-Barre (*HSJ*, May 31, 1884, 5)
Goethean Literary Society, Franklin and Marshall College, Lancaster (*HSJ*, June 21, 1884, 2)
Lincoln Literary Society, Chambersburg (*HSJ*, July 26, 1884, 1)
Samuel Slater Literary Society, Wilkes-Barre (*HSJ*, July 26, 1884, 4)
AME Zion Literary Society, Wilkes-Barre (*HSJ*, November 8, 1884, 1)
Union Literary Society, Wilkes-Barre (1886) (*NYF*, December 18, 1886, 1)
Phillis Wheatley Literary Society, New London (*NYF*, January 23, 1886, 4)
Garrison Literary Society, Middletown (*NYF*, May 15, 1886, 4)
Catto Lyceum, Philadelphia (*NYF*, June 11, 1887, 1)
Literary Society of Allen Chapel, Philadelphia (*NYA*, June 7, 1890, 1)
Union Lyceum, Easton (*NYA*, August 16, 1890, 4)
Amphion Society, Philadelphia (*NYA*, November 1, 1890, 1)
Monumental Literary Society, Philadelphia (1891) (*IF*, March 28, 1891, 2)
Eliza Turner Mission Lyceum, Philadelphia (*IF*, March 7, 1891, 2)
Philosophian Lyceum, Lincoln University, Oxford (*IF*, March 28, 1891, 2)
St. Benedict the Moor Lyceum, Pittsburgh (*CG*, September 2, 1893, 1)
Theological Lyceum and Missionary Society, Lincoln University, Oxford (*IF*, November 18, 1893, 5)
New Era Lyceum, Altoona (*CG*, April 6, 1895, 3)
AME Church Lyceum, Altoona (1896) (*IF*, November 7, 1896, 4)
Tawawa Literary Lyceum, Washington (*CG*, April 23, 1898, 1)
American Negro Historical Society, Philadelphia (*CAW*, March 25, 1899, 8)
Paul Laurence Dunbar Lyceum, Zion Baptist Church, Philadelphia (*CAW*, October 25, 1902, 2)
Aurora Reading Club, Pittsburg (*Minutes of the Eleventh Biennial Convention of the National Association of Colored Women*, 68)

Black Opals, Philadelphia (McHenry, *Forgotten Readers*, 293)[41]
Benjamin Harrison Literary Society, Pittsburgh (*TP*, July 29, 1938, 6)

Rhode Island
Literary Society (1833), Providence (*TL*, October 18, 1839, 166; *FDP*, December 1, 1854, 2; Porter, "Organized Educational Activities," 558)
Colored Female Literary Society, Providence (*TL*, June 1, 1833)
Debating Society (before 1837), Providence (*TL*, June 1, 1833; Porter, "Organized Educational Activities," 558)
Banneker Lyceum, Newport (*WAA*, February 25, 1860, 1)
L'Ouverture Literary Assembly, Providence (*CR*, March 24, 1866)
Historical Literary Association, Providence (*NYF*, December 25, 1886, 4)
Literary and Public Debating Society, Providence (*NYF*, January 29, 1887, 3)
Franklin Lyceum, Providence (*NYF*, March 19, 1887, 4)
Bethel Literary Society, Providence (*NYF*, March 19, 1887, 4)
Pioneer Lyceum, Provincetown (*IF*, April 20, 1895, 3)
Narragansett Lyceum, Narragansett (*CAW*, July 27, 1901, 9)

South Carolina
Crouther Literary Society, Columbia (*G*, November 17, 1883, 2)
Youth's Literary Club, Charleston (*G*, July 12, 1884, 4)
Lucy Laney Lyceum, Charleston (*NYF*, July 24, 1886, 4)
Douglass Literary Society, Charleston (*NYF*, August 21, 1886, 1)
Phyllis Wheatley Literary and Social Club, Charleston (McHenry, *Forgotten Readers*, 243)
Educational School Lyceum, Spartanburg (*IF*, January 31, 1891, 8)

South Dakota
Deadwood and Leed City Literary Society, Deadwood and Leed City (*TP*, July 2, 1915, 4)

Tennessee
Union Literary Society (1868), Fisk University, Nashville (*WL*, May 31, 1879, 2; Logan, *Liberating Language*, 91)
LeMoyne Literary Society, Memphis (Logan, *Liberating Language*, 44)
Beta Kappa Beta Literary Society (1881), Fisk University, Nashville (Little, "The Extra-Curricular Activities of Black College Students," 43)
Nashville Institute Literary Society (*HG*, December 24, 1881, 3)
Young Ladies Lyceum, Fisk University, Nashville (Little, "The Extra-Curricular Activities of Black College Students," 43)
Duodecem Literae Virgines, Fisk University, Nashville (Little, "The Extra-Curricular Activities of Black College Students," 43)
Memphis Lyceum, Memphis (1883) (*MDA*, February 17, 1884, 4; *CG*, April 4, 1885, 1)[42]
Presbyterian Church Literary Society, Rogersville (*PA*, June 30, 1883, 3)

Howard Chapel Lyceum, Nashville (*G*, August 4, 1883, 2)
Young Men's Lyceum, Union City (*IF*, May 27, 1893, 1)
Salters' Lyceum, Browder's Chapel AME Church, Pierce Station (*IF*, September 8, 1894, 5)
Young People's Lyceum, Dyersburg (1896) (*IF*, March 14, 1896, 4)
West Side Lyceum, Chattanooga (*IF*, April 25, 1896, 8)
Young Ladies' and Gentleman's Lyceum, Jackson (*IF*, June 13, 1896, 5)
Harvest Gleaner Literary Society, South Nashville AME Church, Nashville (*IF*, May 26, 1900, 8)
Frances Harper Literary Circle, Central Tennessee College, Nashville (*IF*, May 26, 1900, 8)
Avery Chapel Lyceum (1901), Memphis (*IF*, February 23, 1901, 1)
High School Lyceum, Dyersburg (*IF*, February 22, 1902, 1)
Memphis Lyceum (1921), Memphis (*SLC*, April 2, 1921, 2)
Kappa Alpha Phi Literary Society, Lane College, Jackson (*KCP*, May 25, 1934, 3)

Texas
The Forney Excelsior Literary Society, Forney (*TA*, February 22, 1880, 1)
Violet Social, Musical and Literary Society, Austin (*G*, March 31, 1883, 4)
Houston Bible and Literary Society, Houston (*ST*, October 26, 1889, 3)
Lone Star Literary Society, Thurber (*LA*, November 2, 1889, 3)
Berean Literary Society, Fort Worth (*TA*, January 17, 1890, 6)
Lawrence Literary Society, Lawrence (*LA*, February 8, 1890, 3)
Gainsville Lyceum, Gainsville (*IF*, May 9, 1891, 3)
Paul-Quinn Literary Society, Austin (*TSL*, November 17, 1893, 1)
Tawawa Literary Society, Galveston (*PWB*, April 21, 1894, 4)
Payne's Literary Society (formerly Tawawa Literary Society), Galveston (*PWB*, May 5, 1894, 4)
Bonham Literary Society, Bonham (*PWB*, January 26, 1895, 3)
Literary Lyceum, Silver Valley (*IF*, March 21, 1896, 3)
Corsicana Lyceum, Corsicana (*IF*, January 30, 1897, 3)
South Hot Springs Literary Society, Hot Springs (*DE*, January 13, 1900, 6)
Albany Literary Society, Albany (*DE*, January 13, 1900, 5)
West Austin Literary Society, Austin (*HI*, January 27, 1900, 1)
Payne Literary Society, Paul Quinn College, Waco (*PQW*, January 27, 1900, 4)
Woman's Reading Club, Gainesville (*Minutes of the Eleventh Biennial Convention of the National Association of Colored Women*, 69)
Lovinggood Literary Society, Samuel Houston College, Austin (*TP*, February 25, 1927, 1)
Johnston Literary Society, St. Philip's College, San Antonio (*KW*, November 20, 1937, 3)

Utah
AME Church Lyceum (1894), Salt Lake City (*IF*, November 24, 1894, 3)

Herber Lyceum, Herber (*BA*, February 22, 1896, 4)[43]
Frederick Douglass Literary Society, Fort Douglass (*IF*, December 24, 1898, 9)
Calvary Baptist Church Literary Society, Salt Lake City (*IF*, January 17, 1903, 8)
Dunbar Literary Society, Salt Lake City (*IF*, December 29, 1906, 5)
W. C. Vernon Society, Salt Lake City (*IF*, March 28, 1908, 4)
Dunbar Literary Society, Ogden (*IF*, April 15, 1911, 3)

Virginia
Banneker Lyceum, Portsmouth (*PA*, July 1, 1876, 2)
Young Men's Literary Debating Society, Herndon (*PA*, April 19, 1879, 3)
Mitchell Lyceum, Alexandria (*PA*, July 12, 1879, 1)
Carthaginian Literary Society, Norfolk (*PA*, November 29, 1879, 3)
Richmond Literary Society, Richmond (*PA*, April 30, 1881, 4)
Lincoln Lyceum, Richmond (*PA*, April 30, 1881, 4)
Petersburg Lyceum, Petersburg (*G*, April 14, 1883, 2)
Acme Literary Society, Richmond (*G*, July 7, 1883, 1)
Harris Lyceum, Norfolk (*G*, September 8, 1883, 4)
Owen Literary Society, Alexandria (*WB*, December 22, 1883, 3)
Chautauqua Literary and Scientific Club, Richmond (*G*, April 5, 1884, 4)
Richmond Institute Lyceum, Richmond (*G*, May 3, 1884, 1)
Virginia Normal and Collegiate Institute Lyceum, Petersburg (*G*, June 28, 1884, 2)
T. T. Fortune Lyceum, Wytheville (*G*, August 16, 1884, 4)
St. John's AME Church Literary Society, Norfolk (*NYF*, August 21, 1886, 4)
Mount Dew Literary Society, Mount Dew (*WB*, December 4, 1886, 3)
Friday Night Literary Club, Alexandria (*L*, February 2, 1889, 5)
Douglass Literary Association, Alexandria (*L*, February 2, 1889, 5)
Garnet Literary, Alexandria (*WB*, February 23, 1889, 3)
Literary Quartette Club, Alexandria (*L*, April 6, 1889, 5)
Literary Society, Hot Springs (*CAW*, August 26, 1899, 1)
Literary Society, Warm Springs (*CAW*, August 26, 1899, 1)
Cooper Literary Society, Evington (*IF*, February 22, 1890, 5)
Ciceronian Lyceum, Danville (*IF*, October 11, 1890, 2)
Authentic Lyceum, Petersburgh (*IF*, November 8, 1890, 2)
L. and G. Lyceum, Elliston (*IF*, March 17, 1894, 7)[44]
Berkley Lyceum, Berkley (*IF*, April 24, 1897, 5)
Epworth League and Lyceum, Alexandria (*CAW*, June 1, 1901, 12)

Washington
Spokane Literary Society, Spokane (*E*, October 18, 1890, 2)
Literary Society, Tacoma (*NA*, December 8, 1906, 5)

Washington, DC
Washington Conventional Society (1834) (*NA*, December 8, 1906, 5; Porter, "Organized Educational Activities," 558)

Debating Society (before 1837) (Porter, "Organized Educational Activities," 558)
Literary Society (before 1837) (Porter, "Organized Educational Activities," 558)
Good Will Literary Association (*WAA*, December 10, 1859, 1)
Pioneer Lyceum at Hillsdale (*E*, June 27, 1874, 2)
Ashbury Sabbath School Lyceum (1877) (*WB*, November 5, 1887, 3)
Literary Club of Union Bethel Sabbath School (*PA*, June 7, 1879, 3)
Bethel Literary and Historical Society (1881) (*PA*, February 25, 1882, 4; *G*, December 15, 1883, 1)
Literary and Musical Society (*PA*, January 1, 1881, 2)
The Monday and Tuesday Night Literary (*WB*, January 13, 1883, 2)
Monday Night Literary Society (*WL*, March 19, 1881, 2; *WB*, June 2, 1883, 2)[45]
Alpha Phi Literary Society, Howard University (*WB*, December 15, 1883, 3)
Ladies' Literary Society, Howard University (*PA*, April 12, 1884, 1)
John Wesley Church Lyceum (*TG*, June 14, 1884, 2)
Galbraith Literary Society (*WB*, January 24, 1885, 3)
Wesley Zion Literary Society (*WB*, February 28, 1885, 3)
Clinton Literary Society (*WB*, August 7, 1886, 3)
Young Men's Literary Association of Israel Bethel Church (*WB*, September 25, 1886, 3)
Second Baptist Church Literary Society (*WB*, October 16, 1886, 3)[46]
Philomathian Literary Society (*WB*, October 30, 1886, 4)
Eureka Literary Society, Howard University (*WB*, February 19, 1887, 1)
Hillsdale Literary Society (*WB*, December 1, 1887, 3)
Plymouth Congregational Afternoon Lyceum (*WB*, February 18, 1888, 3)
Mt. Carmel Baptist Sunday Afternoon Lyceum (*WB*, March 10, 1888, 3)
Plymouth Sunday School Lyceum (*WB*, March 17, 1888, 3)
Zania Literary Society (*WB*, March 24, 1888, 2)
Ebenezer Lyceum (*WB*, October 6, 1888, 3)
Mt. Carmel Sunday Evening Lyceum (*WB*, October 6, 1888, 3)
Mt. Carmel Sunday Afternoon Lyceum (*WB*, October 13, 1888, 3)
Mt. Carmel Literary Society (*WB*, December 15, 1888, 3)
19th Street Baptist Sabbath School Lyceum (1890) (*WB*, January 18, 1890, 3)
Metropolitan Wesley Zion Sunday School Lyceum (1890) (*NYF*, March 22, 1890, 1)
First Baptist Sunday Afternoon Lyceum (1890) (*WB*, June 14, 1890, 3)
Plymouth Argumentative Lyceum (1890) (*NYA*, November 22, 1890, 1)
Second Baptist Sunday School Lyceum (*WB*, February 8, 1890, 3)[47]
Theological Lyceum, Howard University (*WB*, May 17, 1890, 3)
Acanthus Club (*NYA*, December 20, 1890, 1)
Salem Baptist Church Sunday School Lyceum (*WB*, April 7, 1894, 1)
Harriet Beecher Stowe Lyceum, M. Street High School (*LH*, November 24, 1894, 2)
East Washington Lyceum (*WB*, December 8, 1894, 3)
Lutheran Church Lyceum (*WB*, December 8, 1894, 3)
Metropolitan Baptist Lyceum (*IF*, April 13, 1895, 5)
YMCA Lyceum (*BAA*, August 3, 1895, 1)
L'Ouveture Catholic Lyceum (*BAA*, August 17, 1895, 1)

National Congressional Lyceum (1897) (*WB*, December 4, 1897, 5)
Varick Lyceum (1898) (*CAW*, April 2, 1898, 5)
Mt. Horeb Baptist Church Lyceum (*WB*, April 16, 1898, 5)
Guild Lyceum of Lincoln Memorial Congregational Church (*CAW*, May 7, 1898, 8)
Enon Baptist Church Lyceum (*WB*, May 14, 1898, 5)
Union Wesley Lyceum (*WB*, November 19, 1898, 5)
Mt Jezreel Baptist Church Lyceum (*CAW*, December 10, 1898, 6)
Odd Fellows Lyceum (1900) (*CAW*, December 1, 1900, 15)
10th Street Baptist Church Lyceum (1901) (*CAW*, December 14, 1901, 7)
Epsworth League Lyceum, Asbury ME Church (*CAW*, November 9, 1901, 8)
Galbraith AME Zion Church Sunday Lyceum (1902) (*CAW*, September 13, 1902, 7)
Pen and Pencil and Book Lovers Club (*IF*, July 14, 1906, 1)
Richards Literary Society (*WB*, May 16, 1914, 1)

West Virginia
Ashbury Sabbath School Lyceum (1877), Ashbury (*WB*, November 5, 1887, 3)
M. E. Church Lyceum, Charleston (*IF*, July 18, 1891, 5)
Frederick Douglass Lyceum, Charleston (*IF*, September 12, 1891, 3)
White Sulphur Literary Society, White Sulphur Springs (*CAW*, August 12, 1899, 5)
Hasty Pudding Lyceum, Clarksburg (*CAW*, January 20, 1900, 5)

Wisconsin
Burns Lyceum, Burns (*WLA*, February 4, 1887, 3)
Campbell Lyceum, Onalaska (*WLA*, March 4, 1887, 3)
Calvary Baptist Church Literary Society, Milwaukee (*IF*, May 13, 1905, 3)
St. Mark's AME Church Literary Society, Milwaukee (*IF*, May 13, 1905, 3)

Wyoming Territory/Wyoming
Cheyenne Lyceum, Cheyenne (*NYF*, July 17, 1886, 2)
Philosophia Literary Society, Cheyenne (*NYF*, July 24, 1886, 2)
Cheyenne Literary Society, Cheyenne (*TP*, December 4, 1903, 4)

Canada West
Wilberforce Lyceum Educating Society (1850), Cannonsburg (*Constitution and By Laws of the Wilberforce Lyceum Educating Society*; Murray, *Come, Bright Improvement!*, 70)
Provincial Union (1854), Toronto (*PFWA*, August 19, 1854, 3)[48]
Windsor Ladies Club (1854), Windsor (Bristow, "Whatever You Raise in the Ground You Can Sell It in Chatham," 122; Murray, *Come, Bright Improvement!*, 71)[49]
Ladies Literary Society, Chatham (Bristow, "Whatever You Raise in the Ground You Can Sell It in Chatham," 122; Murray, *Come, Bright Improvement!*, 71)[50]
Young Men's Excelsior Literary Association (by 1855), Toronto (*PFWA*, April 7, 1855; Murray, *Come, Bright Improvement!*, 72)
Dumas Literary Society, Chatham[51] (*PFWA*, April 12, 1856; Murray, *Come, Bright Improvement!*, 202)

Dumas Literary Association, Chatham (*PFWA*, April 12, 1856; Murray, *Come, Bright Improvement!*, 70–71)

Mental and Moral Improvement Association (by 1859), Toronto (*Caverhill's Toronto City Directory 1859–1860*, 222)[52]

Barrie Grammar School Literary and Scientific Society, Barrie (*BNA*, November 9, 1859, 2)

Ontario, Canada

Chatham Literary and Debating Society (1872), Chatham (*AE*, November 25, 1887; *Chatham Directory, 1876–1877*)[53]

Chatham Literary Association (1875), Chatham (*P*, February 13, 1891; Shadd, "No 'back-alley clique,'" 79)

Amherstburg Literary Association (1880), Amherstburg (*AE*, January 21, 1881, and January 28, 1881; Murray, *Come, Bright Improvement!*, 73)

Essex Literary Society, Essex (*ER*, January 8, 1880, 1)

Busy Gleanors (1887), Amherstburg (*AE*, November 4, 1887)

Cheerful Workers, Amherstburg (*AE*, November 25, 1887)

Amherstburg Library and Reading Room Association, Amherstburg (*ER*, May 4, 1894, 8)

High School Lyceum, Essex (*EFP*, October 8, 1909, 4)

Amherstburg Reading Club, Amherstburg (*WER*, February 25, 1914, 6)

East Harrow Mutual Improvement Society, Harrow (*AE*, October 12, 1917, 7)

C. C. I. [Chatham Collegiate Institute] Literary Club, Chatham (*CDN*, April 27, 1934, 6)

Tilbury Continuation School Literary Society, Tilbury (*CDN*, September 29, 1934, 6)

Haiti

Government Lyceum, Port-au-Prince (*IF*, May 6, 1893, 6)

Republic of Liberia

Freeman Lyceum, Brewerville (*NYF*, March 19, 1887, 2)

Notes

Introduction

1. Highgate, Letter to the Editor, April 3, 1869.
2. For example, the *Colored American* reported on the Phoenixonian Society (1833–1841), sister literary society to the male Phoenix Society (1833–1839), and the Ladies' Literary Society of New York (founded 1834). Amicus, "Our Literary Societies." The paper also linked literary and benevolent societies in its reporting, such as in its September 1839 report on Poughkeepsie's "2 or 3 female benevolent associations" and the Phoenxionian Library, a "well attended" literary society connected with a debating society in the city. "For the Colored American, Poughkeepsie." A month later, the paper described the Philomathean and Phoenixonian Societies, the Eclectic Fraternity, the Franklin Forum, and the Tyro Association as "praiseworthy literary institutions" of New York City. "Literary Societies."
3. Amicus, "Our Literary Societies"; Muta, "Messrs. Editors." McHenry refers to the *Colored American* as "a great supporter of African American literary societies" and a primary historical record of their formation and work. McHenry, *Forgotten Readers*, 327n63.
4. McHenry, *Forgotten Readers*, 41.
5. "Bethel Literaries." Bethel and AME literary societies are mentioned in the Black press from the late 1870s through the early twentieth century across the country. See, for example, the *People's Advocate*, July 5, 1879; the *New York Globe*, January 13, 1883; the *State Journal* (Harrisburg, PA), December 13, 1883; the *Weekly Pelican* (New Orleans, LA), August 20, 1887; and the *Broad Ax* (Salt Lake City, UT), October 21, 1905.
6. "Summary," 3. Dorothy Porter documented the first women's literary society as the 1831 Philadelphia Female Literary Society. Porter, "The Organized Educational Activities of Negro Literary Societies," 557. See also Muhammad, "The Literacy Development and Practices within African American Literary Societies," 6.
7. Jones, *All Bound Up Together*, 88.
8. McHenry documents the greater growth of women's societies as the century progressed and notes that the number of women's benevolent societies in cities such as Philadelphia nearly doubled those of their male counterparts as early as 1831. McHenry, *Forgotten Readers*, 57.
9. McHenry, *Forgotten Readers*, 56.
10. Foster, "Genealogies of Our Concern," 355.
11. Dunbar, *A Fragile Freedom*, 5.

12. Weare, "Mutual Benefit Societies," 830.

13. See, for example, "Notice. . . . The African Dorcas Association."

14. Horton and Horton, *In Hope of Liberty*, 128.

15. Dunbar, *A Fragile Freedom*, 4; Porter, "The Organized Educational Activities of Negro Literary Societies," 558–59. An undated letter written by a white man to *The Liberator* dates the Philadelphian Minerva Society as being in operation "about 9 months," with Henrietta Matthews then its president. The writer noted that he "frequently visited them on their meeting nights . . . to see and hear my oppressed sisters. read and recite pieces, some of which were original, and which would have done credit to the fairest female in America—the republican land of liberty." J. C. B., "Literary Societies." McHenry refers to such touristic attendance as forming "a steady stream of observers." McHenry, *Forgotten Readers*, 79.

16. Dunbar, *A Fragile Freedom*, 60.

17. Weare, "Mutual Benefit Societies," 830. Weare cites "the Benevolent Daughters (1706), the Daughters of Africa (1812), the American Female Bond Benevolent Society of Bethel (1817), the Female Benezet (1818), and the Daughters of Aaron (1819)" as among the earliest such societies in Philadelphia.

18. "Weekly Scribblings and Gleanings," 138.

19. Perkins, "Black Women and Racial 'Uplift,'" 327.

20. Jones, *All Bound Up Together*, 221n69.

21. Weare, "Mutual Benefit Societies," 830.

22. C. B. R., "For the Colored American." On this trip, $100 was raised "from the Colored Citizens of Buffalo," although the Dorcas society is the only organization named. For reports on the Female Dorcas Association of New York City, see *Freedom's Journal*, February 1, 1828; February 15, 1828; March 7, 1828; September 26, 1828; October 3, 1828; November 21, 1828; January 9, 1829; February 7, 1829; and March 14, 1829. For reports on the Female Dorcas Society of Buffalo, see the *Weekly Advocate*, February 11, 1837; and the *Colored American*, November 4, 1837.

23. See the *Colored American*, January 20, 1838, 7; and Porter, "The Organized Educational Activities of Negro Literary Societies," 569.

24. On mental feasts, see McHenry, *Forgotten Readers*, 78. For example, the *Christian Recorder* reported on the Philadelphia Dorcas Society in the early 1860s: see *Christian Recorder*, November 23, 1861; November 22, 1862; and November 29, 1862.

25. Porter, "The Organized Educational Activities of Negro Literary Societies," 558; Newman, *Black Founders*, 11. In four years, the Troy Female Benevolent Society grew from ten to sixty-one members and accumulated $236.10 in savings. Troy also supported a United Sons and Daughters of Zion's Benevolent Society, in operation since 1833, with forty-eight members and an account worth $112. Miter, "Colored People of Troy," 1.

26. De Vera, "'We the ladies . . . have been deprived of a voice,'" 3–4.

27. Weare, "Mutual Benefit Societies," 830.

28. Weare, "Mutual Benefit Societies," 830–31.

29. Logan, *Liberating Language*, 65.

30. Philadelphia was home to at least fourteen literary societies between 1828 and 1841 (see the appendix).

31. For example, Providence, which had an African American population of 1,210 in 1830, was home to two literary societies in 1833 and a debating society sometime before 1837 (see the appendix). On the 1830 population of the five counties of Rhode Island, see the *Colored American*, April 1, 1837; and Porter, "The Organized Educational Activities of Negro Literary Societies," 558.

32. See the appendix for state-by-state listings of literary societies drawn from historical African American newspapers.

33. Douglass and Forten were members of the PFLA. Stewart was a member of the Ladies' Literary Society of New York after she left Boston in 1833. Elizabeth Jennings Jr. addressed that society in the fall of 1837, reading an address written by her mother, Elizabeth, Sr., and in 1854 she successfully sued against racial segregation on public transportation in the city. On Jennings Jr., see Logan, *Liberating Language*, 74; on Stewart, see Richardson, *Maria W. Stewart*, 81.

34. Duster, *Crusade for Justice*, 22–24; Logan, *Liberating Language*, 4.

35. Logan, *Liberating Language*, 56, 87. Cooper also addressed Washington's Odd Fellows Lyceum, giving "Colored Women as Wage Earners" on April 3, 1904. "Budget of Interesting News," 2.

36. Cooper delivered "The High School Idea" to the Bethel Historical and Literary Society on May 20, 1902. "City Paragraphs," 16.

37. At its original founding, the Bethel Historical and Literary Society counted "about seventy-five members." Annie E. Geary was the first vice president of the executive committee, which also included Amanda R. [Mattie] Bowen as second vice president, Chanie A. Patterson as librarian, and Julia R. Bush and Belle Nickens. Patterson, along with her sister Mary Jane, went on to debate Alexander Crummell and Robert Purvis at the Bethel on the question of professional versus trade education. Cromwell, *History of the Bethel Literary and Historical Association*, 4; *People's Advocate*, March 3, 1884.

38. "Bethel Literaries"; "Bethel Closes," 6.

39. "After the Colored Vote," 3.

40. On Shadd and Terrell at the Bethel, see McHenry, *Forgotten Readers*, 184–85, 361n94. For a notice of Terrell's election to president, see "Our Journalists and Literary Folks," 6.

41. Terrell published in the *A.M.E. Church Review*, the Indianapolis *Freeman*, the Baltimore *Afro-American*, the *Norfolk Journal and Guide*, the *Washington Tribune*, the *Chicago Defender*, the *New York Age*, and the *Voice of the Negro*. She also published in the *Southern Workman*, the *Evening Star* (Washington, DC), and the *Washington Post*.

42. Coppin was a member of the National League of Colored Women in Washington, DC, and later the NACWC, along with Carrie Clifford.

43. Frances Harper was a nationally recognized poet, an activist in the Free Soil movement and the Underground Railroad, a crusader for temperance, and a suffragist affiliated with the American Woman Suffrage Association. See Foster, *Brighter Coming Day*; and Boyd, *Discarded Legacy*.

44. Carrie Clifford, a suffragist, was a member of the NAACP and contributed to the special suffrage number of *The Crisis* (August 1915). From March 1903 to June 1905

she wrote the woman's column of the *Cleveland Journal* (Cleveland, OH; 1903–1912) and edited its special Woman's Edition in February 1905. From May to August 1905, she also wrote Of Interest to Women, a column in *Alexander's Magazine*.

45. Lucy Craft Laney founded the first kindergarten for African American children in Augusta, Georgia, and the Haines Normal and Industrial Institute (1883), of which she was principal for fifty years. Laney was also active in the Black women's club movement, the NAACP, the Niagara Movement, and the Interracial Commission.

46. Along with Coppin, Clifford, and Laney, Coralie Franklin Cook was a member of the Colored Woman's League. She was also superintendent of the Washington Home for Destitute Children and was active in both the NAWSA and the NAACP. Terborg-Penn, *African-American Women*, 64.

47. Lucy Moten was a central figure in education in Washington, DC, as were Anna Julia Cooper and Nannie Helen Burroughs. She was the first African American principal of the Miner Normal School, a teacher training school where Moten educated virtually every African American teacher in the city from 1883 to 1920. "Dr. Lucy E. Moten."

48. Ida Gibbs, born in Victoria, British Columbia, Canada, graduated from Oberlin in 1884 along with Mary Church Terrell and Anna Julia Cooper. Gibbs taught at the M Street High School, where Cooper served as principal from 1901 to 1906. She was a co-organizer with W. E. B. Du Bois of the Pan-African Congresses and delivered "The Colored Races and the League of Nations" at the third congress in 1923. Gibbs was also active in the Niagara Movement and the NAACP. She wrote for *The Crisis* under the pen name Iola Gibson. Alexander, *Parallel Worlds*.

49. Hallie Quinn Brown addressed the World's Congress of Representative Women in 1892, as did Anna Julia Cooper, Frances Harper and Fannie Barrier Williams. The daughter of formerly enslaved parents, Brown was educated at Wilberforce University (class of 1873). She became dean of Allen University in Columbia, South Carolina (1885–1887), and principal of Tuskegee Institute (1892–1893). She was a cofounder of the Colored Woman's League in Washington, DC, and served as president of the Ohio State Federation of Colored Women's Clubs (1905–1912) and the NACWC (1920–1924); and was known internationally as a powerful speaker on temperance, suffrage, and civil rights. Majors, *Noted Negro Women*, 231–32; Davis, *Lifting as They Climb*, 174–76.

50. Nannie Helen Burroughs's activism was informed by her membership in the Baptist church, which she opened to women's voices and concerns by cofounding the Women's Convention, Auxiliary to the National Baptist Convention (1900) and serving as its president for over a decade. The daughter of formerly enslaved parents, she migrated from Virginia to Washington, DC, in 1883, attending the M Street High School where she met Terrell and Cooper. She founded the National Training School for Women and Girls in Washington, DC, in 1909. Burroughs was active in the NAACP, the NACWC, the International Council of Women of the Darker Races, and the National Association of Wage Earners. Moore, *Leading the Race*, 164. See also Harley, "Nannie Helen Burroughs"; Graves, *Nannie Helen Burroughs*.

51. Mattie [Amanda R.] Bowen was the director of the Sojourner Truth Home for Working Girls in Washington, DC, which offered young working women an affordable

and safe place to live; was a teacher in Washington, DC; was active in the NACWC; and was well known for her lectures to Black women's church groups on African American women and their accomplishments. Moore, *Leading the Race*, 163.

52. Wright, *Centennial Encyclopaedia of the African Methodist Episcopal Church*, 368. Fannie Jackson Coppin delivered "The Duty of the Hour" to the Bethel Literary and Historical Society on October 26, 1897. *New York Freeman*, October 23, 1897, 1. Terrell and Shadd Cary formally addressed the Bethel and participated in its activities as members. The Woman's Night, held on March 20, 1897, included Terrell, Rosetta Lawson, Anna E. Murray, and Mattie Bowen. "Matters in Brief," 1; "A Symposium on Woman," 1. Ida Gibbs addressed the Bethel as part of its symposium on education on the evening of April 5, 1898. "Bethel's Spring Season," 1. Coralie Franklin Cook, Alice Strange Davis, Mary Church Terrell, and Lucy Moten addressed the Bethel on the arts in the spring of 1899. "Doings of the Literaries," 7. On December 11, 1900, Terrell, Jennie Conner, and Ida Gibbs addressed the society on the influence of Oberlin College. "Bethel Literary and Historical Scholarly Discussion," 13. Coralie Franklin Cook, Terrell, Rosetta Lawson, and Ida Gibbs all were part of the society's program on Robert Burns held the evening of January 29, 1901. "A Treat at the Bethel," 16. Carrie Clifford gave a talk on segregation in theaters, restaurants, and transportation titled "Some Thoughts on the Great American Problem" in late December 1908. "Thompson's Review," 3. Frances Harper addressed the Bethel on January 9, 1883 and February 6, 1883. *New York Globe*, January 20, 1883, 1; *Washington Bee*, February 10, 1883, 2. Hallie Quinn Brown gave "The Divine Art" before the Bethel on December 11, 1888, and on November 23, 1920, she delivered "Our Women, Present and Future." *Washington Bee*, December 8, 1888, 3; "Bethel Literary," *Washington Bee*, November 13, 1920, 1; "Bethel Literary," *Washington Bee*, November 20, 1920, 1. As part of her public lecturing to raise funds for the National Training School for Women and Girls in Washington, DC, Nannie Helen Burroughs presented "The Way Out" before the Bethel on February 20, 1906. She also addressed the society on February 23, 1909, and November 28, 1911. *New York Freeman*, February 24, 1906, 1, and February 20, 1909, 1; *Washington Bee*, December 2, 1911, 5. For the text of part of her November 28, 1911, address, see "Education that Counts," 1.

53. Fanny Jackson Coppin and Ida B. Wells were both born with slave status; Carrie Clifford, Ida Gibbs, Frances Harper, Lucy Moten, and Mary Ann Shadd were born with free status to parents with free status; Hallie Quinn Brown, Nannie Hellen Burroughs, Coralie Franklin Cook, and Lucy Laney were born with free status to parents who had been enslaved.

54. Harper, *Brighter Coming Day*, 271, 285–92.

55. Johnson, "The Half Has Never Been Told," 838.

56. Hopkins was active in the Black women's club movement and "represented the Woman's Era Club [of Boston] at the Annual Convention of New England Federation of Woman's Clubs" in 1898. Dworkin, "Biography of Pauline E. Hopkins"; McHenry, *Forgotten Readers*, 361n89.

57. Gere and Robbins, "Gendered Literacy in Black and White," 674.

58. Harley, "Fleetwood, Sara Iredell," 72–73; Sterling, *We Are Your Sisters*, 430; Forbes, *African American Women during the Civil War*, 82, 131.

59. Knupfer, *Toward a Tenderer Humanity*, 122.

60. Hine, *When the Truth Is Told*, 36; Ferguson, "Woman's Improvement Club," 1278.

61. As an example of what might form part of women's lyceum programs, the Lucy Laney Lyceum debated whether "females should receive a collegiate education." "Charleston News," 4. See also *The Topeka Plaindealer*, December 26, 1913, 2; "Frances Harper Anniversary," 5; "Saloon Brawl," 7.

62. Bacon, *Freedom's Journal*, 53; Fraser, "Emancipatory Cosmology," 264.

63. Foreman, *Activist Sentiments*, 139.

64. Han, "All Roads Lead to San Francisco," 3; Han, "Making a Black Pacific," 31.

65. For examinations of this goal and how particular periodicals pursued it, see Fraser, *Star Territory*; Spires, *The Practice of Citizenship*; Fagan, *The Black Newspaper and the Chosen Nation*; and Gardner, *Black Print Unbound*.

66. Gallon, "The Black Press." The *Weekly Advocate*, renamed *The Colored American*, was in print from 1837 to 1842, *Freedom's Journal* was published from 1827 to 1829, and *The North Star* was published from 1847 to 1851.

67. Foster, "Genealogies of Our Concerns," 355.

68. Similar to the direct action beauty culturalists engaged in to distribute publications such as *The Messenger*, some magazines existed to promote Black beauty products. For example, Anthony Overton's *Half-Century Magazine* (1916–1925), edited by Katherine Williams-Irvin, and the *Sunday Chicago Bee* (1925–1942), edited by Olive Diggs, were responsible for the success of his High Brown cosmetic product empire. See Gill, *Beauty Shop Politics*, 56, 58; Halliday, "Centering Black Women in the Black Chicago Renaissance."

69. Gill, *Beauty Shop Politics*, 51–53. *The Messenger* was read "in the eastern and western Caribbean, the Philippines, Great Britain, Japan, Germany, Austria and Italy," and had a "circulation [of] 26,000 at its height." Digby-Junger, "The *Guardian*, *Crisis*, *Messenger*, and *Negro World*," 267, 41. For more on the Madam C. J. Walker Hair Culturalists Union of America and the political organizing of beauty culturalists, see Gill, *Beauty Shop Politics*, 32–60.

70. Sheehan, "To Exist Serially," 40.

71. Gallon offers a very useful sketch of scholarship in "The Black Press." Gardner's focus on subscribers to the *Christian Recorder* in *Black Print Unbound* and Gallon's *Pleasure in the News* are notable exceptions, along with biographically based studies of women editors, such as Jane Rhodes's *Mary Ann Shadd Cary* and Ula Taylor's *The Veiled Garvey*.

72. I have found Cohen and Stein's definition of African American print culture helpful, particularly their consideration of "print in relation to the oral, visual, and manuscript mediations that nevertheless persist in a world where print has become commonplace," rather than privileging print as an object distinct within this communicative and expressive environment. Also very helpful is their distinction between print and print culture: "We distinguish between 'print,' a technology that fixes impressions, and 'print culture,' a world in which print both integrates with other practices and assumes a life of its own. This conceptual distinction emphasizes that print does not merely function as an instrument of human needs; it directs our

attention instead to the ways that print affects (and sometimes effects) personhood, circulates to unintended readers, is subject to reiteration and reappropriation, solicits publics that may not yet recognize themselves as such, and allows equally for representation and misrepresentation. Cohen and Stein, "Introduction," 7.

73. Dann, *The Black Press*, 13, 17.

74. Jones, *All Bound Up Together*, 103.

75. Foster, "A Narrative of the Interesting Origins," 735, 715.

76. Foster, "A Narrative of the Interesting Origins," 726, 721.

77. Foreman, "Black Organizing, Print Advocacy, and Collective Authorship," 23–24.

78. McHenry, *Forgotten Readers*, 84–85. Chapter 1 and this book's appendix will make clear the geographic and temporal range of such societies.

79. Jones, *All Bound Up Together*, 4–5.

80. Here, Jones was building on the foundational work of Black feminist scholars such as Elsa Barkley Brown, who argued that Black women in the Progressive Era were working to regain, not attain for the first time, their place in Black public politics. See Brown, "Negotiating and Transforming the Public Sphere."

81. McHenry, *Forgotten Readers*, 86.

82. Foreman, "Black Organizing, Print Advocacy, and Collective Authorship," 22. See also Woo, "Deleted Name But Indelible Body"; and "Exhibits," Colored Conventions Project, https://coloredconventions.org/exhibits/.

83. Foreman, "Black Organizing, Print Advocacy, and Collective Authorship," 44.

84. Foreman, "Black Organizing, Print Advocacy, and Collective Authorship," 44; Jim Casey, personal correspondence. See also Casey, "Editing Forms," which traces connections between the Black press and the convention movement, such as the founding of the *Mirror of the Times* as an outcome of California's first colored convention in 1855 and newspaperman Philip Bell's repeat convention attendance alongside his co-editorship of *The Colored American* (New York, NY), the *Pacific Appeal*, and the San Francisco *Elevator*.

85. See, for example, Dann, *The Black Press*. For more historiography and scholarship that takes the convention movement as the primary site of Black press development, see Foreman, "Black Organizing, Print Advocacy, and Collective Authorship,"; Fagan, *The Black Newspaper and the Chosen Nation*; Fagan, "The Organ of the Whole"; Durrance et al., "The Early Case for a Black National Press."

86. Foreman, "Black Organizing, Print Advocacy, and Collective Authorship," 43–44.

87. Senchyne, "Under Pressure," 116.

88. Liddle, "Method in Periodical Studies."

89. Brooks, "The Early American Public Sphere and the Emergence of a Black Counterpublic," 73. Cohen and Stein affirm that for African Americans, entering the public sphere, as, for example, in a political movement, is underwritten not necessarily by the economic but by the social. They also offer a very useful overview of the print-capitalism thesis. Cohen and Stein, "Introduction," 14.

90. In my use of the term "white supremacist settler colonialism," I take seriously Andrea Smith's argument that critical race theory and Indigenous studies each need to learn from and incorporate the analysis of the other into their own understandings of

how racialization and settler colonialism are intertwined in their operations to maintain what she calls the "three pillars" of white supremacy. See Smith, "Indigeneity, Settler Colonialism, White Supremacy," 30–38.

91. Ardis, "Towards a Theory of Periodical Studies." Ardis's and Liddle's thoughts on media ecology and following the genre arose from a 2013 MLA conference roundtable focused on the question of conceptualizing and theorizing the periodical as an object of study, which responded to Sean Latham and Robert Scholes's modernist journal–focused article "The Rise of Periodical Studies." Discussion raised the following topics as important points of focus for future periodical studies: an "explicit discussion of methodology and common practices"; a desire not to silo studies by geographic or temporal particularity; an attention to the ways chosen objects of study will suggest or determine our conceptualization of the periodical itself; "social action as an important concept for periodical studies"; and the need to "theorize sameness just as we theorize difference." Ball, Summary of "Session 384—What Is a Journal?"

92. Peterson, "Subject to Speculation," 114, 116.

93. For example, although *The Black Republican* (New Orleans, LA) was in print for only a month (during the spring of 1865), its April 15 issue had a print run of 5,000 copies and the paper claimed 300 subscribers in Mobile, Alabama, alone in that issue. "Advertisement," 2; "The Black Republican in Mobile," 2.

94. Still, "Miss M. A. Shadd."

95. Rhodes, *Mary Ann Shadd Cary*, 100.

96. Gardner, *Black Print Unbound*, 276n64.

97. Gardner notes that "by the January 14, 1865, issue, Weaver estimated that it now cost 'over two hundred dollars per week to get the *Recorder* out.' Given prices in 1865—$2.50 for an annual subscription or six cents for a single copy—the paper would need either 4,160 paid full-year subscriptions or over 173,000 single-copy sales to reach the $10,400 that Weaver's somewhat off-hand weekly estimate suggests." Gardner, *Black Print Unbound*, 73.

98. Gardner, *Black Print Unbound*, 84. See also McGill, *American Literature and the Culture of Reprinting*; Jackson, *The Business of Letters*; Garvey, *Writing with Scissors*; Cordell, "Reprinting, Circulation, and the Network Author."

99. Thornbrough, "American Negro Newspapers," 487.

100. The *Colored American* was in print from March 4, 1837, to December 25, 1842. It was edited by Samuel Cornish (former coeditor of *Freedom's Journal*) until his retirement in 1839, when Charles B. Ray became editor. The paper's staff included Phillip Bell, who later edited the *Pacific Appeal* and the San Francisco *Elevator*, and James McCune Smith. Fagan, "'Americans as They Really Are,'" 97–119.

101. McHenry, *Forgotten Readers*, 50.

102. The white-owned and white-edited abolitionist press also relied on these societies for content. For example, William Lloyd Garrison began a regular Ladies' Department in *The Liberator* by publishing work that the members of the all-Black Philadelphia Female Literary Association had created. See Garrison, "Female Literary Association."

103. On reprinting, see McGill, *American Literature and the Culture of Reprinting*.

104. Wahl-Jorgensen, "A 'Legitimate Beef' or 'Raw Meat,'" 90–91.
105. Madera, *Black Atlas*, 6; Warner, *Publics and Counterpublics*, 119.
106. Gilmore, "Fatal Couplings of Power and Difference," 22.
107. See Fagan, *The Black Newspaper and the Chosen Nation*.
108. Fraser, "Emancipatory Cosmology," 256.
109. Spires, *The Practice of Citizenship*, 9.
110. Fielder and Senchyne, *Against a Sharp White Background*, 9.
111. Bass, "On the Sidewalk," 1.

CHAPTER ONE: **Recirculation and African American Feminisms**

1. The *Blade* was a four-page weekly with a reported circulation of 1,200 in 1899. Earlier editions of *Ayer's* do not note circulation. See *Ayer's American Newspaper Annual*, 1899. The paper circulated through subscription via agents who were paid a 25 percent commission. Its greatest number of agents was listed in May 1894: twelve agents in Texas, two of whom were women; two in Indian Territory; three in Montana; two in its home state of Kansas; and one in Iowa. Colophon, *Parsons Weekly Blade*, May 12, 1894, 2.
2. "In Defense of Our Women," 2.
3. "Miss Wells' Crusade," 2.
4. Wells, *Southern Horrors*, 17; McMurray, *To Keep the Waters Troubled*, 189; Zackodnik, *Press, Platform, Pulpit*, 133–34.
5. Ella Mahammitt wrote the Woman's Column for the *Enterprise*, which she also edited. Peavler, "African Americans in Omaha," 341. Mahammitt also operated a catering business and the Mahammitt School of Cookery; see Mahammitt, *Recipes and Domestic Service*.
6. McHenry, *Forgotten Readers*, 13.
7. Fisher, *Black Literate Lives*, 25.
8. I do not use remediation to name this practice because I seek both to highlight the movement of Black women's texts and their circulation as essential to the viability of a fledgling Black press and to avoid suggesting that the print publication of such texts altered their meaning or achieved a more developed media form.
9. For such operative definitions of recirculation in current scholarship, see, for example, Garvey, *Writing with Scissors*; Sommers, "Harriet Jacobs and the Recirculation of Print Culture"; Leavell, "'Not Intended Exclusively for the Slave States.'" Sometimes recirculation is used as a synonym for reprinting in periodical studies. Although this was a standard journalistic practice in the nineteenth-century press both in the United States and the United Kingdom, it cannot be said to have been inherently politicized. See, for example, Garvey, "The Power of Recirculation," 219.
10. Gaonkar and Povinelli, "Technologies of Public Forms," 386.
11. Warner, *Publics and Counterpublics*, 11–12, 67; emphasis in the original.
12. Warner, *Publics and Counterpublics*, 96.
13. Lee and LiPuma, "Cultures of Circulation," 194.
14. Warner, *Publics and Counterpublics*, 108.
15. Hutton, *The Early Black Press in America*, 39. In the larger context of American journalism, circulation figures for the Black press approach those of the average

weeklies and dailies. From the 1830s to the 1860s, "the great mass of weeklies had only a few hundred circulation each, and most of the dailies only a few thousand." Mott, *American Journalism*, 303.

16. Detweiler, *Negro Press*, 6–7; Logan, *Liberating Language*, 69.
17. McHenry, *Forgotten Readers*, 13.
18. Letter to the Editor, *Christian Recorder*, January 18, 1877, 6.
19. McGill, *American Literature and the Culture of Reprinting*, 107, 41.
20. Warner, *Publics and Counterpublics*, 95–96.
21. Lee and LiPuma, "Cultures of Circulation," 192; emphasis in the original.
22. On newspaper readers as aware of themselves within a larger community of others engaged in a "ritual" of mass simultaneity, see Anderson, *Imagined Communities*.
23. Kelley, "'Talents Committed to Your Care,'" 48, 69. Amy Matilda (Williams) married Joseph Cassey in 1827. Cassey was a free immigrant from the West Indies, a barber and real estate entrepreneur who founded the Pennsylvania Anti-Slavery Society. He was also a sales agent for *The Liberator*. Dunbar, "A Mental and Moral Feast," 83.
24. The paper printed such cautions as in "Observer No. V," and "A Sketch of Comfort."
25. "Matilda," "Messrs. Editors," 2; emphasis added. Although Joycelyn Moody has attributed this letter to Stewart and Waters has followed suit, Kelley documents it as authored by Amy Matilda Cassey.
26. "To Our Patrons," 1.
27. Walker, *Walker's Appeal*, 37.
28. "Beatrice," "By a Young Lady."
29. "A." [Sarah Forten], "By a Member of the Female Literary Association."
30. Dunbar, "Mental and Moral Feast," 105.
31. "Third Anniversary of the Ladies' Literary Society"; emphasis in the original. Jennings's mother was also named Elizabeth, which may explain why scholarship has attributed authorship of this address to the daughter (not the mother), despite her young age when she delivered it. See, for example, Foner and Branham, *Lift Every Voice*, 166–68; Logan, *Liberating Language*, 74; Kelley, *Learning to Stand and Speak*, 143–44. Elizabeth Jennings Sr. was a founding member of the New York Ladies' Literary Society along with Henrietta Ray, Sarah Ennals, and Sarah Elson. Alexander, *African or American?*, 91.
32. A Colored Lady in Medford, "Reflections on Slavery"; Anna Elizabeth, "A Short Address to Females of Color"; Mapps Douglass, "Emigration to Mexico"; Mapps Douglass, "Address."
33. "High School for Young Colored Ladies and Misses"; de Vera, "'We the ladies,'" 3.
34. Stewart was indentured as result of being orphaned at the age of five. Bolden, "Maria W. Stewart."
35. Richardson, *Maria W. Stewart*, 126n68. Martha Jones documents that by 1836, women "were seated as delegates and [were] signing petitions" at the colored conventions. Jones, *All Bound Up Together*, 45.
36. Sophanisba, "Extract from a Letter."

37. Richardson, *Maria W. Stewart*, 81. Dorothy Porter documents two Black women's literary societies in New York City in the 1830s: the Ladies' Literary Society of the City of New York and the New York Female Literary Society. Porter, "The Organized Educational Activities of Negro Literary Societies," 557. See the appendix to this volume for seven possible literary societies (not all of them female only) that Stewart could have joined in Baltimore in the period from 1852 to 1861 and the three in Washington, DC, that operated when Stewart lived in that city from 1861 until her death in 1879. Kirstin Waters speculates that Stewart may have been a member of Boston's interracial Female Anti-Slavery Society, formed in 1833 the year she left Boston, whose members included Maria Weston Chapman, Lavinia Hilton, Lydia Maria Child, and Susan Paul, quite likely because Stewart and Paul were friends. Waters, *Maria W. Stewart and the Roots of Black Political Thought*, 240.

38. Garfield, "Literary Societies," 113. For a very useful definition of print culture, see Sommers:

> As the proliferation of its usage suggests, print culture is an expansive and expanding term that encompasses the technology of print (with all its requisite tools and materials), the literary and non-literary products produced by this technology (books, newspapers, pamphlets, primers, posters, and broadsides), and the people involved at every stage of these processes (typesetters, editors, printers, writers, booksellers, readers, and newsboys). Yet African American print culture is not something limited to material processes and products—it also exists in the imaginative space of literature. This view of print culture manifests when printed documents are incorporated into the world of a narrative or kept at a distance through ekphrastic description. . . . Acknowledging the presence of print culture within African American literature yields new sites for investigating early African American writers' assertions of authority.

Sommers, "Harriet Jacobs," 136. See also Cohen and Stein, "Introduction," 7.

39. Waters, *Maria W. Stewart and the Roots of Black Political Thought*, 179, 183.

40. Jones, *All Bound Up Together*, 25; Stewart, *Religion and the Pure Principles of Morality*, 21.

41. Stewart, "Cause for Encouragement," 110.

42. Stewart, *Religion and the Pure Principles of Morality*, 30; "A Colored Lady in Medford"; May, "Letter to the Editor." See also Phila., "Letter to the Editor," on women's respectability in antislavery activities; and S., "Letter to the Editor," praising the paper. Phila's letters join two letters to the editor by Sarah Mapps Douglass, writing as Zillah: "To a Friend" and "Dear Brother." These letters were part of a larger discourse on freedom and the rights of "the race" that was pursued in women's literary societies in the early 1830s.

43. Lee and LiPuma define a performative as "a self-reflexive use of reference that, in creating a representation of an ongoing act, also enacts it." Lee and LiPuma, "Cultures of Circulation," 195.

44. "A Short Address."

45. McHenry, *Forgotten Readers*, 68.

46. In 1833, the colored convention movement proposed a mechanical arts high school and a college for men in New Haven, Connecticut. This was the same year that Prudence Crandall founded her academy for Black women in Canterbury, Connecticut, after her school for girls, first established in 1831, drew censure because she had admitted an African American pupil. Whatever the social stigma against educating Black male youth, the education of Black girls and women was regarded as much more controversial in the 1830s. Martha Jones refers to the fact that Black women's literary societies "cloaked" women's education "in domesticity" even as they were its "primary avenue." Jones, *All Bound Up Together*, 32, 34.

47. See "Address to the Female Literary Association of Philadelphia."

48. Fagan, "'Americans as They Really Are,'" 99; Pride and Wilson, *History of the Black Press*, 26. On circulation figures for *Freedom's Journal*, see Bacon, *Freedom's Journal*; and McHenry, *Forgotten Readers*, 89. On the circulation and readership of the *Colored American*, see Johnson, *The Fear of French Negroes*, 170, 236n5. On *The Liberator*, see Quarles, *Black Abolitionists*, 20.

49. "Agents."

50. Mayer, *All on Fire*, 117.

51. Rorbach, "Truth Stranger than Fiction," 730.

52. Mayer, *All on Fire*, 121–23.

53. Garrison, "Female Literary Association."

54. These pseudonyms have fostered a degree of disagreement among scholars. Julie Winch has speculated that Ella was either Sarah Mapps Douglass or her mother Grace Douglass, but Marie Lindhorst has "uncovered nothing to make that identification with any certainty." Winch, *Philadelphia's Black Elite*; Lindhorst, "Politics in a Box," 278n29. Dorothy Sterling identified Sarah Mapps Douglass as Sophanisba and Zillah, and this identification has been widely followed in scholarship on African American women's contributions to *The Liberator*. Sterling, *We Are Your Sisters*, 110–11. However, Mary Kelley cites Winch as she attributes the pseudonyms Ella and Sophanisba to Mapps Douglass while leaving Zillah as an unattributable pseudonym. Kelley, "'Talents Committed to Your Care,'" 43. Gay Gibson Cima believes that Ella was a sufficiently common pseudonym that it may have been used by a variety of women, yet she also argues that Mapps Douglass used it in *The Liberator*. Cima, *Performing Anti-Slavery*, 112–14, 133–34n60. Todd Gernes contests attributing literary contributions signed "Ada" to Sarah Forten after 1834, noting that a white Quaker poet, Eliza Earle, also signed herself Ada at that time. Gernes, "Poetic Justice," 229.

55. Logan, *Liberating Language*, 69.

56. Peterson, *"Doers of the Word,"* 68.

57. Richardson, "Introduction," 24.

58. Garrison, "Female Literary Association."

59. Yee, *Black Women Abolitionists*, 21. Mapps Douglass's mother, Grace Bustill Douglass, helped found this antislavery society in 1833.

60. Stewart, "Establishing a Girls' Department," 85–86.

61. Zillah (Mapps Douglass), "Moonlight."

62. A Colored Female of Philadelphia, "Emigration to Mexico."

63. Zillah (Mapps Douglass), "Extract from a Letter to a Friend."
64. Horton and Horton, *In Hope of Liberty*, 197–99, 211.
65. Zillah (Mapps Douglass), "Reply to Woodby."
66. *The Emancipator* was a weekly publication of the American Anti-Slavery Society. In 1849 and 1850, as the corresponding secretary of the Women's Association of Philadelphia, Sarah Mapps Douglass reported on the group's activities to Frederick Douglass's paper *The North Star*, and in the spring of 1859 she wrote under her own signature for the new monthly *Anglo-African Magazine*. See Mapps Douglass, "For the Pennsylvania Freeman"; Mapps Douglass, "Pennsylvania A. S. Fair"; Mapps Douglass, "Appeal of the Philadelphia Association"; Mapps Douglass, "The North Star Fair"; Mapps Douglass, "A Good Habit Recommended"; and Mapps Douglass, "A General View of Hayti."
67. "Constitution of the Afric-American Female Intelligence Society of Boston," 162–63.
68. Reed, *Platform for Change*, 77–78.
69. Stewart, *Religion and the Pure Principles of Morality*, 41; emphasis in the original.
70. Stewart, "An Address Delivered before the Afric-American Female Intelligence Society of Boston," 2.
71. Glaude, *Exodus!* 6 (emphasis added), 111.
72. Stewart, "An Address Delivered before the Afric-American Female Intelligence Society of Boston," 2. The rhetorical strategy Stewart used most frequently was the Black jeremiad, which is why she is so often understood as influenced by David Walker's *Appeal*. On her work with this rhetorical form, see, for example, May, *Evangelism and Resistance in the Black Atlantic*; Harrell, "A Call to Political and Social Activism"; Ampadu, "Maria W. Stewart and the Rhetoric of Black Preaching"; Utley, "A Woman Made of Words."
73. Rael, *Black Identity and Black Protest*, 266–67.
74. Stewart, "An Address Delivered before the Afric-American Female Intelligence Society of Boston," 2.
75. See, for example, Peterson, *"Doers of the Word,"* 68; Richardson, "Maria W. Stewart," 24.
76. Stewart, "An Address Delivered before the Afric-American Female Intelligence Society of Boston," 2; emphasis added.
77. Richardson, "What If I Am a Woman?," 193.
78. Stewart, *Religion and the Pure Principles of Morality*, 29; Stewart, "Lecture Delivered at the Franklin Hall"; Stewart, "An Address, Delivered at the African Masonic Hall . . . (Concluded)."
79. Stewart, *Religion and the Pure Principles of Morality*; "For Sale at This office, a Tract"; Stewart, "Mrs. Steward's [sic] Essays"; Stewart, *Meditations*; "Just Published, and for Sale at This Office"; Stewart, "An Address Delivered before the Afric-American Female Intelligence Society."
80. Stewart, "An Address, Delivered at the African Masonic Hall"; Stewart, "An Address, Delivered at the African Masonic Hall . . . (Concluded)." Both installments of Stewart's address were published in the section titled Literary, Miscellaneous and

Moral on the paper's last page. Stewart's September 18, 1833, farewell address delivered at the Belknap Street schoolroom (of the African Meeting House on Beacon Hill) was not published in *The Liberator*, but it was published in her *Productions of Mrs. Maria W. Stewart*, signed with "New York, April 14, 1834."

81. Stewart, "Lecture. Delivered at the Franklin Hall"; "Notice. A Lecture on African Rights and Liberty"; "Notice. Mrs. Stewart, Will Deliver Her Farewell Address"; "Mrs. Stuart's [sic] Farewell Address . . . Was Delivered."

82. Richardson, "What If I Am a Woman?," 204; Richardson, "Introduction," 27. Kirstin Waters speculates that Stewart's reasons for leaving Boston may have been more complex, including the fact that schoolteaching may have been open to her in New York. Waters, *Maria W. Stewart and the Roots of Black Political Thought*, 244. Streitmatter presents her teaching as an outgrowth of her literary society activities in New York, which in turn led to her appointment "as assistant principal for the Williamsburg section of Brooklyn," a position she lost in 1852. After that, she moved to Baltimore. Streitmatter, "Maria W. Stewart," 56–57. She also attended the Women's Anti-Slavery Convention of 1837. Richardson, "Introduction," 27.

83. Qtd. in Sterling, *We Are Your Sisters*, 158–59.

84. Richardson, "What If I Am a Woman?," 205n1. *The Repository*, which at first was a quarterly based in Indianapolis that was edited by Elisha Weaver, moved to Baltimore in 1861 under the editorship of John Mifflin Brown when Weaver began editing the *Christian Recorder*. With that move, it also shifted to monthly publication. See Gardner, *Unexpected Places*, chapter 2. The *Repository* sold for $1 for a yearly subscription and 25 cents per copy. The paper serialized Stewart's short story, "The First Stage of Life," in three installments that ran from April through October in 1861. See also Wright, *Black Girlhood*, 70.

85. Stewart and Gardner, "Two Texts," 156.

86. McHenry, *Forgotten Readers*, 138; Gardner, *Unexpected Places*, 86.

87. McHenry, *Forgotten Readers*, 133, 132.

88. McHenry, *Forgotten Readers*, 139.

89. "Letter from William C. Nell," 3.

90. "Meditations, by Mrs. Maria W. Stewart." Stewart moved to Washington, DC, in 1861 to teach. After the war, she became the director of housekeeping at the Freedmen's Hospital there, and in 1871 she raised funds to open an Episcopal Sunday school. Streitmatter, "Maria W. Stewart," 58. In 1878, she successfully claimed eligibility for an $8 monthly pension as "widow of a veteran of the War of 1812." Richardson, *Maria W. Stewart*, 79. She died in the Freedmen's Hospital in Washington, DC, on December 17, 1879.

91. Streitmatter, "Maria W. Stewart," 58.

92. Foster, "Narrative," 726, 721.

93. Harper, *Enlightened Motherhood*.

94. On "The Elevation and Education of Our People" as the address that became "The Colored People in America" in *Poems on Miscellaneous Subjects* (1854), see Foster, "Introduction," 11. Foster also notes that many of Harper's antislavery addresses formed a repertoire "that she delivered extemporaneously and modified with references to

recent or local events." Foster, "Introduction," 37. On Stewart's address "Christianity," see Peterson, *"Doers of the Word,"* 133.

95. For example, Harper's address for the fourth anniversary of the New York City Anti-Slavery Society, delivered on the evening of May 13, 1857, in the City Assembly Rooms in New York, was recirculated in abridged form in the *National Anti-Slavery Standard*. This address has since become known and anthologized as "Could We Trace the Record of Every Human Heart." For further examples of Harper's use of recirculation, see Yerrington, "Speech of Miss Frances Ellen Watkins"; "An Appeal to Christians throughout the World"; M. R. L., "Mrs. Frances E. W. Harper on Reconstruction," a report of Harper's speech (a mix of transcription and summary) given on February 1, 1864, in Roger Williams Church in Providence, RI. "Coloured Women of America," published in *Englishwoman's Review*, reports Harper's speech at the Women's Congress in Philadelphia and notes: "We transcribe a portion of the essay ['paper read by Mrs. Harper, of Philadelphia'] for our readers." See "Coloured Women of America."

96. Washington, "Frances Ellen Watkins," 61–67, 71.

97. Mathews was integral to the formation of the National Federation of Afro-American Women in 1895 and to its merger a year later with the National Colored Women's League, which became the NACWC. She also founded the White Rose Industrial Association in 1897 to support Black women as they migrated north. Logan, "Victoria Earle Matthews."

98. Archivists have speculated that "The Value of Race Literature" was published as a pamphlet from Boston in 1895, although the document notes neither press nor publication date. See Matthews, *The Value of Race Literature*. Logan documents that the Society of Christian Endeavor had become "an international, interdenominational youth movement with a membership of more than 1.5 million by 1893." Logan, "Victoria Earle Mathews."

99. Wells had *A Red Record* published by Donohue & Henneberry in Chicago in 1894. Wells's address at the AME Church in Washington, DC, on February 3, 1893, was recirculated in the *American Citizen*, February 17, 1893. Frederick Douglass invited her to make that address and Mary Church Terrell introduced her to the audience. Two of her Birmingham addresses on lynch law in the United States, given at meetings on May 16, 1894, were recirculated as "Lynch Law in the United States" and "Lynch Law in America." Wells's Birmingham address on lynching and anti-Black and anti-Asian racism, delivered on May 17, 1894, was recirculated as both excerpts and summary in an editorial titled "The Lesson of Toleration" in the *Birmingham Daily Gazette*. Her address at the Bethel AME Church in New York City on July 29, 1894, was recirculated in the *New York Times*, the New York *Sun*, the New York *Herald Tribune*, and the *Memphis Commercial Appeal* on July 30, 1894, and in the *Hawaiian Gazette* on August 21, 1894. Wells's "Remarks to President McKinley," delivered March 21, 1898, was recirculated in the *Cleveland Gazette*.

100. Hutchinson, *Anna J. Cooper*, 89. Cooper appeared on the masthead of the *Southland* as coeditor with S. G. Atkins.

101. Cooper, *A Voice from the South*, 9; "Protestant Episcopal Ministers in Convention," 2; Hutchinson, *Anna J. Cooper*, 87.

102. "Colored Women as Wage Earners," which Cooper gave several times from the late 1890s to 1904 at literary societies and lyceums, was recirculated in the *Southern Workman* as an essay, which was then reprinted in excerpted form in the *Washington Bee*. She again delivered "Colored Women as Wage Earners" to the Odd Fellows Lyceum in Washington, DC, on April 3, 1904, and this version was excerpted in the Indianapolis *Freeman* two weeks later. Cooper, "Colored Women as Wage Earners," *Southern Workman*, 285–98; "Colored Women as Wage Earners," Indianapolis *Freeman*, 4; and "Colored Women as Wage Earners," *Washington Bee*, 2; "Second Baptist," 1. Her February 17, 1907, address "Program of Education" for the Second Baptist Church Lyceum in Washington, DC, became the basis of the three-part "Educational Programmes" published in *McGirt's Magazine* in January 1908, April 1908, and May 1908. For mention of *McGirt's* publication of this series, see Murray, "The In-Look," January 1, 1908, 25; Murray, "The In-Look," May 1, 1908, 29; Murray, "The In-Look," June 1, 1908, 27. The issues of *McGirt's* in which this series of publications appeared may not have survived and are not preserved in any library with *McGirt's Magazine* holdings listed on WorldCat.

103. This address was published in *World's Congress of Representative Women* and then self-published as the pamphlet *The Present Status and Intellectual Progress of Colored Women*.

104. Washington, "We Must Have a Cleaner 'Social Morality.'"

105. "Our Women. Meeting of the American Woman Suffrage Association—Mrs. Terrell's Address," 4; "Progress of Colored Women," March 12, 1898, 4; "Progress of Colored Women," March 19, 1898, 2; Terrell, *The Progress of Colored Women*. The pamphlet's first seventeen pages can be downloaded at "The Progress of Colored Women," https://www.loc.gov/item/90898298/.

106. Terrell, "The International Congress of Women." Terrell's "What It Means to Be Colored in the Capital of the United States," delivered on October 10, 1906, to the United Women's Club of Washington, DC, was recirculated in *The Independent* (New York, NY). Terrell, "What It Means to Be Colored in the Capital," 181–86.

107. McHenry, *Forgotten Readers*, 20.

108. Ball, *To Live an Antislavery Life*, 4, 52–54.

109. Porter, "The Organized Educational Activities of Negro Literary Societies," 562; "From the Pennsylvania Freeman."

110. Charlotte K. wrote that these male organizations "destroyed the New York Literary Societies" and offered "nothing but . . . Balls and Suppers" that drained Lodge benevolent funds. Charlotte K., "Mr. Editor," 3.

111. See, for example, "A Fred. Douglass Literary Society in New York Takes Note of the Embree Affair."

112. "Our Girls."

113. "Letter from C. J. Hardstew."

114. The National Independent Political League (1908–1920) was founded by activist and journalist Monroe Trotter and was regarded as militant in its politics. Trotter had resigned from the Niagara Movement because of W. E. B. Du Bois's pacifist approach. The League's leadership was all-Black and former members of the Niagara

Movement, the National Afro-American Council, and the Constitutional League, and it pursued Black civil rights and anti-lynching.

115. De Vera notes that at an 1850 colored convention, "'the Ladies attending the Convention proposed to defray the expenses of the house,' and in 1856, the 'Ladies of AME Church' donated five dollars to help with the cost of renting a hall and publishing the minutes. . . . During the 1858 Cincinnati convention, delegates decided to form an anti-slavery society and Frances Ellen Watkins [Harper] was among those who donated a large sum." Lucy Stanton [Day Sessions] and Mary J. Hopkins pledged funds to publish the minutes of the 1851 Columbus, Ohio, colored convention. de Vera, "'We the ladies . . . have been deprived of a voice,'" 8, 8n22. See also *Minutes of the State Convention of the Colored Citizens of Ohio*.

116. Melvin and Richards, "Sir"; Dunbar, "Mental and Moral Feast," 95.

117. Jones, *All Bound Up Together*, 83. Shirley Yee notes that the association's inaugural meeting was held in Rachel Lloyd's home. Yee, *Black Women Abolitionists*, 108. Sarah Mapps Douglass, Amy Matilda Cassey, Hester Bustill, Lydia Ann Bustill, and Hetty Burr were among the thirteen members of the association listed in Mapps Douglass, "Appeal of the Philadelphia Association," 3. See also Mapps Douglass, "The North Star Fair," 2.

118. "Circular by the Provisional Committee of the *Impartial Citizen*," 38–41. See also Hunter, "The Rev. Jermain Loguen"; Hunter, *To Set the Captives Free*; Rev. Jermain Loguen, *The Rev. J. W. Loguen*; Sernett, *North Star Country*.

119. Bastien and Tompkins, "To the Friends of Freedom and the Press," 4. See also Streitmatter, *Raising Her Voice*, 57.

120. Still, "From the Ladies." Not a small sum, $20 in 1861 would have a relative value of $714 in 2024. See https://www.measuringworth.com/calculators/uscompare/. For notices of *Recorder* agents that included Still, see "Our City Canvas"; "Notice." See also Gardner, *Black Print Unbound*, 91–92.

121. Qtd. in Gardner, *Black Print Unbound*, 76.

122. Grice, "Elevator Aid Association," 2; emphasis added. Grice had recently attended a meeting of the Elevator Aid Association, where he learned of the donation campaign to support the paper.

123. Mary, "A Response," 2. Mary had written in response to Mrs. D. D. Carter's proposition that women "contribute a dollar each" to sustain the *Elevator*.

124. Nubia, "Progress of the Colored People," 4; Snorgrass, "The Black Press in the San Francisco Bay Area," 306. Snorgrass also contests the scholarly consensus that the *Mirror* began publication in 1857 by indicating that "volume numbers and dates of the issues available (provided the paper was published on a regular basis) indicate the *Mirror* was first published October 31, 1856." He contends that the paper was established as a result of the first colored convention of California in Sacramento in 1855 (306).

125. Logan, *Liberating Language*, 91–93.

126. See, for example, "Col. J. Perry." Gordon Fraser argues that "unlike isolated mutual aid or literary societies in the North, *Freedom's Journal* and *The Rights of All* enabled a mobile network connecting North and South." However, reports like this in the Indianapolis *Freeman* make clear that the sustained connections between the Black

press and literary societies formed a broader mobile network for both institutions. Fraser, "Emancipatory Cosmology," 280.

127. "There is a need of energy among our young people here."

128. On Williams, see Mulcahy, "Professional Anxiety."

129. See, for example, Gilmore, *Gender and Jim Crow*; Beatty, "Black Perspectives of American Women." Other Black women journalists who wrote about their colleagues include Lucy Wilmot Smith ("Some Female Writers") and Katherine Tillman ("Afro-American Women"). Tillman edited the women's column of the *Iowa State Bystander* (Des Moines) in the late 1890s.

130. See, for example, "Triana. Personal and General," 3; "Good Political Speaking," 1; "Philadelphia Dots," 8; "Literary Society," 1; "Albany, TX," 5; "From Our Correspondents. Weekly Paragraphs," 4; "Bethel, Literary Society," 4; "Mt. Zion Baptist," 1; "Metropolitan Baptist," 6. See also the appendix to this book.

131. The Garrison Lyceum was reorganized in 1890; see the *New York Age*, October 18, 1890, 1. In 1891, Ida B. Wells and others were working to reorganize the Memphis Lyceum. See the Indianapolis *Freeman*, May 2, 1891, 4.

132. African American literacy was growing at spectacular rates by the late nineteenth century. While 30 percent of the Black population was considered literate by 1880, that figure rose to 42.9 percent in 1890 and 55.5 percent in 1900. Detweiler, *The Negro Press in the United States*, 61. From 450,000 to 500,000 Southern African Americans relocated to Northern urban centers in 1915 to 1918, and another 700,000 migrated north during the 1920s. Arnesen, *Black Protest and the Great Migration*, 1. Thomas Maloney notes that migration virtually tripled from 1911 to 1920, when 70 of every 1,000 African Americans migrated north, in contrast to 25 per 1,000 from 1901 to 1910. Maloney also found that "increased probability of Northern residence was concentrated among literate women," making Black female literacy central if we are crediting the exponential growth of the Black press partly to migration. Maloney, "African American Migration to the North," 2, 5.

133. Bacon and McClish, "Reinventing the Master's Tools," 22.

134. See the *Weekly Pelican*, July 30, 1887, 2; and the *Commonwealth* (Baltimore, MD; 1915), July 24, 1915, 3, for the Opelousa Literary Society of Opelousa, Louisiana, and the Pikesville Literary Society of Pikesville, Maryland, taking the paper as their "chief organ." See the *Huntsville Gazette*, November 5, 1892, 3, for the Gateway Literary Society of Decatur, Alabama, taking the *Gazette*, in which it also planned to publish its proceedings. See the *New York Age*, May 3, 1890, 4, for the Zion Lyceum of Paterson, New Jersey, subscribing to it; and the Indianapolis *Freeman*, April 7, 1894, 5, for the L. and G. Lyceum of Elliston, Virginia, taking the paper as its organ.

135. Kennedy, "New Era Club," 879; Coleman, "The Woman's Era, 1894–1897," 36.

136. Salem, "National Association of Colored Women," 845; Harrison, "Mississippi State Federation of Colored Women's Clubs," 802; Herron, "Mississippi State Federation of Women's Clubs."

137. Scharf, *The Chronicles of Baltimore*, 108. The Galbraith Lyceum was founded by 1859, judging from its coverage in the Black press. See the *Weekly Anglo-African*, September 7, 1859, 2, and the *Washington Bee*, April 11, 1885, 2. On the *Lyceum Observer*

(Baltimore, MD), see Logan, *Liberating Language*, 19. On the Freeman Lyceum in Brewerville, Liberia, see the *New York Freeman*, March 19, 1887, 2. On the Government Lyceum in Port au Prince, Haiti, see the Indianapolis *Freeman*, May 6, 1893, 6.

138. Publishing the doings of literary societies and lyceums across the nation continued when William Pope sold *The Topkea Call* to Joseph Bass in 1896, who then sold it in 1898 to Nick Chiles, who renamed it the *Plaindealer*. The Indianapolis *Freeman* also continued to publish reports on literary societies after Edward Elder Cooper sold it to George L. Knox in 1892.

139. *American Citizen*, April 5, 1889, 4; *New York Freeman*, January 5, 1889, 5; Indianapolis *Freeman*, June 3, 1893, 4. Mary E. Lambert's (Mary Eliza Tucker Lambert) writing also appears in the *A.M.E. Church Review*.

140. I have been unable to locate these lyceum papers' publication date ranges, which is a common problem for historical African American periodicals and for those published by literary societies and lyceums in particular. See Penn, *The Afro-American Press, and Its Editors*.

141. Reese, *Women of Oklahoma*, 160, 172–73, 154.

142. Gilmore, "North Carolina Federation of Women's Clubs," 883.

143. Warner, *Publics and Counterpublics*, 119.

CHAPTER TWO: **Making Place**

1. Gardner, *Black Print Unbound*, 159.

2. Forten, "Letter from St. Helena's Island," *Boston Evening Transcript*, 1; Forten, "Letter from St. Helena's Island," *Salem Register*; Forten, "Letter from St. Helena's Island," *The Liberator*; "Interesting Letter from Miss Charlotte L. Forten," *The Liberator*; Forten, "Life on the Sea Islands," parts I and II. For more on the continuities between these letters and the *Atlantic Monthly* essays, see Barnes, "Teaching to Resist."

3. Forten Grimké, "Colored People in New England," 37.

4. For Annie M. Smith's letters in the *Christian Recorder* from December 1864 through November 1865 on education, charity, reading, women's roles, and respectability; Sallie Daffin's letters on education, the freedpeople, self-sufficiency, and migration in the *Recorder* from April 1864 through March 1869; Lizzie Hart's writing on Black civil rights, education, the Civil War, and freedpeople in the *Recorder* from July 1864 through December 1865; and Jennie Carter writing as Semper Fidelis and Ann Trask in the *Elevator* from July 1867 through December 1874, see Gardner, *Unexpected Places*; Gardner, "Remembered (Black) Readers."

5. Shadd Cary, "Trade for Our Boys"; Wells, "Freedom of Political Action"; Wells, "Our Women"; Terrell, "To the Editor," *Charleston News and Courier* and "To the Editor," *Evening Star* (Washington, DC). The Mary Church Terrell Papers have archived some letters to the editor Terrell wrote among her correspondence. For example, from 1904 to 1925 she wrote to the editors of the *North American Review*, the *Saturday Evening Post*, the *New Republic*, *Collier's*, *Harper's*, the *Charleston News and Courier*, the *Evening Star*, the *Washington Post*, the *New York Age*, and the *Baltimore American*.

6. As Karin Wahl-Jorgensen has noted, "the letters section is perhaps the oldest forum for public debate—some form of letters-to-the-editor feature has existed as long

as newspapers have been in mass circulation." Wahl-Jorgensen, "A 'Legitimate Beef' or 'Raw Meat,'" 91. Gaul and Harris base their contention that letters to the editor is American journalism's foundational genre on the fact that the original content of early newspapers (i.e., content not reprinted from another publication) was almost exclusively letters. Gaul and Harris "Introduction," 10.

7. Wahl-Jorgensen, "A 'Legitimate Beef' or 'Raw Meat,'" 90–91. See also Snyder and Sorensen, "Letters to the Editor as a Serial Form"; Nielsen, "Participation through Letters to the Editor"; Delap, "The Freewoman"; Green, "Complaints of Everyday Life."

8. The print-capitalism thesis was developed by Benedict Anderson, who argued that nationalisms are developed and sustained through imagined communities in which disparate members of a nation, geographically distant from one another, experience themselves as united through a shared vocabulary. Anderson posited that print, particularly the "convergence of capitalism and print technology," was central to the formation and function of imagined communities. Anderson, *Imagined Communities*, 49. See also Habermas, *The Structural Transformation of the Public Sphere*.

9. Brooks, "The Early American Public Sphere and the Emergence of a Black Counterpublic," 73; emphasis added.

10. Gardner, *Black Print Unbound*, 167.

11. Fraser, "Emancipatory Cosmology," 264; Fagan, *The Black Newspaper and the Chosen Nation*.

12. Spires, *The Practice of Citizenship*, 9–10.

13. Foreman, "Black Organizing, Print Advocacy, and Collective Authorship," 48, 52.

14. David Roediger reminds us of John Locke's "grounding of natural rights in property" and his "hesitant embrace of 'possessive individualism'" as delimited by his view that not all men possessed their bodies and could sell their labor, which together formed the basis of his "straightforward endorsement of the 'possessive investment in whiteness.'" Locke was an "architect of policies enabling colonial slavery" in the United States through his work as a Carolina landgrave on the colony's Board of Trade and Plantations. Part of enabling slavery was, of course, to enable settler colonialism, and Locke promoted settler colonialism by characterizing the relationship of Indigenous peoples to land as dysfunctional because they did not "subdue" or "improv[e] it by labor," since they neither inhabited nor farmed it but instead migrated through it. Therefore, for Locke, Indigenous peoples "forfeited their right to land," either as individual possession or in common. Locke is but one example of the ways in which anti-Black racemaking and racialization of land and space in the United States was foundationally anti-Indigenous. Roediger, *How Race Survived U.S. History*, 11, 16–17.

15. Hartman, *Scenes of Subjection*, 118.

16. Byrd, *The Transit of Empire*, 202–3.

17. Byrd has introduced "arrivant" into Indigenous studies, a term adopted from the work of Edward Kamau Brathwaite that disrupts the binary of "settler" and "native." Byrd, *The Transit of Empire*, xix. See also Brathwaite, *The Arrivants*. Work in Black studies on Black life and western ontologies of "the human," includes that of Saidiya Hartman, David Marriott, Katherine McKittrick, Fred Moten, Jared Sexton, Christina Sharpe, Hortense Spillers, Frank Wilderson, Michelle Wright, and Sylvia Wynter.

18. See Lefebvre, *The Production of Space*; Crawley, "Introduction to the Academy and What Can Be Done?"

19. Data visualization is the representation of information or data, in graph, chart, geospatial, or network forms, and is typically employed to analyze and represent a large amount of information.

20. Warner, *Publics and Counterpublics*, 119.

21. Dahn, *Jim Crow Networks*, 83.

22. Shadd, a schoolteacher, hailed from an abolitionist family that was active in the Underground Railroad. She was also active in abolition, which she continued in both Canada West and later in the United States by advocating for the rights of self-emancipated African Americans.

23. Shadd, "Wilmington, Jan. 25, 1849."

24. There is no extant copy of this pamphlet. See Rhodes, *Mary Ann Shadd Cary*, 22–23.

25. M. R. D. [Martin R. Delany], "In the Lecturing Field"; J. B. Y., "Miss Shadd's Pamphlet."

26. Peterson, *"Doers of the Word,"* 111.

27. Jones, *All Bound Up Together*, 105. Samantha de Vera draws attention to Amelia Freeman as a delegate. Freeman moved to Chatham in 1856 and shortly thereafter married Isaac Shadd, Mary Ann Shadd's brother. De Vera, "'We the ladies,'" 5.

28. *Proceedings of the National Emigration Convention of Colored People*, 20.

29. "American Slavery."

30. De Vera, "'We the ladies,'" 8.

31. J. B. Y., "Miss Shadd's Pamphlet."

32. Delany, *Condition, Elevation, Emigration, and Destiny*, 131.

33. As Rhodes points out, Delany's pamphlet went on to become "a classic text of black nationalism," while Shadd's "quickly lapse[d] into obscurity." Shadd's pamphlet seems to have sold poorly, receiving little notice in the Black or abolitionist press, much as was the case with *Hints*. Rhodes, *Mary Ann Shadd Cary*, 50. Richard Almonte notes that neither sales figures nor figures about print run exist for *A Plea for Emigration*. Almonte, "Introduction," 21.

34. "Plea for Emigration"; Bibb, "A Plea for Emigration."

35. Almonte, "Introduction," 21. See also Bearden and Butler, *Shadd*, 132, which quotes the *Pennsylvania Freeman*, May 26, 1853, regarding one of these lectures.

36. The paper weathered interruptions to its publication with moves from Windsor to Toronto and then to Chatham.

37. Rhodes, *Mary Ann Shadd Cary*, 74, 88; Logan, *Liberating Language*, 65. Shadd continued her activist career after leaving the *Freeman*. During the mid- to late 1850s, she lectured on abolition and emigration, and during the late 1860s and early 1870s, she advocated for women's interests and participation in fields such as the Black labor movement. In 1880, she formed the Colored Women's Progressive Franchise Association to promote women's political and economic rights. Rhodes, *Mary Ann Shadd Cary*, 199.

38. *Poems on Miscellaneous Subjects* (1854) was reviewed in *Frederick Douglass' Paper* with an excerpt from William Lloyd Garrison's preface just two weeks later; "Poems on

Miscellaneous Subjects by Frances Ellen Watkins." The volume sold more than 10,000 copies and was reprinted by Yerrinton and Son in 1855. By 1871, it had gone to twelve editions.

39. Washington, "Frances Ellen Watkins," 59.

40. Linton, "The Power of the Newspaper Press"; "Meeting to Organize the Provincial Union."

41. Douglass, "Canada" (editorial).

42. Jones, *All Bound Up Together*, 103.

43. Rhodes, *Mary Ann Shadd Cary*, 199; "Bethel Literary," *The People's Advocate*, 2. Abraham Shadd worked as an agent for both William Lloyd Garrison's *The Liberator* and the American Anti-Slavery Society's *Emancipator*. He also operated an Underground Railway station in the family's homes in Wilmington, Delaware, and Westchester, Pennsylvania.

44. Jones, *All Bound Up Together*, 4; Foreman, "Black Organizing, Print Advocacy, and Collective Authorship," 43.

45. While Ward was nominal editor, Shadd wrote letters to the editor under her own signature, such as "Your obedient servant" and "Dear 'C'."

46. Z. H. M., "Dear Freeman."

47. Warner, *Publics and Counterpublics*, 67, 95.

48. Bangs, "Mr. Freeman"; W—S, "Mr. Editor"; A Spectator, "My Dear Madam."

49. "Woman's Rights"; Norton, "One of Our Legal Fictions."

50. Jones, *All Bound Up Together*, 88. For more on Shadd's staged letters to the editor focused on woman's rights, see Zackodnik, *Press, Platform, Pulpit*, chapter 5.

51. Shadd, "Remarks"; M. A. S., "Dear 'C'"; Shadd, "Adieu."

52. Wolseley, *The Black Press*, 38; Gayles, "Black Women Journalists in the South," 139. See Mossell, "Our Woman's Department . . . Women and Journalism"; Smith, "Some Female Writers of the Negro Race"; Langston, "Women in Journalism."

53. Qtd. in Logan, *Liberating Language*, 67.

54. Sigma, "Letter from Hartford," *Weekly Anglo-African*, December 3, 1859, 1.

55. McHenry, *Forgotten Readers*, 135–36. Thomas Hamilton edited and published the short-lived *People's Press* (1843) before he established the monthly *Anglo-African Magazine* and later the *The Weekly Anglo-African*. The *Weekly Anglo-African* was critical of colonization schemes and advocated for improving the condition of African Americans in the United States. Upon Hamilton's death in 1861, the paper was sold to James Redpath, who advocated migration to Haiti.

56. Warner, *Publics and Counterpublics*, 105.

57. Anderson, *Imagined Communities*, 35. Anderson's contention that newspaper readers imagined this ritual to be simultaneous has been challenged by scholars such as Trish Loughran, who has argued that in the United States, the postal service was unreliable as a newspaper distribution technology, which made for irregular reception and consumption. See Loughran, *Republic in Print*.

58. Lee and LiPuma, "Cultures of Circulation," 194. See also Habermas, *The Structural Transformation of the Public Sphere*.

59. Gaonkar and Povinelli, "Technologies of Public Forms," 387; emphasis in original.

60. Gaonkar and Povinelli, "Technologies of Public Forms," 396.

61. Han, "Making a Black Pacific," 33.
62. Qtd. in Gardner, *Black Print Unbound*, 168.
63. Gardner, *Black Print Unbound*, 168–70.
64. Gardner, *Black Print Unbound*, 167; Gardner, "Remembered (Black) Readers," 248–49. Similarly, the letters column in the *Southern Workman* could occupy half that publication's print space, and the *Workman* published several different letters columns in each edition. I offer the *Recorder* and the *Workman* as examples, since Black women's letters to them constitute the most significant subset of my data across the largest sweep of time (42 percent, published in the 1860s–1870s).
65. C. A. Cook and Co.'s *United States Newspaper Directory*, 11, 171; Gardner, *Black Print Unbound*, 111–12.
66. Thorton, "Pleading Their Own Cause," 168–69.
67. Madera, *Black Atlas*, 13.
68. Madera, *Black Atlas*, 218.
69. Eric Gardner brought Highgate's *Recorder* and *Tribune* letters to light. In addition to chapter 6 of *Black Print Unbound*, he published two posts on his blog *Black Print Culture*: "Edmonia Highgate in Mississippi: A 'New' Letter" (May 8, 2017) and "Edmonia Highgate, the New Orleans Massacre, & Christian Recording" (September 18, 2015). Unfortunately, *Black Print Culture* is no longer available. Highgate was published as the *Colored Tennessean's* New Orleans Correspondent in the March 14, 1866, edition under the name E. Goodelle Highgate, which she also used in the *Christian Recorder* as a correspondent. She also published in the *Christian Recorder* as E. Goodelle H.
70. Gardner, *Black Print Unbound*, 186.
71. Gardner, *Black Print Unbound*, 189.
72. Highgate, "Letter from New Orleans"; Highgate, "New Orleans Correspondence," *Colored Tennessean*. I determined the names of the First Nations mentioned in this section and in chapter 3 by consulting Native Land Digital (https://native-land.ca).
73. Highgate, "A Spring Day Up the James."
74. Highgate, "On Horse Back—Saddle Dash, No. 1."
75. Madera, *Black Atlas*, 217.
76. Brooks, "The Unfortunates," 52; emphasis added.
77. Brooks, "The Early American Public Sphere and the Emergence of a Black Counterpublic," 75.
78. Madera, *Black Atlas*, 5.
79. Gardner, *Black Print Unbound*, 178.
80. Madera, *Black Atlas*, 6. Derrick Spires helps us understand "political commoning" as also a model of Black citizenship early in the nineteenth century with his attention to Hosea Easton's theorization of "citizenship as a commons (rather than a private possession) essential to the functioning of any society and the livelihood of individuals within that society" in *A Treatise on the Intellectual Character, and Civil and Political Condition of the Colored People of the U. States* (1837). Spires, *The Practice of Citizenship*, 16–17.
81. Cooper, *A Voice from the South*, 31.
82. This was a common theme in the political arguments of Progressive Era Black feminists, and it is central to Anna Julia Cooper's 1892 manifesto *A Voice from the South*.

83. These 293 letters have been drawn from two databases: Readex African American Newspapers, Series 1, 1827–1998 and Accessible Archives. From African American Newspapers, Series 1 alone, I read 1,700 letters. My dataset is limited by the search protocols and tagging of these databases; by the "dirty data" resulting from the limitations of optical character recognition and its facility with the microfilm quality of historical papers in varying conditions; and by the parameters I used to create the dataset. These visualizations do not include letters for which I cannot determine the letter's place of origin. Anonymous and pseudonymous signatures, and signatures consisting only of initials, also proved challenging for determining the gender of the letter writer.

84. Pride and Wilson, *A History of the Black Press*, 26. See Thorton, "Pleading Their Own Cause," 170, for a reminder to attend to class, gender, and location (suburban versus city) as determinants of who wrote letters to the editor. His caution reminds us that this press form will not give researchers straightforward access to what African Americans actually thought at any given historical moment.

85. Each of these papers also account for the highest number of such letters: the *Christian Recorder* (83), the San Francisco *Elevator* (72), and the *Southern Workman* (54).

86. Eric Gardner's work with both the *Elevator* and the *Christian Recorder*, letters that together comprise 53 percent of my dataset, enables their verification as written by women and not fabricated by editors. The letters in my dataset from the *Southern Workman* were verified with research in Hampton school publications. Other women in my dataset are known Black female activists and journalists who signed their names or used known pen names, or are women who signed their names in ways that made it possible to determine the gender of the writer as female.

87. David Paul Nord notes that letters to the editor are "cued" or "prompted but not at all guided by the text" a reader encounters in the periodical. Nord, *Communities of Journalism*, 252.

88. The Black population of the West (dating from the first census in the region), ranged from 0.7 percent in 1850 to 0.6 percent in 1880, the lowest Black population of any region in the country during these decades. Gibson and Jung, "Historical Census Statistics," 19–23, 25, 28.

89. Han, "Making a Black Pacific," 31; Han, "All Roads Lead to San Francisco," 3, 8. The *Elevator*'s first agent for China and Japan was John C. Plummer (Yokohama) in 1868; William Everson, a barber, was an agent in Yokohama from 1869 to 1871; and Mrs. William M. Thomas was a distributor of the paper in Yokohama in 1873. See Colophon, *The Elevator*, April 10, 1868; Colophon, *The Elevator*, February 26, 1869; Colophon, *The Elevator*, December 29, 1871; "Japan." B. S. Fuller was the paper's agent in Honolulu in 1872; see Colophon, *The Elevator*, April 27, 1872. No agents are listed by the paper for New Zealand or Australia, indicating distribution in these countries was informal and, as Han documents, facilitated by the "one of every ten African Americans in San Francisco . . . working aboard a steamer" while the *Elevator* was in publication. Han, "Making a Black Place," 36.

90. See Kelley, *Freedom Dreams*.

91. See, for example, the work of Robin D. G. Kelley, Elsa Barkely Brown, Xiomara Santamarina, and James C. Scott.

92. Foster and Haywood, "Christian Recordings," 22.

93. Newman, "Faith in the Ballot"; emphasis added.

94. See, for example, Lincoln and Mamiya's foundational assertion: "No other area of black life received a higher priority from black churches than education." Lincoln and Mamiya, *The Black Church*, 251.

95. Jones, *All Bound Up*, 76.

96. The letters in my dataset were drawn from three sources: Readex African American Newspapers, 1827–1998, HathiTrust, and Accessible Archives.

97. Patrick Collier speculates that the study of periodicals requires a combination of close reading, distant or machine reading, and surface reading. Collier, "What Is Modern Periodical Studies?"

98. Conversation with the author, Wisconsin Historical Society, Madison, September 17, 2014.

99. A notable title in this category is *Our Women and Children Magazine*, which I. Garland Penn mentions several times in his chapter on Black women journalists as published in Louisville. Kentucky. Journalists Mary E. Britton, Mary V. Cook ("Grace Ermine"), Lucy Wilmot Smith, Georgia Mabel De Baptiste, Katherine Davis Chapman, Lucretia Newman Coleman, Lillian Lewis ("Bert Islew"), Gertrude Mossell, Ida B. Wells, and Ione E. Wood wrote articles, edited departments, or were regular contributors to this magazine. Mrs. C. C. Stum, a journalist who wrote articles for the *Bowling Green Watchman* and the *Hub and Advocate*, acted as Philadelphia agent for the magazine. No extant copies have yet surfaced of *Our Women and Children Magazine*, which Penn notes was founded and edited by Rev. William J. Simmons, president of the State University of Kentucky (now known as Simmons College of Kentucky), from 1880 to 1890. Penn, *The Afro-American Press*, 374–418. Jennifer Harris notes that Simmons edited the *American Baptist*, which published *Our Women and Children* from 1888 to 1891. Harris, "Hidden in Plain Sight," 234.

100. Drucker, "Humanities Approaches to Graphical Display"; emphasis in the original. See also Lavin, "Why Digital Humanists Should Emphasize Situated Data over Capta."

101. Gallon, "Making a Case for the Digital Humanities," 46–47.

102. Morris, "Document to Database and Spreadsheet," 149.

103. McPherson, "Why Are the Digital Humanities So White?," 154.

104. Gallon, "Making a Case for the Digital Humanities," 44.

105. Liddle, "Method in Periodical Studies."

106. As Jeff Drouin puts it, "The point is not that digital methods in distant reading should replace traditional techniques, but rather that they should show us where to apply them or suggest answers where the print trail is inconclusive. . . . The computer shows us interesting patterns that can shape our inquiry, prompt us to ask new questions, and test assumptions." Drouin, "Close- and Distant-Reading," 111.

107. Maria DiCenzo has provocatively suggested that the field of periodical studies has become divided between close and distant reading protocols. DiCenzo, "Remediating the Past."

108. Madera, *Black Atlas*, 13.

CHAPTER THREE: **Geographies of Racialization, Occupation, and Refusal in the** *Southern Workman*

1. Painter, *Sojourner Truth*, 203. Truth met with Lincoln on October 29, 1864 (204).
2. Painter, *Sojourner Truth*, 213–17.
3. Painter, *Sojourner Truth*, 234.
4. Truth, "Letter from Sojourner Truth—Land for the Freed-People." Painter notes that the petition was likely never presented to Congress. Painter, *Sojourner Truth*, 242.
5. Truth, "Letter from Sojourner Truth—Land for the Freed-People."
6. Painter, *Sojourner Truth*, 236, 241. Painter notes that Truth was somewhat unique in suggesting the West. Wendell Phillips and A. M. Powell also spoke on freedpeople resettlement at the National Colored Labor Convention in Washington, DC, in December 1869. Frederick Douglass opposed such resettlement plans (238–45).
7. A series of acts aimed at incorporating Indigenous peoples as citizens of the nation-state by eradicating their status as citizens of their nations or "tribes" includes the Dawes Act (1887), which focused on severalty to convert tribal land ownership into individual land ownership; the Lacey Act (1906), which gave individuals control of a pro-rata share of tribal funds; and the Sells Declaration (1917), which provided for the issuance of fee-simple titles to reservation land to so-called competent individuals, thus transforming over one million acres of collectively held lands to individually held tracts, a process that was represented as the gaining of "freedom." See Hoxie, *A Final Promise*.
8. Of these 236 letters, twenty-three were written by Indigenous women students or graduates from the Arikaree, Cherokee, Gros Ventre, Omaha, Oneida, Ptedutawin, Seneca, Santee Sioux, Sioux, and Winnebago Nations; twenty-one by Indigenous men students or graduates from the Arapaho, Cherokee, Cheyenne, Menomonee, Pima, Shawnee, Sioux, Wichita, and Winnebago Nations; fifty-six by African American men students or graduates, and 136 by African American women students or graduates. Without place names, signatures, initials, or references to fellow students, graduates, or a graduating class, I could not determine a letter writer's location and it could not be mapped in a geospatial visualization. In many cases, these gaps were not addressable by cross-referencing letters with other sources on Hampton's student body.
9. I use the term "interscale" to refer to the process of combining close reading of the content and form of a text, a technique long employed in literary studies (attending to the significance of a document's word choice, formal devices, etc.), and what is conventionally called distant reading, or reading a large corpus of texts with the aid of computer-assisted data analysis that makes it possible to discern patterns.
10. Gilmore, "Fatal Couplings of Power and Difference," 22; Cheng and Shabazz, "Introduction," 5.
11. Cantiello, "Harper's Educational Reservations," 577. See also "Dawes Act (1887)."
12. Cantiello, "Harper's Educational Reservations," 579–80.
13. Lindsey, *Indians at Hampton Institute*, 33. See, for example, Armstrong, "The Cherokee Strip," 13. Armstrong's articles and correspondence shifted to a nearly exclusive focus on Indigenous education. Lindsey, *Indians at Hampton Institute*, 53, 56–57. Donal F. Lindsey notes that "school authorities estimated that they received twice as much for the education of Indians from charity as from the government" (42).

14. For Black leaders such as Martin Delany, Alexander Crummell, and Frederick Douglass arguing "for African American superiority" based on physical strength or "forbearing under wrong and violence" from 1865 through to 1880, see Cantiello, "Harper's Educational Reservations," 578–79.

15. Gourgey focuses on a range of papers, including the *AME Church Review*, the *Baptist Headlight* (Wichita, KS; 1893–1894), the *San Francisco Vindicator* (1884–1906), the *Free Man's Press* (Galveston, TX; 1868) and the *Afro-Independent* (St. Paul, MN; 1888). Gourgey, "Poetics of Memory and Marginality."

16. Ahern, "An Experiment Aborted," 271, 264, 266.

17. Jackson and Nunn, *Historically Black Colleges and Universities*, 14. The Morrill Land-Grant Act provided states with funding and land to establish universities "with the purpose of the production of agricultural, military, and technically oriented citizens." The Morrill Land-Grant Act, the Homestead Act, and the Pacific Railroad Act, all of which Congress passed in the same year, hastened the expansion of white westward migration and settler colonialism. See Bateau, "American University Consensus," 27.

18. The AMA was founded in 1846 by abolitionists, members of the American Home Missionary Society and members of the American Board of Commissioners for Foreign Missions. Composed of white and African American members, the AMA advocated for abolition and organized education for African Americans before, during, and after the Civil War and during Reconstruction. The AMA established more schools for freedpeople than the Freedman's Bureau and organized the Freedman's Aid Society to recruit Northern teachers to their Southern schools.

19. Lindsey, *Indians at Hampton Institute*, 7.

20. Neverdon-Morton, *Afro-American Women of the South*, 16, 32.

21. Lindsey, *Indians at Hampton Institute*, 20. Lindsey documents that Armstrong first proposed that the "entire Nez Perce tribe, or 'not less than 150 Indians'" be enrolled at Hampton for three years, "at a per annum rate of $250 each," which he followed with a "more modest proposition . . . to educate twenty-five Nez Perce youth" (21).

22. Carlisle, Pennsylvania, was also a stop on the Underground Railroad. Lindsey documents that Harriet Beecher Stowe "taught a few of the prisoners' classes" at Carlisle, writing about the experience in the April 18 and 25, 1877, editions of the *Christian Union*. A connection between abolition and settler colonization and occupation is further evident in Lydia Maria Childs's estate purchase of "250 acres . . . for $4,500" near Hampton's 400-acre farm, Shellbanks. The school named that land "Canebreaks," and "intended [it] for Indian education, although Hampton graduates soon operated both of these former slave plantations and black students alone largely worked the farm." Lindsey, *Indians at Hampton Institute*, 30, 47n32, 47n43.

23. See, for example, Wexler, *Tender Violence*; and Fear-Segal, *White Man's Club*.

24. Lindsey, *Indians at Hampton Institute*, 32.

25. Du Bois, "Hampton."

26. Lindsey, *Indians at Hampton Institute*, 32.

27. Pratt had used a version of the outing system at St. Augustine and "claimed the black experience of slavery as his model, believing that the domestic and industrial habits

of 'civilized' Christian life, learned by blacks during slavery, could be duplicated with Indians under the milder system of outing." Lindsey, *Indians at Hampton Institute*, 37.

28. Lindsey, *Indians at Hampton Institute*, 37–38.

29. On racial engulfment, see Smith, "Indigeneity, Settler Colonialism, White Supremacy," 30–38.

30. Seniors, "Cole and Johnson's *The Red Moon*," 24; Lindsey, *Indians at Hampton Institute*, 30–31.

31. McPherson qtd. in Lindsey, *Indians at Hampton Institute*, 6.

32. John Estes (Sioux) wrote to the *Southern Workman* about his work at the Iapi Ouye press at the Yankton Agency in Dakota Territory. The press published Rev. A. W. Williamson's Dakota dictionary and vocabulary book in the 1870s and 1880s. Pilling, *Bibliography of the Siouan Languages*, 77. From 1886 to 1907, Indigenous students also wrote, illustrated, and produced *Talks and Thoughts of the Hampton Indian Students*. On school periodicals as understudied despite their proliferation by the early twentieth century, see Wood, "Transforming Student Periodicals."

33. Colophon, *The Southern Workman*, 2.

34. "Already the 'Southern Workman' . . . ," 2; emphasis in the original.

35. "During the Month of April . . . ," 2.

36. In her work on *Talks and Thoughts*, Jacqueline Emery documents that Harry Hand (Crow Creek Sioux), who attended Hampton from 1889 to 1894, "founded his own newspaper, the *Crow Creek Herald* [,] upon returning to the Crow Creek Reservation, and by 1898 was publishing the *Crow Creek Chief*." Emery, "Writing against Erasure," 190.

37. See the March 1873 issue for reference to a speech by Frederick Douglass on "annex[ing] San Domingo"; "Our Exchanges," 3. By 1886, Gertrude Mossell's column Our Woman's Department, written for T. Thomas Fortune's *New York Freeman*, was being reprinted in the *Workman*.

38. See Cooper, "Paper by Mrs. Anna J. Cooper"; Washington, "Southern Plantation Work"; Cooper, "The American Negro Academy"; Matthews, "Some Dangers Confronting Southern Girls in the North"; Laney, "The Burden of the Educated Colored Woman"; Terrell, "Club Work of Colored Women"; Williams, "The Relation of the Trained Nurse to the Negro Home"; Williams, "The Problem of Employment for Negro Women"; Murray, "In Behalf of the Negro Woman"; Fernandis, "A Colored Social Settlement"; Fernandis, "Neighborhood Interpretations of a Social Settlement"; Barrett, "Social Settlement for Colored People."

39. "Gleanings," 1; "Newspapers," 1.

40. By the opening years of the twentieth century, the *Workman* had been redesigned so that these letters columns were no longer staples of the paper. When students' and graduates' letters were included, they were no longer reprinted in full but selectively excerpted, editorialized with framing narratives, and published in the Personal Notes or Notes from the Field departments. This redesign coincided with a more deliberate emphasis on Hampton as a model for industrial education in the United States and on the Caribbean and Pacific as imperial US interests. See Zackodnik, "Empire and Education in Hampton's *Southern Workman*."

41. The *Workman* also ran serialized Academic Department columns that offered reports on the school's pedagogy, editorials by Armstrong, illustrations from plates

shared by *Harper's*, and reprints from exchanges with periodicals such as the *Atlantic Monthly*, the *Farmer's Review*, the *Educational Journal of Virginia*, *Scribner's Monthly*, *Harper's Weekly*, and the *Paper Trade Journal*. This combined content made the *Southern Workman* a mix of reporting on the school, articles on the trades and sectors it educated its students for, and articles of interest to a general readership.

42. Serafini, "Black, White, and Native," 75.

43. Neverdon-Morton, *Afro-American Women of the South*, 31. David Paul Nord notes that letters to the editor as a press genre are "cued" or "prompted but not at all guided by the text" a reader encounters or by an editor. Nord, *Communities of Journalism*, 252.

44. Nord, *Communities of Journalism*, 253.

45. See, for example, R.'s letter noting that he worked at Hampton during his vacation, which enabled him "to continue in school this term." R., "Dear Friend," 21. See also the scholarship letter written by the daughter of an enslaved woman detailing her journey via Norfolk, where her brother nearly died of smallpox. V., "Dear Friend," 21.

46. Serafini reserves this phrase for Hampton students and graduates only, but I suggest that letters to the editor as a press form are always contingent, given they are always chosen for publication by a periodical editor. Serafini, "Black, White, and Native," 66.

47. Madera, *Black Atlas*, 69–71. African American thinkers who linked freedom to extranational territory included Mary Ann Shadd, Martin Delaney, Alexander Crummel, James Holly, Henry Bibb, William Wells Brown, and Samuel Ringgold Ward.

48. Madera, *Black Atlas*, 75, 96.

49. Madera, *Black Atlas*, 108.

50. "Dear Teacher," 2; P., "Dear Teacher," 18; emphasis in the original.

51. B., "Miss R. H. T.," 17; "Hard Times Improving," 17. B. wrote from somewhere in Texas, but the anonymous letter did not indicate where the hard times were. The *Workman* often published letters that did not include signature, date, or place.

52. Alvarado et al., "Conversación los Abajocomunes."

53. The school requested that its graduates who were teaching in Virginia report on the November 1879 elections. The *Workman* presented their letters in December 1879 and January 1880 issues as "showing the arguments by which the great majority of the colored vote was secured by the Readjusters. Most would have voted for entire repudiation if they had had the chance, while many, utterly confused by the split of the party, stayed away from the polls, for fear they should vote wrongly." "Letters from Hampton Graduates," 6.

54. See, for example, a graduate's letter indicting the Democrats of West Virginia for refusing to build a schoolhouse for African Americans where he taught. Even though the Democrats had been petitioned over "the last ten years[,] . . . they have refused on the ground that they have no money." "A Hampton graduate teaching in West Va. . . ." 14. See also I.'s letter dated May 30, 1878, defending Hampton from the critique of the AME's *Christian Recorder* and C.'s letter dated March 18, 1878, on sharecropping in Norfolk County, Virginia, both in the *Southern Workman*, July 1878, 52.

55. Claytor, "Our Workers in the Far South," 140; E., "Miss A. E. Cleveland, Dear Teacher," 141; I., "Graduate Teachers in the North, 141.

56. Collins, "Sidelights on the 'Other Half,'" 140–41.

57. See I., "From a Colored Juror," 54; I., "A Better Report in Some Respects," 54.
58. D., "Causes of Crime," 54; emphasis in the original.
59. D., "Causes of Crime," 54.
60. See Wright, *Physics of Blackness*; Cohen, *Semi-Citizenship in Democratic Politics*; Melish, *Disowning Slavery*; Hartman, *Scenes of Subjection*.
61. Knadler, "Antebellum African American Freemen's Narratives," 25–47. See also Day, *Alien Capital*; Willse, *The Value of Homelessness*; Cacho, *Social Death*; Melamed, *Represent and Destroy*; Gilmore, *Golden Gulag*; Robinson, *Black Marxism*.
62. Byrd et al., "Predatory Value," 2, 3; emphasis in the original.
63. Jackson, "Humanity beyond the Regime of Labor."
64. Patterson, *Slavery and Social Death*.
65. Alvarado et al., "Conversación Los Abajocomunes."
66. Veracini, *Settler Colonialism*; Day, *Alien Capital*, 113; Vowel, *Indigenous Writes*, 24. Scholarship is pressing on the imperative to recognize that the slave trade was not a form of migration, however much it set in motion a diaspora. See, for example, Sexton, "The Social Life of Social Death."
67. Byrd et al., "Predatory Value," 5.
68. Byrd, *The Transit of Empire*, xv, xvi–xvii.
69. Barker, "Territory as Analytic," 21.
70. Oshkeneny, "Dear Friend," 104. See also Oshkenney, "Dear Friend and Teacher," 90.
71. Ahern, "An Experiment Aborted," 270.
72. See Fear-Segal, *White Man's Club*.
73. *Twenty-Two Years' Work of the Hampton Normal and Agricultural Institute*, 328.
74. Ma-ah-chis Soaring Eagle, "My Dear Friend Miss L."
75. La Flesche, "Yonder is a man . . ." Suzette LaFlesche was the sister of Susan LaFlesche Picotte (Omaha), the first Indigenous woman to earn a medical degree in the United States. Their father, Iron Eye (Ponca and Quebecois), became chief in 1855 and their mother was Mary Gale (Omaha-Oto-Iowa). Marguerite, Suzette and Susan LaFlesche were at Hampton in the mid-1880s. See Tong, *Susan LaFlesche Picotte, M.D.*
76. King, "Dear Friend."
77. See, for example, R., letter dated March 12, 1882, from Elizabeth City County, Virginia, 102; Robinson, letter from Thaxton's Switch, Bedford County, Virginia; W. letter dated February 5, 1881, from Mathews County, Virginia. A letter written by S. L. Dutton dated January 17, 1873, mentioned William Henry Wilkins, who taught in Bedford, Southampton, Norfolk, and Portsmouth Counties in Virginia and owned land in Portsmouth. Many Hampton graduates writing from communities in which they were teaching endorsed land and home ownership as markers of African American advancement following the Civil War.
78. Pattee, letter from the Cheyenne River Agency, South Dakota, 213.
79. Batker, *Reforming Fictions*, 8.
80. Excellent work on letters to the editor that, however, follows the print-capitalism thesis includes Nielsen, "Participation through Letters to the Editor"; Delap, "The Freewoman"; and Green, "Complaints of Everyday Life."

81. Some Indigenous students went on to study at Carlisle and other residential or boarding schools, but the vast majority were returned to their reservations from Hampton with the goal of teaching others what they had learned at the school.

82. See Byrd, *The Transit of Empire*.

83. Goeman, "Land as Life," 81.

84. Cresswell, "Towards a Politics of Mobility," 18.

85. Everuss, "New Mobilities Paradigm," 288–89.

86. Hague, "'The Right to Enter Every Other State,'" 333–34.

87. The eight letter-writers are Ann Anderson (class of 1885) from Bellevue, Bedford County, Virginia; Lucy Boulding (class of 1881) from Burkeville, Virginia; Sarah Collins [Fernandis] (class of 1882) from Baltimore, Maryland; Henrietta C. Hunter [Evans] (class of 1876) from Norfolk, Virginia; Mary Robinson (class of 1872) from King William County, Virginia; Julia Rutledge (class of 1872) from Charleston, South Carolina; Lucy E. Smith (class of 1879) from Williamsburg, Virginia; and Rebecca Wright (class of 1878) from Warwick County, Virginia.

88. Smith, "They Would Not Let Us Have Schools," 112.

89. Caroline Smith's testimony, Atlanta, Georgia, October 21, 1871, in *Testimony Taken by the Joint Select Committee to Inquire into the Condition of Affairs in the Late Insurrectionary States*, 400–401.

90. Anderson, letter dated March 1895, from Houston, Texas, 39; Collins, undated letter from Springfield, Tennessee, 31. Ann Anderson (class of 1885), originally from Bellevue, Bedford County, Virginia, relocated six times, including her move to Hampton for her education. In March 1895, she wrote to the *Workman* from Houston, Texas, where she had been teaching since 1891. Collins wrote from Springfield, Tennessee, likely in 1884 (her letter is undated). According to Hampton records, she went on to teach in an industrial school in St. Augustine, Florida.

91. Lerner, *Black Women in White America*, 119.

92. Finch, "Sarah Collins Fernandis," 221–23. See also Hollie, "Fernandis, Sarah Collins"; Peebles-Wilkins, "Fernandis, Sarah A. Collins"; Honey, *Shadowed Dreams*, 107; Fernandis, "A Social Settlement in South Washington," 64–66.

93. See Boulding, undated letter from Staunton, Virginia, 21; Boulding, undated letter from Lynchburg, Virginia, 47; and Symms, "First Three Lynchburg African American Women Voters." In 1902, the state legislature "curtail[ed] the collegiate program" and changed the school's name to Virginia Normal and Industrial, and in 1920, it moved the state's "land-grant program for Blacks" from "Hampton Institute, where it had been since 1872, to Virginia Normal and Industrial Institute." The college program was restored in 1923, and the school's name was changed to Virginia State College for Negroes in 1930. This school would eventually become Virginia State University in 1979. Boulding would have witnessed the land-grant program's move from Hampton during her time in Lynchburg. "History of VSU."

94. Matthews, "Some Dangers Confronting Southern Girls in the North." This speech was originally delivered in the Woman's Conference at the second annual Hampton Negro Conference of 1898. See also its recirculation in the September 1898 issue of the *Workman*. Matthews was New York correspondent for the *National Leader* in the late 1880s.

95. Cresswell, "The Production of Mobilities," 19; Hague, "'The Right to Enter Every Other State,'" 334; Larsen, Urry, and Axhausen, *Mobilities, Networks, Geographies*, 11. Larsen and colleagues also argue that "relational economies of commitments and obligations" to family and community further complicate readings of mobility as individually exercised autonomy.

96. Guittet, "Unpacking the New Mobilities Paradigm," 209.

97. Sheller, *Mobility Justice*, 9.

98. Madera, *Black Atlas*, 217.

99. McKittrick, *Demonic Grounds*, xv.

100. Snyder and Sorensen argue that "the serial form of the letters page lends itself to an open-ended conversation." Snyder and Sorensen, "Letters to the Editor as a Serial Form," 130.

101. McKittrick, *Demonic Grounds*, xiv; emphasis in the original.

102. The Piegan (Pikuni, Pikani, or Piikáni) are the largest of three nations known as the Blackfoot Confederacy along with the Kainai and Siksika Nations. Piegan territory spanned much of the Great Plains in what is now known as Canada and the United States. The Blackfeet were not consulted in the Fort Laramie Treaty (1851), which first affected their territory; in 1865 and 1868, treaties not ratified by Congress negotiated for their land south of the Missouri River; and in "1873 and 1874, the Blackfeet southern boundary was moved 200 miles north by Presidential orders and Congressional Acts" to open their southern lands to white settlement. In 1888, the US government established boundaries between the "Blackfeet, Fort Belknap and Fort Peck Reservations," and in 1896 the government sought the further ceding of land in what is now the Glacier National Park and Lewis and Clark National Forest, which is currently under dispute. Montana Office of Public Instruction, Division of Indian Instruction, *Montana Indians, Their History and Location*, 8–9.

103. John L. Brudvig, "Hampton Normal & Agricultural Institutes: American Indian Students, 1878–1923," compiled and edited from American Indian student files held in the archives of Hampton University in Hampton, Virginia, 1994 and 1996, http://www.twofrog.com/hamptonfem1.txt. Grant Institute opened in 1884 and was later known as the Genoa Indian Industrial School. Haskell Institute (1887) resulted from the renaming of the United States Indian Industrial Training School, originally founded in 1884. Both schools operated on military training and industrial education models derived from Carlisle. Grant/Genoa also published a monthly newspaper, *The Indian News*.

104. Ketosh, "The following letter . . . ," 505.

105. Henderson, "Our Indian Salutatorian of '90," 185–86.

106. Chalcraft, *Assimilation's Agent*, 99. Chalcraft was hired in 1883 by the Bureau of Indian Affairs and worked as a superintendent for nearly four decades. Even this detail of her life in *Twenty-Two Years Work* registers Kate Henderson's removals; it lists her as an orphan and her name appears in its own untitled section between "Oneidas Brought by Dr. A. L. Johnson, July 9, 1888, from Oneida, WIS" and "From Indian Territory, Brought by Dudley Talbot, Oct. 13, 1888." *Twenty-Two Years' Work of the Hampton Normal and Agricultural Institute*, 471. Albert Howe lists her parents as "killed in Custer

massacre." Howe, "Notes on the Returned Indian Students of the Hampton Normal and Agricultural Institute," 11.

107. Folsom, "Returned Indian Students," 53.

108. Chalcraft, *Assimilation's Agent*, 100–101. Fort Belknap Agency was created in 1888 on "ancestral territory of the Blackfeet and Assiniboine Nations." It is home to Assinboine and Gros Ventre peoples. See "Welcome to Fort Belknap Indian Community, Home of the Nakoda and Aaniiih Nations," 2024, https://ftbelknap.org/history. The Puyallup Agency was created in 1854 on what is now known as Tacoma, Washington. The Yakima Reservation of 1,130,000 acres on the east side of the Cascade Mountains in what is now known as southern Washington state was formed on a portion of the more than 12 million acres of land that the Yakama ostensibly ceded in an 1855 treaty that they fought until 1859 in the Yakima War. Don Healy, "The Yakima or Yakama Nation," Yakama Nation History, https://www.yakama.com/about/. The 405-square-mile Devil's Lake Reservation (now known as Spirit Lake Reservation) was formed by treaty with the Sisseton Wahpeton Sioux in 1867 in what is now known as east-central North Dakota. "Spirit Lake Nation."

109. See, for example, T. B., undated letter from Reynoldson, Gates County, North Carolina. T. B. named four other Hampton graduates teaching near him. See also Robert Dungey's letter mentioning he teaches near a person he identified as W.; Dungey, undated letter from unnamed place in Virginia.

110. Washington, undated letter from Mt. Meigs, Alabama, 116–17.

111. McKittrick, *Demonic Grounds*, 7.

112. Serafini, "Black, White, and Native," 80.

113. For example, see Josephine Barnaby's letter likening the view of the water from Winona Lodge at Hampton to the beauty of seeing Chippewa students at the government school on the Fond du Lac reservation in Minnesota, where she was teaching. She closed a description of Chippewa with "they are very different people from the Sioux and Omahas, my own tribes. But I like them. . . . I should dearly like to come back to Hampton next summer, but that is a long way off." Barnaby, undated letter from the Fond du Lac reservation, 247.

114. *Twenty-Two Years' Work of the Hampton Normal and Agricultural Institute*, 456–57.

115. Pay-Pay, "From Another Indian Daughter of Hampton," 61. Mrs. Carrie Paypay's family surname before marriage was Half.

116. Pay-Pay, "A Letter from Cheyenne River," 31. *Talks and Thoughts* was a Hampton periodical for which Indigenous students and graduates wrote all the content, and it was edited and printed by Indigenous students. The periodical was published from March 1886 until July 1907. Emery, *Recovering Native American Writings in the Boarding School Press*, 325n6. The *Workman* at times printed letters that students wrote to *Talks and Thoughts*.

117. *Domestic and Foreign Mission Society of the Protestant Episcopal Church*, 72.

118. When South Dakota entered the Union in 1889, the Cheyenne River Agency, which was created that same year, bordered the Standing Rock Agency to the north. "Fort Bennett."

119. Goeman, "Land as Life," 73–74.

120. See, for example, C., who writes of reading the paper for news of White's mission. C., "Letter dated November 14, 1877 from Henry County, Virginia."

121. The AMA operated missions in Hawaii, Thailand (then Siam), and Egypt. It also served self-liberated African Americans who had migrated to Canada, liberated Blacks in Jamaica, and Chinese immigrants in California. Before the Civil War, it provided aid to abolitionist churches in the North and in border states in the South. Sullivan, "Historical Note."

122. Yannielli, "John Brown in Africa."

123. Lindsey, *Indians at Hampton Institute*, 55.

124. Seniors, "Cole and Johnson's *The Red Moon*," 28.

125. Van Orden and Zackodnik, "Visualizing the Racialization of Space."

126. For Black Studies deliberations on "the human," see the foundational work of Sylvia Wynter and Hortense Spillers and recent work in Afro-pessimism and Black optimism such as Marquis Bey's *The Problem of the Negro as a Problem for Gender*, Denise Ferreira da Silva's *Toward a Global Idea of Race*, Saidiya Hartman's *Scenes of Subjection*, Zakiyyah Iman Jackson's *Becoming Human*, Fred Moten's *Stolen Life*, Alexander Weheliye's *Habeas Viscus*, and Frank Wilderson's *Red, White and Black*. For Indigenous studies deliberations on recognition and refusal, see, for example, Coulthard, *Red Skin, White Masks*; and Simpson, *Mohawk Interruptus*.

127. My use of "situated data" is informed by Lavin, "Why Digital Humanists Should Emphasize Situated Data over Capta."

128. Gallon, "Making a Case for the Black Digital Humanities," 44.

129. See McPherson, "Why Are the Digital Humanities So White?" The very terminology we continue to use, such as "racialized," keeps doing the work of white supremacist settler colonialism, since its use typically ignores that whiteness is a racialized subject position.

130. The Powhatan Confederacy territory is now known as the states of North Carolina, Virginia, and Maryland, and the District of Columbia. For a map, see "Powhatan," Native Land Digital, https://native-land.ca/maps/territories/powhatan-2/. The confederacy comprised at least thirty Algonquian-speaking tribal nations. Late in August of 1619, twenty to thirty enslaved Africans aboard the privateer *White Lion* arrived at Port Comfort, now the site of Fort Monroe in Hampton, Virginia. They were from Kabasa, the royal capital of the Kingdom of Ndongo, located in what is now Angola. The captain of the privateer traded the Africans for supplies. A few days later, the *Treasurer* brought more enslaved Africans to Virginia. English privateers from the Spanish slaver *San Juan Bautista* had captured both groups. The enslaved people from these two ships are the first recorded Africans who were trafficked to England's mainland colonies. Austin, "1619: Virginia's First Africans," 2. See also Stapleton, *A Military History of Africa*.

131. Perdue, "The Legacy of Indian Removal," 4. Patrick Wolfe reminds us that "Indian removal" dates from at least the Royal Proclamation of 1763 and that treaties, removal, and slavery went hand in hand: "The extension of the slave-plantation economy in Georgia, Tennessee, Arkansas, Louisiana, Mississippi, Alabama and the Florida panhandle was conditional upon Indian removal. The [Louisiana] Purchase

provided the territory west of the Mississippi that the US government exchanged for the homelands that removing tribes were obliged to surrender by way of treaties." Wolfe, "After the Frontier," 16–17.

132. Rumsey and Williams, "Historical Maps," 16.

133. Whose Land (www.whose.land) is a project that "uses GIS technology to assist users in identifying Indigenous Nations, Territories, and Indigenous communities across Canada." Whose Land partnered with Victor G. Temprano's Native Land (https://native-land.ca) to produce and share maps of worldwide Indigenous territories. "Native Land Digital is a registered Canadian not-for-profit organization," that maintains a web-hosted and interactive digital map of Indigenous territories based on its continuously updated database. The organization has "a majority-Indigenous Board of Directors, representing people who have close ties to land bases, communities, and deep knowledge about Indigenous ways of being and knowing. The Board of Directors is further informed by an Advisory Council, consisting of a variety of specialists in mapmaking, GIS, relations with Indigenous communities, and more." "How It Works," Native Land Digital, https://native-land.ca/about/how-it-works/#:~:text=How%20To%20Use%20Native%2DLand,appear%20with%20different%20nation%20names.

134. Keating, "Indigenous Geographies Overlap."

135. White, "What Is Spatial History?"; emphasis in the original.

136. Gitelman and Jackson argue that "starting with data often leads to an unnoticed assumption that data are transparent, that information is self-evident, the fundamental stuff of truth itself. . . . Our zeal for more and more data can become a faith in their neutrality and autonomy, their objectivity." Gitelman and Jackson, "Introduction," 16.

137. On distant reading, see, for example, Bode, *Reading by Numbers*; English, "Everywhere and Nowhere"; Hayles, "How We Read"; Jockers, *Macroanalysis*; Moretti, *Distant Reading*. Ted Underwood's definition of distant reading as part of the "same representational strategies that are transforming social science," and that treat writing "as a field of relations to be modeled," usefully questions the tendency to oppose distant reading to close reading, thereby confining its development to shifts in literary studies. Underwood, "Distant Reading and Recent Intellectual History," 531. Alan Liu cautions us that this distinction or debate between close and distant reading, the debate's apparent "newness," and its source in the digital turn, obscure its much earlier emergence. The "debate serves as a proxy for the present state of the running battle between New Critical method and post-May 1968 cultural criticism. . . . Close reading came into dominance only after the New Critics fought polemical battles against a prior age of cultural criticism whose methods were in their own way distant reading." Liu, "Where Is Cultural Criticism in the Digital Humanities?," 492.

CHAPTER FOUR: **Feminist Black Internationalism in *The Crisis* and *Negro World***

1. McKittrick, *Demonic Grounds*, 41–42.
2. Lipsitz, *How Racism Takes Place*, 9.
3. Detweiler, *The Negro Press in the United States*, 61.
4. Gayles, "Black Women Journalists in the South," 1410.

5. Blain and Gill identify these as central questions for future work on Black internationalisms. Blain and Gill, "Introduction," 3–5.

6. Important exceptions include Blain and Gill, *To Turn the Whole World Over*; Blain, *Set the World on Fire*; Higashida, *Black Internationalist Feminism*; Davies, *Left of Karl Marx*; Edwards, *The Practice of Diaspora*; and Sharpley-Whiting, *Negritude Women*.

7. A critical study focused on Amy Jacques Garvey did not appear until Ula Taylor's *The Veiled Garvey* (2002), even though scholarship on Marcus Garvey and the Garvey movement has been ongoing for some sixty years. Even scholarship lauded as the strongest on the UNIA, such as Adam Ewing's, continues to occlude the important work women accomplished in the movement. See Ewing, *The Age of Garvey*; see also Blain, "Uncovering the Silences of Black Women's Voices."

8. Oppel, "W. E. B. Du Bois, Nazi Germany, and the Black Atlantic," 101; Edwards, *The Practice of Diaspora*, 7. Michelle Stephens argues that historicizing and analyzing Black internationalisms as both a politics and a social formation "depends on . . . the 'fits' between different instances, different periods and epochs, indeed different periodicities. . . . In such a history, the 'Black internationalism' of the interwar years becomes historicized as one of multiple instances of a Black, radical, global critique of empire that has operated transatlantically from the seventeenth century until the present." Stephens, "Disarticulating Black Internationalisms," 106. See also Stephens, *Black Empire*. For examinations of the influence of the Haitian Revolution on African American political imaginaries and activism that trace Black internationalist thinking and politics back into the nineteenth century, see Nwankwo, *Black Cosmopolitanism*; Daut, *Tropics of Haiti*.

9. Stephens, "Disarticulating Black Internationalisms," 104.

10. Hanchard, "Translation, Political Community, and Black Internationalism," 118. Hanchard calls for further work on "the tension between Black internationalism and nationalism, particularly the conventional trajectories and political projects associated with nationalist mobilization." Scholars such as Stephens, Kelley, and Oppel have also marked that tension. Kelley and Stephens have argued that Black nationalist and internationalist desire and politics were fueled by the experience of being denied access to the rights and privileges of full citizenship. Stephens credits the Garvey movement with harnessing those "desires for statehood and nationality," while Kelley looks to the Black nationalist politics of Martin Delany, Samuel Ringgold Ward, and Mary Ann Shadd in the 1850s. Stephens, *Black Empire*, 94; Kelley, "'But a Local Phase of a World Problem,'" 148; Kelley, *Race Rebels*.

11. Shadd's *Notes on Canada West* and Martin Delany's *The Condition, Elevation, Emigration and Destiny of the Colored People of the United States, Politically Considered* were both published in 1852, yet Shadd is rarely discussed in historiographies of Black nationalism or Black internationalism.

12. West, Martin, and Wilkins, "Preface," xi (first quote); West and Martin, "Introduction," 2 (second quote).

13. West and Martin, "Introduction," 5. Although work to elaborate a history of Black internationalism that predates the interwar years is crucial, periodizing politics

according to waves creates blind spots. For example, the waves attributed to American feminism and to Black internationalism have occluded Black feminist politics.

14. Patterson and Kelley underscore that Black internationalism "does not always come out of Africa, nor is it necessarily engaged with Pan-Africanism," but "sometimes it lives through or is integrally tied to other kinds of international movements— socialism, communism, feminism, surrealism, religions such as Islam, and so on." Patterson and Kelley, "Unfinished Migrations," 27.

15. Work on Fauset's interest in global citizenship is an important exception; see Allen, *Black Women Intellectuals*; Popp, "Where Confusion Is."

16. Although scholarship on Fauset's work rarely mentions her journalism with *The Crisis*, Sylvander speculates that she "undoubtedly had extensive power and influence" in its "day-to-day running . . . from November 1918 to April of 1926, excluding her months in Europe in 1921 and 1924–25." Sylvander, *Jessie Redmon Fauset*, 59.

17. Wall, *Women of the Harlem Renaissance*, 46. W. E. B. Du Bois's "Essay toward a History of the Black Man in the Great War" headlined that issue, which also included "The Atlanta Negro Vote," on the NAACP's voter registration drive in Atlanta, Georgia, and "The Anti-Lynching Conference," which covered the NAACP's conference at Carnegie Hall in New York City.

18. Hutchinson, *The Harlem Renaissance in Black and White*, 141. The first issue established its mandate: "The Crisis. . . . will record important happenings and movements in the world which bear on the great problem of inter-racial relations, and especially those which affect the Negro-American. Secondly, it will be a review of opinion and literature, recording briefly books, articles, and important expressions of opinion in the white and colored press on the race problem. Thirdly, it will publish a few short articles. Finally, its editorial page will stand for the rights of men, irrespective of color or race, for the highest ideals of American democracy, and for reasonable but earnest and persistent attempt to gain these rights and realize these ideals." Du Bois, "Editorial," 10.

19. Ardis, "Making Middlebrow Culture," 22.

20. Fultz, "'The Morning Cometh,'" 132. Hutchinson explains that decline as one of waning influence on the New Negro movement. Fauset's departure as literary editor coincided with "the new vehemence of the magazine's attacks on the rising appeal to white 'decadence' in art concerning the Negro" and Du Bois's "attacks" on Harlem Renaissance writers for "'pandering' to a white audience." Hutchinson, *The Harlem Renaissance in Black and White*, 166–67. *The Crisis* was also competing for readers; over fifty new Black-edited magazines aimed at an African American readership emerged between 1910 and 1930, as Fultz notes.

21. Ardis, "Making Middlebrow Culture," 23; Digby-Junger, "The *Guardian, Crisis, Messenger,* and *Negro World*," 267. Digby-Junger observes that periodicals such as the *Messenger,* the *Crusader,* and *Negro World* are frequently referred to as more radical than *The Crisis*. Regardless of whether we call *The Crisis* middlebrow or elite, "articles, commentary, graphics, and even the advertising spoke to a lifestyle unknown to the vast majority of early-20th-century African Americans" (267).

22. Hutchinson, *The Harlem Renaissance in Black and White*, 142, 156.

23. Digby-Junger, "The *Guardian, Crisis, Messenger,* and *Negro World,*" 267.

24. In this chapter "the Negro" appears in quotation marks because I am quoting Fauset's, Jacques Garvey's or *Negro World* readers' uses of it. This term was also in use by Black intellectuals, activists, and writers at the time, along with "the New Negro." Throughout this chapter, I do not sanitize language I am quoting since it was used at the time with political intent.

25. Qtd. in Digby-Junger, "The *Guardian, Crisis, Messenger,* and *Negro World,*" 273.

26. Fauset's contemporaries include Alice Dunbar Nelson, whose columns "Une femme dit" and "As in a Looking Glass" ran from the mid-1920s and onward in the *Pittsburgh Courier* (1910–1966) and the *Washington Eagle: National Negro Weekly* (Washington, DC; 1913–?). Nelson's columns, like most women's columns in the Black press, were presented with a single authorial voice although she covered a variety of issues and seemed to deliberately juxtapose disparate topics in her columns.

27. Carroll, "Protest and Affirmation," 89; Castronovo, "Beauty along the Color Line," 1452.

28. Ardis, "Making Middlebrow Culture," 26.

29. Fauset did not raise the condition of Indigenous peoples or the United States itself as US colonial-imperial conquests. Amy Jacques Garvey, in contrast, included reprints critical of settler colonialism in her women's column. See, for example, "Story of Indian Heiress," 7.

30. Qtd. in Carroll, "Protest and Affirmation," 93.

31. Fauset, "As to Lynching," 279, 281.

32. Fauset, "Race Superiority," 24.

33. Fauset, "Race Superiority," 24.

34. Weinbaum, *Wayward Reproductions*, 190.

35. Melamed, "The Spirit of Neoliberalism," 12–13.

36. Du Bois qtd. in Weinbaum, *Wayward Reproductions*, 200.

37. Fauset, "Colored Laborers," 129.

38. Fauset, "Colored Laborers," 130.

39. Significantly, readers are never told that the Empire Mattress Company is located in the North.

40. Fauset, "Colored Women in Industry," 94.

41. The investigation led to a campaign to abolish and preempt work-or-fight laws and an expanded NAACP presence in the South. Hunter, *To 'Joy My Freedom*, 230.

42. Grant, *The Way It Was in the South*, 306.

43. Hunter, *To 'Joy My Freedom*, 227. Hunter notes that the NAACP investigations "confirm[ed] that when workers quit or took time out of the labor market temporarily, demanded higher wages, or expressed discontent in any way, employers summoned 'work or fight' laws to retaliate against them" (231).

44. Grant, *The Way It Was in the South*, 306.

45. Fauset, "'The Work or Fight' Edict," 97.

46. Fauset, "The Restless South African," 238.

47. Qtd. in Maynard, "'In the interests of our people,'" 11. Fauset "wrote hundreds of signed and unsigned stories, poems, dialogues, biographies, articles, and did the

editing of manuscripts and correspondence with contributors" for all twenty-four issues of *The Brownies' Book: A Monthly Magazine for Children of the Sun* (New York, NY; 1920–1921). Although it circulated as edited by Du Bois, August Dill, and Fauset, the "day-to-day labor fell to Fauset." Sylvander, *Jessie Redmon Fauset*, 115. *The Crusader Magazine* (New York, NY; 1918–1922) was Cyril Briggs's periodical, established in September 1918 to promote the emigration of Blacks to Africa. In 1919, the paper's focus shifted to linking the Black and white working class and indictments of capitalism. Founded and edited by James Edward McCall in Montgomery, Alabama, *The Emancipator: A National Weekly* (1917–1929) folded when McCall, threatened by the Ku Klux Klan, moved to Detroit and opened the offices of the *Detroit Tribune* (1922–1966). He sold that paper in 1943. McCall's papers advocated for the rights of African Americans, particularly Black workers.

48. Garvey, "Negro's Greatest Enemy," 5 (first quote); Rolinson, *Grassroots Garveyism*, 3 (second quote).

49. Hill and Bair, *Marcus Garvey*, xxvii.

50. Rolinson, *Grassroots Garveyism*, 3.

51. James, *Holding Aloft the Banner of Ethiopia*, 12, 52, 96.

52. James, *Holding Aloft the Banner of Ethiopia*, 70–71.

53. James, *Holding Aloft the Banner of Ethiopia*, 136. A UNIA division in New Waterford, Canada, is mentioned in the *Negro World*, for example.

54. Rolinson, *Grassroots Garveyism*, 3, 2, 4. See also Dalrymple, "'Reclaiming the Fallen'"; and Harold, *The Rise and Fall of the Garvey Movement*.

55. Rolinson, *Grassroots Garveyism*, 3–4, 8. In the South, the UNIA spread "like wildfire"; "as many as 80 percent of its divisions and chapters in the South [were] organized . . . between July 1919 and August 1921." Some of Garvey's strongest constituencies were longshoremen and other organized laborers in the coastal areas of the South. Rolinson, *Grassroots Garveyism*, 86.

56. James, *Holding Aloft the Banner of Ethiopia*, 80–81. James documents the literacy of Caribbean migrants at 98.6 percent in 1923, rising to 99.0 percent by 1932. By comparison, "the illiteracy rates for Black American adults in 1920 and 1930 were 27.4 percent, and 20.0 percent respectively. The corresponding figures for white Americans were 5.0 and 3.4 percent." For James, such figures underscore "the profoundly selective character of the Caribbean migration" to the United States (78). For more information on these migrants, see James; for information on the migratory routes of workers in the circum-Caribbean (who were also highly literate) and to the United States, see Putnam, *The Company They Kept*.

57. The paper was banned and/or labeled seditious in British Honduras, Belize, British Guiana, St. Vincent, the Windward Islands, Grenada, St. Lucia, Trinidad, Barbados, Bahamas, and the Leeward Islands. For details on these bills and for British, Swiss, and American intelligence warnings of the power of the *Negro World* to incite unrest, see Elkins, "Marcus Garvey, the *Negro World*, and the British West Indies."

58. Rolinson, *Grassroots Garveyism*, 73, 17. Carnegie documents that *Negro World* was distributed from Hawaii to South Africa by Black sailors. He estimates its circulation

during 1918–1933 as 50,000 to 200,000 and argues that its influence far exceeded its circulation figures. Carnegie, "Garvey and the Black Transnation," 60–61. The lack of accurate records on UNIA membership and *Negro World* circulation can be seen in the scholarship. Although Rolinson cites the *Negro World*'s highest circulation as 75,000, quoting Robert Hill's edition of *The Marcus Garvey Papers*, the paper is routinely said to have had a circulation between 50,000 and 200,000. An August 1922 report from the Belgian vice-consul in New York City cited a claimed circulation of "more than one million," which he characterized as exaggerated. Hallaert, "Report by Charles Hallaert," 571.

59. See Digby-Junger, "The *Guardian, Crisis, Messenger*, and *Negro World*," on these distinctions between *Negro World* and other US-based Black periodicals in print at the time.

60. Broussard, "Exhortation to Action," 88.

61. In a memorandum dated October 11, 1919, J. Edgar Hoover indicted *Negro World* for "uphold[ing] 'Soviet Russian Rule' and . . . openly advocat[ing] Bolshevism." Elkins, "Marcus Garvey, the *Negro World*, and the British West Indies," 75. Rolinson also documents "complaints to federal authorities" about the paper's content. Rolinson, *Grassroots Garveyism*, 56.

62. Our Women was not published in the *Negro World* from the March 20, 1926, issue through the April 24, 1926, issues due to Amy Jacques Garvey's ill health. It also does not appear in the December 18, 1926, and May 7, 1926 issues.

63. James, *Holding Aloft the Banner of Ethiopia*, 154.

64. James, *Holding Aloft the Banner of Ethiopia*, 138.

65. Bair, "True Women, Real Men," 157 (first quote); Martin, "Women in the Garvey Movement," 70 (second quote). For more information on women's roles in the UNIA, see Taylor, *The Veiled Garvey*; Leeds, "Toward the 'Higher Type of Womanhood'"; and Reddock, "The First Mrs. Garvey."

66. Ford-Smith, "Women and the Garvey Movement in Jamaica," 78.

67. Qtd. in James, *Holding Aloft the Banner of Ethiopia*, 138–39.

68. James, *Holding Aloft the Banner of Ethiopia*, 139–40. For further details on who supported the recommendations at the convention, see Bair, "True Women, Real Men," 160–61.

69. Jacques Garvey, "Do Negro Women Want to Express Themselves?," 7.

70. James, *Holding Aloft the Banner of Ethiopia*, 141–42.

71. Taylor, "'Negro Women Are Great Thinkers,'" 109.

72. Taylor, *The Veiled Garvey*, 66; Bair, "True Women, Real Men," 162.

73. De Veyra, "Activities of Filipino Women," 10.

74. For readings of this repeated call Jacques Garvey made to her readers, see Taylor, *The Veiled Garvey*, 115; and Corbould, *Becoming African Americans*.

75. Jacques Garvey, "Have a Heart," 12.

76. Nicholas was secretary of the New York City division of the UNIA.

77. Holly was the daughter of Anglican bishop and Black emigrationist James Theodore Holly. She was an editorial writer for the *Negro World* in 1925. Hill, *Marcus Garvey*, 11:ccxx.

78. Sayers, a Black Cross Nurse in the New York City division, provided administrative assistance to Jacques Garvey during Marcus Garvey's incarceration and was her traveling companion on trips for the organization. Hill, *Marcus Garvey*, 7:44.

79. Sayers, "Woman as Educator," 10; Nichols, "Lady Delegate in Convention Demands Single Standard for All," 16. Other women who submitted more than one contribution, whether an article or letter, were Ida Jacques (Amy Jacques Garvey's sister) in 1924; Carrie Mero Ledeatt (associate secretary of the UNIA Ladies' Division from 1917 to 1918, listed on the UNIA's certificate of incorporation) in 1924 and 1925; Saydee E. Parham (a law student in New York City) in 1924; Mabel M. Douglass in 1925; Eva Aldred Brooks in 1925; Virginia Weston in 1925; Lula Belle Robinson in 1926; Mrs. Walter Ferguson in 1926 and 1927; and Ethel Collins (a beautician who emigrated from Jamaica in 1919 and served as acting secretary of the UNIA in the late 1920s) in 1926 and 1927, including an article in the paper outside the women's column. Collins is credited with helping Mme de Mena revive the UNIA in Jamaica in the early 1950s. Lady President Henrietta Vinton Davis and Mme M. L. T. de Mena also contributed to Our Women in 1925 (three articles) and 1926 (two articles). For more information on some of these Garveyites, see Blain, *Set the World on Fire*.

80. Jacques Garvey reissued her call for contributors through the month of May 1924, twice in June 1924, in August 1924 (with an extended call in her editorial "Have a Heart"), and again in mid-September 1924.

81. Jacques Garvey, "Our Page Is Three Years Old," 7.

82. Women contributed the most articles to "Our Women" in 1925 (twenty-nine) and 1926 (fifteen). In the October 31, 1925, issue, Madame de Mena published Our Women, registering a frustration similar to Jacques Garvey's: "It is an awful calamity when we realize the many intelligent women in the Universal Negro Improvement Association, who are capable of contributing an article to the 'Woman's page' in The *Negro World* and will not do so. . . . Women of the UNIA are called upon at this time to put in every spare moment in fitting themselves for real service." De Mena, "Our Women," 7.

83. Lee and LiPuma, "Cultures of Circulation," 192.

84. Taylor, "Negro Women Are Great Thinkers," 108.

85. Maynard, "'In the interests of our people,'" 1–2, 10.

86. Maynard, "'In the interests of our people,'" 1. Maynard refers to Lacey as "Tom Lacey," although he signed himself "L. Lacey."

87. Lacey, "Australia Sends Greetings," 3.

88. Maynard, "'In the interests of our people,'" 14.

89. See chapter 1 for late nineteenth- and early twentieth-century women's columns in the Black press that formed the horizon for Amy Jacques Garvey's innovations, including Gertrude Mossell inviting readers of her columns in the Indianapolis *World* and the *New York Freeman* to make suggestions to improve and increase their usefulness and Pauline Hopkins inviting reader contributions to her Woman's Department in *Colored American Magazine*. These are exceptions; women's pages or columns in the Black press typically did not invite reader collaboration.

90. See Rooks, *Ladies' Pages*, for an analysis of the politics of fashion and domesticity as presented in periodicals to Black women.

91. "Advice to Expectant Mothers," 7.
92. De Mena, "Part Women Must Play," 7; Leeds, "Toward the 'Higher Type of Womanhood,'" 6, 4.
93. Henkin, *The Postal Age*, 43; Gaul and Harris, *Letters and Cultural Transformations*, 8.
94. Henkin, *The Postal Age*, 21, 45.
95. Bannet, *Empire of Letters*, 46–47.
96. Roughly one-third of all letters to the page came from the urban Northeast, including New York City. One-third came from the Eastern and Western Caribbean, and roughly one-seventh came from the US South.
97. See Lewis, "The Black Woman's Part in Race Leadership," 10. On the New Negro as masculinist, see Ross, *Manning the Race*.
98. McReeves, "Fifteen-Year-Old Girl," 16.
99. Jacques Garvey, "It's Up to You!" 13.
100. Leeds, "Toward the 'Higher Type of Womanhood,'" 13.
101. Lewis, "The Black Woman's Part in Race Leadership," 10. Garvey saw the Chicago area as a UNIA "stronghold" with thousands of members and "some of the largest . . . divisions (locals) in the world." Black women played a vital role in those divisions. McDuffie, "Chicago, Garveyism, and the History of the Diasporic Midwest," 130.
102. According to the 1920 federal census, James Lewis Sr. worked as a foundry laborer in Chicago; his occupation in the 1930 census was office building porter. His income may have been sufficient to sustain their $35 per month home rental and the family without Eunice joining the workforce; in both the 1920 and 1930 censuses, she is listed as not working. In the 1920 census, Eunice, James Sr., and James Jr. are listed as living with Eunice's sister, Katherine Robinson. By the 1930 census, Eunice's mother, Julia Robinson (b. ca. 1854 as Julia Nation in Decatur, Alabama), her sister Katherine (who was by then married and listed as Katherine Cole), and Katherine's two children, Wilmer (age 9) and Arthur (age 7), were living with James Sr. and Eunice at the same address. Katherine was listed as working as a waitress and Eunice as not employed. James Lewis Jr. no longer lived with them. Julia Nation Robinson died on May 16, 1935; Eunice Lewis died on March 29, 1936; and James Lewis Sr. died on February 12, 1937. Entries for James Lewis and Eunice Lewis, United States census, 1920, FamilySearch, https://www.familysearch.org/ark:/61903/1:1:MJSJ-K6N; entries for James Lewis and Eunice Lewis, United States census, 1930, FamilySearch, https://www.familysearch.org/ark:/61903/1:1:XSRB-HW3. They are all buried at Restvale Cemetery in Cook County, Illinois. Entries for Eunice Lewis and William Robinson, March 29, 1936, "Illinois, Cook County Deaths, 1871–1998," FamilySearch, https://www.familysearch.org/ark:/61903/1:1:Q2M6-J776.
103. Drake and Cayton qtd. in McDuffie, "Chicago, Garveyism, and the History of the Diasporic Midwest," 133.
104. Langhorne, "Girls Should Be Taught," 10.
105. Taylor, "Negro Women Are Great Thinkers," 112.
106. Ingleton, "Four Essential Qualities," 12. Ingleton was a Black Cross Nurse in the San Juan, Honduras, division.
107. Ingleton, "Let Us Hold Our Own," 16.

108. Stephens, *Black Empire*, 8.
109. Stephens, *Black Empire*, 92. Carnegie differs from Stephens by asserting that Garvey espoused a "*hybrid* nationalism . . . that was decidedly ambivalent on the question of territorial integrity." Carnegie, "Garvey and the Black Transnation," 53; emphasis in the original.
110. Stephens, *Black Empire*, 92; emphasis in the original.
111. Putnam, *The Company They Kept*, 64.
112. Ingleton, "Let Us Hold Our Own," 16.
113. Nyberg, "Greetings from Australia," 12.
114. Zeleza, "African Diasporas and Academics," 89.
115. Hiery, *The Neglected War*, 214. Copra is dried coconut flesh from which coconut oil is extracted.
116. Augustin, "Economic Pressure," 8.
117. Augustin, "Economic Pressure," 8. Leeds argues that West Indians who had migrated to Cuba and Central America developed a "new anticolonial consciousness" resulting from "race-based [immigration] restrictions" in the United States and developments such as a 1934 banana contract that banned Black workers from the new Pacific Zone in the region. Leeds, "Toward the 'Higher Type of Womanhood,'" 11, 10.
118. McLeod, "Garveyism in Cuba," 132, 134. The UNIA reached out to Afro-Cubans through the Spanish page of *Negro World*, through translating UNIA materials into Spanish, through sailing the Black Star steamer *Frederick Douglass* to Cuba in 1919, and through visits by Marcus Garvey, Henrietta Vinton Davis, and John Sydney de Bourg in the spring of 1921.
119. McLeod, "Garveyism in Cuba," 136.
120. McLeod, "Garveyism in Cuba," 136. "British West Indians tended to settle in . . . urban areas of eastern Cuba, including Camagüey, Santiago, and Guantánamo, as well as in the larger mill towns" (137).
121. Taylor, "Negro Women Are Great Thinkers," 109.
122. Gaul and Harris, "Introduction," 9.
123. Gerber, *Authors of Their Lives*, 103.
124. Gerber, *Authors of Their Lives*, 102.
125. Jacques Garvey, "How to Help," 8. See also her April 1924 editorial, which offers a reprint from the *Union Messenger* critiquing the Emigrant Laborers Act of 1924 as "designed to keep the laborers in the Colony by conferring arbitrary powers on the Governor to place all obstacles in their way if they attempt to emigrate." Jacques Garvey, "St. Kitts Newspaper," 10.
126. Materson, "African American Women's Global Journeys," 36.

CHAPTER FIVE: **Intermedial Fugitivity and the "New Negro" Woman in *The Colored American Magazine***

1. Desrochers, "Periphery as Center," 2. An earlier version of this chapter was published in *American Periodicals*. I thank Joycelyn Moody and Eric Gardner for their generative questions and suggestions that improved that version and Mark Simpson for suggesting the concept of double rendition as productive for this chapter.
2. Waldstreicher, "Reading the Runaways," 247.

3. Latham and Scholes, "The Rise of Periodical Studies"; Philpotts, Description of the roundtable "What Is a Journal? Towards a Theory of Periodical Studies." On the question of methodology as articulated most strongly through attention to (white-edited) modernist periodicals, see Collier, "What Is Modern Periodical Studies?" The opposition between "description" and "explanation" reflects debates over reading protocols that oppose surface reading to critique. See, for example, Best and Marcus, "Surface Reading."

4. Liddle, "Method in Periodical Studies."

5. Latham, "Affordance and Emergence."

6. Sylvia Wynter's work has been central to theorizing the category of "human" as imbricated in technologies of modernity. Wynter, "The Ceremony Must Be Found"; Wynter, "Unsettling the Coloniality of Being/Power/Truth/Freedom." See also Chun, "Race and/as Technology"; Nakamura, *Digitizing Race*; Eubanks, *Digital Dead End*; Nakamura and Chow-White, *Race after the Internet*; Weheliye, *Habeas Viscus*; McGlotten, "Black Data"; Wade, "New Genres of Being Human"; Noble, *Algorithms of Oppression*; Litwack, "The Closed World and the Open Society."

7. Fagan, "Chronicling White America," 12. Fagan cites Chronicling America and the Making of America databases, which, although public, are "lily white." His points about the risks of conflating research insights drawn from such databases with all of American periodical production are vital, as is his attention to Black periodicals as the monetized content of paywalled, private corporation databases such as Readex and Accessible Archives.

8. Hopwood, "Discoverability and the Problems of Access," 7–10.

9. See, for example, Fagan, "Chronicling White America"; Cordell, "What Has the Digital Meant to American Periodicals Scholarship?"; Leary, "Response: Search and Serendipity."

10. See, for example, Gitelman, *Always Already New*; Liu, "Imagining the New Media Encounter." Maria DiCenzo has identified the "rhetoric of newness" as mobilizing "self-reinforcing narratives about emergence and innovation" that "miss or dismiss decades of valuable scholarship." DiCenzo, "Remediating the Past," 23–24.

11. See, for example, Tavia Nyong'o's notion of "tenseless time" in *Afro-Fabulations*; Wright, *Physics of Blackness*; McKittrick, *Demonic Grounds*.

12. Shukin, *Animal Capital*, 22.

13. My terminology here is in keeping with scholarship focused on "slave ads," "slave advertisements," engravings of "runaways," and wood block or metal cast type used to advertise enslaved people for sale or recapture. A broader array of what we might call slavery advertising, which exceeds my focus here, would encompass what Desrochers calls "subsidiary economic activities that slavery helped support," including "shipping; insurance; provisioning; and . . . the distilling industry." Desrochers, "Periphery as Center," 5.

14. Ardis, "Towards a Theory of Periodical Studies," 1.

15. Senchyne, "Bottles of Ink and Reams of Paper," 141–42.

16. Ardis, "Towards a Theory of Periodical Studies," 1. Ardis quotes this from Matthew Philpotts's description of the roundtable.

17. Mussell, "The Matter with Media," 5.
18. Mussell, "The Matter with Media," 5.
19. Liddle, "Method in Periodical Studies," 4.
20. Wilson, *Whither the Black Press?*, 20.
21. Thomas, *The History of Printing in America*, 130n2. See also Jonathan Senchyne's work on Primus Fowle, "Type, Paper, Glass, and Screws," and Senchyne, "Under Pressure."
22. Senchyne, "Under Pressure," 118.
23. Hardesty, *Unfreedom*, 157.
24. Thomas, *The History of Printing in America*, 122–23, 99.
25. McMurtrie, *A History of Printing in the United States*, 454.
26. Thomas, *The History of Printing in America*, 130n2. It is not clear from Thomas's reference whether Cain was freeborn or enslaved at some point in his past prior to Pennsylvania's 1780 emancipation act.
27. De Groft, "Eloquent Vessels/Poetics of Power," 250. For more on Dave the Potter, see the essays collected in Chaney, *Where Is All My Relation?*
28. Schweiger, *A Literate South*, 60–61. See also McGee, "*Spirit of the Age*."
29. Schweiger, *A Literate South*, 61–62.
30. Gardner, *Black Print Unbound*, 66.
31. Bradley, *Slavery, Propaganda, and the American Revolution*, xxi. Although Thomas does not identify enslaved people as among those "employed" in paper mills or rag collecting to produce paper, he does note that by 1810, 195 mills were in operation in a combination of slave and free states and territories and that an average mill with two vats would "employ twelve or more persons." He estimates that "collecting rags, making paper, &c., may be said to give employment to not less than 2,500 persons." Thomas, *The History of Printing in America*, 25–26. It is highly likely that not all those so "employed," particularly in slave states, were free workers.
32. Desrochers, "Slave-For-Sale Advertisements and Slavery in Massachusetts," 635; Desrochers, "Periphery as Center," 8.
33. Waldstreicher, *Runaway America*, 23–24.
34. "Explore Advertisements," The Geography of Slavery, http://www2.vcdh.virginia.edu/gos/browse/browse_ads.php?year=1790&%20month=6&page=0. Online database collections of slavery advertising tend to be limited to runaway ads and provide perspectives that augment print scholarship. In North Carolina newspapers that have been digitized, there are "more than 2,300" runaway advertisements for the period from 1751 to 1840. By 1790, roughly 3,700 enslaved persons lived in the New England colonies, where about 1 percent of white families owned slaves at the time. In comparison, in 1790, 100,000 enslaved persons were living in North Carolina. See "North Carolina Runaway Slave Notices, 1750–1865," Digital Library on American Slavery, https://dlas.uncg.edu/notices/.
35. Hall, "Missing Dolly, Mourning Slavery," 80.
36. McGee, "*Spirit of the Age*."
37. Bradley, *Slavery, Propaganda, and the American Revolution*, 43–44.
38. Bradley, *Slavery, Propaganda, and the American Revolution*, 26, 30–31.

39. Prude, "To look upon the 'lower sort,'" 143.

40. Waldstreicher, "Reading the Runaways," 250.

41. Franklin and Schweninger, *Runaway Slaves*, 2. Even a scholar like Waldstreicher, one of the few who considers slave advertising as a print culture genre, speculates that "runaway advertisements, in effect, were the first slave narratives—the first published stories about slaves and their seizure of freedom," although he goes on to say that their difference from that genre is that "the advertisements attempted to use print to bolster confidence in slavery, rather than confidence in African Americans and their narratives." Waldstreicher, "Reading the Runaways," 247. Art historian Charmaine Nelson also reads slave advertising, in part, as biographical texts. See Nelson, *Creolization and Transatlantic Blackness*.

42. See, for example, Frey, *Water from the Rock*; Hodges and Brown, *"Pretends to Be Free"*; Donnan, *Documents Illustrative of the History of the Slave Trade*; McManus, *Black Bondage in the North*; Mullin, *Flight and Rebellion*; Parker, *Running for Freedom*; White, *Somewhat More Independent*; Windley, *Runaway Slave Advertisements*; and Smith and Wojtowicz, *Blacks Who Stole Themselves*. Major slave advertisement databases include The Geography of Slavery in Virginia (University of Virginia); "North Carolina Runaway Slave Notices, 1750–1865" (Digital Library on American Slavery); the Texas Runaway Slave Project (East Texas Digital Archives); and the ambitious Freedom on the Move project (Cornell University, University of Alabama, University of New Orleans, and University of Kentucky), which aims to "compile all North American slave runaway ads and make them available for statistical, geographical, textual, and other forms of analysis"; "Freedom on the Move. A Database on Fugitives from North American Slavery," H-Slavery, https://networks.h-net.org/node/11465/links/145380/freedom-move-database-fugitives-north-american-slavery. For a listing of runaway slave ad databases, see Crystal Edding, "On the Lives of Fugitives: Runaway Slave Advertisements Databases," HASTAC, March 30, 2017, https://publishing-archives.hastac.hcommons.org/2017/03/30/on-the-lives-of-fugitives-runaway-slave-advertisement-databases/.

43. Nelson, "Introduction"; Costa, "What Can We Learn From a Digital Database of Runaway Slave Advertisements?," 40. Nelson is director of the Digital Scholarship Lab at the University of Richmond, and Costa has created The Geography of Slavery, a digital database of more than 4,000 advertisements for runaway slaves and indentured white servants drawn from newspapers in Virginia and Maryland from 1736 to 1803.

44. Greene, "The New England Negro as Seen in Advertisements," 127.

45. Costa, "What Can We Learn From a Digital Database of Runaway Slave Advertisements?," 40.

46. Moody, "Tactical Lines in Three Black Women's Visual Portraits," 9.

47. Waldstreicher, "Reading the Runaways," 247.

48. Desrochers, "Slave-For-Sale Advertisements and Slavery in Massachusetts," 623.

49. Moody, "Tactical Lines in Three Black Women's Visual Portraits," 9.

50. See Lacey, "Visual Images of Blacks in Early American Imprints," 137–80.

51. Desrochers, "Slave-For-Sale Advertisements and Slavery in Massachusetts," 623; Wood, *Blind Memory*, 89. Wood notes that "the print cultures of eighteenth- and nineteenth-century Brazil, the Caribbean, and the Southern United States teemed with notices for runaway slaves. They were also current in the late eighteenth-century

English newspapers published in slave ports, most significantly Liverpool." Wood, *Blind Memory*, 80.

52. Wood, *Blind Memory*, 89. Wood describes the runaway icons that have become most familiar to us today and that were "largely standardized over two continents and two centuries" as follows: "A male was represented by a running clothed figure, carrying a bundle of goods on a stick and passing a tree. A female was represented, most commonly, by a seated clothed figure, resting, and holding a bundle" (80).

53. Wood, *Blind Memory*, 87.

54. Moody, "Tactical Lines in Three Black Women's Visual Portraits," 10.

55. Blackwood, "Fugitive Obscura," 94.

56. "Ambrotypes," 2.

57. On January 7, 1836, Louis-Jacques-Mandé Daguerre presented his daguerreotype process to the French Académie des Sciences. In 1839, Sir John Herschel coined the word "photography" for his production of the first glass negative. In 1841, William Fox Talbot patented his negative-positive process of producing a translucent negative that made it possible to print multiple copies of the same exposure (the talbotype or calotype), the prototype for analog photography. This process produced less detailed images than the dauguerreotype, and others sought to arrive at processes that would enable higher-quality reproducible images. The result was Gustave Le Gray's invention of the wet collodion in 1850. Wet collodion processes enabled the development of the ambrotype, patented by James Ambrose Cutting in 1854, which was an "underexposed glass negative placed against a dark background" that "create[d] a positive image." Dry-plate technology was invented in 1871 by Dr. Richard Maddox, using gelatin as the plate material. Daniel, "Daguerre (1787–1851) and the Invention of Photography"; and "Ambrotypes and Tintypes," Liljenquist Family Collection of Civil War Photographs, Library of Congress, https://www.loc.gov/collections/liljenquist-civil-war-photographs/articles-and-essays/ambrotypes-and-tintypes/.

58. Darrah, *Cartes de Visite*, 48–53, 19. See also Perry, "The Carte de Visite in the 1860s"; and Volpe, "The Middle Is Material."

59. Darrah, *Cartes de Visite*, 10.

60. Dinius, *The Camera and the Press*, 209.

61. See, for example, Darrah, *Cartes de Visite*; Painter, *Sojourner Truth*; and Wallace and Smith, *Pictures and Progress*.

62. Hill notes that Douglass "allowed his supporters in England to buy his legal emancipation" in 1841; Hill, "'Rightly Viewed,'" 48. John Stauffer, Zoe Trodd, and Celeste-Marie Bernier estimate that Douglass sat for his portrait "on average once every sixteen weeks from 1845–1895," producing at least "168 separate photographs . . . as defined by *distinct* poses, rather than multiple copies of the same image." Stauffer, Trodd, and Bernier, "Introduction," ii, 215n3; emphasis in the original.

63. See, for example, "Letter from Sojourner Truth," and "Letter from Sojourner Truth. The Story of Her Interview with the President." Nearly twenty years later, Truth noted that her photographs were still for sale in a letter to the editor of Chicago's *Daily Inter-Ocean*. See Truth, "To the Editor of *The Inter-Ocean*," reprinted in Fitz and Mandziuk, *Sojourner Truth as Orator*, 201–2.

64. Qtd. in Mabee, *Sojourner Truth*, 216.

282 Notes to Pages 167–169

65. See, for example, the Library of Congress Print and Photographs online catalog of Sojourner Truth's photographic portraits; http://www.loc.gov/pictures/search/?q=truth%2C%20sojourner (accessed July 23, 2019). See also Grigsby, *Enduring Truths*; Painter, *Sojourner Truth*; Peterson, *"Doers of the Word"*; Collins, "Shadow and Substance."

66. Hill, "'Rightly Viewed,'" 48.

67. Douglass delivered "Lecture on Pictures" in the Fraternity Course series at Boston's Tremont Temple on December 3, 1861, but it was advertised in the press as "Pictures and Progress," explaining perhaps why no title of any lecture or fragment in the ninety-page digitized manuscript of his lectures on photography is given as "Pictures and Progress" in the Library of Congress; see "Frederick Douglass Papers: Speech, Article, and Book File, 1846–1894; Speeches and Articles by Douglass, 1846–1894; 1861, 'Lecture on Pictures,' title varies," Library of Congress, https://www.loc.gov/resource/mss11879.22004/?sp=1&r=-1.526,0,4.052,1.59,0 (hereafter Douglass, "Lecture on Pictures"). These lectures are the basis for scholars' assertions that Douglass was a theorist of photography. The questions Jasmine Nicole Cobb raises regarding Truth's interest in photography suggest that what is often referred to as her "savvy" praxis should be revised to considerations of her theory: "Did the repeated sale of Truth—three owners in one year—inform her attitude about pricing or repetition? Did a penchant for evidence, both in slavery and the legal system, deepen Truth's commitment to photography as an 'objective' medium?" In raising pricing, repetition, and evidence, Cobb's questions also point to the need for greater attention to Truth's use of the periodical press as a medium for circulating, naturalizing, and capitalizing on her self-authorized persona. Cobb, "Review of *Enduring Truths*," 528. On Douglass as a theorist of photography, see Blackwood, "Fugitive Obscura"; Hill, "'Rightly Viewed'"; Meehan, *Mediating American Autobiography*; Stauffer, "Race and Contemporary Photography"; Stauffer, "Daguerreotyping the National Soul"; Wexler, "'A More Perfect Likeness.'"

68. Douglass, "Lecture on Pictures," 2, 9, 28–29.

69. See "Selections from Gleason's Pictorial Daguerrian Gallery of the West," 1. The *New Orleans Daily Creole* also ran stories on photographic technologies; see, for example, "Ambrotypes," 2.

70. Dinius, *The Camera and the Press*, 195–96.

71. Douglass, "Oh Liberty!," 2.

72. Douglass, "Lecture on Pictures," 12.

73. I take this phrase from Petry, "Complicity Chapter Five: Slavery and the *Courant*." On July 4, 2000, the *Courant* published a front-page apology for running and profiting from slave advertising. Leavenworth and Canfield, "Courant Complicity," 1. As Ira Berlin notes, following this front-page apology the paper then "reprised the history of slavery in Connecticut in a seventy-nine-page supplement to its Sunday edition." Berlin, "American Slavery in History and Memory," 1254.

74. Moody, "Tactical Lines in Three Black Women's Visual Portraits," 2; Wood qtd. in Moody, "Tactical Lines in Three Black Women's Visual Portraits," 2.

75. Chaney, *Fugitive Vision*, 37.

76. Hill, "'Rightly Viewed,'" 49.

77. For a reading of Henry Bibb's author frontispiece, engraved by P. H. Reason, and woodcut illustrations, see Wood, *Blind Memory*, 117–30. Wood elsewhere refers to Bibb's narrative as "one of the most heavily illustrated of all slave narratives." Wood, *Black Milk*, 114.

78. Wood, *Blind Memory*, 130.

79. Wright, "Photography in the Printing Press," 37.

80. Stauffer, "Creating an Image in Black," 68.

81. Dinius, *The Camera and the Press*, 4.

82. Sekula, "The Body and the Archive," 10, 12.

83. McCandless, "The Portrait Studio and the Celebrity," 49. Mathew Brady's award-winning exhibition of daguerreotype portraits, *Illustrious Americans*, at the Crystal Palace Exposition in London in 1851 was the basis for the "model Americans" he offered for emulation in his book of lithographs, *Gallery of Illustrious Americans* (1850). Smith, *American Archives*, 165. See also Taft, *Photography and the American Scene*, chapters 3 and 4. There is a rich body of work on portrait photography as securing, rather than leveling, American social hierarchies based on class and race. See particularly Wexler, *Tender Violence*; Smith, *American Archives*; and Smith, *Photography on the Color Line*.

84. Kelley, "Foreword," in *Reflections in Black*, ix, x.

85. Thomas Junius Calloway, a former Fisk undergraduate who became the assistant principal at Tuskegee, was Du Bois's friend. He had coedited the *Fisk Herald* with Du Bois when they were at Fisk. When Calloway asked Du Bois to participate in the exhibit, Du Bois chose to focus on Georgia as the state "with the largest nonwhite population." Du Bois presented Georgia as paradigmatic of the situation of African Americans in the South. Lewis, "A Small Nation of People," 23–24, 28. The materials assembled for the exhibit, including Du Bois's charts and graphs, can be viewed at "African American Photographs Assembled for 1900 Paris Exposition: Search Results," Library of Congress, http://www.loc.gov/pictures/search/?sp=1&co=anedub&st=grid.

86. Lewis, "A Small Nation of People," 30. The portraits of individuals were numbered, but identifying names and names of photographers were not included in the exhibit and were not recorded for later study.

87. Howard, "The American Negro Exhibit," 6.

88. Du Bois qtd. in Smith, *Photography on the Color Line*, 5.

89. Smith, *Photography on the Color Line*, 4.

90. Smith, *Photography on the Color Line*, 2.

91. Foreman, "Reading/Photographs," 263, 261.

92. Foreman, "Reading/Photographs," 262. Foreman notes that the photographs of editors that accompany their reports in Josephine St. Pierre Ruffin's *Woman's Era* from 1894 to 1896 were part of an editorial shift at the periodical.

93. See "Our Woman's Number," a special issue of *The Voice of the Negro*, and "Votes for Women," a special issue of *The Crisis*.

94. Dworkin, "Biography of Pauline E. Hopkins."

95. Hazel Carby calls Hopkins a cofounder of the magazine. Other scholars, such as Alisha Knight and Lois Brown, refer to her joining its staff in 1900. Carby, *Reconstructing Womanhood*, 125; Knight, *Pauline Hopkins and the American Dream*, 37; Brown, *Pauline Elizabeth Hopkins*, 2.

96. See Wallinger, *Pauline E. Hopkins*, 60–65.

97. Smith, "Chicago Notes," 1; Hopkins, "Josephine St. Pierre Ruffin at Milwaukee," 210–13.

98. Scholars who have documented this shift in the ownership and politics of Black periodical publication in the Northeast at the time under Washington's consolidating influence and control, and its link to Hopkins's departure from the magazine, include Alisha R. Knight, Sigrid Anderson Cordell, Hannah Wallinger, Sabina Matter-Seibel, Jill Bergman, and Lois Brown.

99. Dahn and Sweeney, "A Brief History of the *Colored American Magazine*."

100. Carby, *Reconstructing Womanhood*, 125.

101. Cordell, "'The Case Was Very Black Against' Her," 53. Cordell also quotes Walter Wallace as saying that "fully one third of our subscribers are white" (58).

102. Brown, *Pauline Elizabeth Hopkins*, 297.

103. "Editorial and Publishers' Announcements," 61.

104. Carby, *Reconstructing Womanhood*, 124, 126.

105. Knight, "Commentary."

106. Elliot, "The Story of Our Magazine," 43. Carby draws a very useful comparison between *The Colored American Magazine* and T. Thomas Fortune's *New York Age* (recognized as the first national Black weekly), which in 1892 boasted "a circulation of 4,500." Carby, *Reconstructing Womanhood*, 193n12.

107. Carby, *Reconstructing Womanhood*, 123. Jill Bergman notes that under Hopkins's tenure, the magazine ran ads for products and services focused on women, such as hair straighteners, facial bleach, clothing, and a women's sanitarium, but the advertising shifted its gender focus once she left, with ads for cigars and men's tailors accompanying its cover portraits of men and articles focused on businesses owned by Black men. Bergman, "'Everything we hoped she'd be,'" 192–94.

108. "Announcement." For more details on how the magazine sustained itself through political alliances prior to its covert purchase by Washington, see Brown, *Pauline Elizabeth Hopkins*, chapter 10.

109. "Here and There," 57; emphasis added.

110. March, "Reframing Blackness,"128.

111. Mitchell, "Negating the Nadir," 46n21. Skeete's cover design replaced that of staff artist Hanson, whose last cover was the November 1900 issue.

112. The one exception is the October 1901 issue, which offered a Skeete-signed lithograph of a male steelworker. Scholars agree that it is difficult to determine Hopkins's influence at the magazine precisely, and I would suggest that the inconsistent or incomplete listing of editorial staff at *The Colored American Magazine* is an indication of just how involved she was, rather than inconclusive evidence of her editorial role as it has been taken to be thus far. There is an established history of women editors in the black press veiling their roles so that their publications might have a better chance of success. Cordell notes that Hopkins is listed "in a senior editorial capacity from at least 1902 onwards," and as "literary editor from May/June 1903 through April 1904," as well as "once as general editor on the masthead" (March 1904). Cordell, "'The Case Was Very Black Against' Her," 54–55.

113. "Announcement."

114. Even though Alain Locke's pronouncements about the New Negro in the 1925 issue of *Survey Graphic* and in his *New Negro* anthology are usually cited as the definition of the figure, his was only one voice in a debate that included both African Americans and Caribbean immigrants, all of whom edited radical periodicals.

115. Hopkins, "Address at the Citizens' William Lloyd Garrison Centenary Celebration," 356; Hopkins, "Address at The Two Days of Observance of the One Hundredth Anniversary," 359.

116. Hopkins, "Address at the Citizens' William Lloyd Garrison Centenary Celebration," 356.

117. In the opening of her Garrison address, Hopkins asserted: "I am a daughter of the Revolution, you do not acknowledge black daughters of the Revolution but we are going to take that right." Hopkins, "Address at the Citizens' William Lloyd Garrison Centenary Celebration," 355.

118. Hopkins, "Famous Women of the Negro Race, IV," 277.

119. Tagg, *The Burden of Representation*, 36.

120. Lalvani, *Photography, Vision, and the Production of Modern Bodies*, 48, 52.

121. Lalvani, *Photography, Vision, and the Production of Modern Bodies*, 52.

122. Smith, *Photography on the Color Line*, 3.

123. Douglass, "A Tribute to the Negro."

124. Raiford, *Imprisoned in a Luminous Glare*, 9.

125. Raiford, *Imprisoned in a Luminous Glare*, 9.

126. Cordell writes that race magazines' "goal of racial advancement required three main elements: a forum for promoting African American arts and literature; a black readership to support that forum and to prove that blacks were advanced enough to appreciate such a journal; and a larger white audience to witness the magazine's cultural impact and be converted by it." Cordell, "'The Case Was Very Black Against' Her," 57–58.

127. Ardis, "Towards a Theory of Periodical Studies," 2–3.

Coda

1. Bass, "Address by Mrs. Charlotta A. Bass."

2. Freer, "L. A. Race Woman," 609. See also Gill, "'Win or Lose—We Win.'"

3. Streitmatter, *Raising Her Voice*, 100. Regina Freer notes that Los Angeles's Black population in 1920 was 15,579, which meant that the subscription base for the *Eagle* well exceeded the size of the city's Black communities. Freer, "L. A. Race Woman," 610.

4. Streitmatter documents that the Office of the Secretary of War monitored African American papers from 1940 to 1947, that the FBI interrogated Bass at the *Eagle* offices in the spring of 1942 and thereafter surveilled her public speeches and the content of the *Eagle*, and that after the US Post Office conducted an investigation of the paper in 1943, it recommended that the Department of Justice revoke Bass's mailing permit because she was publishing "subversive material." Streitmatter, *Raising Her Voice*, 102–3. Bass was "targeted by Senator Tenney during the House Un-American Activities Committee hearings" and "accused of being a member of the Communist Party." Johnson, "Constellations of Struggle," 162.

5. Freer, "L. A. Race Woman," 609.
6. Bass, "On the Sidewalk," 1.
7. Bass, *Forty Years*, 27; Streitmatter, *Raising Her Voice*, 96.
8. Bass, *Forty Years*, 30.
9. Joseph Bass edited the *Topeka Call* from 1896 to 1898, when he sold the paper to Nick Chiles, who renamed it the *Topeka Plaindealer*. Bass worked with Chiles until 1905, when he moved to Helena, Montana. In 1906, Bass established the *Montana Plaindealer*, which he published until financial difficulties forced it to close in 1911. He then migrated to Los Angeles in late 1912 by way of San Francisco and visited the *Eagle*'s offices shortly after arriving in Los Angeles. Charlotta Spears hired him in 1913 as a writer, and at the end of that year she offered him a position as managing editor. The two were married in August 1914. Joseph Bass died in 1934. See Lang, "The Nearly Forgotten Blacks."
10. Bass, *Forty Years*, 28.
11. Bass scholars variously give her year of birth as 1874, 1879, 1880, or 1890 and her birthplace as Rhode Island, Ohio, or South Carolina.
12. Taylor, "Read[ing] Men and Nations," 75.
13. See for example Tobert, *Ideology and Community*.
14. See Freer on Bass as a leader in both the UNIA and the NAACP. Freer notes that Bass and others in Los Angeles's UNIA division broke from it less than a year after it formed, disputing "local control of finances." Freer, "L. A. Race Woman," 610–14. Douglass Flamming documents this dispute as one over UNIA, not local, finances and possible fraud. Los Angeles Division president Noah Thompson discovered that the "UNIA was effectively broke" and had misspent $250,000 of UNIA members' money on Black Star Line ships that "were only worth scrap." Flamming, *African Americans in the West*, 139.
15. Streitmatter, *Raising Her Voice*, 96.
16. Du Bois, "Editorial. Southern California," 131. Los Angeles's population grew from 319,000 in 1910 to 576,573 in 1920. See Bunch, "'The Greatest State for the Negro,'" 138.
17. Bunch, "'The Greatest State for the Negro,'" 111. Bunch documents that the African American population of Los Angeles "(7,599 residents in 1910) quickly outpaced that of both San Francisco (1,642) and Oakland (3,055)" (111). See also Flamming, *Bound for Freedom*; Sides, *L.A. City Limits*; and Smith, *The Great Black Way*.
18. Bass, *Forty Years*, 35–36.
19. Bass, *Forty Years*, 37–42, 46–53.
20. Bass, "Industry 1934," 5. Washington had migrated from Kansas to Los Angeles in 1928, urged by his cousin, Loren Miller, who later bought the *Eagle* from Bass. Washington joined the *Eagle* staff as the paper's advertising manager in 1930 and left to establish the *Los Angeles Sentinel* in 1933. Although the *Sentinel* soon became a rival publication, Charlotta and Joseph Bass continued to collaborate with Washington on this campaign. Leonard, *The Battle for Los Angeles*, 16. By the late 1940s, he was leading direct action boycotts of white-owned businesses in majority-Black neighborhoods that refused to employ African Americans, reviving the "Don't spend your money where you can't work" slogan. Washington is said to have left the *Eagle* over disputes regarding his advertising commissions. See "Black Leadership in Los Angeles," 78.

21. Bass, *Forty Years*, 57, 59.
22. Bass, *Forty Years*, 66–68.
23. Streitmatter, *Raising Her Voice*, 102.
24. Johnson, "Constellations of Struggle," 158, 155. Johnson describes Guatemalan-born Moreno as "among the most visible women in labor and civil rights activism in the United States from the 1930s to 1950" (156).
25. Johnson, "Constellations of Struggle," 158.
26. Johnson, "Constellations of Struggle," 162–63.
27. California Legislature, Senate, *Un-American Activities in California*, 217.
28. California Legislature, Senate, *Eleventh Report of the Senate Fact-Finding Subcommittee on Un-American Activities in California*, 45.
29. Founded in 1946 in Detroit by William Patterson, a Communist Party USA leader, the Civil Rights Congress was composed of working and unemployed African Americans and leftist whites. It focused on the police brutality and justice system discrimination that African Americans faced in the 1940s and 1950s. The Congress also defended anyone charged under the Smith Act, which targeted members of the Communist Party USA and the Socialist Worker's Party.
30. Johnson, "Constellations of Struggle," 164. See also Freer, "L. A. Race Woman," 626–27.
31. Bass, *Forty Years*, 95–113.
32. See "Articles of Incorporation."
33. Streitmatter, *Raising Her Voice*, 104. It is worth noting that Bass kept Black feminist editorial company in this with Ida B. Wells. In January 1919, the FBI recommended that Passport Control deny Wells a passport for travel to the Paris Peace Conference. The FBI referred to her as "one of the most dangerous negro agitators" based on her speeches that "endeavor[ed] to impress upon" African American audiences "that they are a downtrodden race and that now is the time for them to demand and secure their proper position in the world." Acting Chief, FBI to R. W. Flournoy, Chief, Division of Passport Control, Bureau of Citizenship, January 11, 1919, case number 123754, https://www.fold3.com/image/1433054/mrs-ida-well-barmett-123754-page-1-us-fbi-case-files-1908-1922?terms=wells,ida,well. This letter was signed only "Acting Chief," although William E. Allen was acting chief or acting director of the FBI in 1919. Wells was denied a passport through this action.
34. Lynn, "Deportation of Claudia Jones." Lynn also documents the seizure of Paul Robeson's passport under the Immigration and Nationality Act of 1952 because he refused to sign an affidavit attesting he was not a member of the Communist Party.
35. Castledine, *Cold War Progressives*, 99. See also McDuffie, "A 'New Freedom Movement.'"
36. Qtd. in Lieberman, "The Missing Peace."
37. Streitmatter, *Raising Her Voice*, 105.
38. Rapp, "A Marginalized Voice for Racial Justice," 234.
39. Streitmatter, *Raising Her Voice*, 106. Streitmatter notes that the FBI file on Bass is 563 pages long.
40. Freer, "L. A. Race Woman," 623. See also Johnson, *Spaces of Conflict*.
41. See, for example, Streitmatter, *Raising Her Voice*, 105.

42. The *Eagle* had California's first Black-owned linotype in 1917. Regester, "Introduction," 3.

43. The April 4, 1930, issue announced that the contest was converting to cash prizes; the first prize was $500 and all others would receive a 25 percent commission for the subscriptions they raised, whether they were for new customers or renewals. Bass, "California Eagle: Prizes in Campaign," 11. For the extension of the contest, see Bass, "$500 Cash Is the Prize," 11.

44. "They Are Off to a Fresh Start in Everybody Wins Campaign," *California Eagle*, May 23, 1930, 11. The prize schedule makes it difficult to know what the vote tally the *Eagle* reported translated to in terms of subscriptions secured, since it operated in three segments with, for example, a three-year subscription beginning at 25,000 votes if it was secured in the first twenty-four days of the contest but falling to 15,000 votes if it was secured in the final nine days. The final published tally of 3,117,000 "votes" may have amounted to from 124 three-year to 1,039 one-year subscriptions if most were secured in the first twenty-four days of the contest or from 156 three-year subscriptions to 1,559 one-year subscriptions if most were secured in the middle twelve days of the contest. It is impossible to know how many renewed or new subscriptions Bass generated with this contest nor how much she paid contestants in the 25 percent commission scheme. See "$500 Cash Is the Prize," 11, for an explanation of the three tiers of the subscription contest as it ran from March 7 until it closed.

45. See *California Eagle*, June 20, 1930.

46. Jeter, "Rough Flying," 11.

47. Cano was paid from a low of $13.34 for the week of December 14, 1929, to a high of $28 in the weeks of June 10 and 28, 1930. Prowd and Hamilton were paid an average weekly salary of $30, while Williams's average weekly salary was $20. Solomon was paid $25 weekly in 1929 and 1930 and from $10 to $13 weekly in 1933. Financial Records, Charlotta Bass Collection.

48. An undated *Eagle* record of press equipment notes four pounds of ink. The canceled checks to General Paper in December 1929, May and June 1930, and March and April 1933 total $88.44; those to Morrell Ink dated November 14, 1932, and April 12, 1933, total $57.96. Canceled checks also indicate that Bass purchased from Sierra Paper Co. (San Francisco), Sabine Robbins Paper (Middletown, Ohio, producer of fine paper), Penn Card and Paper (Philadelphia, producer of chipboards for bookbinding), Fred H. French Paper (Los Angeles), and Blake Moffit and Towne paper and printing company (San Francisco). Sierra Paper was her regular fine paper supplier from 1929 through 1933. See Financial Records, Charlotta Bass Collection.

49. Bond, *The Negro in Los Angeles*, 32.

50. Jeter, "Rough Flying," 9.

51. Financial Records, Charlotta Bass Collection.

52. Object description of a photograph captioned "The staff of 'The California Eagle Hour' prepare for their weekly radio broadcast, circa 1940," Charlotta Bass/*California Eagle* Photograph Collection, 1880–1986, Southern California Library for Social Studies and Research, Los Angeles.

53. Smith, *The Great Black Way*, 22.

54. Object description of photograph, "The staff of 'The California Eagle Hour' prepare for their weekly radio broadcast, circa 1940."

55. *N. W. Ayer & Son's Directory . . . 1940*, 84.

56. Rapp, "A Marginalized Voice for Racial Justice," 130.

57. Carl Bigsby owned Compton Printing, which initially refused to pay new National Recovery Act (1933) union-negotiated scales in 1934. The threat of a strike secured his compliance. Perry and Perry, *History of the Los Angeles Labor Movement*, 294.

58. Compton Printing Company invoice to the *Eagle*, January 9, 1957.

59. Brodie to Bass, May 5, 1948. Brodie's letter noted that among other employees, Cyril Briggs was seeking $115 from Bass for unpaid "two weeks' vacation in 1947"; the *Eagle's* society editor "Miss Jessie Mae Brown . . . should have been paid a total of $515.70"; and "Edward Banbridge . . . [was] owed a total of $936.35."

60. Bass to Brodie, Los Angeles Newspaper Guild, May 19, 1948, Additional Box 1, Letters to, 1940s, Charlotta Bass Collection.

61. Bass to Brodie, October 4, 1948, Additional Box 1, Letters to, 1940s, Charlotta Bass Collection. An October 22, 1947, check made out to June Hilyard for the sum of $873.53 in the *Eagle's* financial files also bears the notation "Compton Press" and may reflect payment of an invoice or past invoices to Compton Press and not back pay to Hilyard. Financial Records, Charlotta Bass Collection.

62. Margolis to the Los Angeles Newspaper Guild, October 12, 1948, Additional Box 1, Letters to, 1940s, Charlotta Bass Collection.

63. California Legislature, Senate, *Un-American Activities in California*, 155.

64. Wealthy whites living in West Adams Heights sued thirty-one Black residents, including Oscar winner Hattie McDaniel, in 1945 to enforce the neighborhood's racially restrictive housing covenant and evict them. The neighborhood had become popularly known as Sugar Hill for the African American upper class and wealthy who lived there, including McDaniel, Louise Beavers, and Ethel Waters. McDaniel and the NAACP organized these residents to fight back, and Justice Thurmond Clarke ruled that housing covenants in Sugar Hill violated the Fourteenth Amendment. The Sugar Hill case is regarded as a legal precedent that contributed to the 1948 Supreme Court decision ruling restrictive housing covenants unconstitutional. See "Los Angeles: Sugar Hill," Segregation by Design, https://www.segregationbydesign.com/los-angeles/sugar-hill.

65. *N. W. Ayer & Son's Directory . . . 1950*, 90.

66. Compton Printing carried the *Eagle's* balance and accepted interest-only payments. Items 13 through 33, Compton Printing Company Correspondence, Mold Box 2, Loren Miller Papers, 1876–2003, The Huntington Library.

67. Bingham, "Strange Death," 29.

68. Bingham, "Strange Death," 28.

69. Jeter, "Rough Flying," 19.

70. Bass retained ownership of the *Eagle* offices in Los Angeles, and it was one of three properties, including her home in Lake Elsinore, that were foreclosed on to pay her debts upon her death. See Rapp, "A Marginalized Voice for Racial Justice," 235.

71. Mangun, "'As citizens of Portland we must protest,'" 385.

72. Miller, "Oregon Is the Best State in the Union," 1.

73. Miller, "Oregon Is the Best State in the Union," 1; "Mrs. Cannady Sees End of Race Trouble."

74. Mangun, "'As citizens of Portland we must protest,'" 387–399.

75. Mangun, "'As citizens of Portland we must protest,'" 393, 386.

76. "Marcus Garvey," 1; "Dean Wm. Pickens Pleads for Release of Garvey," 1.

77. Mangun, "The (Oregon) *Advocate*," 17.

78. See Sayers, "Los Angeles Social Circle," 3; Reid, "Arrow Tips," 1. Sayers's column was also syndicated by the Pacific Coast News Bureau.

79. Sayers, "Los Angeles Social Circle," 3.

80. Mangun, "The (Oregon) *Advocate*," 18.

81. Mangun, "Boosting the Bottom Line," 41.

82. Mangun, "Boosting the Bottom Line," 42.

83. "Pay Your Subscription," 4.

84. Mangun, "Boosting the Bottom Line," 43–44. Mangun speculates that Cannady could not possibly have secured the new subscriptions she would have needed to break even on the car alone.

85. Mangun, "'As citizens of Portland we must protest,'" 404.

Appendix

1. The Progressive Lyceum's first debate was on the rights of women. *E*, February 19, 1869, 3.

2. In 1892, the Gateway Literary Society was planning to have all members subscribe to and have the *Huntsville Gazette* publish their proceedings. *HG*, November 5, 1892, 3.

3. Formerly St. Mark's Literary Society. Knupfer, *Toward a Tenderer Humanity*, 119.

4. The Fort Scott Lyceum published a paper titled *The Gleaner*. *AC*, April 5, 1889, 4.

5. This society was also known as the Allen Literary Society. *TC*, November 8, 1891, 1.

6. This society was also known as the Paola Lyceum. *FP*, March 10, 1899, 3.

7. This society was also known as the Banaque Literary Society. *TP*, December 13, 1901, 3.

8. This society was also known as the Baneka Literary Society. *TP*, February 7, 1902, 4.

9. The N. U. G. literary society became the N. U. G. Black Women's Club.

10. Mount Olive Literary Society in Quindaro was also known as Mount Olive Baptist Literary Society. *KCA*, September 8, 1916, 4.

11. The Citizens' Lyceum was organized by Nannie Helen Burroughs. *IF*, November 25, 1905.

12. The Opelousa Literary Society was organized by farmers and took the New Orleans *Weekly Pelican* as its "chief organ." *WP*, July 30, 1887, 2.

13. The Galbreth (variously spelled "Galbreath" or "Galbraith") Lyceum published the *Lyceum Observer*, which was in print by 1863. It was "the first paper published by, and devoted exclusively to, the colored race in Baltimore." Scharf, *Chronicles of Baltimore*, 108.

14. In 1915, the Pikesville Literary Society was planning to take the *Weekly Pelican* (1886–1889) as its chief organ. *BC*, July 24, 1915, 3.

15. The Garrison Lyceum was reorganized in 1890. *NYA*, October 18, 1890, 1.

16. Virginia Lambert edited the *St. Matthew's Lyceum Journal* and contributed to the *AME Church Review*. *IF*, January 5, 1889, 5.

17. The Ladies' Lyceum of Ypsilanti was a parlor lyceum. *P*, March 20, 1891, 4.
18. Haven Institute was instrumental in establishing the 13th Street Colored Library in Meridian in 1913. *ST*, December 18, 1897, 3.
19. This literary society was also known as the Baptist Athenian. *TO*, March 26, 1892, 3.
20. The Progressive Age Literary Club was the first literary society organized in Omaha. *OE*, April 4, 1896, 3.
21. The Zion Lyceum took the *New York Age* as its official organ. *NYA*, May 3, 1890, 4.
22. Quaker women established the African Clarkson Society mission school in New York City to help African Americans make the transition to freedom. Harris, *In the Shadow*, 93.
23. The Female Lundy Society was organized on June 19, 1833. Howell, *Bi-centennial History of Albany*, 726.
24. The Phoenixonian Society was renamed The Hamilton Lyceum sometime between July 3 and December 25, 1841. McHenry, *Forgotten Readers*, 327n63.
25. Sydna E. R. Frances was president of the Ladies' Literary and Progressive Association in 1848. Foreman, "Black Organizing," 38.
26. This society pledged to support *Frederick Douglass' Paper*. *FDP*, February 9, 1855, 3.
27. This literary society was also known as the Youth's Association. *WAA*, March 3, 1860, 3.
28. This literary society was also known as the Wendell Phillips Lyceum. *NYF*, November 27, 1886, 4.
29. C. M. Stewart Jr. edited the lyceum-published *American Progressive*, which "claim[ed] to be the first official organ of the Afro-American League." *NYF*, January 18, 1890, 5.
30. The newspaper of the Lincoln Lyceum of Wilmington was the *Lincoln Gazette*; Moses Alston was the editor and Sarah Butler was the associate editor. *IF*, June 3, 1893, 4.
31. See also Ladies' Literary Society (Aelioian, L.L.S.) Records, 1846–1953, Oberlin College Archives, Oberlin College, Oberlin, Ohio.
32. The Minerva Reading Club, which was founded by seven women, including Carrie W. Clifford, became part of the National Association of Colored Women in 1898. "Carrie Williams Clifford, A Sketch," *CAW*, February 1, 1902.
33. The meetings of the Trefoil Literary Society were held in the home of Luella Alexander. *CG*, June 10, 1905, 1.
34. This society was also known as the William P. Lawrence Dunbar Literary Society.
35. This society was also known as the Philadelphia Female Literary Association. *TL*, November 29, 1834, 190.
36. This society was also known as the Philadelphia Association for Moral and Intellectual Improvement of the People of Color. *NECA*, January 21, 1837, 78.
37. Porter lists the founding of the Demosthenian Institute as 1837, but correspondence to the *Colored American* lists the date of its founding as January 10, 1838, by seven men at the house of John P. Burr. By 1841 the Demosthenian Institute had forty members and a small library, and had plans to publish a weekly paper for 1 cent per copy. *CA*, April 24, 1841, 30. The Demosthenian Institute was publishing the weekly *Demosthenian Shield* by late July 1841 and had an agent in New York City. *CA*, July 24, 1841, 82.

38. Sarah Mapps Douglass and Martin Delaney cofounded the Women's Association of Philadelphia. Jones, *All Bound Up Together*, 110.

39. This literary society was also known as the Progressive Workmen's Club. *G*, October 6, 1883, 1.

40. The Hannibal Literary Society dissolved January 2, 1884. *HSJ*, January 12, 1884, 4.

41. The Black Opals of Philadelphia published *Black Opals* magazine (1927–1928). McHenry, *Forgotten Readers*, 293.

42. The Memphis Lyceum published *The Evening Star*, which Ida B. Wells edited in 1884. In 1891, Wells and others try to reorganize this lyceum under the same name. See *IF*, May 2, 1891, 4.

43. The Herber Lyceum published the *Herber Lyceum Eclipse*. *BA*, March 7, 1896, 1.

44. The L. and G. Lyceum read the *Freeman* (Indianapolis). *IF*, April 7, 1894, 5.

45. This literary society was also known as the Monday Night Literary Club. *WL*, March 19, 1881, 2.

46. The Second Baptist Church Literary Society became the Philomathian Literary Society in October 1886. *WB*, October 16, 1886, 3.

47. Anna Julia Cooper read a paper at a meeting of the Second Baptist Sunday School Lyceum on July 27, 1890, in which she argued that whiskey was to blame for nine-tenths of crime. *WB* August 2, 1890, 3.

48. The Ladies Committee of the Provincial Union supported the *Provincial Freeman*. *PFWA*, August 19, 1854, 3.

49. The Windsor Ladies Society was sometimes referred to as the Windsor Mutual Aid Society. The group was founded by Mary Bibb. Bristow, "Whatever You Raise in the Ground You Can Sell It in Chatham," 122; Murray, *Come, Bright Improvement!*, 71.

50. The Ladies Literary Society was founded by Amelia Freeman Shadd. Bristow, "Whatever You Raise in the Ground You Can Sell It in Chatham," 122.

51. With confederation in 1867, Canada West became the province of Ontario, Canada. Murray documents more literary societies, lyceums, and debating societies organized by Black Canadians than are listed here. I list only those mentioned in newspapers that have been preserved. See Murray, *Come, Bright Improvement!*

52. The Mental and Moral Improvement Association met at 120 Yonge Street. Murray, *Come, Bright Improvement!*, 72; Murray, "A Black Literary Society," 163.

53. The Chatham Literary and Debating Society, also known as the Chatham Lyceum, had "about 80 members" and met Friday evenings. *Chatham Directory, 1876–1877*, 68. It became the Kent County Civil Rights League in 1891 and agitated for school desegregation. Clark, "The Globalization of Civil Society," 17.

Bibliography

A. [Sarah Forten]. "By a member of the Female Literary Association." *The Liberator*, November 22, 1834.
"An Able Paper by Mrs. Pryor Read Before the Bishop Worthington Lyceum." *The Parsons Weekly Blade*, May 12, 1894, 4.
"Address to the Female Literary Association of Philadelphia, on Their First Anniversary: by a Member." *The Liberator*, October 13, 1832.
"Advertisement." *The Black Republican*, April 15, 1865, 2.
"Advice to Expectant Mothers by the Black Cross Nurses of New York." *Negro World*, January 23, 1926, 7.
"The *Advocate*'s 24th Anniversary." *The Advocate*, September 3, 1927, 4.
"After the Colored Vote. It Is the Women This Time Whose Ballots Are Wanted—Prominent Speakers." *The Cleveland Gazette*, March 24, 1888, 3.
"Agents." *The Liberator*, April 27, 1833.
Ahern, Wilbert H. "An Experiment Aborted: Returned Indian Students in the Indian School Service, 1881–1908." *Ethnohistory* 44 (1997): 263–304.
"Albany, TX." *The Dallas Express*, January 13, 1901, 5.
Alexander, Adele Logan. *Parallel Worlds: The Remarkable Gibbs-Hunts and the Enduring (In)Significance of Melanin*. Charlottesville: University of Virginia Press, 2010.
Alexander, Leslie M. *African or American? Black Identity and Political Activism in New York City, 1784–1861*. Urbana: University of Illinois Press, 2008.
"All Aboard! Ohio Railroad History." Ohio Memory. www.ohiomemory.org.
Allen, Carol. *Black Women Intellectuals: Strategies of Nation, Family, and Neighborhood in the Works of Pauline Hopkins, Jessie Fauset, and Marita Bonner*. New York: Garland, 1998.
Almonte, Richard. "Introduction." In *A Plea for Emigration; Or, Notes of Canada West*, edited by Richard Almonte, 9–41. Toronto: The Mercury Press, 1998.
"Already the 'Southern Workman' . . ." *The Southern Workman*, March 1872, 2.
Alvarado, Yollotl Gómez, Juan Pablo Anaya, Luciano Concheiro, Cristina Rivera Garza, and Aline Hernández. "Conversación Los Abajocomunes: Stefano Harney and Fred Moten in Conversation on the Occasion of the Spanish Translation of *The Undercommons*." *The New Inquiry*, September 5, 2018. https://thenewinquiry.com/conversacion-los-abajocomunes/.
"Ambrotypes." *New Orleans Daily Creole*, November 14, 1856, 2.
"American Slavery." *British Banner*, November 20, 1855.

Amicus. "Our Literary Societies." *The Colored American* (New York, NY), March 11, 1837.
Ampadu, Lena. "Maria W. Stewart and the Rhetoric of Black Preaching: Perspectives on Womanism and Black Nationalism." In *Black Women's Intellectual Traditions: Speaking Their Minds*, edited by Kristin Waters and Carol B. Conaway, 38–54. Burlington: University of Vermont Press, 2007.
Anderson, Ann. Letter dated March 1895, from Houston, Texas. *The Southern Workman*, May 1895, 39.
Anderson, Benedict. *Imagined Communities: Reflections on the Origin and Spread of Nationalism*. London: Verso, 1983.
Anna Elizabeth. "A Short Address to Females of Color." *The Liberator*, June 18, 1831.
"Announcement." *The Colored American Magazine* 1, no. 1 (May 1900): 1.
"An Appeal to Christians Throughout the World." *Cincinnati Daily Gazette*, February 4, 1860. Reprinted in *The Weekly Anglo-African*, February 11, 1860.
Ardis, Ann. "Making Middlebrow Culture, Making Middlebrow Literary Texts Matter: The Crisis, Easter 1912." *Modernist Cultures* 6, no. 1 (2011): 18–40.
Ardis, Ann. "Towards a Theory of Periodical Studies." Presented as part of "What Is a Journal? Toward a Theory of Periodical Studies Roundtable," Modern Languages Association, Boston, MA, January 3–6, 2013. https://seeeps.princeton.edu/wp-content/uploads/sites/243/2015/03/mla2013_ardis.pdf.
Armstrong, Samuel. "The Cherokee Strip." *The Southern Workman*, January 1892, 13.
Arnesen, Eric. *Black Protest and the Great Migration*. Boston: Bedford, 2003.
"Articles of Incorporation of Negro Press Foundation (A Non-Profit, Non-Stock Membership Corporation)." Negro Press Foundation, Addition Box 1, Charlotta Bass Collection, Southern California Library for Social Studies and Research.
Augustin, Ethel. "Economic Pressure Put upon the Negro." *Negro World*, December 13, 1924, 8.
Austin, Beth. "1619: Virginia's First Africans." Hampton History Museum. https://hampton.gov/DocumentCenter/View/24075/1619-Virginias-First-Africans?bidId=.
Ayer's American Newspaper Annual. Philadelphia: N. W. Ayer and Son, 1899.
B. "Miss A. E. C." Letter dated November 10, 1887. *The Southern Workman*, February 1888, 17.
B. "Miss R. H. T." *The Southern Workman*, February 1888, 17.
Bacon, Jacqueline. *Freedom's Journal: The First African-American Newspaper*. Lanham, MD: Lexington Books, 2007.
Bacon, Jacqueline, and Glen McClish. "Reinventing the Master's Tools: Nineteenth-Century African-American Literary Societies of Philadelphia and Rhetorical Education." *RSQ: Rhetoric Society Quarterly* 30, no. 4 (2000): 19–47.
Bair, Barbara. "True Women, Real Men: Gender, Ideology, and Social Roles in the Garvey Movement." In *Gendered Domains: Rethinking Public and Private in Women's History*, edited by Dorothy O. Helly and Susan M. Reverby, 154–166. Ithaca, NY: Cornell University Press, 1992.
Ball, Cheryl E. Summary of "Session 384—What Is a Journal? Toward a Theory of Periodical Studies." Digital Rhetoric Collaborative, February 28, 2013, https://www

.digitalrhetoriccollaborative.org/2013/02/28/session-384-what-is-a-journal-toward-a-theory-of-periodical-studies/.
Ball, Erica L. *To Live an Antislavery Life: Personal Politics and the Antebellum Black Middle Class*. Athens: University of Georgia Press, 2012.
Bangs, Dolly. "Mr. Freeman." *The Provincial Freeman*, April 29, 1854.
Bannet, Eve Tavor. *Empire of Letters: Letter Manuals and Transatlantic Correspondence, 1680–1820*. Cambridge: Cambridge University Press, 2005.
Barker, Joanne. "Territory as Analytic: The Dispossession of Lenapehoking and the Subprime Crisis." *Social Text* 36, no. 2 (June 2018): 19–39.
Barnaby, Josephine. Undated letter from the Fond du Lac reservation. *The Southern Workman*, December 1898, 247.
Barnes, Mollie. "Teaching to Resist, Teaching to Recover: Charlotte Forten's Sea Islands Archives across Private and Public Forms." *Legacy: A Journal of American Women Writers* 37, no. 2 (2020): 235–62.
Barrett, Janie Porter. "Social Settlement for Colored People." *The Southern Workman*, September 1912, 516–20.
Bass, Charlotta A. "Address by Mrs. Charlotta A. Bass." American Labor Party Rally, Madison Square Garden, October 27, 1952, Progressive Party Campaign, 1952—Speeches, Charlotta Bass Collection, Southern California Library for Social Studies and Research, Los Angeles.
Bass, Charlotta A. "California Eagle: Prizes in Campaign Are With Drawn in Favor of All Cash Prizes." *California Eagle*, April 4, 1930, 11.
Bass, Charlotta A. "$500 Cash Is the Prize." *California Eagle*, April 11, 1930, 11.
Bass, Charlotta A. *Forty Years: Memoirs from the Pages of a Newspaper*. Los Angeles: Charlotta A. Bass, 1960.
Bass, Charlotta A. "Industry 1934." Additional Box 1, Articles 1930s, Charlotta Bass Collection, Southern California Library for Social Studies and Research, Los Angeles.
Bass, Charlotta A. "On the Sidewalk." *California Eagle*, January 31, 1946, 1.
Bass, Charlotta A. To William H. Brodie, Los Angeles Newspaper Guild, May 19, 1948. Additional Box 1, Letters to, 1940s, Charlotta Bass Collection, Southern California Library for Social Studies and Research, Los Angeles.
Bass, Charlotta A. To William H. Brodie, Los Angeles Newspaper Guild, October 4, 1948. Additional Box 1, Letters to, 1940s, Charlotta Bass Collection, Southern California Library for Social Studies and Research, Los Angeles.
Bastien, Emeline, and Fanny Tompkins. "To the Friends of Freedom and the Press." *The North Star*, April 12, 1850, 4.
Bateau, Courtney Moffett. "American University Consensus and the Imaginative Power of Fiction." *Critical Ethnic Studies* 4, no. 1 (Spring 2018): 84–106.
Batker, Carol J. *Reforming Fictions: Native, African, and Jewish American Women's Literature and Journalism in the Progressive Era*. New York: Columbia University Press, 2000.
Bearden, Jim, and Linda Jean Butler. *Shadd: The Life and Times of Mary Shadd*. Toronto: NC Press, 1977.
Beatrice. "By a Young Lady of Color. For the Liberator. Female Education." *The Liberator*, July 7, 1832.

Beatty, Bess. "Black Perspectives of American Women: The View from Black Newspapers 1865–1900." *The Maryland Historian* 9, no. 2 (1978): 39–50.

Bergman, Jill. "'Everything we hoped she'd be': Contending Forces in Hopkins Scholarship." *African American Review* 38, no. 2 (2004): 181–99.

Berlin, Ira. "American Slavery in History and Memory and the Search for Social Justice." *Journal of American History* 90, no. 4 (2004): 1251–69.

Best, Stephen, and Sharon Marcus. "Surface Reading: An Introduction." *Representations* 108, no. 1 (2009): 1–21.

"Bethel, Literary Society." *Washington Bee*, May 13, 1911, 4.

"Bethel Closes." *The Colored American* (Washington, DC), May 14, 1898, 6.

"Bethel Literaries." *The Christian Recorder*, January 31, 1884.

"Bethel Literary." *The People's Advocate*, October 20, 1883, 2.

"Bethel Literary." *Washington Bee*, November 13, 1920, 1.

"Bethel Literary." *Washington Bee*, November 20, 1920, 1.

"Bethel Literary and Historical Scholarly Discussion. Oberlin College Next Attraction." *The Colored American* (Washington, DC), December 8, 1900, 13.

"Bethel's Spring Season." *The Colored American* (Washington, DC), March 26, 1898, 1.

Bey, Marquis. *The Problem of the Negro as a Problem for Gender*. Minneapolis: University of Minnesota Press, 2020.

Bibb, Henry. "A Plea for Emigration." *Voice of the Fugitive*, July 17, 1852.

Bingham, Joseph. "Strange Death of a Negro Newspaper." *Bronze America* 2, no. 2 (April 1965): 29.

"Black Leadership in Los Angeles: Ruth Washington." Transcript of interview by R. B. Hopkins. The Oral History Program, University of California Los Angeles. Los Angeles: Regents of the University of California, 1991.

Blain, Keisha N. *Set the World on Fire: Black Nationalist Women and the Global Struggle for Freedom*. Philadelphia: University of Pennsylvania Press, 2018.

Blain, Keisha N. "Uncovering the Silences of Black Women's Voices in the Age of Garvey." *Black Perspectives* (blog), November 29, 2015. https://www.aaihs.org/uncovering-the-silences/.

Blain, Keisha N., and Tiffany M. Gill. "Introduction: Black Women and the Complexities of Internationalism." In *To Turn the Whole World Over: Black Women and Internationalism*, edited by Keisha N. Blain and Tiffany M. Gill, 1–12. Urbana: University of Illinois Press, 2019.

Blain, Keisha N., and Tiffany M. Gill, eds. *To Turn the Whole World Over: Black Women and Internationalism*. Urbana: University of Illinois Press, 2019.

"The *Black Republican* in Mobile." *The Black Republican*, May 13, 1865, 2.

Blackwood, Sarah. "Fugitive Obscura: Runaway Slave Portraiture and Early Photographic Technology." *American Literature* 81, no. 1 (2009): 93–125.

Bode, Katherine. *Reading by Numbers*. London: Anthem, 2014.

Bolden, Tonya. "Maria W. Stewart (1803–1879)." Digital Schomburg African American Women Writers of the 19th Century. http://digital.nypl.org/schomburg/writers_aa19/bio2.html.

Bond, J. M. *The Negro in Los Angeles*. San Francisco: R and E Research Association, 1972.

Boulding, Lucy. Undated letter from Lynchburg, Virginia. *The Southern Workman*, April 1897, 47.
Boulding, Lucy. Undated letter from Staunton, Virginia. *The Southern Workman*, February 1884, 21.
Boyd, Melba Joyce. *Discarded Legacy: Politics and Poetics in the Life of Frances E. W. Harper 1825–1911*. Detroit: Wayne State University Press, 1994.
Bradley, Patricia. *Slavery, Propaganda, and the American Revolution*. Jackson: University Press of Mississippi, 1998.
Brathwaite, Edward Kamau. *The Arrivants: A New World Trilogy—Rights of Passage/Islands/Masks*. New York: Oxford University Press, 1988.
Bristow, Peggy. "'Whatever You Raise in the Ground You Can Sell It in Chatham': Black Women in Buxton and Chatham, 1850–65." In *We're Rooted Here and They Can't Pull Us Up: Essays in African Canadian Women's History*, edited by Peggy Bristow, Dionne Brand, Linda Carty, Afua P. Cooper, Sylvia Hamilton, and Adrienne Shadd, 69–142. Toronto: University of Toronto Press, 1994.
Brodie, William H., Los Angeles Newspaper Guild. To Charlotta A. Bass, May 5, 1948. Additional Box 1, Letters to, 1940s, Charlotta Bass Collection, Southern California Library for Social Studies and Research, Los Angeles.
Brooks, Joanna. "The Early American Public Sphere and the Emergence of a Black Counterpublic." *William and Mary Quarterly* 62, no. 1 (January 2005): 67–98.
Brooks, Joanna. "The Unfortunates: What the Life Spans of Early Black Books Tell Us about Book History." In *Early African American Print Culture*, edited by Lara Langer Cohen and Jordan Alexander Stein, 40–52. Philadelphia: University of Pennsylvania Press, 2012.
Broussard, Jinx Colman. "Exhortation to Action: The Writings of Amy Jacques Garvey, Journalist and Black Nationalist." *Journalism History* 32, no. 2 (2006): 87–95.
Brown, Elsa Barkley. "Negotiating and Transforming the Public Sphere: African American Political Life in the Transition from Slavery to Freedom." In *The Black Public Sphere*, edited by the Black Public Sphere Collective, 111–50. Chicago: University of Chicago Press 1995.
Brown, Lois. *Pauline Elizabeth Hopkins: Black Daughter of the Revolution*. Chapel Hill: University of North Carolina Press, 2008.
"Budget of Interesting News." *The Freeman* (Indianapolis, IN), April 16, 1904, 2.
Bunch, Lonnie G. "'The Greatest State for the Negro', Jefferson L. Edmonds, Black Propagandist of the California Dream." In *Seeking El Dorado: African Americans in California*, edited by Lawrence B. de Graaf, Kevin Mulroy, and Quintard Taylor, 129–48. Seattle: University of Washington Press, 2001.
Byrd, Jodi A. *The Transit of Empire: Indigenous Critiques of Colonialism*. Minneapolis: University of Minnesota Press, 2011.
Byrd, Jodi, Alyosha Goldstein, Jodi Melamed, and Chandan Reddy. "Predatory Value: Economies of Dispossession: Indigeneity, Race, Capitalism." *Social Text* 36, no. 2 (2018): 1–18.
C. Letter dated March 18, 1878. *The Southern Workman*, July 1878, 52.

C. Letter dated November 14, 1877, from Henry County, Virginia. *The Southern Workman*, January 1878.

Cacho, Lisa. *Social Death: Racialized Rightlessness and the Criminalization of the Unprotected*. New York University Press, 2012.

C. A. Cook and Co.'s *United States Newspaper Directory: Containing Correct Lists of All the Newspapers and Periodicals Published in the United States, Territories and British Provinces*. Chicago: C. A. Cook and Co., 1876.

California Legislature. Senate. *Eleventh Report of the Senate Fact-Finding Subcommittee on Un-American Activities*. University of California, 1961. http://content.cdlib.org/view?docId=kt396n99b3&brand=calisphere&doc.view=entire_text.

California Legislature. Senate. *Un-American Activities in California: Report of Joint Fact-Finding Committee on Un-American Activities in California*. Sacramento: California State Printing, 1943.

Cantiello, Jessica Wells. "Frances E. W. Harper's Educational Reservations: The Indian Question in Iola Leroy." *African American Review* 54, no. 4 (2012): 575–92.

Carby, Hazel V. *Reconstructing Womanhood: The Emergence of the Afro-American Woman Novelist*. New York: Oxford University Press, 1987.

Carnegie, Charles V. "Garvey and the Black Transnation." *Small Axe* 5 (1999): 48–71.

Carroll, Anne. "Protest and Affirmation: Composite Texts in the *Crisis*." *American Literature* 76, no. 1 (March 2004): 89–116.

Casey, Jim. "Editing Forms: The Emergence of Editorship in Nineteenth-Century U.S. Periodicals." PhD diss., University of Delaware, 2017.

Castledine, Jacqueline. *Cold War Progressives: Women's Interracial Organizing for Peace and Freedom*. Champaign: University of Illinois Press, 2012.

Castronovo, Russ. "Beauty along the Color Line: Lynching, Aesthetics, and the *Crisis*." *PMLA* 121, no. 5 (2006): 1443–59.

Caverhill's Toronto City Directory 1859–1860. Toronto: Lovell and Gibson, 1859.

C. B. R. "For the Colored American." *The Colored American* (New York, NY), November 4, 1837.

Chalcraft, Edwin L. *Assimilation's Agent: My Life as a Superintendent in the Indian Boarding School System*. Edited by Cary C. Collins. Lincoln: University of Nebraska Press, 2004.

Chaney, Michael. *Fugitive Vision: Slave Image and Black Identity in Antebellum Narrative*. Bloomington: Indiana University Press, 2008.

Chaney, Michael, ed. *Where Is All My Relation? The Poetics of Dave the Potter*. New York: Oxford University Press, 2018.

"Charleston News." *The New York Freeman*, July 24, 1886, 4.

Chatham Directory, 1876–1877. Toronto: William W. Evans, 1876.

Cheng, Wendy, and Rashad Shabazz. "Introduction: Race, Space and Scale in the Twenty-First Century." *Occasion* 8 (2015): 1–7.

Chun, Wendy. "Race and/as Technology: Or, How to Do Things with Race." *Camera Obscura* 70, no. 24 (2009): 6–35.

Cima, Gay Gibson. *Performing Anti-Slavery: Activist Women on Antebellum Stages*. Cambridge: Cambridge University Press, 2014.

"Circular by the Provisional Committee of the *Impartial Citizen*." August 1849. In *The Black Abolitionist Papers*, vol. 4, edited by C. Peter Ripley, Roy E. Finkenbine, Michael F. Hembree, and Donald Yacovone, 38–41. Chapel Hill: University of North Carolina Press, 1992.

"City Paragraphs." *The Colored American* (Washington, DC), May 10, 1902, 16.

Clark, John D. "The Globalization of Civil Society." In *Critical Mass: The Emergence of the Global Civil Society*, edited by James W. St. G. Walker and Andrew Thompson, 3–23. Waterloo, ON: Wilfrid Laurier University Press, 2008.

Claytor, Mr. and Mrs. W. J. "Our Workers in the Far South." *The Southern Workman*, September 1893, 140.

Cobb, Jasmine Nichole. "Review of *Enduring Truths: Sojourner's Shadows and Substance*, by Darcy Grimaldo Grigsby." *The Art Bulletin* 98, no. 4 (2016): 52.

Cohen, Elizabeth. *Semi-Citizenship in Democratic Politics*. New York: Cambridge University Press, 2009.

Cohen, Lara Langer, and Jordan Alexander Stein. "Introduction: Early African American Print Culture." In *Early African American Print Culture*, edited by Lara Langer Cohen and Jordan Alexander Stein, 1–16. Philadelphia: University of Pennsylvania Press, 2012.

Coleman, Willie M. "*The Woman's Era*, 1894–1897: Voices from Our 'Womanist' Past." *SAGE: A Scholarly Journal on Black Women*, 1, no. 2 (Fall 1984): 36–47.

"Col. J. Perry." *The Freeman* (Indianapolis, IN), December 24, 1892.

Collier, Patrick. "What Is Modern Periodical Studies?" *Journal of Modern Periodical Studies* 6, no. 2 (2015): 92–111.

Collins, Kathleen. "Shadow and Substance: Sojourner Truth." *History of Photography* 7, no. 3 (1983): 183–205.

Collins, Sadie C. "Sidelights on the 'Other Half,' . . . Dear Gen. Armstrong." *The Southern Workman*, September 1893, 140–41.

Collins, Sarah. Undated letter from Springfield, Tennessee. *The Southern Workman*, March 1884, 31.

Colophon. *The Elevator*, April 10, 1868, 1.

Colophon. *The Elevator*, April 27, 1872, 1.

Colophon. *The Elevator*, December 29, 1871, 2.

Colophon. *The Elevator*, February 26, 1869, 2.

Colophon, *The Elevator*, March 8, 1873, 3.

Colophon. *Parsons Weekly Blade*, May 12, 1894, 4.

Colophon. *The Southern Workman*, May 1872, 2.

A Colored Female of Philadelphia. "Emigration to Mexico: Mr. Editor." *The Liberator*, January 28, 1832.

"A Colored Lady in Medford." *The Liberator*, April 9, 1831.

"Colored Women as Wage Earners." *The Colored American* (Washington, DC), November 12, 1898, 5.

"Colored Women's International Council." *The Southern Workman*, 52 (January 1923): 7–10.

"Coloured Women of America." *Englishwoman's Review*, January 15, 1878.

Compton Printing Company Correspondence, items 13 through 33, Mold Box 2, Loren Miller Papers (1876–2003), The Huntington Library. https://hdl.huntington.org/digital/collection/p15150coll7/id/32859/rec/1.

Compton Printing Company invoice to the *Eagle*, January 9, 1957. Compton Printing Company Correspondence, Mold Box 2, Loren Miller Papers (1876–2003), The Huntington Library. https://hdl.huntington.org/digital/collection/p15150coll7/id/32860.

Constitution and By Laws of the Wilberforce Lyceum Educating Society: For Moral and Mental Improvement, Cannonsburg Township of Colchester, Province of Canada, British North America. Amherstburg, ON: I. B. Boyle, 1850.

"Constitution of the Afric-American Female Intelligence Society of Boston." *The Liberator*, January 7, 1832. Reprinted in *Genius of Universal Emancipation* 2, no. 10 (March 1832): 162–63.

Cooper, Anna Julia. "The American Negro Academy." *The Southern Workman*, February 1898, 35–36.

Cooper, Anna Julia. "Colored Women as Wage Earners." *The Freeman* (Indianapolis, IN), April 16, 1904, 2.

Cooper, Anna Julia. "Colored Women as Wage Earners." *The Southern Workman*, August 28, 1899, 295–98. Reprinted in *Washington Bee*, August 26, 1899, 4.

Cooper, Anna Julia. "Paper by Mrs. Anna J. Cooper." *The Southern Workman*, July 1894, 131–33.

Cooper, Anna Julia. *A Voice from the South. By a Black Woman of the South*. Xenia, OH: Aldine, 1892.

Corbould, Clare. *Becoming African Americans: Black Public Life in Harlem, 1919–1939*. Cambridge, MA: Harvard University Press, 2009.

Cordell, Ryan. "What Has the Digital Meant to American Periodicals Scholarship?" *American Periodicals: A Journal of History & Criticism* 26, no. 1 (2016): 2–7.

Cordell, Sigrid Anderson. "'The Case Was Very Black Against' Her: Pauline Hopkins and the Politics of Racial Ambiguity at the *Colored American Magazine*." *American Periodicals* 16, no. 1 (2006): 52–73.

Cordell, Sigrid Anderson. "Reprinting, Circulation, and the Network Author in Antebellum Newspapers." *American Literary History* 27, no. 3 (2005): 417–45.

Cornelius, Elizabeth. "A Letter from Elizabeth Cornelius." *The Southern Workman*, November 1903, 573–74.

Cornelius, Elizabeth. "You who are still sheltered . . ." *The Southern Workman*, February 1903, 122.

Costa, Tom. "What Can We Learn from a Digital Database of Runaway Slave Advertisements?" *International Social Science Review* 76, nos. 1 and 2 (January 2001): 36–43.

Coulthard, Glen. *Red Skin, White Masks: Rejecting the Colonial Politics of Recognition*. Minneapolis: University of Minnesota Press, 2014.

Crawley, Ashon. "Introduction to the Academy and What Can Be Done?" *Critical Ethnic Studies* 4, no. 1 (2018): 4–19.

Cresswell, Timothy. "The Production of Mobilities." *New Formations* 43, no. 1 (2001): 11–25.

Cresswell, Timothy. "Towards a Politics of Mobility." *Environment and Planning D: Society and Space* 28, no. 1 (2010): 17–31.

Cromwell, John W. *History of the Bethel Literary and Historical Association.* Washington, D.C.: Press of R. L. Pendleton, 1896.

D. "Causes of Crime." Letter dated March 16, 1884, from Staunton, Virginia. *The Southern Workman*, May 1884, 54.

Da, Nan Z. "The Computational Case against Computational Literary Studies." *Critical Inquiry* 45, no. 3 (2019): 601–39.

Dahn, Eurie. *Jim Crow Networks: African American Periodical Cultures.* Amherst: University of Massachusetts Press, 2021.

Dahn, Eurie, and Brian Sweeney. "A Brief History of the *Colored American Magazine*." The Colored American Magazine Project. http://coloredamerican.org/?page_id=70.

Dalrymple, Daniel A "'Reclaiming the Fallen': The University Negro Improvement Association Central Division, New York, 1935–1942." *Journal of Black Studies* 45, no. 1 (2014): 1–18.

Daniel, Malcolm. "Daguerre (1787–1851) and the Invention of Photography." The Metropolitan Museum of Art, 2000. https://www.metmuseum.org/toah/hd/dagu/hd_dagu.htm.

Danky, James P., and Maureen E. Hady. *African-American Newspapers and Periodicals: A National Bibliography.* Cambridge, MA: Harvard University Press, 1998.

Dann, Martin E., ed. *The Black Press, 1827–1890: The Quest for National Identity.* New York: G. P. Putnam's Sons, 1971.

Darrah, William C. *Cartes de Visite in Nineteenth-Century Photography.* Gettysburg, PA: W. C. Darrah, 1981.

Daut, Marlene L. *Tropics of Haiti: Race and the Literary History of the Haitian Revolution in the Atlantic World, 1789–1865.* Liverpool: University of Liverpool Press, 2015.

Davies, Carole Boyce. *Left of Karl Marx: The Political Life of Black Communist Claudia Jones.* Durham, NC: Duke University Press, 2008.

Davis, Elizabeth Lindsey. *Lifting as They Climb.* 1933. Reprint, New York: G. K. Hall, 1996.

"Dawes Act (1887)." Milestone Documents, National Archives. https://www.archives.gov/milestone-documents/dawes-act.

Day, Iyko. *Alien Capital: Asian Racialization and the Logic of Settler Colonial Capitalism.* Durham, NC: Duke University Press, 2016.

"Dean Wm. Pickens Pleads for Release of Garvey." *The Advocate*, August 13, 1927, 1.

"Dear Teacher." *The Southern Workman*, April 1873, 2.

De Groft, Aaron. "Eloquent Vessels/Poetics of Power: The Heroic Stoneware of 'Dave the Potter.'" *Winterthur Portfolio* 33, no. 4 (1998): 249–60.

Delany, Martin R. *The Condition, Elevation, Emigration, and Destiny of the Colored People of the United States; and, Official Report of the Niger Valley Exploring Party.* Edited by T. Falola. 1852. Reprint, Amherst, MA: Humanity Books, 2004.

Delap, Lucy. "The Freewoman: Individualism and Introspection." In *Feminist Media History*, edited by Maria DiCenzo with Lucy Delap and Leila Ryan, 159–93. New York: Palgrave Macmillan, 2011.

De Mena, M. L. T. "Our Women." *Negro World*, October 31, 1925, 7.

De Mena, M. L. T. "Part Women Must Play in the Organization." *Negro World*, January 23, 1926, 7.

Desrochers, Robert E., Jr. "Periphery as Center: Slavery, Identity, and the Commercial Press in the British Atlantic, 1704–1765." In *British North America in the Seventeenth and Eighteenth Centuries*, edited by Stephen Foster, 170–94. Oxford: Oxford University Press, 2013.

Desrochers, Robert E., Jr. "Slave-For-Sale Advertisements and Slavery in Massachusetts, 1704–1781." *William and Mary Quarterly* 59, no. 3 (July 2002): 623–64.

Detweiler, Frederick. *The Negro Press in the United States*. Chicago: University of Chicago Press, 1922.

De Vera, Samantha. "'We the ladies . . . have been deprived of a voice': Uncovering Black Women's Lives through the Colored Conventions Archive." *C19: Interdisciplinary Studies in the Long Nineteenth Century* 27 (2018): 1–19.

De Veyra, Sofia R. "Activities of Filipino Women in Public Life are Potent Forces in the Progress of Nation." *Negro World*, February 9, 1924, 10.

DiCenzo, Maria. "Remediating the Past: Doing 'Periodical Studies' in the Digital Era." *English Studies in Canada* 41, no. 1 (2015): 19–39.

Digby-Junger, Richard. "The *Guardian*, *Crisis*, *Messenger*, and *Negro World*: The Early 20th-Century Black Radical Press." *Howard Journal of Communications* 9, no. 3 (1998): 263–82.

Dinius, Marcy J. *The Camera and the Press: American Visual and Print Culture in the Age of the Daguerreotype*. Philadelphia: University of Pennsylvania Press, 2012.

"Doings of the Literaries." *The Colored American* (Washington, DC), May 13, 1899, 7.

The Domestic and Foreign Mission Society of the Protestant Episcopal Church in the United States of America, Triennial Report of the Board of Managers, Annual Report of the Board of Managers, Reports of Standing Committees, Recognized Auxiliaries, Missionary Bishops, etc., for the Year Ending August 31, 1889. New York: Bible House, 1889.

Donnan, Elizabeth, ed. *Documents Illustrative of the History of the Slave Trade to America*. 4 vols. Washington, DC: Carnegie Institution, 1930–1932.

Douglass, Frederick. "Canada." *Frederick Douglass' Paper*, July 4, 1856.

Douglass, Frederick. *The Life and Times of Frederick Douglass, from 1817–1882*. London: Christian Age, 1882.

Douglass, Frederick. "Oh Liberty! What Deeds Are Done in Thy Name!" *The North Star*, February 22, 1850, 2.

Douglass, Frederick. "A Tribute to the Negro." *The North Star*, April 7, 1849.

"Dr. Lucy E. Moten." Women's History Month at the District of Columbia. https://www.udc.edu/2017/03/13/womens-history-month-dr-lucy-e-moten/.

Drouin, Jeff. "Close- and Distant-Reading Modernism: Network Analysis, Text Mining, Pedagogy, and *The Little Review*." *Journal of Modern Periodical Studies* 5, no. 1 (2014): 110–35.

Drucker, Johanna. "Humanities Approaches to Graphical Display." *digital humanities quarterly* 5, no. 1 (2011). http://www.digitalhumanities.org/dhq/vol/5/1/000091/000091.html.

Du Bois, W. E. B. "Editorial." *The Crisis* 1, no. 1 (November 1910): 10–11.
Du Bois, W. E. B. "Editorial. Southern California." *The Crisis* 6, no. 3 (July 1913): 131.
Du Bois, W. E. B. "Hampton." *The Crisis* 15 (November 1917): 10–12.
Dunbar, Erica Armstrong. *A Fragile Freedom: African American Women and Emancipation in the Antebellum City*. New Haven, CT: Yale University Press, 2008.
Dunbar, Erica Armstrong. "A Mental and Moral Feast: Reading, Writing, and Sentimentality in Black Philadelphia." *Journal of Women's History* 16, no. 1 (2004): 78–102.
Dungey, Robert. Undated letter from unnamed place in Virginia. *The Southern Workman*, January 1878.
"During the Month of April . . ." *The Southern Workman*, May 1872, 2.
Durrance, Ashley, Hannah Harkins, Nicholas Palombo, Leslie Rewis, Melanie Berry, Christy Hutcheson, Eli Jones, and Morgan Shaffer. "The Early Case for a National Black Press." Digital exhibit. Colored Conventions Project, 2016. http://coloredconventions.org/exhibits/show/national-press-1847.
Duster, Alfreda M., ed. *Crusade for Justice: The Autobiography of Ida B. Wells*. Chicago: University of Chicago Press, 1970.
Dutton, S. L. Letter dated January 17, 1873. *The Southern Workman*, February 1873.
Dworkin, Ira. "Biography of Pauline E. Hopkins (1859–1930)." The Pauline Elizabeth Hopkins Society. https://www.paulinehopkinssociety.org/biography.
E. "Miss A. E. Cleveland, Dear Teacher." *The Southern Workman*, September 1893, 141.
"Editorial and Publishers' Announcements." *The Colored American Magazine* 1, no. 1 (May 1900): 60–64.
"Education that Counts." *Washington Bee*, December 30, 1911, 1.
Edwards, Brent Hayes. *The Practice of Diaspora: Literature, Translation, and the Rise of Black Internationalism*. Cambridge, MA: Harvard University Press, 2003.
Elkins, E. F. "Marcus Garvey, the *Negro World,* and the British West Indies: 1919–1920." *Science & Society* 36, no. 1 (Spring 1972): 63–77.
Elliot, R. S. "The Story of Our Magazine." *The Colored American Magazine*, May 1901, 43.
Emery, Jacqueline. *Recovering Native American Writings in the Boarding School Press*. Lincoln: University of Nebraska Press, 2017.
Emery, Jacqueline. "Writing against Erasure: Native American Students at Hampton Institute and the Periodical Press." *American Periodicals* 22, no. 2 (2012): 178–98.
English, James F. "Everywhere and Nowhere: The Sociology of Literature after 'The Sociology of Literature.'" *New Literary History* 41, no. 2 (2010): v–xxiii.
Eubanks, Virginia. *Digital Dead End*. Cambridge, MA: MIT Press, 2011.
Everuss, Louis. "The New Mobilities Paradigm and Social Theory." In *Routledge Handbook of Social and Cultural Theory*, 2nd ed., edited by Anthony Elliott, 287–305. London: Routledge, 2020.
Ewing, Adam. *The Age of Garvey: How a Jamaican Activist Created a Mass Movement and Changed Global Black Politics*. Princeton, NJ: Princeton University Press, 2014.
Fagan, Benjamin. "'Americans As They Really Are': The *Colored American* and the Illustration of National Identity." *American Periodicals* 21, no. 2 (2011): 97–119.
Fagan, Benjamin. *The Black Newspaper and the Chosen Nation*. Athens: University of Georgia Press, 2016.

Fagan, Benjamin. "Chronicling White America." *American Periodicals: A Journal of History & Criticism* 26, no. 1 (2016): 10–13.

Fagan, Benjamin. "The Organ of the Whole: Colored Conventions, the Black Press, and the Question of National Authority." In *The Colored Convention Conventions Movement: Black Organizing in the Nineteenth Century*, edited by P. Gabrielle Foreman, Jim Casey, and Sarah Lynn Patterson, 195–210. Chapel Hill: University of North Carolina Press, 2021.

Fauset, Jessie Redmon. "As to Lynching." *The Crisis* 16, no. 6 (October 1918): 279, 281.

Fauset, Jessie Redmon. "Colored Laborers." *The Crisis* 17, no. 3 (January 1919): 129–130.

Fauset, Jessie Redmon. "Colored Women in Industry." *The Crisis* 18, no. 2 (June 1919): 94–97.

Fauset, Jessie Redmon. "Race Superiority." *The Crisis* 16, no. 6 (October 1918): 24.

Fauset, Jessie Redmon. "The Restless South African." *The Crisis* 17, no. 5 (March 1919): 238.

Fauset, Jessie Redmon. "The 'Work or Fight' Edict." *The Crisis* 18, no. 2 (June 1919): 97.

Fauset, Jessie Redmon, ed. "The Looking Glass." *The Crisis* 17, no. 1 (November 1918): 22–27.

Fear-Segal, Jacqueline. *White Man's Club: Schools, Race, and the Struggle of Indian Acculturation*. Lincoln: University of Nebraska Press, 2007.

Ferguson, Earline Rae. "Woman's Improvement Club, Indianapolis." In *Black Women in America: An Historical Encyclopedia*, vol. 2, edited by Darlene Clark Hine, Elsa Barkley Brown, and Rosalyn Terborg-Penn, 1278. Brooklyn: Carlson, 1993.

Fernandis, Sarah Collins. "A Colored Social Settlement." *The Southern Workman*, June 1904, 346–50.

Fernandis, Sarah Collins. "Neighborhood Interpretations of a Social Settlement." *The Southern Workman*, January 1906, 46–48.

Fernandis, Sarah Collins. "A Social Settlement in South Washington." In *The Negro in the Cities of the North*, edited by Edward T. Devine, 64–66. New York: Charity Organization Society, 1905.

Ferreira da Silva, Denise. *Toward a Global Idea of Race*. Minneapolis: University of Minnesota Press, 2007.

Fielder, Brigitte and Jonathan Senchyne, eds. *Against a Sharp White Background: Infrastructures of African American Print*. Madison: University of Wisconsin Press, 2019.

Financial Records. Charlotta Bass Collection, Southern California Library for Social Studies and Research, Los Angeles.

Finch, Jacqueline Brice. "Sarah Collins Fernandis." In *Notable Black American Women*, book 2, edited by Jessie Carney Smith, 221–23. New York: Gale Research, 1996.

Fisher, Maisha T. *Black Literate Lives: Historical and Contemporary Perspectives*. New York: Routledge, 2009.

Fitz, Suzanne Pullon, and Roseann M. Mandziuk, eds. *Sojourner Truth as Orator: Wit, Story, and Song*. Westport, CT: Greenwood Press, 1997.

Flamming, Douglass. *African Americans in the West*. Santa Barbara, CA: ABC-Clio, 2009.

Flamming, Douglass. *Bound for Freedom: Black Los Angeles in Jim Crow America*. Berkeley: University of California Press, 2005.

Folsom, C. M. "Returned Indian Students." In *Hampton Normal and Agricultural Institute Annual Reports for the Academical and Fiscal Year Ending June 30, 1888*, 49–54. Hampton, VA: Normal School Steam Press Print, 1888.

Foner, Philip S., and Robert J. Branham, *Lift Every Voice: African American Oratory 1787–1900*. Tuscaloosa: University of Alabama Press, 1998.

Forbes, Ella. *African American Women during the Civil War*. New York: Garland, 1998.

Ford-Smith, Honor. "Women and the Garvey Movement in Jamaica." In *Garvey: His Work and Impact*, edited by Rupert Charles Lewis and Patrick Bryan, 73–83. Trenton, NJ: Africa World Press, 1991.

Foreman, P. Gabrielle. *Activist Sentiments: Reading Black Women in the Nineteenth Century*. Urbana: University of Illinois Press, 2005.

Foreman, P. Gabrielle. "Black Organizing, Print Advocacy, and Collective Authorship: The Long History of the Colored Conventions Movement." In *The Colored Convention Conventions Movement: Black Organizing in the Nineteenth Century*, edited by P. Gabrielle Foreman, Jim Casey, and Sarah Lynn Patterson, 21–71. Chapel Hill: University of North Carolina Press, 2021.

Foreman, P. Gabrielle. "Reading/Photographs: Emma Dunham Kelley-Hawkins's *Four Girls at Cottage City*: Victoria Earle Mathews and *The Woman's Era*." *Legacy* 24, no. 3 (2007): 248–77.

"For Sale at This Office, a Tract." *The Liberator*, October 8, 1831.

"Fort Bennett." South Dakota State Historical Archives. https://history.sd.gov/archives/forms/military/Fort%20Bennett.pdf.

Forten, Charlotte. "Letter from St. Helena's Island, Beaufort, S.C." *Boston Evening Transcript*, December 5, 1862, 1.

Forten, Charlotte. "Letter from St. Helena's Island, Beaufort, S.C." *The Liberator*, December 12, 1862.

Forten, Charlotte. "Letter from St. Helena's Island, Beaufort, S.C." *Salem Register*, December 8, 1862.

Forten, Charlotte. "Life on the Sea Islands." Part I. *The Atlantic Monthly* 13, no. 79 (May 1864): 587–96.

Forten, Charlotte. "Life on the Sea Islands." Part II. *The Atlantic Monthly* 13, no. 80 (June 1864): 666–76.

Forten Grimké, Charlotte. "Colored People in New England." Letter to the editor dated Washington, D.C., October 10, 1889. Manuscripts for the Grimké Book, 37. https://dh.howard.edu/ajc_grimke_manuscripts/37.

"For the Colored American, Poughkeepsie, Sept 19th 1839." *The Colored American* (New York, NY), September 28, 1839.

Foster, Frances Smith. "Genealogies of Our Concerns, Early (African) American Print Culture, and Transcending Tough Times." *Early American Literature* 45, no. 2 (2010): 347–59.

Foster, Frances Smith. "Introduction." In *Brighter Coming Day: A Frances Ellen Watkins Harper Reader*, edited by Frances Smith Foster, 3–42. New York: Feminist Press, 1990.

Foster, Frances Smith. "A Narrative of the Interesting Origins and (Somewhat) Surprising Developments of African American Print Culture." *American Literary History* 17, no. 4 (2005): 714–40.

Foster, Frances Smith, ed. *Brighter Coming Day: A Frances Ellen Watkins Harper Reader.* New York: Feminist Press, 1990.

Foster, Frances Smith, and Chanta Haywood. "Christian Recordings: Afro-Protestantism, Its Press, and the Production of African American Literature." *Religion and Literature* 27, no. 1 (1995): 15–33.

"Frances Harper Anniversary." *The Savannah Tribune*, February 11, 1911, 5.

Francis, Sydna E. R. "Buffalo, April 5th, 1850. Mr. Editor." *The North Star*, April 5, 1850.

Francis, Sydna E. R. "To a Charitable Public." *The North Star*, February 22, 1850.

Franklin, John Hope, and Loren Schweninger. *Runaway Slaves: Rebels on the Plantation.* New York: Oxford University Press, 1999.

Fraser, Gordon. "Emancipatory Cosmology: Freedom's Journal, The Rights of All, and the Revolutionary Movements of Black Print Culture." *American Quarterly* 68, no. 2 (2016): 263–86.

Fraser, Gordon. *Star Territory: Printing the Universe in Nineteenth-Century America.* Philadelphia: University of Pennsylvania Press, 2021.

"A Fred. Douglass Literary Society in New York Takes Notice of the Embree Affair." *The American Citizen*, August 11, 1899.

Freer, Regina. "L. A. Race Woman: Charlotta Bass and the Complexities of Black Political Development in Los Angeles." *American Quarterly* 56, no. 3 (2004): 607–32.

Frey, Sylvia. *Water from the Rock: Black Resistance in a Revolutionary Age.* Princeton, NJ: Princeton University Press, 1991.

"From Our Correspondents. Weekly Paragraphs." *The Topkea Plaindealer*, November 8, 1901, 4.

"From the Pennsylvania Freeman." *The Colored American* (New York, NY), June 29, 1839.

Fultz, Michael. "'The Morning Cometh': African-American Periodicals, Education, and the Black Middle-Class, 1900–1930." In *Print Culture in a Diverse America*, edited by James P. Danky and Wayne A. Wiegand, 129–48. Champaign: University of Illinois Press, 1998.

Gallon, Kim. "The Black Press." In *Oxford Research Encyclopedia of American History.* New York: Oxford University Press, 2021. https://oxfordre.com/americanhistory/view/10.1093/acrefore/9780199329175.001.0001/acrefore-9780199329175-e-851.

Gallon, Kim. "Making a Case for the Black Digital Humanities." In *Debates in the Digital Humanities*, edited by Matthew K. Gold and Lauren F. Klein, 42–49. Minneapolis: University of Minnesota Press, 2016.

Gallon, Kim. *Pleasure in the News: African American Readership and Sexuality in the Black Press.* Champaign: University of Illinois Press, 2020.

Gaonkar, Dilip Parameshwar, and Elizabeth A. Povinelli, "Technologies of Public Forms: Circulation, Transfiguration, Recognition." *Public Culture* 15, no. 3 (2003): 385–97.

Gardner, Eric. *Black Print Unbound: The Christian Recorder, African American Literature, and Periodical Culture.* New York: Oxford University Press, 2015.

Gardner, Eric. "Edmonia Highgate, the New Orleans Massacre, & Christian Recording." *Black Print Culture.* Last modified September 18, 2015, accessed December 18, 2020.

Gardner, Eric. "Edmonia in Mississippi: A 'New' Letter." *Black Print Culture.* Last modified May 8, 2017, accessed December 18, 2020.

Gardner, Eric. "Remembered (Black) Readers: Subscribers to the *Christian Recorder*, 1864–1865." *American Literary History* 23 (2011): 229–59.

Gardner, Eric. *Unexpected Places: Relocating Nineteenth-Century African American Literature*. Jackson: University Press of Mississippi, 2009.

Garfield, Michelle N. "Literary Societies: The Work of Self-Improvement and Racial Uplift." In *Black Women's Intellectual Traditions: Speaking Their Minds*, edited by Kristin Waters and Carol B. Conaway, 113–28. Burlington: University of Vermont Press, 2007.

Garrison, William Lloyd. "Female Literary Association." *The Liberator*, June 30, 1832.

Garvey, Ellen Gruber. "The Power of Recirculation: Scrapbooks and the Reception of the Nineteenth-Century Press." In *New Directions in American Reception Study*, edited by Philip Goldstein and James L. Machor, 211–32. New York: Oxford University Press, 2008.

Garvey, Ellen Gruber. *Writing with Scissors: American Scrapbooks from the Civil War to the Harlem Renaissance*. New York: Oxford University Press, 2012.

Garvey, Marcus. "The Negro's Greatest Enemy." [1923.] In *The Marcus Garvey and Universal Negro Improvement Association Papers*, edited by Robert A. Hill, 3–12. Berkeley: University of California Press, 1983.

Gaul, Teresa Strouth, and Sharon M. Harris. "Introduction." In *Letters and Cultural Transformations in the United States, 1760–1860*, edited by Teresa Strouth Gaul and Sharon M. Harris, 1–14. New Brunswick, NJ: Routledge, 2009.

Gayles, Gloria Wade. "Black Women Journalists in the South, 1880–1905: An Approach to the Study of Black Women's History." *Callaloo* 4, nos. 11–13 (1981): 138–52.

Gerber, David A. *Authors of Their Lives: The Personal Correspondence of British Immigrants to North America in the Nineteenth Century*. New York: New York University Press, 2006.

Gere, Anne Reggles, and Sarah R. Robbins. "Gendered Literacy in Black and White: Turn-of-the-Century African-American and European-American Club Women's Printed Texts." *Signs: Journal of Women in Culture and Society* 21, no. 3 (1996): 643–58.

Gernes, Todd S. "Poetic Justice: Sarah Forten, Eliza Earle, and the Paradox of Intellectual Property." *New England Quarterly* 71 (June 1998): 229–65.

Gibson, Campbell, and Kay Jung. "Historical Census Statistics on Population Totals by Race, 1790 to 1990, and by Hispanic Origin, 1970 to 1990, for the United States, Regions, Divisions, and States." Population Division, Working Paper no. 56. U.S. Census Bureau, September 2002. https://www.census.gov/content/dam/Census/library/working-papers/2002/demo/POP-twps0056.pdf.

Gill, Gerald. "'Win or Lose—We Win': The 1952 Vice-Presidential Campaign of Charlotta A. Bass." In *The Afro-American Woman: Struggles and Images*, edited by Sharon Harley and Rosalyn Terborg-Penn, 109–18. Port Washington, NY: Kennikat, 1978.

Gill, Tiffany. *Beauty Shop Politics: African American Women's Activism in the Beauty Industry*. Urbana: University of Illinois Press, 2010.

Gilmore, Glenda. *Gender and Jim Crow: Women and the Politics of White Supremacy in North Carolina, 1896–1920*. 2nd ed. Chapel Hill: University of North Carolina Press, 2019.

Gilmore, Glenda. "North Carolina Federation of Colored Women's Clubs." In *Black Women in America: An Historical Encyclopedia*, vol. 2, edited by Darlene Clark Hine, Elsa Barkley Brown, and Rosalyn Terborg-Penn, 881–82. Brooklyn, NY: Carlson, 1993.

Gilmore, Ruth Wilson. "Fatal Couplings of Power and Difference: Notes on Racism and Geography." *Professional Geographer* 54, no. 1 (2002): 15–24.

Gilmore, Ruth Wilson. *Golden Gulag: Prisons, Surplus, Crisis, and Opposition in Globalizing California*. Berkeley: University of California Press, 2006.

Gitelman, Lisa. *Always Already New: Media, History, and the Data of Culture*. Cambridge, MA: MIT Press, 2008.

Gitelman, Lisa, and Virginia Jackson. "Introduction." In *"Raw Data" Is an Oxymoron*, edited by Lisa Gitelman, 1–14. Cambridge, MA: MIT Press, 2013.

Glaude, Eddie S., Jr. *Exodus! Religion, Race, and Nation in Early Nineteenth-Century Black America*. Chicago: University of Chicago Press, 2000.

"Gleanings." *The Southern Workman*, May 1872, 1.

Goeman, Mishuana. "Land as Life: Unsettling the Logics of Containment." In *Native Studies Keywords*, edited by Stephanie Nohelani Teves, Andrea Smith, and Michelle H. Raheja, 71–89. Tuscon: University of Arizona Press, 2015.

"Good Political Speaking." *The Freeman* (Indianapolis, IN), October 6, 1894, 1.

Gourgey, Hannah. "Poetics of Memory and Marginality: Images of the Native American in African American Newspapers, 1870–1900 and 1970–1990." In *The Black Press: New Literary and Historical Essays*, edited by Todd Vogel, 104–20. New Brunswick, NJ: Rutgers University Press, 2001.

Grant, Donald L. *The Way It Was in the South: The Black Experience in Georgia*. Edited by Jonathan Grant. Athens: University of Georgia Press, 1993.

Graves, Kelisha B., ed. *Nannie Helen Burroughs: A Documentary Portrait of an Early Civil Rights Pioneer, 1900–1959*. Notre Dame, IN: University of Notre Dame Press, 2019.

Green, Barbara. "Complaints of Everyday Life: Feminist Periodical Culture and Correspondence Columns in the *Woman Worker*, *Women Folk*, and the *Freewoman*." *Modernism/modernity* 19, no. 3 (2012): 461–85.

Greene, Lorenzo J. "The New England Negro as Seen in Advertisements for Runaway Slaves." *Journal of Negro History* 29, no. 2 (1944): 125–46.

Grice, F. H. "Elevator Aid Association." *The Elevator*, October 16, 1868, 2.

Grigsby, Darcy Grimaldo. *Enduring Truths: Sojourner's Shadows and Substance*. Chicago: University of Chicago Press, 2015.

Guittet, Emmanuel-Pierre. "Unpacking the New Mobilities Paradigm." In *Security/Mobility: Politics of Movement*, edited by Matthias Leese and Stef Wittendorp, 209–15. Manchester: Manchester University Press, 2017.

Habermas, Jürgen. *The Structural Transformation of the Public Sphere: An Inquiry into a Category of Bourgeois Society*. Translated by Thomas Burger. Cambridge, MA: MIT Press, 1989.

Hague, Euan. "'The Right to Enter Every Other State'—The Supreme Court and African American Mobility in the United States." *Mobilities* 5, no. 3 (2010): 331–47.

Hall, Rachel. "Missing Dolly, Mourning Slavery: The Slave Notice as Keepsake." *Camera Obscura* 61 (May 2006): 71–103.

Hallaert, Charles, "Report by Charles Hallaert, Belgian Vice Consul, New York City." [August 16, 1922.] In *The Marcus Garvey and Universal Negro Improvement Association Papers*, edited by Robert A. Hill, 571–73. Berkeley: University of California Press, 1983.

Halliday, Aria S. "Centering Black Women in the Black Chicago Renaissance: Katherine Williams-Irvin, Olive Diggs, and 'New Negro Womanhood.'" In *Against a Sharp White Background: Infrastructures of African American Print*, edited by Brigitte Fielder and Jonathan Senchyne, 240–58. Madison: University of Wisconsin Press, 2019.

"A Hampton graduate teaching in West Va. . . ." *The Southern Workman*, February 1877, 14.

Han, Eunsun Celeste. "All Roads Lead to San Francisco: Black Californian Networks of Community and the Struggle for Equality, 1849–1877." PhD diss., Brown University, 2015.

Han, Eunsun Celeste. "Making a Black Pacific: African Americans and the Formation of Transpacific Community Networks, 1865–1872." *Journal of African American History* 101, nos. 1–2 (2016): 23–48.

Hanchard, Michael. "Translation, Political Community, and Black Internationalism: Some Comments on Brent Hayes Edwards's *The Practice of Diaspora*." *Small Axe* 9, no. 1 (2005): 112–19.

Hardesty, Jared. *Unfreedom: Slavery and Dependence in Eighteenth-Century Boston*. New York: New York University Press, 2016.

"Hard Times Improving." *The Southern Workman*, February 1888, 17.

Harley, Sharon. "Fleetwood, Sara Iredell (1849–1908)." In *Facts on File Encyclopedia of Black Women in America: Science, Health, and Medicine*, edited by Darlene Clark Hine, 72–73. New York: Facts on File, 1997.

Harley, Sharon. "Nannie Helen Burroughs: 'The Black Goddess of Liberty.'" *Journal of Negro History* 81, nos. 1–4 (1996): 6–71.

Harold, Claudrena A. *The Rise and Fall of the Garvey Movement in the Urban South, 1918–1942*. New York: Routledge, 2007.

Harper, Frances Ellen Watkins. *Enlightened Motherhood: An Address by Mrs. Frances E. W. Harper before the Brooklyn Literary Society*. [November 15, 1892.] Brooklyn, NY, 1892.

Harrell, Willie J., Jr. "A Call to Political and Social Activism: The Jeremiadic Discourse of Maria Miller Stewart, 1831–1833." *Journal of International Women's Studies* 9, no. 3 (2008): 300–319.

Harris, Jennifer. "Hidden in Plain Sight: Uncovering the Career of Lucretia Howe Newman Coleman." *Legacy* 34, no. 2 (2017): 227–52.

Harris, Leslie. *In the Shadow: African Americans in New York City, 1626–1863*. Chicago: University of Chicago Press, 2003.

Harrison, Alferdteen B. "Mississippi State Federation of Colored Women's Clubs." In *Black Women in America: An Historical Encyclopedia*, vol. 2, edited by Darlene Clark Hine, Elsa Barkley Brown, and Rosalyn Terborg-Penn, 801–2. Brooklyn, NY: Carlson, 1993.

Hartman, Saidiya. *Scenes of Subjection: Terror, Slavery, and Self-Making in Nineteenth-Century America*. New York: Oxford University Press, 1997.

Hayles, N. Katherine. "How We Read: Close, Hyper, Machine." *ADE Bulletin* 150 (2010): 62–79.

Henderson, Kate. "Our Indian Salutatorian of '90 . . . My dear Winona-Mother." *The Southern Workman*, December 1892, 185–86.

Henkin, David M. *The Postal Age: The Emergence of Modern Communications in Nineteenth-Century America*. Chicago: University of Chicago Press, 2006.

"Here and There." *The Colored American Magazine*, May 1900, 57.

Herron, Kaimara. "Mississippi State Federation of Women's Clubs." *Mississippi Encyclopedia*. http://mississippiencyclopedia.org/entries/mississippi-state-federation-of-colored-womens-clubs/.

Hiery, Hermann Joseph. *The Neglected War: The German South Pacific and the Influence of World War I*. Honolulu: University of Hawai'i Press, 1995.

Higashida, Cheryl. *Black Internationalist Feminism: Women Writers of the Black Left, 1945–1995*. Urbana: University of Illinois Press, 2011.

Highgate, Edmonia G. "Letter from New Orleans." *The Christian Recorder*, March 17, 1866.

Highgate, Edmonia G. Letter to the Editor. *National Antislavery Standard*, April 6, 1869.

Highgate, Edmonia G. "New Orleans Correspondence." *The Christian Recorder*, August 8, 1866.

Highgate, Edmonia G. "On Horse Back—Saddle Dash, No. 1." *The Christian Recorder*, November 3, 1866.

Highgate, Edmonia G. "A Spring Day Up the James." *The Christian Recorder*, May 27, 1865.

Highgate, E. Goodelle. [Edmonia G. Highgate]. "New Orleans Correspondence." *The Colored Tennessean*, March 24, 1866.

"High School for Young Colored Ladies and Misses." *The Liberator*, March 2, 1833.

Hill, Ginger. "'Rightly Viewed': Theorization of Self in Frederick Douglass's Lectures on Pictures." In *Pictures and Progress: Early Photography and the Making of African American Identity*, edited by Maurice O. Wallace and Shawn Michelle Smith, 411–82. Durham, NC: Duke University Press, 2012.

Hill, Robert A., ed. *Marcus Garvey and the Universal Negro Improvement Association Papers*. Vols. 7, 9, and 11. Berkeley: University of California Press, 1990.

Hill, Robert A., and Barbara Bair, eds. *Marcus Garvey: Life and Lessons. A Centennial Companion to the Marcus Garvey and Universal Negro Improvement Association Papers*. Berkeley: University of California Press, 1987.

Hine, Darlene Clark. *When the Truth Is Told: A History of Black Women's Culture and Community in Indiana, 1875–1950*. Indianapolis, IN: National Council of Negro Women, Indianapolis Section, 1981.

"History of VSU." Virginia State University. https://www.vsu.edu/about/history/history-vsu.php.

Hodges, Graham Russell, and Alan Edward Brown, eds. *"Pretends to Be Free": Runaway Slave Advertisements from Colonial and Revolutionary New York and New Jersey*. New York: Garland, 1994.

Hollie, Donna Tyler. "Fernandis, Sarah Collins." Oxford African American Studies Center, May 31, 2013. https://doi:10.1093/acref/9780195301731.013.35626.

Honey, Maureen. *Shadowed Dreams: Women's Poetry of the Harlem Renaissance*. New Brunswick, NJ: Rutgers University Press, 2006.

Hopkins, Pauline E. "Address at the Citizens' William Lloyd Garrison Centenary Celebration (December 11, 1905)." In *Daughter of the Revolution: The Major Nonfiction Works of Pauline E. Hopkins*, edited by Ira Dworkin, 355–57. New Brunswick, NJ: Rutgers University Press, 2007.

Hopkins, Pauline E. "Address at the Two Days of Observance of the One Hundredth Anniversary of the Birth of Charles Sumner (January 6, 1911)." In *Daughter of the Revolution: The Major Nonfiction Works of Pauline E. Hopkins*, edited by Ira Dworkin, 358–60. New Brunswick, NJ: Rutgers University Press, 2007.

Hopkins, Pauline E. "Famous Women of the Negro Race, IV. Some Literary Workers." *The Colored American Magazine* 4, no. 4 (March 1902): 277.

Hopkins, Pauline E. "Josephine St. Pierre Ruffin at Milwaukee, 1900." *The Colored American Magazine* 5, no. 3 (July 1902): 210–13.

Hopwood, Elizabeth. "Discoverability and the Problems of Access: Thoughts on Responsive Digital-Research Interfacing." *American Periodicals: A Journal of History & Criticism* 26, no. 1 (2016): 7–10.

Horton, James Oliver, and Lois E. Horton. *In Hope of Liberty: Culture, Community and Protest among Northern Free Blacks, 1700–1860*. New York: Oxford University Press, 1997.

Howard, J. I. "The American Negro Exhibit." *The Colored American* (Washington, DC), September 1, 1900, 6.

Howe, Albert. "Notes on the Returned Indian Students of the Hampton Normal and Agricultural Institute." December 1891. In United States Department of the Interior, *Letter from the Secretary of the Interior: In Response to Senate Resolution of February 28, 1891, Forwarding Report Made by the Hampton Institute Regarding Its Returned Indian Students*, 3–87. 52nd Congress, First Session. Executive Document No. 31. Washington, DC: Government Printing Office, [1892].

Howell, George Rogers. *Bi-Centennial History of Albany*. Vol. 2, *History of the County of Albany, N.Y., from 1609 to 1886*. New York: W. W. Munsell and Co., 1886.

"How It Works." Native Land Digital, https://native-land.ca/about/how-it-works/.

Hoxie, Frederick E. *A Final Promise: The Campaign to Assimilate the Indians, 1880–1920*. Oklahoma: University of Nebraska Press, 2001.

Hunter, Carol M. "The Rev. Jermain Loguen: A Narrative of Real Life." *Afro-Americans in New York Life and History* 13 (July 1989): 33–46.

Hunter, Carol M. *To Set the Captives Free: Reverend Jermain Wesley Loguen and the Struggle for Freedom in Central New York, 1835–1872*. New York: Garland, 1993.

Hunter, Tera W. *To 'Joy My Freedom: Southern Black Women's Lives and Labors after the Civil War*. Cambridge, MA: Harvard University Press, 1997.

Hutchinson, George. *The Harlem Renaissance in Black and White*. Cambridge, MA: Belknap Press of Harvard University Press, 1995.

Hutchinson, Louise Daniel. *Anna J. Cooper*. Washington, DC: Smithsonian Institution Press, 1981.

Hutton, Frankie. *The Early Black Press in America, 1827–1860*. Westport, CT: Greenwood Press, 1993.

I. "A Better Report in Some Respects." Letter dated March 19, 1884 from Palmer's Springs, Va. *The Southern Workman*, May 1884, 54.

I. "From a Colored Juror." Letter dated March 21, 1884, from Danville, Virginia. *The Southern Workman*, May 1884, 54.

I. "Graduate Teachers in the North, Dear Miss Cleveland." *The Southern Workman*, September 1893, 141.

I. Letter dated May 30, 1878. *The Southern Workman*, July 1878, 52.
"In Defense of Our Women." *The Parson's Weekly Blade*, December 9, 1893, 2.
Ingleton, Matilda. "Four Essential Qualities in a Negro Woman. To the Editor of the Woman's Page." *Negro World*, August 2, 1924, 12.
Ingleton, Matilda. "Let Us Hold Our Own in World Affairs. To the Editor of the Woman's Page." *Negro World*, August 23, 1924, 16.
"Interesting Letter from Miss Charlotte L. Forten." *The Liberator*, December 19, 1862.
Jackson, Cynthia L., and Eleanor F. Nunn. *Historically Black Colleges and Universities: A Reference Handbook*. Santa Barbara, CA: ABC-Clio, 2003.
Jackson, Leon. *The Business of Letters: Authorial Economies in Antebellum America*. Stanford, CA: Stanford University Press, 2008.
Jackson, Shona N. "Humanity beyond the Regime of Labor: Antiblackness, Indigeneity, and the Legacies of Colonialism in the Caribbean." *Decolonization: Indigeneity, Education and Society*, June 6, 2014. https://decolonization.wordpress.com/2014/06/06/humanity-beyond-the-regime-of-labor-antiblackness-indigeneity-and-the-legacies-of-colonialism-in-the-caribbean/.
Jackson, Zakiyyah Iman. *Becoming Human: Matter and Meaning in an Antiblack World*. New York: New York University Press, 2020.
Jacques Garvey, Amy. "Do Negro Women Want to Express Themselves?" *Negro World*, April 11, 1925, 7.
Jacques Garvey, Amy. "Have a Heart." *Negro World*, August 2, 1924, 12.
Jacques Garvey, Amy. "How to Help Better the Economic Condition of the West Indies." *Negro World*, January 10, 1925, 8.
Jacques Garvey, Amy. "It's 'Up to You!'" *Negro World*, September 13, 1924, 1.
Jacques Garvey, Amy. "Our Page Is Three Years Old." *Negro World*, February 12, 1927, 7.
Jacques Garvey, Amy. "St. Kitts Newspaper Exposes Legislative Measure to Rob Nations of Their Liberty." *Negro World*, April 19, 1924, 10.
Jacques Garvey, Amy. "Women of the Negro Race!" *Negro World*, February 9, 1924, 10.
James, Winston. *Holding Aloft the Banner of Ethiopia: Caribbean Radicalism in Early Twentieth-Century America*. London: Verso, 1998.
"Japan." *The Elevator*, August 23, 1873, 3.
J. B. Y. "Miss Shadd's Pamphlet." *The North Star*, June 8, 1849.
J. C. B. "Literary Societies." *The Liberator*, August 30, 1834.
Jeter, James Philip. "Rough Flying: *The California Eagle*, 1879–1965." In *Proceedings of the American Journalism Historians' Association Conference*, 36–62. Salt Lake City, UT, October 5–7, 1993.
Jockers, Matthew L. *Macroanalysis: Digital Methods and Literary History*. Urbana: University of Illinois Press, 2013.
Johnson, Gaye Theresa. "Constellations of Struggle: Luisa Moreno, Charlotta Bass, and the Legacy for Ethnic Studies." *Aztlán: A Journal of Chicano Studies* 33, no. 1 (2008): 155–72.
Johnson, Gaye Theresa. *Spaces of Conflict, Sounds of Solidarity: Music, Race, and Spatial Entitlement in Los Angeles*. Berkeley: University Press of California, 2013.

Johnson, Sara E. *The Fear of French Negroes: Transcolonial Collaboration in the Revolutionary Americas.* Berkeley: University of California Press, 2012.

Johnson, Val Marie. "'The Half Has Never Been Told': Maritcha Lyons' Community, Black Women Educators, the Woman's Loyal Union, and 'the Color Line' in Progressive Era Brooklyn and New York." *Journal of Urban History* 44, no. 5 (2018): 835–61.

Jones, Martha S. *All Bound Up Together: The Woman Question in African American Public Culture, 1830–1900.* Chapel Hill: University of North Carolina Press, 2007.

"Just Published, and for Sale at This Office." *The Liberator*, March 31, 1832.

K., Charlotte. "Mr. Editor." *Frederick Douglass' Paper*, March 3, 1854, 3.

Keating, Cecilia. "Indigenous Geographies Overlap in This Colorful Online Map." *Atlas Obscura*. https://www.atlasobscura.com/articles/native-land-map-of-indigenous-territories.

Kelley, Mary. *Learning to Stand and Speak: Women, Education, and Public Life in America's Republic.* Chapel Hill: University of North Carolina Press, 2012.

Kelley, Mary. "'Talents Committed to Your Care': Reading and Writing Radical Abolitionism in Antebellum America." *The New England Quarterly* 88, no. 1 (2015): 37–72.

Kelley, Robin D. G. "'But a Local Phase of a World Problem': Black History's Global Vision 1883–1950." *Journal of American History* 86, no. 3 (1999): 1045–77.

Kelley, Robin D. G. "Foreword." In *Reflections in Black: A History of Black Photographers, 1840 to the Present*, edited by Deborah Willis, ix–xi. New York: W. W. Norton, 2000.

Kelley, Robin D. G. *Freedom Dreams: The Black Radical Tradition.* Boston: Beacon Press, 2002.

Kelley, Robin D. G. *Race Rebels: Culture, Politics, and the Black Working Class.* New York: Free Press, 1994.

Kennedy, Shelagh Rebecca. "New Era Club." In *Black Women in America: An Historical Encyclopedia*, vol. 2, edited by Darlene Clark Hine, Elsa Barkley Brown, and Rosalyn Terborg-Penn, 879–81. Brooklyn, NY: Carlson, 1993.

Ketosh, Juanita Espinosa. "The following letter . . ." *The Southern Workman*, September 1902, 505.

King, John. "Dear Friend." Letter dated January 12, 1881, from Shawneetown, Indian Territory. *The Southern Workman*, February 1881, 21.

Knadler, Stephen. "Antebellum African American Freemen's Narratives and Semi-Citizenship." In *African American Literature in Transition*, vol. 5, *1850–1865*, edited by Teresa Zackodnik, 25–47. Cambridge: Cambridge University Press, 2021.

Knight, Alisha R. "Commentary." *The Colored American Magazine* 1, no. 2 (June 1900). The Colored American Magazine Project. http://coloredamerican.org/?page_id=685.

Knight, Alisha R. *Pauline Hopkins and the American Dream: An African American Writer's (Re)Visionary Gospel of Success.* Knoxville: University of Tennessee Press, 2014.

Knupfer, Anne Meis. *Toward a Tenderer Humanity and a Nobler Womanhood: African American Women's Clubs in Turn-of-the-Century Chicago.* New York: New York University Press, 1996.

Lacey, Barbara E. "Visual Images of Blacks in Early American Imprints." *William and Mary Quarterly* 53, no. 1 (January 1996): 137–80.

Lacey, L. "Australia Sends Greetings to the Fourth International." *Negro World*, August 2, 1924, 3.

La Flesche, Suzette. "Yonder is a man . . ." *The Southern Workman*, April 1879, 44.

Lalvani, Suren. *Photography, Vision, and the Production of Modern Bodies*. Albany: State University of New York Press, 1996.

Lamontagne, Kori. "A Study of Black Intellectual and Literary Societies in Antebellum Boston." Primary Research: Local History, Closer to Home. http://primaryresearch.org/a-study-of-black-intellectual-and-literary-societies-in-antebellum-boston/#_edn9.

Laney, Lucy Craft. "The Burden of the Educated Colored Woman." *The Southern Workman*, September 1899, 37–43.

Lang, William L. "The Nearly Forgotten Blacks on Last Chance Gulch, 1900–1912." *Pacific Northwest Quarterly* 70 (April 1979): 50–57.

Langhorne, Mrs. P. A. "Girls Should Be Taught to Keep House Properly. To the Editor of the Women's Section." *Negro World*, April 19, 1924, 10.

Langston, Carrie. "Women in Journalism." *The Atchison Blade*, September 10, 1892.

Larsen, Jonas, John Urry, and Kay Axhausen. *Mobilities, Networks, Geographies*. Aldershot, UK: Ashgate, 2006.

Latham, Sean. "Affordance and Emergence: Magazine as New Media." Paper presented at the Modern Language Association, Boston, MA, January 3–6, 2013. https://seeeps.princeton.edu/wp-content/uploads/sites/243/2015/03/mla2013_latham.pdf.

Latham, Sean and Robert Scholes. "The Rise of Periodical Studies." *PMLA* 121, no. 2 (2006): 517–31.

Lavin, Matthew. "Why Digital Humanists Should Emphasize Situated Data over Capta." *digital humanities quarterly* 15, no. 2 (2021). http://www.digitalhumanities.org/dhq/vol/15/2/000556/000556.html.

Leary, Patrick. "Response: Search and Serendipity." *Victorian Periodicals Review* 48, no. 2 (2015): 267–72.

Leavell, Lori. "'Not Intended Exclusively for the Slave States': Antebellum Recirculation of David Walker's Appeal." *Callaloo: A Journal of African Diaspora Arts and Letters* 38, no. 3 (2015): 679–95.

Leavenworth, Jesse, and Kevin Canfield. "Courant Complicity in an Old Wrong." *Hartford Courant*, July 4, 2000, 1.

Lee, Benjamin, and Edward LiPuma. "Cultures of Circulation: The Imaginations of Modernity." *Public Culture* 14, no. 1 (2002): 191–213.

Leeds, Asia. "Toward the 'Higher Type of Womanhood': The Gendered Contours of Garveyism and the Making of Redemptive Geographies in Costa Rica, 1922–1941." *Palimpsest: A Journal on Women, Gender, and the Black International* 2, no. 1 (2013): 1–27.

Lefebvre, Henri. *The Production of Space*. Translated by Donald Nicholson-Smith. Oxford: Basil Blackwell, 1991.

Leonard, Kevin Allen. *The Battle for Los Angeles: Racial Ideology and World War II*. Albuquerque: University of New Mexico Press, 2006.

Lerner, Gerda, ed. *Black Women in White America: A Documentary History*. 1972. Reprint, New York: Vintage Books, 1992.

"The Lesson of Toleration." *The Birmingham Daily Gazette*, May 18, 1894.

"Letter from C. J. Hardstew." *The Savannah Tribune*, January 6, 1917.

"Letter from Sojourner Truth." *National Anti-Slavery Standard*, February 13, 1864.

"Letter from William C. Nell." *The Liberator*, March 5, 1852, 3.

"Letters from Hampton Graduates." *The Southern Workman*, January 1880, 6.

Letter to the Editor. *The Christian Recorder*, January 18, 1877, 6.

Lewis, David Levering. "A Small Nation of People: W. E. B. Du Bois and Black Americans at the Turn of the Twentieth Century." In Library of Congress, *A Small Nation of People: W. E. B. Du Bois and African American Portraits of Progress*, 23–50. New York: Harper Collins, 2003.

Lewis, Eunice. "The Black Woman's Part in Race Leadership." *Negro World,* April 19, 1924, 10.

Library of Congress. *A Small Nation of People: W. E. B. Du Bois and African American Portraits of Progress*. New York: Harper Collins, 2003.

Liddle, Dallas. "Method in Periodical Studies: Follow the Genre." Presented as part of "What Is a Journal? Towards a Theory of Periodical Studies Roundtable," Modern Languages Association, Boston, MA, January 3–6, 2013. https://seeeps.princeton.edu/wp-content/uploads/sites/243/2015/03/mla2013_liddle.pdf.

Lieberman, Robbie. "The Missing Peace: Charlotta Bass and the Vision of the Black Left in the Early Cold War Years." In *Lineages of the Literary Left: Essays in Honor of Alan M. Wald*, edited by Howard Brick, Robbie Lieberman, and Paula Rabinowitz. Ann Arbor: Michigan Publishing, 2015. https://quod.lib.umich.edu/m/maize/13545968.0001.001/1:13/--lineages-of-the-literary-left-essays-in-honor-of-alanm-wald?rgn=div1;view=fulltext.

Lincoln, C. Eric, and Lawrence H. Mamiya. *The Black Church in the African American Experience*. Durham, NC: Duke University Press, 1990.

Lindhorst, Marie. "Politics in a Box: Sarah Mapps Douglass and the Female Literary Association, 1831–1833." *Pennsylvania History* 65 (1998): 263–78.

Lindsey, Donal F. *Indians at Hampton Institute, 1877–1923*. Urbana: University of Illinois Press, 1995.

Linton, J. J. E. "The Power of the Newspaper Press—Slavery." *The Provincial Freeman*, July 31, 1856.

Lipsitz, George. *How Racism Takes Place*. Philadelphia: Temple University Press, 2011.

"Literary Societies." *The Colored American* (New York, NY), October 5, 1839.

"Literary Society." *Illinois Record*, January 8, 1898, 1.

Little, Monroe H. "The Extra-Curricular Activities of Black College Students, 1868–1940." *Journal of African American History* 87 (2002): 43–55.

Litwack, Michael. "The Closed World and the Open Society: Cybernetics and Racial Liberalism from Wiener to Wynter." Unpublished manuscript, November 26, 2016, typescript.

Liu, Alan. "Imagining the New Media Encounter." In *A Companion to Digital Literary Studies*, edited by Susan Schreibman and Ray Siemens. Oxford: Blackwell, 2008. http://www.digitalhumanities.org/companion/view?docId=blackwell/9781405148641/9781405148641.xml&chunk.id=ss1-3-1.

Liu, Alan. "Where Is Cultural Criticism in the Digital Humanities?" In *Debates in the Digital Humanities*, edited Matthew K. Gold, 490–510. Minneapolis: University of Minnesota Press, 2012.

Logan, Shirley Wilson. *Liberating Language: Sites of Rhetorical Education in Nineteenth-Century Black America*. Carbondale: Southern Illinois University Press, 2008.

Logan, Shirley Wilson. "Victoria Earle Matthews." In *American Women Prose Writers, 1870–1920*, edited by Sharon M. Harris. Republished by Gale Literature Resource Center (Gale, 2000). https://www.gale.com/c/literature-resource-center.

Loughran, Trish. *The Republic in Print: Print Culture in the Age of US Nation Building, 1770–1870*. New York: Columbia University Press, 2007.

Loguen, Jermain. *The Rev. J. W. Loguen, as a Slave and as a Freeman*. 1859. Reprint, New York: Negro University Press, 1968.

"Lynch Law in America." *Birmingham Daily Post*, May 17, 1894.

"Lynch Law in the United States, Protest by Birmingham Audiences." *Birmingham Daily Post*, May 17, 1894.

Lynn, Denise. "The Deportation of Claudia Jones." *Black Perspectives* (blog), October 5, 2018. https://www.aaihs.org/the-deportation-of-claudia-jones/.

Ma-ah-chis Soaring Eagle. "My Dear Friend Miss L." Letter dated August 1, 1878. *The Southern Workman*, October 1878.

M. A. S. [Mary Ann Shadd]. "Dear 'C.'" *Provincial Freeman*, October 21, 1854.

Mabee, Carleton, with Susan Mabee Newhouse. *Sojourner Truth: Slave, Prophet, Legend*. New York: New York University Press, 1993.

Madera, Judith. *Black Atlas: Geography and Flow in Nineteenth-Century African American Literature*. Durham, NC: Duke University Press, 2015.

Mahammitt, Mrs. T. P. *Recipes and Domestic Service: The Mahammitt School of Cookery*. Omaha, NE, 1939.

Majors, Monroe. *Noted Negro Women: Their Triumphs and Activities*. Chicago: Donohue and Henneberry, 1893.

Maloney, Thomas N. "African American Migration to the North: New Evidence for the 1910s." *Economic Inquiry* 40, no. 1 (2002): 1–11.

Mangun, Kimberley. "'As citizens of Portland we must protest': Beatrice Morrow Cannady and the African American Response to D. W. Griffith's 'Masterpiece.'" *Oregon Historical Quarterly* 107, no. 3 (Fall 2006): 382–409.

Mangun, Kimberley. "Boosting the Bottom Line: Beatrix Morrow Cannady's Tactics to Promote *The Advocate*, 1923–1933." *American Journalism* 25, no. 1 (2008): 31–69.

Mangun, Kimberley. "The (Oregon) Advocate: Boosting the Race and Portland, Too." *American Journalism* 23, no. 1 (2006): 7–34.

Mapps Douglass, Sarah. "Address" ["The Cause of the Slave Became My Own"]. *The Liberator*, July 21, 1832.

Mapps Douglass, Sarah. "Appeal of the Philadelphia Association." *The North Star*, September 7, 1849. 3.

Mapps Douglass, Sarah. "Emigration to Mexico." *The Liberator*, January 28, 1832.

Mapps Douglass, Sarah. "For the Pennsylvania Freeman." *The Pennsylvania Freeman*, June 21, 1838.

Mapps Douglass, Sarah. "A General View of Hayti." *The Liberator*, June 19, 1863.

Mapps Douglass, Sarah. "A Good Habit Recommended." *The Anglo-African Magazine*, May 1859.

Mapps Douglass, Sarah. "The North Star Fair." *The North Star*, September 5, 1850, 2.
Mapps Douglass, Sarah. "Pennsylvania A. S. Fair." *National Anti-Slavery Standard*, December 20, 1849.
Marano, Carla. "'We All Used to Meet at the Hall': Assessing the Significance of the Universal Negro Improvement Association in Toronto, 1900–1950." *Journal of the Canadian Historical Association* 25, no. 1 (2014): 143–75.
March, Deborah. "Reframing Blackness: The Photograph and African American Literary Modernism at the Turn of the Twentieth Century." PhD diss., Yale University, 2012.
"Marcus Garvey." *The Advocate*, May 14, 1927, 1.
Margolis, Ben. To Los Angeles Newspaper Guild, October 12, 1948. Additional Box 1, Letters to, 1940s, Charlotta Bass Collection, Southern California Library for Social Studies and Research, Los Angeles.
Martin, Tony. "Women in the Garvey Movement." In *Garvey: His Work and Impact*, edited by Rupert Charles Lewis and Patrick Bryan, 67–72. Trenton, NJ: Africa World Press, 1991.
Materson, Lisa G. "African American Women's Global Journeys and the Construction of Cross-Ethnic Racial Identity." *Women's Studies International Forum* 32 (2009): 35–42.
Mary. "A Response." *The Elevator*, February 14, 1868, 2.
Matilda [Amy Matilda Cassey]. "Messrs. Editors." *Freedom's Journal*, August 10, 1827, 2.
"Matters in Brief." *The New York Freeman*, March 13, 1897, 1.
Matthews, Victoria Earle. *The Awakening of the Afro-American Woman*. Brooklyn, NY: Victoria Earle Matthews, 1897.
Matthews, Victoria Earle. "Some Dangers Confronting Southern Girls in the North." *Hampton Negro Conference* 2 (July 1898): 62–69. Reprinted in *The Southern Workman*, September 1898, 173–75.
Matthews, Victoria Earle. *The Value of Race Literature: An Address Delivered at the First Congress of Colored Women of the United States, at Boston, Mass., July 30th, 1895*. Boston, 1895.
May. "Letter to the Editor." *The Liberator*, October 27, 1832.
May, Cedrick. *Evangelism and Resistance in the Black Atlantic, 1760–1835*. Athens: University of Georgia Press, 2008.
Mayer, Henry. *All on Fire: William Lloyd Garrison and the Abolition of Slavery*. New York: St. Martin's Press, 1998.
Maynard, John. "'In the interests of our people': The Influence of Garveyism on the Rise of Australian Aboriginal Political Activism." *Aboriginal History* 29 (2005): 1–22.
McCandless, Barbara. "The Portrait Studio and the Celebrity." In *Photography in Nineteenth-Century America*, edited by Martha A. Sandweiss, 49–72. New York: Harry N. Abrams, 1991.
McDuffie, Erik S. "Chicago, Garveyism, and the History of the Diasporic Midwest." *African and Black Diaspora: An International Journal* 8, no. 2 (2015): 129–45.
McDuffie, Erik S. "A 'New Freedom Movement of Negro Women': Sojourning for Truth, Justice, and Human Rights During the Early Cold War." *Radical History Review* 101 (Spring 2008): 81–106.

McGee, David. "*Spirit of the Age.*" In *Encyclopedia of North Carolina*, edited by William S. Powell. Chapel Hill: University of North Carolina Press, 2006. https://www.ncpedia.org/spirit-age.

McGill, Meredith. *American Literature and the Culture of Reprinting, 1834–1853*. Philadelphia: University of Pennsylvania Press, 2003.

McGlotten, Shaka. "Black Data." In *No Tea, No Shade: New Writings in Black Queer Studies*, edited by E. J. Johnson, 262–86. Durham, NC: Duke University Press, 2016.

McHenry, Elizabeth. *Forgotten Readers: Recovering the Lost History of African American Literary Societies*. Durham, NC: Duke University Press, 2002.

McKittrick, Katherine. *Demonic Grounds: Black Women and the Cartographies of Struggle*. Minneapolis: University of Minnesota Press, 2006.

McLeod, Marc. "Garveyism in Cuba, 1920–1940." *Journal of Caribbean History* 30, nos. 1–2 (1996): 132–68.

McManus, Edgar J. *Black Bondage in the North*. Syracuse, NY: Syracuse University Press, 1973.

McMurray, Linda O. *To Keep the Waters Troubled: The Life of Ida B. Wells*. Oxford: Oxford University Press, 1998.

McMurtrie, Douglas C. *A History of Printing in the United States: The Story of the Introduction of the Press and of Its History and Influences during the Pioneer Period in Each State of the Union*. Vol. 2. New York: R. R. Bowker, 1936.

McPherson, Tara. "Why Are the Digital Humanities So White? Or Thinking the Histories of Race and Computation." In *Debates in the Digital Humanities*, edited by Matthew K. Gold, 139–60. Minneapolis: University of Minnesota Press, 2012.

McReeves, Lillie. "Fifteen-Year-Old Girl Wide Awake." *Negro World*, August 23, 1924, 16.

"Meditations, by Mrs. Maria W. Stewart, Matron of the Freedman's Hospital." *The People's Advocate*, August 30, 1879.

Meehan, Sean Ross. *Mediating American Autobiography: Photography in Emerson, Thoreau, Douglass, and Whitman*. Columbia: University of Missouri Press, 2008.

"Meeting to Organize the Provincial Union." *Provincial Freeman*, August 19, 1854.

Melamed, Jodi. *Represent and Destroy: Rationalizing Violence in the New Racial Capitalism*. Minneapolis: University of Minnesota Press, 2011.

Melamed, Jodi. "The Spirit of Neoliberalism: From Racial Liberalism to Neoliberal Multiculturalism." *Social Text* 89, no. 4 (Winter 2006): 1–24.

Melish, Joanne Pope. *Disowning Slavery: Gradual Emancipation and "Race" in New England, 1780–1860*. Ithaca, NY: Cornell University Press, 1998.

Melvin, Sarah B., and Eliza D. Richards. "Sir,—The Ladies' Literary Society of New York Send You the Enclosed Sum." *The Colored American* (New York, NY), January 20, 1838.

"Metropolitan Baptist." *The Plaindealer* (Kansas City, KS), July 7, 1933, 6.

Miller, Clifford L. "Oregon Is the Best State in the Union, Says Mrs. E. D. Cannady, of Portland, Who Is in the East as a Delegate to the Pan-African Congress." *The Advocate*, September 10, 1927, 1. Reprinted from New York *Amsterdam News*.

Miller, Kelly. "After Marcus Garvey: What of the Negro?" [1927]. In *Marcus Garvey and the Vision of Africa*, edited by John Henrik Clarke, 242–47. New York: Vintage, 1974.

Minutes of the Eleventh Biennial Convention of the National Association of Colored Women, July 8–13, 1918 at Shorter Chapel AME Church, Denver, Colo. Microfilm. In *Records of the National Association of Colored Women's Clubs, 1895–1922*, part 1, *Minutes of National Conventions, Publications and President's Office Correspondence*, edited by Lillian Serece Williams and Randolph Bohem, frames 0481–0591. Bethesda, MD: University Publications of America, 1994.

Minutes of the State Convention of the Colored Citizens of Ohio. N.p., 1851. https://omeka.coloredconventions.org/items/show/249.

"Miss Wells' Crusade. How She Started Out on an Anti-Lynching Crusade." *Omaha World-Herald*, September 20, 1894, 2.

Mitchell, Patricia Pugh. "Negating the Nadir: The Smoky City Newspaper Series as a Forum for Black Perspectives." *Western Pennsylvania History* 89, no. 4 (Winter 2006–2007): 31–47.

Miter, J. J. "Colored People of Troy." *The Colored American* (New York, NY), April 1, 1837, 1.

Montana Office of Public Instruction, Division of Indian Instruction. *Montana Indians, Their History and Location*. Montana Office of Public Instruction, n.d. https://opi.mt.gov/Portals/182/Page%20Files/Indian%20Education/Indian%20Education%20101/Montana%20Indians%20Their%20History%20and%20Location.pdf.

Moody, Joycelyn K. *Sentimental Confessions: Spiritual Narratives of Nineteenth-Century African American Women*. Athens: University of Georgia Press, 2001.

Moody, Joycelyn K. "Tactical Lines in Three Black Women's Visual Portraits, 1773–1849 / Líneas tácticas en los retratos visuals de tres mujeres negras, 1773–1849." *A/b: Auto/Biography Studies* 30, no. 1 (2015): 67–98.

Moore, Jacqueline M. *Leading the Race: The Transformation of the Black Elite in the Nation's Capital, 1880–1920*. Charlottesville: University of Virginia Press, 1999.

Moretti, Franco. *Distant Reading*. New York: Verso, 2013.

Morris, R. J. "Document to Database and Spreadsheet." In *Research Methods for the Arts and Humanities: Research Methods for History*, edited by Simon Gunn and Lucy Faire, 141–67. Edinburgh: Edinburgh University Press, 2016.

Mossell, Mrs. N. F. [Gertrude Mossell]. "Our Woman's Department . . . Women and Journalism." *The New York Freeman*, May 8, 1886.

Mossell, Mrs. N. F. *The Work of the African American Woman*. Philadelphia: George S. Ferguson, 1908.

Moten, Fred. *Stolen Life*. Durham, NC: Duke University Press, 2018.

Mott, Frank Luther. *American Journalism, A History: 1690–1960*. 3rd ed. New York: Macmillan, 1962.

M. R. D. [Martin R. Delany]. "In the Lecturing Field." *The North Star*, February 16, 1849.

M. R. L. "Mrs Frances E. W. Harper on Reconstruction." *The Liberator*, March 3, 1864.

"Mrs. Cannady Sees End of Race Trouble." *Chicago Defender*, August 20, 1927.

"Mrs. Stuart's [sic] Farewell Address . . . Was Delivered." *The Liberator*, September 28, 1833.

"Mt. Zion Baptist." *The Negro Star*, December 10, 1926, 1.

Muhammad, Gholnecsar E. "The Literacy Development and Practices within African American Literary Societies." *Black History Bulletin* 75, no. 1 (2012): 6–13.

Mulcahy, Monica Clare. "Professional Anxiety: African American Female Journalists Writing Their Way to Legitimacy, 1880–1914." PhD diss., University of Alberta, 2017.

Mullin, Gerald W. *Flight and Rebellion: Slave Resistance in Eighteenth-Century Virginia*. New York: Oxford University Press, 1972.

Murray, Anna E. "In Behalf of the Negro Woman." *The Southern Workman*, April 1904, 232–34.

Murray, F. H. M. "The In-Look." *Horizon: A Journal of the Color Line*, January 1, 1908, 25.

Murray, F. H. M. "The In-Look." *Horizon: A Journal of the Color Line*, May 1, 1908, 29.

Murray, F. H. M. "The In-Look." *Horizon: A Journal of the Color Line*, June 1, 1908, 27.

Murray, Heather. "A Black Literary Society." In *The Ward Uncovered: The Archaeology of Everyday Life*, edited by John Lorinc, Holly Martelle, Michael McClelland, and Tatum Taylor, 163–66. Toronto: Coach House Press, 2018.

Murray, Heather. *Come, Bright Improvement! The Literary Societies of Nineteenth-Century Ontario*. Toronto: University of Toronto Press, 2002.

Mussell, James. "The Matter with Media." Paper presented at the Modern Language Association, Boston, MA, January 3–6, 2013. https://seeeps.princeton.edu/wp-content/uploads/sites/243/2015/03/mla2013_mussell.pdf.

Muta. "Messrs. Editors." *Freedom's Journal*, July 27, 1827.

Nakamura, Lisa. *Digitizing Race: Visual Cultures of the Internet*. Minneapolis: University of Minnesota Press, 2010.

Nakamura, Lisa, and Peter A. Chow-White, eds. *Race after the Internet*. New York: Routledge, 2013.

Nelson, Charmaine A. *Creolization and Transatlantic Blackness: The Visual and Material Cultures of Slavery*. London: Routledge, 2025.

Nelson, Robert. "Introduction." Mining the Dispatch, updated November 2020. http://dsl.richmond.edu/dispatch/introduction.

Neverdon-Morton, Cynthia. *Afro-American Women of the South and the Advancement of the Race, 1895–1925*. Knoxville: University of Tennessee Press, 1991.

Newman, Richard S. *Black Founders: The Free Black Community in the Early Republic*. Philadelphia: The Library Company of Philadelphia, 2008.

Newman, Richard S. "Faith in the Ballot: Black Shadow Politics in the Antebellum North." *Common-Place* 9, no. 1 (October 2008). https://commonplace.online/article/faith-in-the-ballot/.

"Newspapers." *The Southern Workman*, January 1873, 1.

"New York City Anti-Slavery Society Fourth Anniversary." *National Anti-Slavery Standard*, May 23, 1857.

Nichols, Hannah. "Lady Delegate in Convention Demands Single Standard for All. Says Negro Women Should Insist upon Right Living in Interests of Posterity." *Negro World*, August 23, 1924, 16.

Nielsen, Rasmus Kleis. "Participation through Letters to the Editor: Circulation, Considerations, and Genres in the Letters Institution." *Journalism: Theory, Practice, and Criticism* 11, no. 1 (2010): 21–35.

Noble, Safiya Umoja. *Algorithms of Oppression*. New York: New York University Press, 2018.

Nord, David Paul. *Communities of Journalism: A History of American Newspapers and Their Readers*. Indianapolis: University of Illinois Press, 2001.

Norton, Caroline. "One of Our Legal Fictions." *Provincial Freeman*, June 10, 1854.

"Notice." *The Christian Recorder*, January 2, 1864.

"Notice. A Lecture on African Rights and Liberty, Will Be Delivered." *The Liberator*, March 2, 1833.

"Notice. Mrs. Stewart, Will Deliver Her Farewell Address." *The Liberator*, September 14, 1833.

"Notice. . . . The African Dorcas Association." *Freedom's Journal*, February 1, 1828.

Nubia [William Newby]. "Progress of the Colored People of San Francisco." *Frederick Douglass' Paper*, September 22, 1854, 4.

Nwankwo, Ifeoma Kiddoe. *Black Cosmopolitanism: Racial Consciousness, and Transnational Identity in the Nineteenth-Century Americas*. Philadelphia: University of Pennsylvania Press, 2005.

N. W. Ayer & Son's Directory: Newspapers and Periodicals, 1940. Philadelphia: N. W. Ayer and Son, 1940.

N. W. Ayer & Son's Directory: Newspapers and Periodicals, 1950. Philadelphia: N. W. Ayer and Son, 1950.

Nyberg, Sister E. "Greetings from Australia. To the Editor of the Woman's Page." *Negro World*, August 2, 1924, 12.

Nyong'o, Tavia. *Afro-Fabulations: The Queer Drama of Black Life*. New York: New York University Press, 2019.

"Object of the Phoenix Society of New York." In Members of the Executive Committee of the American Anti-Slavery Society, *Address to the People of Color of the City of New York*, 12. New York: S. W. Benedict, 1834.

"Observer No. V." *Freedom's Journal*, October 5, 1827.

Oppel, Christina. "W. E. B. Du Bois, Nazi Germany, and the Black Atlantic." *GHI Bulletin Supplement* 5 (2008): 99–122.

Oshkeneny, Michael-Young Man. "Dear Friend." Letter dated February 6, 1883. *The Southern Workman*, October 1883, 104.

Oshkeneny, Michael-Young Man. "Dear Friend and Teacher." Letter dated March 3, 1884, from Keshena, WI. *The Southern Workman*, August 1884, 90.

"Our City Canvas." *The Christian Recorder*, June 28, 1862.

"Our Exchanges." *The Southern Workman*, March 1873, 3.

"Our Girls." *Lyceum Echo*. Reprinted in *The Freeman* (Indianapolis, IN), March 21, 1891.

"Our Journalists and Literary Folks." *The Freeman* (New York, NY), February 11, 1893, 6.

"Our Woman's Number." *Voice of the Negro* 1, no. 7 (July 1904).

"Our Women. Meeting of the American Woman Suffrage Association.—Mrs. Terell's Address." *Washington Bee*, February 26, 1898, 4.

P. "Dear Teacher." *The Southern Workman*, February 1879, 18.

Painter, Nell Irvin. *Sojourner Truth: A Life, A Symbol*. New York: W. W. Norton, 1996.

Parker, Freddie L. *Running for Freedom: Slave Runaways in North Carolina, 1775–1840*. New York: Garland, 1993.

Pattee, Capt. John P. Letter from the Cheyenne River Agency, South Dakota. *The Southern Workman,* July 1891, 213.

Patterson, Orlando. *Slavery and Social Death: A Comparative Study.* Cambridge, MA: Harvard University Press, 1982.

Patterson, Tiffany Ruby, and Robin D. G. Kelley. "Unfinished Migrations: Reflections on the African Diaspora and the Making of the Modern World." *African Studies Review* 43, no. 1 (2000): 11–45.

Pay-Pay [Paypay], Mrs. Carrie. "From Another Indian Daughter of Hampton." *The Southern Workman,* April 1893, 61.

Pay-Pay [Paypay], Mrs. Carrie. "A Letter from Cheyenne River." *The Southern Workman,* February 1893, 31.

"Pay Your Subscription." *The Advocate,* June 13, 1925, 4.

Peavler, David J. "African Americans in Omaha and the 1898 Trans-Mississippi and International Exposition." *Journal of African American History* 93, no. 3 (2008): 337–61.

Peebles-Wilkins, Wilma. "Fernandis, Sarah A. Collins." *Encyclopedia of Social Work* 11 (June 2013). htpps://doi:10.1093/acrefore/9780199975839.013.686.

Penn, I. Garland. *The Afro-American Press, and Its Editors.* Springfield, MA: Willey and Co., 1891.

Perdue, Theda. "The Legacy of Indian Removal." *Journal of Southern History* 78, no. 1 (2012): 3–36.

Perkins, Linda. "Black Women and Racial 'Uplift' Prior to Emancipation." In *The Black Woman Cross-Culturally,* edited by Filomina Chioma Steady, 317–34. Rochester, NY: Schenkman, 1981.

Perry, Lara. "The Carte de Visite in the 1860s and the Serial Dynamic of the Photographic Likeness." *Art History* 35 (2012): 728–49.

Perry, Louis B., and Richard S. Perry. *A History of the Los Angeles Labor Movement, 1911–1941.* Berkeley: University of California Press, 1963.

Peterson, Carla L. *"Doers of the Word": African-American Women Speakers and Writers in the North (1830–1880).* New York: Oxford University Press, 1995.

Peterson, Carla L. "Subject to Speculation: Assessing the Lives of African American Women in the Nineteenth Century." In *Women's Studies in Transition: The Pursuit of Interdisciplinarity,* edited by Kate Conway-Turner, Suzanne Cherrin, Jessica Schiffman, and Kathleen Doherty Turkel, 109–117. Newark: University of Delaware Press, 1998.

Petry, Liz. "Complicity Chapter Five: Slavery and the *Courant,* Promoting and Protecting Human Bondage." Courant.com, September 29, 2002. www.courant.com/news/special-reports/hc-newcourant.artsep29,0,3988959.story.

"Phila." Letter to the Editor. *The Liberator,* March 17, 1834.

"Philadelphia Dots." *Washington Bee,* March 27, 1897, 8.

Philpotts, Matthew. Description of the roundtable "What Is a Journal? Towards a Theory of Periodical Studies" convention of the Modern Languages Association, Boston, MA, January 3–6, 2013. *Journal of Victorian Culture Online.* https://jvc.oup.com/2012/12/24/what-is-a-journal-mla2013/.

Pilling, James Constantine. *Bibliography of the Siouan Languages.* Washington, DC: Government Printing Office, 1887.

"Plea for Emigration." *Voice of the Fugitive*, June 3, 1852.
"Poems on Miscellaneous Subjects by Frances Ellen Watkins, Boston: J. B. Yerrinton and Son Printers, 1854." *Frederick Douglass' Paper*, September 15, 1854.
Popp, Valerie. "Where Confusion Is: Transnationalism in the Fiction of Jessie Redmon Fauset." *African American Review* 43, no. 1 (2009): 131–44.
Porter, Dorothy. "The Organized Educational Activities of Negro Literary Societies, 1828–1846." *Journal of Negro Education* 5, no. 4 (October 1936): 555–76.
Pride, Armistead S., and Clint C. Wilson II. *A History of the Black Press*. Washington, DC: Howard University Press, 1997.
Proceedings of the National Emigration Convention of Colored People Held at Cleveland, Ohio, on Thursday, Friday, and Saturday, the 24th, 25th, and 26th of August, 1854. Pittsburgh: A. A. Anderson, 1854.
"Progress of Colored Women. Mrs. Mary Church Terrell's Eloquent Plea before the Woman Suffragist Convention." *The Broad Ax*, March 12, 1898, 4.
"Progress of Colored Women. Mrs. Mary Church Terrell's Eloquent Plea before the Woman Suffragist Convention." *The Broad Ax*, March 19, 1898, 2.
"Protestant Episcopal Ministers in Convention." *The Freeman* (Indianapolis, IN), October 9, 1886, 2.
Prude, Jonathan. "To look upon the 'lower sort': Runaway Advertisements and the Appearance of Unfree Laborers in America, 1750–1800." *Journal of American History* 78, no. 1 (June 1991): 124–59.
Putnam, Lara. *The Company They Kept: Migrants and the Politics of Gender in Caribbean Costa Rica, 1870–1960*. Chapel Hill: University of North Carolina Press, 2002.
Quarles, Benjamin. *Black Abolitionists*. New York: Oxford University Press, 1969.
R. "Dear Friend." *The Southern Workman*, February 1881, 21.
R. Letter dated March 12, 1882, from Elizabeth City Co., Virginia. *The Southern Workman*, October 1882, 102.
Rael, Patrick. *Black Identity and Black Protest in the Antebellum North*. Chapel Hill: University of North Carolina Press, 2002.
Raiford, Leigh. *Imprisoned in a Luminous Glare: Photography and the African American Freedom Struggle*. Chapel Hill: University of North Carolina Press, 2011.
Rapp, Anne Barbara. "A Marginalized Voice for Racial Justice: Charlotta Bass and Oppositional Politics, 1914–1960." PhD diss., University of California, Santa Barbara, 2005.
Reddock, Rhoda. "The First Mrs. Garvey: Pan-Africanism and Feminism in the Early 20th Century British Colonial Caribbean." *Feminist Africa* 19 (2014): 58–77.
Reed, Harry. *Platform for Change: The Foundations of the Northern Free Black Community, 1775–1865*. East Lansing: Michigan State University Press, 1994.
Reese, Linda Williams. *Women of Oklahoma, 1890–1920*. Norman: University of Oklahoma Press, 1997.
Regester, Charlene B. "Introduction." In *Black Entertainers in African American Newspaper Articles*, vol. 2, *An Annotated and Indexed Bibliography of the Pittsburgh Courier and the California Eagle, 1914–1950*, edited by Charlene B. Regester. Jefferson, NC: McFarland and Co., 2010.

Reid, Kit. "Arrow Tips." *The Advocate*, June 18, 1927, 1.

Rhodes, Jane. *Mary Ann Shadd Cary: The Black Press and Protest in the Nineteenth Century*. Bloomington: Indiana University Press, 1998.

Richardson, Marilyn. "Introduction." In *Maria W. Stewart, America's First Black Woman Political Writer*, edited by Marilyn Richardson, 1–27. Bloomington: Indiana University Press, 1987.

Richardson, Marilyn. "Maria W. Stewart: America's First Black Woman Political Writer." In *Black Women's Intellectual Traditions: Speaking Their Minds*, edited by Kristin Waters and Carol B. Conaway, 13–37. Burlington: University of Vermont Press, 2007.

Richardson, Marilyn. "'What If I Am a Woman?': Maria W. Stewart's Defense of Black Women's Political Activism." In *Courage and Conscience: Black and White Abolitionists in Boston*, edited by Donald M. Jacobs, 191–206. Bloomington: Indiana University Press, 1993.

Richardson, Marilyn, ed. *Maria W. Stewart, America's First Black Woman Political Writer: Essays and Speeches*. Bloomington, Indiana University Press, 1987.

Ripley, C. Peter, Roy E. Finkenbine, and Paul A. Cimbala, eds. *The Black Abolitionist Papers*. Vol. 2, *Canada, 1830–1865*. Chapel Hill: University of North Carolina Press, 1986.

Robbins, James C. "Our Evening Study." *The Southern Workman*, October 1878.

Robinson, Cedric. *Black Marxism: The Making of the Black Radical Tradition*. Chapel Hill: University of North Carolina Press, 2000.

Robinson, Mary. Letter from Thaxton's Switch, Bedford County, Virginia. *The Southern Workman*, February 1873.

Roediger, David R. *How Race Survived U.S. History: From Settlement and Slavery to the Obama Phenomenon*. London: Verso, 2008.

Rolinson, Mary G. *Grassroots Garveyism: The Universal Negro Improvement Association in the Rural South, 1920–1927*. Chapel Hill: University of North Carolina Press, 2007.

Rollin, Frank A. *Life and Public Services of Martin R. Delany*. Boston: Lee and Shepard, 1881.

Rooks, Noliwe. *Ladies' Pages: African American Women's Magazines and the Culture That Made Them*. New Brunswick, NJ: Rutgers University Press, 2005.

Rorbach, Augusta. "Truth Stranger than Fiction: Reexamining William Lloyd Garrison's *The Liberator*." *American Literature* 73 (2001): 727–55.

Ross, Marlon B. *Manning the Race: Reforming Black Men in the Jim Crow Era*. New York: New York University Press, 2004.

Rowell, George P. *Geo. P. Rowell and Co.'s American Newspaper Directory*. New York: Geo. P. Rowell, 1870.

Rumsey, David, and Meredith Williams. "Historical Maps in GIS." In *Past Time, Past Place: GIS for History*, edited by Anne Kelly Knowles, 1–18. Redlands, CA: ESRI Press, 2002.

"S." Letter to the Editor. *The Liberator*, March 22, 1831.

Salem, Dorothy. "National Association of Colored Women." In *Black Women in America: An Historical Encyclopedia*, vol. 2, edited by Darlene Clark Hine, Elsa Barkley Brown, and Rosalyn Terborg-Penn, 846–48. Brooklyn, NY: Carlson, 1993.

"Saloon Brawl." *The Freeman* (Indianapolis, IN), December 7, 1895, 7.

Sayers, Amelia. "Woman as Educator: Man Is the Brain, Woman the Heart of Humanity." *Negro World*, November 8, 1924, 10.

Sayers, Emma Lue. "Los Angeles Social Circle." *The Advocate*, June 18, 1927, 3.

Scharf, Col. J. Thomas. *The Chronicles of Baltimore; Being a Complete History of "Baltimore Town" and Baltimore City from the Earliest Period to the Present Time*. Baltimore, MD: Turnbull Brothers, 1874.

Schweiger, Beth Barton. *A Literate South: Reading before Emancipation*. New Haven, CT: Yale University Press, 2019.

"Second Baptist." *Washington Bee*, February 23, 1907, 1.

Sekula, Allan. "The Body and the Archive." *October* 39 (Winter 1986): 3–64.

"Selections from Gleason's Pictorial Daguerrian Gallery of the West." *Frederick Douglass' Paper*, May 5, 1854, 1.

Senchyne, Jonathan. "Bottles of Ink and Reams of Paper: *Clotel*, Racialization and the Material Cultures of Print." In *Early African American Print Culture*, edited by Lara Langer Cohen and Jordan Alexander Stein, 140–58. Philadelphia: University of Pennsylvania Press, 2012.

Senchyne, Jonathan. "Type, Paper, Glass, and Screws: Reading Surfaces and the Materialities of Communication." Lecture at Bard Graduate Center, March 12, 2018. https://www.youtube.com/watch?v=7uzinkHXQsI.

Senchyne, Jonathan. "Under Pressure: Reading Material Textuality in the Recovery of Early African American Print Work." *Arizona Quarterly: A Journal of American Literature, Culture, and Theory* 75, no. 3 (2019): 109–132.

Seniors, Paula Marie. "Cole and Johnson's *The Red Moon*, 1908–1910: Reimagining African American and Native American Female Education at Hampton Institute." *Journal of African American History* 93, no. 1 (2008): 21–35.

Serafini, Sidonia. "Black, White, and Native: The Multiracial Writing Community of Hampton Institute's *Southern Workman*." *Southern Quarterly* 56, no. 2 (2019): 63–81.

Sernett, Milton. *North Star Country*. Syracuse, NY: Syracuse University Press, 2002.

Sexton, Jared. "The Social Life of Social Death: On Afro-Pessimism and Black Optimism." *InTensions* 5 (2011): 1–47.

Shadd, Adrienne. "No 'back-alley clique': The Campaign to Desegregate Chatham's Public Schools, 1891–1893." *Ontario History* 99, no. 1 (2007): 77–95.

Shadd, Mary Ann. "Adieu." *Provincial Freeman*, June 30, 1855.

Shadd, Mary Ann. "Remarks." *Provincial Freeman*, August 26, 1854.

Shadd, Mary Ann. "Wilmington, Jan. 25, 1849, Frederick Douglass." *The North Star*, March 23, 1849.

Shadd, Mary Ann. "Your obedient servant." *Provincial Freeman*, July 22, 1854.

Shadd Cary, Mary Ann. "Trade for Our Boys." *New National Era*, March 21, 1872.

Sharpley-Whiting, T. Denean. *Negritude Women*. Minneapolis: University of Minnesota Press, 2002.

Sheehan, Elizabeth M. "To Exist Serially: Black Radical Magazines and Beauty Culture, 1917–1919." *Journal of Modern Periodical Studies* 9, no. 1 (2018): 30–52.

Sheller, Mimi. *Mobility Justice: The Politics of Movement in an Age of Extremes*. London: Verso, 2018.

"She Pleads for Her Race. Miss Ida B. Wells Talks about Her Anti-Lynching Campaign." *New York Herald Tribune*, July 30, 1894.

"A Short Address." *The Liberator*, May 11, 1833.

Shukin, Nicole. *Animal Capital: Rendering Life in Biopolitical Times*. Minneapolis: University of Minnesota Press, 2009.

Sides, Josh. *L.A. City Limits: African American Los Angeles from the Great Depression to the Present*. Berkeley: University of California Press, 2003.

Simms, Hunter. "First Three Lynchburg African American Women Voters." *Lynchburg Museum blog*, February 12, 2019. https://www.lynchburgmuseum.org/blog/2019/2/12/first-three-lynchburg-african-american-women-voters.

Simpson, Audra. *Mohawk Interruptus: Political Life across the Borders of Settler States*. Durham, NC: Duke University Press, 2014.

"A Sketch of Comfort." *Freedom's Journal*, June 22, 1827.

Smith, Albreta M. "Chicago Notes." *The Colored American Magazine* 2, no. 2 (December 1900): 1.

Smith, Andrea. "Indigeneity, Settler Colonialism, White Supremacy." In *Racial Formation in the Twenty-First Century*, edited by Daniel Martinez HoSang, Oneka LaBennett, and Laura Pulido, 30–38. Berkeley: University of California Press, 2012.

Smith, Billy G., and Richard Wojtowicz, eds. *Blacks Who Stole Themselves: Advertisements for Runaways in the Pennsylvania Gazette, 1728–1790*. Philadelphia: University of Pennsylvania Press, 1989.

Smith, Caroline. "They Would Not Let Us Have Schools." In *Black Women in White America: A Documentary History*, edited by Gerda Lerner, 112. 1972. Reprint, New York: Vintage Books, 1992.

Smith, Lucy Wilmot. "Some Female Writers of the Negro Race." *The Journalist*, January 26, 1889, 4–6. Reprinted as "Women as Journalists." *The Freeman* (Indianapolis, IN), February 23, 1889, 4.

Smith, R. J. *The Great Black Way: L. A. in the 1940s and the Lost African-American Renaissance*. New York: Public Affairs, 2006.

Smith, Shawn Michelle. *American Archives: Gender, Race, and Class in Visual Culture*. Princeton, NJ: Princeton University Press, 1999.

Smith, Shawn Michelle. *Photography on the Color Line: W. E. B. Du Bois, Race, and Visual Culture*. Durham, NC: Duke University Press, 2004.

Snorgrass, J. William. "The Black Press in the San Francisco Bay Area, 1856–1900." *California History* 60, no. 4 (1981–1982): 306–17.

Snyder, Carey, and Leif Sorensen. "Letters to the Editor as a Serial Form." *Journal of Modern Periodical Studies* 9, no. 1 (2018): 123–46.

Sommers, Samantha. "Harriet Jacobs and the Recirculation of Print Culture." *MELUS* 40, no. 3 (2015): 134–49.

"Sophanisba." [Sarah Mapps Douglass]. "Extract from a Letter." *The Liberator*, July 14, 1832.

A Spectator. "My Dear Madam." *Provincial Freeman*, June 30, 1855.

Spires, Derrick R. *The Practice of Citizenship: Black Politics and Print Culture In the Early United States*. Philadelphia: University of Pennsylvania Press, 2019.

"Spirit Lake Nation." Spirit Lake Tribe. http://www.spiritlakenation.com/history/.
"The staff of 'The California Eagle Hour' prepare for their weekly radio broadcast, circa 1940." Charlotta Bass/*California Eagle* Photograph Collection, 1880–1986. Southern California Library for Social Studies and Research, Los Angeles, Los Angeles.
Stapleton, Timothy J. *A Military History of Africa*. 3 vols. Santa Barbara, CA: Praeger, 2013.
Stauffer, John. "Creating an Image in Black: The Power of Abolition Pictures." In *Beyond Blackface: African Americans and the Creation of American Popular Culture, 1890–1930*, edited by Brundage W. Fitzhugh, 66–94. Chapel Hill: University of North Carolina Press, 2011.
Stauffer, John. "Daguerreotyping the National Soul: The Portraits of Southworth & Hawes, 1843–1860." In *Young America: The Daguerreotypes of Southworth & Hawes*, edited by Grant Romer and Brian Wallis, 57–74. New York: International Center of Photography, George Eastman House, and Steidl, 2005.
Stauffer, John. "Race and Contemporary Photography: Willie Robert Middlebrook and the Legacy of Frederick Douglass." *21st: The Journal of Contemporary Photography and Culture* 1 (1998): 55–60.
Stauffer, John, Zoe Trodd, and Celeste-Marie Bernier. "Introduction." In *Picturing Frederick Douglass: An Illustrated Biography of the Nineteenth Century's Most Photographed American*, 2nd ed., edited by John Stauffer, Zoe Trodd, and Celeste-Marie Bernier, ix–xlvii. New York: Liveright, 2017.
Stephens, Michelle Ann. *Black Empire: The Masculine Global Imaginary of Caribbean Intellectuals in the United States, 1914–1962*. Durham, NC: Duke University Press, 2005.
Stephens, Michelle Ann. "Disarticulating Black Internationalisms: West Indian Radicals and the Practice of Diaspora." *Small Axe* 9, no. 1 (2005): 100–111.
Sterling, Dorothy, ed. *We Are Your Sisters: Black Women in the Nineteenth Century*. New York and London: W. W. Norton, 1984.
Stewart, Maria W. "An Address, Delivered at the African Masonic Hall in Boston, Feb. 27, 1833. By Mrs. Maria W. Stewart." *The Liberator*, April 27, 1833.
Stewart, Maria W. "An Address, Delivered at the African Masonic Hall in Boston, Feb. 27, 1833. By Mrs. Maria W. Stewart (Concluded)." *The Liberator*, May 4, 1833.
Stewart, Maria W. "An Address Delivered before the Afric-American Female Intelligence Society of Boston. By Mrs. Maria W. Stewart." *The Liberator*, April 28, 1832.
Stewart, Maria W. "Cause for Encouragement; Composed upon Hearing the Editor's Account of the Late Convention in Philadelphia." *The Liberator*, July 14, 1832.
Stewart, Maria W. "Establishing a Girls' Department in the Institute for Colored Youth: Sarah Mapps Douglass." In *Black Women in White America: A Documentary History*, edited by Gerda Lerner, 85–86. New York: Vintage, 1972.
Stewart, Maria W. "Lecture. Delivered at the Franklin Hall, Boston, September 21st, 1832. By Mrs. Maria W. Stewart." *The Liberator*, November 17, 1832.
Stewart, Maria W. *Meditations: From the Pen of Mrs. Maria W. Stewart*. Boston: Garrison and Knapp, 1832.
Stewart, Maria W. "Mrs Steward's [sic] Essays." *The Liberator*, January 7, 1832.
Stewart, Maria W. *Productions of Mrs. Maria W. Stewart*. Boston: Published by Friends of Freedom and Virtue, 1835.

Stewart, Maria W. *Religion and the Pure Principles of Morality, the Sure Foundation on Which We Must Build, Productions from the Pen of Mrs Maria W. Steward [sic] Widow of the Late James W. Steward, of Boston*. Boston: Garrison and Knapp, 1831. Reprinted in *Maria W. Stewart, America's First Black Woman Political Writer*, edited by Marilyn Richardson, 28–42. Bloomington: Indiana University Press, 1987.

Stewart, Maria, and Eric Gardner. "Two Texts on Children and Christian Education." *PMLA* 123, no. 1 (2008): 156–65.

Still, Mary. "From the Ladies." *The Christian Recorder*, May 11, 1861.

Still, William. "Miss M. A. Shadd." *Provincial Freeman*, March 24, 1855.

"Story of Indian Heiress Reveals System of Plundering Indians' Oil Lands by White Men in Oklahoma." *Negro World*, April 5, 1924, 7.

Streitmatter, Rodger. "Maria W. Stewart: The First Female African-American Journalist." *Historical Journal of Massachusetts* 21, no. 2 (1993): 44–59.

Streitmatter, Rodger. *Raising Her Voice: African-American Women Journalists Who Changed History*. Lexington: University Press of Kentucky, 1994.

Sullivan, Lester. "Historical Note: American Missionary Association." Amistad Research Center, Tulane University. https://amistad-finding-aids.tulane.edu/agents/corporate_entities/427.

"Summary." *Freedom's Journal*, August 24, 1827, 3.

Sylvander, Carolyn Wedin. *Jessie Redmon Fauset: Black American Writer*. Troy, NY: Whitston, 1981.

"A Symposium on Women." *The New York Freeman*, March 27, 1897, 1.

Taft, Robert. *Photography and the American Scene: A Social History, 1839–1889*. New York: Macmillan, 1938.

Tagg, John. *The Burden of Representation: Essays on Photographies and Histories*. Amherst: University of Massachusetts Press, 1988.

Taylor, Ula Y. "'Negro Women Are Great Thinkers as Well as Doers': Amy Jacques-Garvey and Community Feminism in the United States, 1924–1927." *Journal of Women's History* 12, no. 2 (2000): 104–26.

Taylor, Ula Y. "Read[ing] Men and Nations: Women in the Black Radical Tradition." *Souls* 1, no. 4 (Fall 1999): 72–80.

Taylor, Ula Y. *The Veiled Garvey: The Life and Times of Amy Jacques Garvey*. Chapel Hill: University of North Carolina Press, 2002.

T. B. Undated letter from Reynoldson, Gates County, North Carolina. *The Southern Workman*, September 1875, 71.

Terborg-Penn, Rosalyn. *African-American Women in the Struggle for the Vote, 1850–1920*. Bloomington: Indiana University Press, 1998.

Terrell, Mary Church. "Club Work of Colored Women." *The Southern Workman*, August 1901, 435–38.

Terrell, Mary Church. "The International Congress of Women." *Voice of the Negro* 1, no. 10 (October 1904): 454–61.

Terrell, Mary Church. *The Progress of Colored Women. An Address before the National American Women's Suffrage Association, at the Columbia Theater, Washington, D.C.,*

February 18, 1898, on the Occasion of Its Fiftieth Anniversary. Washington, DC: Smith Bros., 1898.

Terrell, Mary Church. "To the Editor." *Charleston News and Courier*, December 1907.

Terrell, Mary Church. "To the Editor." *Evening Star*, January 28, 1908.

Terrell, Mary Church. "What It Means to Be Colored in the Capital of the United States." *The Independent*, January 24, 1907, 181–86.

Testimony Taken by the Joint Select Committee to Inquire into the Condition of Affairs in the Late Insurrectionary States. Georgia. Vol. 6. Washington, DC: Government Printing Office, 1872.

"There is a need of energy among our young people here." *Parsons Weekly Blade*, January 20, 1894, 1.

"They Are Off to a Fresh Start in Everybody Wins Campaign." *California Eagle*, May 23, 1930, 11.

"Third Anniversary of the Ladies' Literary Society of the City of New York." *The Colored American* (New York, NY), September 23, 1837.

Thomas, Isaiah. *The History of Printing in America, with a Biography of Printers, and an Account of Newspapers.* Albany, NY: J. Munsell, 1878.

"Thompson's Review." *The New York Freeman*, January 4, 1908, 3.

Thornbrough, Emma Lou. "American Negro Newspapers, 1880–1914." *The Business History Review* 40, no. 4 (1966): 467–90.

Thorton, Brian. "Pleading Their Own Cause: Letters to the Editor and Editorials in Ten African-American Newspapers, 1929–30." *Journalism History* 32, no. 3 (Fall 2006): 168–78.

Tillman, Katherine. "Afro-American Women and Their Work." *A.M.E Church Review*, April 1895, 477–499.

Tobert, Emory J. *Ideology and Community in the American Garvey Movement.* Los Angeles: UCLA's Center for Afro-American Studies, 1980.

Tong, Benson. *Susan LaFlesche Picotte, M.D.: Omaha Indian Leader and Reformer.* Norman: University of Oklahoma Press, 1999.

"To Our Patrons." *Freedom's Journal*, March 16, 1827, 1.

"A Treat at the Bethel." *The Colored American* (Washington, DC), January 26, 1901, 16.

"Triana. Personal and General." *Huntsville Gazette*, February 23, 1889, 3.

Truth, Sojourner. "Letter from Sojourner Truth." *National Anti-Slavery Standard*, February 13, 1864.

Truth, Sojourner. "Letter from Sojourner Truth—Land for the Freed-People." *National Anti-Slavery Standard*, March 4, 1871.

Truth, Sojourner. "Letter from Sojourner Truth. The Story of Her Interview with the President." *National Anti-Slavery Standard*, December 17, 1864.

Truth, Sojourner. "To the Editor of *The Inter-Ocean*." *Daily Inter-Ocean*, April 16, 1881. Reprinted in *Sojourner Truth as Orator: Wit, Story, and Song*, edited by Suzanne Pullon Fitz and Roseann M. Mandziuk, 201–2. Westport, CT: Greenwood Press, 1997.

Twenty-Two Years' Work of the Hampton Normal and Agricultural Institute, at Hampton, Virginia: Records of Negro and Indian Graduates and Ex-Students. Hampton, VA: Hampton Press, 1893.

Underwood, Ted. "Distant Reading and Recent Intellectual History." In *Debates in the Digital Humanities*, edited by Matthew K. Gold and Lauren F. Klein, 530–33. Minneapolis: University of Minnesota Press, 2016.

Utley, Ebony A. "A Woman Made of Words: The Rhetorical Invention of Maria W. Stewart." In *Black Women's Intellectual Traditions: Speaking Their Minds*, edited by Kristin Waters and Carol B. Conaway, 55–71. Burlington: University of Vermont Press, 2007.

V. "Dear Friend." *The Southern Workman*, February 1881, 21.

Van Orden, Nicholas, and Teresa Zackodnik. "Visualizing the Racialization of Space in Letters to the Editor Using Carto DB." Presented at Digital Diversity 2015: Writing, Feminism, Culture, University of Alberta, Edmonton, Alberta, May 7–9, 2015.

Veracini, Lorenzo. *Settler Colonialism: A Theoretical Overview*. London: Palgrave Macmillan, 2010.

Volpe, Andrea. "The Middle Is Material: Cartes de Visite Photographs and the Culture of Class Formation." In *The Middling Sorts: Explorations in the History of the American Middle Class*, edited by Burton J. Bledstein and Robert D. Johnston, 157–69. New York: Routledge, 2001.

"Votes for Women." Special Issue, *The Crisis* 10, no. 4 (August 1915).

Vowel, Chelsea. *Indigenous Writes: A Guide to First Nations, Métis, and Inuit Issues in Canada*. Winnipeg: HighWater Press, 2016.

W. Letter dated February 5, 1881, from Mathews County, Virginia. *The Southern Workman*, May 1881, 54.

Wade, Ashleigh Greene. "New Genres of Being Human: World Making through Viral Blackness." *The Black Scholar* 47, no. 3 (2017): 33–44.

Wahl-Jorgensen, Karin. "A 'Legitimate Beef' or 'Raw Meat'? Civility, Multiculturalism, and Letters to the Editor." *Communication Review* 7, no. 1 (2004): 89–105.

Waldstreicher, David. "Reading the Runaways: Self-Fashioning, Print Culture, and Confidence in Slavery in the Eighteenth-Century Mid-Atlantic." *William and Mary Quarterly* 56, no. 2 (April 1999): 243–72.

Waldstreicher, David. *Runaway America: Benjamin Franklin, Slavery, and the American Revolution*. New York: Hill and Wang, 2004.

Walker, David. *Walker's Appeal, in Four Articles; Together with a Preamble, to the Coloured Citizens of the World, but in Particular, and Very Expressly, to Those of the United States of America, Written in Boston, State of Massachusetts, September 28, 1829*. 3rd ed. Boston: David Walker, 1830. https://docsouth.unc.edu/nc/walker/walker.html.

Walker, Sarah. Letter from Pittsfield, Massachusetts, August 1880. *The Southern Workman*, October 1880, 103.

Wall, Cheryl A. *Women of the Harlem Renaissance*. Bloomington: Indiana University Press, 1995.

Wallace, Maurice O., and Shawn Michelle Smith, eds. *Pictures and Progress: Early Photography and the Making of African American Identity*. Durham, NC: Duke University Press, 2012.

Wallinger, Hanna. *Pauline E. Hopkins: A Literary Biography*. Athens: University of Georgia Press, 2005.

Warner, Michael. *Publics and Counterpublics*. New York: Zone Books, 2002.
Washington, Georgiana. Undated letter from Mt. Meigs, Alabama. *The Southern Workman*, July 1892, 116–17.
Washington, Josephine Turpin. "Southern Plantation Work." *The Southern Workman*, August 1897, 160–61.
Washington, Margaret. "Frances Ellen Watkins: Family Legacy and Antebellum Activism." *Journal of African American History* 100, no. 1 (2015): 59–86.
Washington, Margaret Murray. "We Must Have a Cleaner 'Social Morality.'" *News and Courier*, September 13, 1898.
Waters, Kirstin. *Maria W. Stewart and the Roots of Black Political Thought*. Jackson: University Press of Mississippi, 2022.
Weare, Walter. "Mutual Benefit Societies." In *Black Women in America: An Historical Encyclopedia*, vol. 2, edited by Darlene Clark Hine, Elsa Barkley Brown, and Rosalyn Terborg-Penn, 829–31. Brooklyn, NY: Carlson, 1993.
"Weekly Scribblings and Gleanings." *The Colored American* (New York, NY), November 13, 1841, 138.
Weheliye, Alexander. *Habeas Viscus: Racializing Assemblages, Biopolitics, and Black Feminist Theories of the Human*. Durham, NC: Duke University Press, 2014.
Weinbaum, Alys Eve. *Wayward Reproductions: Genealogies of Race and Nation in Transatlantic Modern Thought*. Durham, NC: Duke University Press, 2004.
Wells, Ida B. "Freedom of Political Action. A Woman's Magnificent Definition of the Political Situation." *The New York Freeman*, November 7, 1885, 2.
Wells, Ida B. "Lynch Law in America." *Birmingham Daily Post*, May 17, 1894.
Wells, Ida B. "Lynch Law in The United States." Excerpted in "The Lesson of Toleration." *Birmingham Daily Gazette*, May 18, 1894.
Wells, Ida B. "Lynch Law in the United States, Protest by Birmingham Audiences." *Birmingham Daily Post*, May 17, 1894.
Wells, Ida B. "Our Women." *The New York Freeman*, January 1, 1887. Reprinted from *Evening Scimitar*.
Wells, Ida B. *A Red Record. Tabulated Statistics and Alleged Causes of Lynchings in the United States, 1892–1893–1894*. Chicago: Donohue & Henneberry, 1894.
Wells, Ida B. "Remarks to President McKinley." [Delivered March 21, 1898]. *The Cleveland Gazette*, April 9, 1898.
Wells, Ida B. *Southern Horrors: Lynch Law in All Its Phases*. 1892. Reprinted in *Selected Works of Ida B. Wells-Barnett*, edited by Trudier Harris, 14–43. New York: Oxford University Press, 1991.
West, Michael O., and William G. Martin. "Introduction: Contours of the Black International from Toussaint to Tupac." In *From Toussaint to Tupac: The Black International Since the Age of Revolution*, edited by Michael O. West, William G. Martin, and Fanon Che Wilkins, 1–44. Chapel Hill: University of North Carolina Press, 2009.
West, Michael O., William G. Martin, and Fanon Che Wilkins. "Preface." In *From Toussaint to Tupac: The Black International Since the Age of Revolution*, edited by Michael O. West, William G. Martin, and Fanon Che Wilkins, xi–xiii. Chapel Hill: University of North Carolina Press, 2009.

Wexler, Laura. "'A More Perfect Likeness': Frederick Douglass and the Image of the Nation." In *Pictures and Progress: Early Photography and the Making of African American Identity*, edited by Maurice O. Wallace and Shawn Michelle Smith, 18–40. Durham, NC: Duke University Press, 2012.

Wexler, Laura. *Tender Violence: Domestic Visions in an Age of U.S. Imperialism.* Chapel Hill: University of North Carolina Press, 2011.

White, Richard. "What Is Spatial History?" Spatial History Lab, February 1, 2010. https://web.stanford.edu/group/spatialhistory/media/images/publication/what%20is%20spatial%20history%20pub%20020110.pdf.

White, Shane. *Somewhat More Independent: The End of Slavery in New York City, 1770–1810.* Athens: University of Georgia Press, 1991.

Wilderson, Frank B., III. *Red, White and Black: Cinema and the Structure of U.S. Antagonisms.* Durham, NC: Duke University Press, 2010.

Williams, Fannie Barrier. "The Present Status and Intellectual Progress of Colored Women." In *World's Congress of Representative Women*, edited by May Wright Sewall, 696–71. Chicago, 1893.

Williams, Fannie Barrier. *The Present Status and Intellectual Progress of Colored Women.* Chicago, 1893.

Williams, Fannie Barrier. "The Problem of Employment for Negro Women." *The Southern Workman*, September 1903, 432–37.

Williams, Fannie Barrier. "The Relation of the Trained Nurse to the Negro Home." *The Southern Workman*, September 1901, 481–83.

Willse, Craig. *The Value of Homelessness: Managing Surplus Life in the United States.* Minneapolis: University of Minnesota Press, 2015.

Wilson, Clint C., II. *Whither the Black Press? Glorious Past, Uncertain Future.* Bloomington, IN: Xlibris, 2014.

Winch, Julie. *Philadelphia's Black Elite: Activism, Accommodation, and the Struggle for Autonomy, 1787–1848.* Philadelphia: Temple University Press, 1988.

Winch, Julie, ed. *The Elite of Our People: Joseph Willson's Sketches of Black Upper-Class Life in Antebellum Philadelphia, 1841.* University Park: Pennsylvania State University Press, 2000.

Windley, Lathan, ed. *Runaway Slave Advertisements: A Documentary History from the 1730s to 1790.* 4 vols. Westport, CT: Greenwood Press, 1983.

Wolfe, Patrick. "After the Frontier: Separation and Absorption in US Indian Policy." *Settler Colonial Studies* 1, no. 1 (2011): 16–17.

Wolseley, Roland F. *The Black Press, U.S.A.* 2nd ed. Ames: Iowa State University Press, 1990.

"Woman's Rights." *Provincial Freeman*, May 6, 1854.

Woo, Jewon. "Deleted Name but Indelible Body: Black Women at the Colored Conventions in Antebellum Ohio." In *The Colored Convention Conventions Movement: Black Organizing in the Nineteenth Century*, edited by P. Gabrielle Foreman, Jim Casey, and Sarah Lynn Patterson, 179–92. Chapel Hill: University of North Carolina Press, 2021.

Wood, Henrietta Rix. "Transforming Student Periodicals into Persuasive Podiums: African American Girls at Lincoln High School, 1915–1930." *American Periodicals* 22, no. 2 (2012): 199–215.

Wood, Marcus. *Black Milk: Imagining Slavery in the Visual Cultures of Brazil and America*. New York: Oxford University Press, 2013.

Wood, Marcus. *Blind Memory: Visual Representations of Slavery in England and America, 1780–1865*. Manchester: Manchester University Press, 2000.

"The Work Before Us." *The Christian Recorder*, February 23, 1867.

Wright, Helena E. "Photography in the Printing Press: The Photomechanical Revolution." In *Presenting Pictures*, edited by Bernard Finn, 21–42. London: London Science Museum, 2004.

Wright, Michelle M. *Physics of Blackness: Beyond the Middle Passage Epistemology*. Minneapolis: University of Minnesota Press, 2015.

Wright, Nazera Sadiq. *Black Girlhood in the Nineteenth Century*. Champaign: University of Illinois Press, 2016.

Wright, Richard R. *Centennial Encyclopaedia of the African Methodist Episcopal Church*. Philadelphia: AME Book Concern, 1916.

W—S, Henrietta. "Mr. Editor." *Provincial Freeman*, April 22, 1854.

Wynter, Sylvia. "The Ceremony Must Be Found: After Humanism." *boundary 2* 12, no. 3 (1984): 19–70.

Wynter, Sylvia. "Unsettling the Coloniality of Being/Power/Truth/Freedom: Towards the Human, After Man, Its Overrepresentation—An Argument." *CR: The New Centennial Review* 3, no. 3 (2003): 257–337.

Yannielli, Joseph. "John Brown in Africa." Presented at the Antislavery Useable Past workshop, Wilberforce Institute for the Study of Slavery and Emancipation, Hull, England, October 16–17, 2015.

Yannielli, Joseph. "The Logic of the Antislavery Movement." Digital Histories@Yale, October 21, 2015. http://digitalhistories.yctl.org/tag/mendi-mission/.

Yee, Shirley. *Black Women Abolitionists: A Study in Activism, 1828–1860*. Knoxville: University of Tennessee Press, 1992.

Yerrington, J. M. W. "Speech of Miss Frances Ellen Watkins." *National Anti-Slavery Standard*, May 22, 1858.

Zackodnik, Teresa. "Empire and Education in Hampton's *The Southern Workman*: The South Pacific, the Caribbean and the Reconstruction South." In *Victorians and Oceania*, edited by Richard Fulton and Peter Hoffenberg, 156–76. London: Routledge, 2018.

Zackodnik, Teresa. *Press, Platform, Pulpit: Black Feminist Publics in the Era of Reform*. Knoxville: University of Tennessee Press, 2011.

Zeleza, Paul Tiyambe. "African Diasporas and Academics: The Struggle for a Global Epistemic Presence." In *The Study of Africa*, vol. 2, *Global and Transnational Engagements*, edited by Paul Tyambe Zeleza, 86–111. Senegal: CODESRIA, 2007.

Z. H. M. "Dear Freeman." *Provincial Freeman*, June 9, 1855.

Zillah. [Sarah Mapps Douglass]. "Dear Brother." Letter dated September 30, 1837, from Philadelphia. *The Liberator*, October 6, 1837.

Zillah. "Extract from a Letter Written to a Friend, Feb. 23d. 1832." *The Liberator*, July 21, 1832.

Zillah. "Moonlight." *The Liberator*, April 7, 1832.

Zillah. "Reply to Woodby." *The Liberator*, August 18, 1832.

Zillah. "To a Friend." *The Liberator*, June 30, 1832.

Index

abolition: in Black women's letters to the editor, 52–53, 73–74, 77; Pauline Hopkins on reviving, 179–80; literary societies and, 2, 15, 24, 26, 37. *See also* Harper, Frances E. W.; Shadd (Cary), Mary Ann; Stewart, Maria

advertising: Black press and, 16, 194. *See also* print illustration; slave advertising

Advocate, The (Portland, OR; 1903–1936), 197–99. *See also* Cannady, Beatrice

Afric-American Female Intelligence Society (AAFIS, Boston, MA), 5, 36–37. *See also* Riley, Elizabeth; Stewart, Maria

African American migration, 49, 105, 147, 188, 198; and labor, 126, 127–30; and settler colonialism, 65–66, 83–84, 92–93. See also *Colored American Magazine, The*; *Crisis, The*; New Negro politics

Afro-Caribbean migrants: to Harlem, 132–33; labor of, 133, 149–53; literacy of, 133–34; politicization of, 133. *See also* Garvey, Amy Jacques; *Negro World*; United Negro Improvement Association

A.M.E. Church Review (Philadelphia, PA; Nashville, TN; Atlanta, GA; 1884–), 9. *See also* Harper, Frances E. W.; Matthews, Victoria Earle; Terrell, Mary Church; Williams, Fannie Barrier

American Colonization Society, 33, 45. *See also* emigration

American imperialism: critiqued by Black women editors, 120, 125–26, 136

American Missionary Association (AMA), 86, 113–14, 261n18, 268n121. *See also* Hampton Normal and Agricultural Institute; Highgate, Edmonia

Anderson, Benedict: imagined community, 63, 256n57; print capitalism thesis, 14, 21, 54, 254n8

Armstrong, General Samuel, 86–89, 260n13, 261n21. *See also* Hampton Normal and Agricultural Institute; *Southern Workman, The*

Bass, Charlotta Spears: activism, 188–89, 191–92; bankruptcy, 195–96; as editor of *California Eagle*, 21–22, 187, 189; FBI surveillance of, 186–87, 191; garage reading room of, 192; Los Angeles Newspaper Guild violation allegations against, 195–97; as Los Angeles Press Club president, 199; as Negro Press Foundation of California founding director, 191; politics of, 186, 187, 189; Progressive Party, 186, 191; Red Scare and, 189–91, 195, 196; Sojourners for Truth and Justice, 191–92. *See also California Eagle*

benevolent societies, 77; Black women's organizing, 2–5, 11–15, 17, 51; as networked, 44–45. *See also* literary societies and lyceums

Bethel Literary and Historical Association (Washington, DC), 6, 237n37; Black feminist members of 6–7, 60; Black feminist speakers at, 7, 239n52; Bethel literaries, 2

Black church, 75, 78, 79; Black women on, 57, 75, 77–79; gender and reforms to, 75, 79

Black convention movement. *See* Colored Conventions

Black diaspora. *See* Garvey, Amy Jacques; *Negro World*; United Negro Improvement Association

Black feminism(s): co-constitutive with the Black press, 11, 14–15, 24–25, 28, 46–47, 64; collectivizing, 11–12, 14–15, 31, 52; networked, 8–9, 14, 24–25, 51, 119–20; politics of in print, 70–82. *See also* Black internationalism; recirculation

Black geographies, 111; in Black print, 106, 111, 114–15; as rupture, 119, 156

Black internationalism, 119–22, 270n8, 270n10; Black feminism(s) and, 119–20, 121–22, 153–54; emergence of, 120–22; gender and scholarship on, 120–21, 153–54; International Council of Women of the Darker Races, 153. See also Fauset, Jessie Redmon; Garvey, Amy Jacques

Black labor: agricultural, 84, 93–94; in the Caribbean, 133, 149–53; in Cuba, 151–52; in the diaspora, 147–51; industrial, 125–26, 128–29; organizing, 130–31; in South Africa, 127–31. See also African American migration; Afro-Caribbean migrants; Fauset, Jessie Redmon; Garvey, Amy Jacques; Hampton Normal and Agricultural Institute; *Negro World*; *Southern Workman, The*

Black nationalism, 33–34, 37–38. See also emigration; feminist Black nationalism; United Negro Improvement Association

Black Pacific, 150–51, 153. See also Garvey, Amy Jacques

Black press: circulation and distribution, 9, 12, 15, 17, 27–28; as collectivist, 19–20, 28–29, 46, 54–55, 75–77; content of, 8–10, 15, 17–18, 64–65; correspondents, 17, 42, 64; exchanges, 17; female correspondents, 42, 53–54, 265n94; financialization by Black women, 4, 10, 24, 46, 60–66; financial precarity of, 10, 16–17, 60, 192–97, 199; gendered historiography of, 10–16; readers, 8–9, 15; reprinting, 17, 27, 122–31, 137–39; sustainability of, 2, 12–15, 49; women journalists, 6, 62–63, 259n99; women's columns in, 47, 49. See also Black feminism(s); literary societies and lyceums

Black public culture, 13, 15. See also public

Black women's club movement, 8, 15, 20, 23–24, 50, 69, 119–20; periodicals of, 50

Boulding, Lucy: activism, 103–5; letters to the editor, 105; literary society organizing, 103. See also Hampton Normal and Agricultural Institute; *Southern Workman, The*

Bowen, Mattie [Amanda R.]: activism, 238–39n51; literary society addresses and membership of, 7, 237n37

Brooklyn Literary Union (Brooklyn, NY), 7, 42. See also Harper, Frances E. W.; Lyons, Maritcha

Brown, Hallie Quinn, 23; literary society addresses and membership of, 7, 238n49, 239n52

Burroughs, Nannie Helen, 173; activism, 153, 238n50; literary society addresses and membership of, 7, 239n52, 290n11

California Eagle (Los Angeles, CA; 1879–1966): advertising, 193–94, 197, 286n20; circulation and distribution, 186, 187, 194, 195, 197; Compton Printing Company, 195, 197; financial difficulties of, 192–97; labor complaints against, 195–96, 286n20; Loren Miller, 194, 197; printing plant, 192–93; radio broadcast, 194–95, 197; Red Scare and, 185–86, 191, 195–96; sale of, 187, 192, 197; staff salaries, 194; subscription contest, 193. See also Bass, Charlotta Spears

Canada West: African American emigration to, 58, 61, 121. See also *Provincial Freeman, The*; Shadd (Cary), Mary Ann

Cannady, Beatrice: activism, 198; as editor of Portland *Advocate*, 197–98; politics of, 198–200; public library and reading room of, 198–99. See also *Advocate, The*

Cary, Mary Ann Shadd. See Shadd (Cary), Mary Ann

Cassey, Amy Matilda (pseud. Matilda): letter to the editor, 28–29, 31, 32, 52, 244n25; literary society membership of, 28, 44, 63. See also *Freedom's Journal*; Philadelphia Female Literary Association

Christian Recorder (Philadelphia, PA; Nashville, TN; 1852–): Black women correspondents, 53; circulation, 65; letters to the editor, 64–65, 66–67, 69, 70–79, 253n4; production costs, 17, 242n97; subscribers, 65; women's columns, 49; women's fundraising to support, 46. See also Highgate, Edmonia; Still, Mary

circulation: as constitutive, 26–28, 51, 63–64, 140; as self-reflexive, 18, 61, 63. See also recirculation

Cleveland *Gazette* (Cleveland, OH; 1883–1945): Black women's letters to the editor in, 70–79; literary societies and, 49

Clifford, Carrie: activism, 7, 237n42, 238n46; literary society addresses and membership of, 7, 239n52, 291n32; as magazine and newspaper columnist, 237–38n44; as magazine and newspaper contributor, 173, 237–38n44

Collins Fernandis, Sarah: activism, 10; letters to the editor, 101–3; oratory, 88. *See also* Hampton Normal and Agricultural Institute; *Southern Workman, The*

Colored American (New York, NY; 1837–1842), 9, 31, 242n100; circulation, 32; literary societies and, 1, 3, 4, 6, 17, 29, 33, 44–45, 235n2; women's fundraising to support, 4, 45, 60, 236n22. *See also* Francis, Sydna E. R.

Colored American (Washington, DC; 1893–1904), 170, 188; financialization of by Black women, 7. *See also* Terrell, Mary Church

Colored American Magazine (Boston, MA; New York, NY; 1900–1909), 172–75; advertising, 175, 284n107; agents, 174–75; circulation, 174–75, 284n101, 285n126; cover design, 175–79, 183–84; founding of, 173; New Negro woman in, 179–84; photographic portraiture in, 21, 157, 174–84; race biography in, 174, 179; relocation of, 174. *See also* Hopkins, Pauline; Skeete, J. Alexandre

Colored Conventions: Black press, 4, 11–12, 13, 241n84; in Black women's letters to the editor, 30, 77; colored conventions movement, 12–14, 60–61; education, 29; female delegates, 11–12, 58, 60; female support of, 45, 60. *See also* Jeffrey, Mary; Shadd (Cary), Mary Ann; Stewart, Maria

Cook Parrish, Mary V. (pseud. Grace Ermine): as journalist and newspaper columnist, 23, 49, 259n99

Cooper, Anna Julia: activism, 6; as coeditor of *The Southland*, 43, 120; literary society addresses and membership of, 6, 8, 237nn35–36, 292n47; oratory, 6, 43, 88, 173, 238n49; use of recirculation, 43, 250n102; *A Voice from the South*, 6, 43, 120, 257n82

Coppin, Fannie Jackson, 7, 237n42, 238n46, 239n52

Crisis, The: A Record of the Darker Races (Baltimore, MD; 1910–), 122–31; advertising, 122–24; agents, 124; Black readership, 124; circulation, 122–24; reprinting, 124–25; subscription, 122. *See also* Du Bois, W. E. B.; Fauset, Jessie Redmon

data visualization: and data, 80–81, 115, 117; limitations of, 68, 115–17; and racialization, 115–16; as reading protocol, 56, 81. *See also* digital humanities

Davis, Henrietta Vinton, 23, 135, 275n79, 277n118. *See also* United Negro Improvement Association

Dawes Act (1887), 86, 260n7. *See also* settler colonialism

Delany, Martin R., 57, 58, 261n14. *See also* Shadd (Cary), Mary Ann

de Mena, Madame Maymie Turpeau, 140; letter to the editor, 144; as newspaper contributor, 275n79, 275n82. *See also* United Negro Improvement Association

Detroit *Plaindealer* (1883–1895): women's columns in, 47

digital humanities: data and, 80, 116; racialization and, 80–81, 117

digitization: accuracy of, 79; African American historical newspapers, 15, 79–80, 156, 278n7. *See also* periodical studies

Douglass, Frederick, 8, 43, 60; literary society addresses of, 6; on photography, 167–68; on slave icon cast type, 168; uses of photographic portraiture, 166–67

Douglass, Sarah Mapps: on emigration, 34–36; fundraising for *The North Star*, 45; letters to the editor, 30, 52; as newspaper contributor, 36, 247n66; pseudonyms of, 36, 246n54. *See also Liberator, The*; Philadelphia Female Literary Association

Du Bois, W. E. B., 120, 127, 186; *Exhibit of American Negros*, 170–72, 283n85; on Los Angeles, 188. *See also* Bass, Charlotta; *Crisis, The*; Fauset, Jessie Redmon

education: of Black men, 246n46; of Black women, 2, 8, 28–33, 63, 76, 246n46; as collective political value 53, 58, 66, 73–75, 77; of freedpeople, 86–87, 101, 103; of Indigenous peoples, 86–87; reform, 73, 79. *See also* American Missionary Association; Cassey, Amy Matilda; Colored Conventions; Forten, Sarah; Hampton Normal and Agricultural Institute; Highgate, Edmonia; Jennings, Elizabeth, Sr.; Stewart, Maria; Walker, David

Elevator, The: A Weekly Journal of Progress (San Francisco, CA; 1865–1904): agents, 72, 258n99; Black women contributors, 9, 53–54; Black women's financial support of, 9, 46, 251n22; Black women's letters to the editor in, 70–79; circulation, 46, 64, 72; informal exchanges, 64

338 Index

emigration: Black women on in 1830s, 33–35; Black women on in 1850s, 52–53, 57–61; destinations for, 15, 34–36, 57–58, 90; National Emigration Conventions and Black women delegates to, 58. *See also* Black nationalism; Douglass, Sarah Mapps; Shadd (Cary), Mary Ann; Stewart, Maria

enslaved pressmen, 158–59

Enterprise, The (Omaha, NE; 1893–1914), 23, 24. *See also* Mahammit, Ella

Fauset, Jessie Redmon: as editor of *The Crisis*, 122, 124; The Looking Glass column, 125–31; pan-Africanism, 125, 131. See also *Crisis, The*; Du Bois, W. E. B.

feedback loop, 18, 24–26, 61

Female Dorcas Societies, 4; and financial support of the *Colored American* (New York, NY), 4, 60

feminist Back nationalism, 33–34, 147–48. *See also* emigration

Fleetwood, Sara Iredell, 8

Forten, Sarah, 5, 28; letters to the editor, 30; literary society membership of, 6, 29; as newspaper contributor, 29; pseudonyms, 29, 246n54

Forten Grimké, Charlotte: at-home literary society, 6; letters to the editor, 52–53; "Life on the Sea Islands," 53

Fox, Lilian Thomas: as journalist, 8

Francis, Sydna E. R., 60. See also *Colored American* (New York, NY; 1837–1842); Colored Conventions

Frederick Douglass' Paper (Rochester, NY; 1851–1860): Black women's letters to the editor in, 52–53, 63, 70–79; literary society financial support of, 291n26; white financial support of, 17

freedom: and Black print, 55, 59; Black women's letters to the editor, 72–74; land in common as, 90; literary societies and, 32, 50; movement as, 66–68, 99–106, 114, 148. *See also* abolition; emigration; movement; settler colonialism

Freedom's Journal (New York, NY; 1827–1829): Black women's letters to the editor in, 28, 70–79; circulation and distribution, 9, 30; female benevolent associations and, 3; literary societies and, 1, 31–33, 49; on racial respectability and Black women, 9, 28

Garnet, Julia Williams: activism, 46; women's fundraising for the *Impartial Citizen* (Syracuse, NY; Boston, MA), 45–46. *See also* Loguen, Caroline Storum

Garrison, William Lloyd. See *Liberator, The*

Garvey, Amy Jacques: as associate editor of *Negro World*, 136; Australian Aboriginal Progressive Association (AAPA), 141–42; Black feminist internationalism of, 132, 140–54. See also *Negro World*; New Negro woman; United Negro Improvement Association

Garvey, Amy Jacques, Our Women and What They Think column: advertisements in, 132, 142, 147; composition and layout, 132, 136–37, 141, 142, 144, 147; editorials of, 136, 139, 140, 146, 153; exchanges of, 137, 149; T. Thomas Fortune as editor of, 140; gender politics of UNIA, 136, 144, 146; letters to the editor in, 140, 144–53; readers' contributions to, 139–53; use of recirculation, 132, 136–38, 141, 144–45

Garvey, Marcus. *See* United Negro Improvement Association

Genius of Universal Emancipation (Baltimore, MD; Hennepin, IL; 1826–1839), 42, 49

Gibbs, Ida (Iola Gibson), 238n48; literary society addresses of, 7, 239n52

Hampton Normal and Agricultural Institute (Hampton, VA), 86–88; critiques of by Black intellectuals, 87; education of African Americans, 86–87, 99–107; education of Indigenous peoples, 86, 89, 95–99, 107–111, 112; ethos and ideology, 88, 90; racial segregation of students, 88, 114–15; as residential school prototype, 87; summer outing program, 87–88, 97. *See also* settler colonialism; *Southern Workman, The*

Harper, Frances E. W., 42; activism, 7, 59, 237n43; letters to the editor, 52–53; literary society addresses of, 7–8, 41–42, 239n52; as newspaper agent, 88; use of recirculation, 41–42, 249n95

Henderson, Kate (Sioux): as educator, 110; letters to the editor, 107, 109, 114; movement of, 109–11. *See also* Hampton Normal and Agricultural Institute; *Southern Workman, The*

Highgate, Edmonia: letters to the editor, 1, 66–68; as newspaper correspondent, 53,

257n69. *See also* American Missionary Association

Hopkins, Pauline: activism, 120, 173, 239n56, 284n12; as editor of *The Colored American Magazine*, 21, 173–74; as journalist, 174; literary society membership, 7–8; oratory, 173, 179–80; pseudonyms, 173; serialized fiction, 173, 179; use of recirculation, 173–74. See also *Colored American Magazine, The*

Huntsville Gazette (Huntsville, AL; 1879–1894): literary societies and, 49, 252n134, 290n2; women's columns in, 49

Impartial Citizen (Syracuse, NY; Boston, MA; 1849–1850): Black women's financial support of, 4, 45–46, 60

Indianapolis *Freeman* (Indianapolis, IN; 1884–1927): Black feminist recirculation in, 43, 250n102; Black women's columns in, 47; literary societies and, 47, 49, 50, 252n134, 292n44

Indigenous geographies, 84–85, 97–99, 106–13

Jeffrey, Mary, 60

Jennings, Elizabeth, Jr.: activism, 53, 237n33; letters to the editor, 52–53; literary society addresses of, 29; newspaper correspondent, 53–54

Jennings, Elizabeth, Sr.: literary society addresses and membership of, 6, 29, 244n31; on women's education, 29, 31

Keckley, Elizabeth, 8, 83

Ketosh, Juanita (Piegan Blackfoot): letter to the editor, 107; movement of, 107–8. *See also* Hampton Normal and Agricultural Institute; *Southern Workman, The*

layout. *See* Fauset, Jessie Redmon; Garvey, Amy Jacques

letters to the editor: as Black place making, 19, 63–79, 81–82, 89–90, 140–41, 144–53, 253n6; as civic or democratic debate, 31, 54, 56, 63–64, 89–90, 115; as collective expression, 54–56, 63–65, 68, 73, 85, 145; cued and editor-curated, 65, 70, 89, 146, 175; liberal individualism and, 54–56, 69, 85, 90, 91, 94–97; newspaper content and, 56, 64; as political praxis of Black women, 18–19, 70–79, 144–45; as relational, 85,

94–118; staged, 61–62. *See also* mobility and movement; *Southern Workman, The*

Lews, Lillian, 10, 47

Liberator, The (Boston, MA; 1831–1865): agents, 256n43; Black subscribers, 32, 69; Ladies' Department, 5, 30–41; notoriety of, 32–33. *See also* Douglass, Sarah Mapps; Forten, Sarah; Stewart, Maria

literary character, 3, 13, 25, 50, 63. *See also* literary societies and lyceums; reading

literary societies and lyceums: activism, 45; Black press circulation and distribution through, 12, 15, 49; Black press content creators, 2, 17–18; Black women's club movement and, 8, 50; Black women's organizing, 2–9, 11, 14, 23–24, 50–51; Black women's political training and, 2–9; civic participation through, 1–2, 13; communal and collective reading, 18, 25–28, 49, 73, 145; coverage of in Black press, 1, 3, 17, 23; emergence of Black print culture through, 12; literacy and, 8, 25, 49, 145; networked with the Black press, 26, 28, 33, 46–47, 49–51; publishers of periodicals, 40, 50, 290n4, 290n13, 290nn29–30, 291n37, 292nn41–42, 292n44, 292n48; subscribers to Black periodicals, 17, 49–50, 59–60, 252n134, 290n2, 290n12, 290n14, 290n16, 290n21, 290n26, 292n43; self-improvement and, 31, 44. *See also* recirculation

Loguen, Caroline Storum: activism, 46; fundraising for the *Impartial Citizen* (Syracuse, NY; Boston, MA), 45–46. *See also* Garnet, Julia Williams; Jeffrey, Mary

Lyons, Maritcha: activism, 7, 24; literary society membership of, 7

Mahammitt, Ella, 24, 243n5. See also *Enterprise, The*

Matthews, Victoria Earle (pseud. Victoria Earle): activism, 7, 23–24, 43, 249n97; addresses of, 88, 105; journalist and newspaper correspondent, 23, 42, 105, 265n94; use of recirculation, 42, 249n98, 265n94

Messenger, The (New York, NY; 1917–1928), 134; Black women's financialization of, 10; circulation and distribution, 10, 240 n69

migration: African American, 55, 84, 92–93, 126–30, 174, 179, 187–88, 198, 252n132; Afro-Caribbean, 132–34, 151–53, 277n117 mobility and movement: as autonomous, 65, 99–111, 113–116, 118, 266n95; and Black deterritorialization, 90–91; of Black politics, 70–79, 81, 134, 140–42, 148–53; of Black women, 66–68, 101–7; of Indigenous peoples, 105–13; of Indigenous women, 113–16; letters to the editor as vectors of, 65–69, 79, 106; racialized, 84, 94–99, 101–5, 107. See also *Christian Recorder*; settler colonialism; *Southern Workman, The*; United Negro Improvement Association

Mossell, Gertrude: activism, 24; as magazine and newspaper contributor, 88, 259n99; as newspaper columnist, 9, 47, 62, 275n89

National Anti-Slavery Standard (New York, NY; Philadelphia, PA; 1840–1870): Black feminist recirculation in, 42, 249n95; Black women's letters to the editor in, 36, 52–53, 83–84

Native Land Digital, 116–17, 269n133

Negro World (New York, NY; 1918–1933): advertising, 10, 134; circulation, 133, 134, 142, 145, 273–74n58; readership, 133–34, 139, 141–42; Spanish page, 277n118; suppression of, 134; Black women published in, 135–42, 145. See also Garvey, Amy Jacques; United Negro Improvement Association; Walker, Madame, C. J.

New Negro politics, 124, 146, 157, 173–74, 179–80, 183–84

New Negro woman: and *The Colored American Magazine*, 179–84; and *Negro World*, 146–48. See also Garvey, Amy Jacques; Hopkins, Pauline; Skeete, J. Alexandre

New York *Age* (1887–1953): Black feminist recirculation in, 43; literary societies and, 47, 49–50, 252n134, 291n21; women journalists, 42; women's columns, 9, 47

New York *Freeman* (1884–1887): Black feminist recirculation in, 239n52; Black women's letters to the editor in, 54; literary societies and, 47, 50, 253n137; women journalists, 62; women's columns, 9, 47, 275n89

North Star, The (Rochester, NY; 1847–1851): Black women's financial support of, 45–46; Black women's letters to the editor in, 36, 57, 70–79; on racial respectability and Black women, 9

Parsons Weekly Blade (Parsons, KS; 1892–1900): circulation, 243n1; literary societies and, 23–24, 47

periodical studies: Black periodical studies, 10–11, 54–55, 85, 157; common methodology, 14–16, 54, 155–57, 184–85, 242n91; digital turn and, 79, 81, 156; racialization and, 155–57, 184–85, 278n3. See also digitization

Philadelphia Female Literary Association, 5, 28. See also Cassey, Amy Matilda; Douglass, Sarah Mapps; Forten, Sarah; *Liberator, The*

photography: debates in the Black press, 165, 168; evidentiary, 170, 183; mass reproduction techniques, 169, 172; as socially transformative, 166, 167–69, 170. See also Douglass, Frederick; photographic portraiture; print illustration

photographic portraiture; daguerreotype, 165–67; and illustrated Black periodicals, 172–73; poses in, 180–83; as self-fashioning, 168. See also *Colored American Magazine, The*; Hopkins, Pauline; Truth, Sojourner; *Woman's Era, The*

place: Black flow, 65, 69, 84; Black place making, 19, 63–79, 81–82, 89–90, 140–41, 144–53, 253n6, as relation, 82, 94. See also letters to the editor; space

print illustration: affordability of, 172; and Black periodicals, 156, 170–74; intermediation of photographic portraiture and print, 15–16, 21, 168–69, 179–84; and racialization, 156; techniques of, 169. See also photography

Provincial Freeman, The (Windsor, Toronto, Chatham, Canada West; 1853–1860): circulation, 59; editorship, 59–60, 62; emigration in, 61, 121; financial sustainability of, 16–17, 59, 292n48; subscription, 59; women's rights in, 61–62. See also Shadd (Cary), Mary Ann

public, 26, 63–64. See also Black public culture

racial capitalism: Black semi-citizenship, 55, 73, 90–94; and periodical studies, 155–56. See also advertising; Hampton Normal and Agricultural Institute; *Southern Workman, The*

racialization. See advertising; mobility and movement; periodical studies; print illustration; settler colonialism

Randolph, Lucille (Green), 10. See also *Messenger, The*
Ray, Henrietta Green Regulas, 60. See also *Colored American* (New York, NY)
reading: communal or collective, 18, 25–28, 49, 73, 145; interscale reading, 56, 66, 68, 72, 85, 115, 117–18. See also data visualization; digital humanities; letters to the editor; literary societies and lyceums
recirculation: Black feminist, 18, 23–40, 41–44, 124–31, 132, 137–38; and Black women's letters to the editor, 144–45. See also Fauset, Jessie Redmon; Garvey, Amy Jacques; literary societies and lyceums
Reconstruction: and Black schools, 66, 68, 101, 103; and Black women's mobility, 66–68, 101–5. See also American Missionary Association; Hampton Normal and Agricultural Institute; racial capitalism
reprinting: and nineteenth-century newspapers, 17, 27, 32–33; as politicized practice, 20, 39, 122, 124–31, 132, 137–38. See also Fauset, Jessie Redmon; Garvey, Amy Jacques; recirculation
Riley, Elizabeth, 3. See also Afric-American Female Intelligence Society
Ruffin, Josephine St. Pierre: activism, 24; as editor of *Woman's Era*, 49–50, 173; as representative of New England Women's Press Association, 173–74

San Francisco *Elevator*. See *Elevator, The: A Weekly Journal of Progress*
San Francisco *Mirror of the Times* (1857–1862), 46. See also *Elevator, The: A Weekly Journal of Progress*
settler colonialism: and Black semi-citizenship, 55, 73, 90–94; and the "human," 96, 115; Indigenous refusal of, 107, 112–13, 115, 116; Indigenous removal, 66, 97–99, 116; land as possession, 90–92, 94, 99; land in severalty, 86, 97, 111, 116; occupation, 66, 84, 91, 92–93, 95, 97–99, 261n22; residential education, 86–89, 95–99, 107–13. See also Armstrong, Samuel; Dawes Act; Hampton Normal and Agricultural Institute; *Southern Workman, The*
Shadd (Cary), Mary Ann: activism, 60, 255n22, 255n37; Colored Conventions, 58, 60; as editor of *The Provincial Freeman*, 16, 57–63; on emigration, 58–59, 61, 121; letters to the editor, 52–53, 54, 57; literary society addresses and membership of, 6–7, 60; as newspaper agent, 62, 63; on women readers, 62; uses of recirculation, 61–62. See also *Colored American Magazine, The; Provincial Freeman, The*
Skeete, J. Alexandre: as artistic director of *The Colored American Magazine*, 175–79, 180–84; at *Boston Herald*, 175
slave advertising: as biography, 160–61, 280n41; digitization of, 159, 161, 279n34; financializing early American print media, 155–56, 159, 162; and racialization, 156, 159–65, 168; as surveillance, 159. See also print illustration; racial capitalism
Southern Workman, The (Hampton, VA; 1872–1910): agents, 88; Black communal or collective reading, 89; Black feminists in, 88, 103; Black students' and graduates' letters in, 89–94, 96, 99–106, 111, 113–15; circulation, 88; Indigenous students' and graduates' letters in, 89–90, 94–99, 107–15; as print production training for students, 88; subscription, 89, 110, 113; uses of by Armstrong, 88, 89, 96; uses of by graduates, 88. See also Armstrong, Samuel; Hampton Normal and Agricultural Institute; settler colonialism
space: public, 69; racialized, 92–95, 97–99; as transparent, 56, 65. See also settler colonialism
Stewart, Maria: and Colored Conventions movement, 30; and David Walker, 29, 30–31; on emigration, 37–39; feminist Black nationalism of, 33, 36–39; letters to the editor, 29–31; literary society addresses and membership of, 30, 40, 46; as magazine contributor, 40; use of recirculation, 37, 39–41; on women's education, 31–33. See also Colored Conventions; *Liberator, The*
Still, Mary: fundraising for the *Christian Recorder* and Female Union Publication Society, 46; as newspaper agent, 46

Terrell, Mary Church: activism, 7, 191–92; as newspaper columnist, 7; feminist Black internationalism of, 153; financial backer of the *Colored American* (Washington, DC), 7; letters to the editor, 54; literary society addresses and membership of, 6–7, 239n52; as magazine and newspaper contributor, 9, 88, 173; use of recirculation, 44, 250nn105–6

Thompson, Grace Lucas: as newspaper columnist, 47. *See also* Indianapolis *Freeman*
Topeka *Plaindealer* (Topeka, KS; 1899–1958): literary societies and, 47, 49, 50
Truth, Sojourner: activism, 83; land for the freedpeople, 83–84; letters to the editor, 52–53, 83–84, 281n63; use of photographic portraiture, 166–67, 168, 282n67. *See also Colored American Magazine, The*; photographic portraiture

United Negro Improvement Association (UNIA): Australia, 141–42; beauty culturalists and, 10; branches and divisions of, 133, 141, 144–45; Cuba, 152, 277n118; founding and relocation of, 132; iconography of, 133; and literacy, 133, 147; membership of, 133; political tenets of, 133, 146, 148–50; and representation of women in organization, 135, 146–47; U.S. regional concentration of, 133, 145; women members, 135–36, 144. *See also* Bass, Charlotta Spears; Davis, Henrietta Vinton; de Mena, Madame Maymie Turpeau; Garvey, Amy Jacques; Walker, Madame C. J.

Walker, David: *Appeal to the Coloured Citizens of the World* (1829), 29; Massachusetts General Colored Association, 30; as newspaper agent, 30. *See also Freedom's Journal*; Stewart, Maria
Walker, Madame C. J.: activism, 10; as financial backer of *Negro World*, 10. *See also* United Negro Improvement Association
Washington, Margaret Murray: activism, 7, 153; as magazine contributor, 173; use of recirculation, 44. *See also* Garvey, Amy Jacques: Black feminist internationalism of

Washington Bee (Washington, DC; 1882–1922): Black feminist recirculation in, 44, 250n102; literary societies and, 49, 239n52, 252n137; Black women contributors, 42; women's columns, 10, 47
Watkins, William J., Jr., 42. *See also Frederick Douglass' Paper*; Harper, Frances E. W.
Watkins, Rev. William, Sr.: as newspaper correspondent, 42. *See also Colored American* (New York, NY); *Freedom's Journal*; *Genius of Universal Emancipation*; Harper, Frances E. W.; *Liberator, The*
Weekly Anglo-African (New York, NY; 1859–1861), 256n55; Black feminist recirculation in, 42; Black women's letters to the editor in, 52–53; literary societies and, 252n137; reading room, 63; women readers, 63
Weekly Pelican (New Orleans, LA; 1886–1889): literary societies and, 49, 252n134, 290n12, 290n14
Wells, Ida B.: activism, 7, 23–24; editorials of, 24; as editor of Memphis *Evening Star*, 6; FBI surveillance of, 287n33; letters to the editor, 54; literary society addresses and membership of, 6, 7, 252n131; use of recirculation, 43, 249n99
Western Outlook (San Francisco, CA; Oakland, CA; 1894–1928): literary societies and, 50
Williams, Ella V. Chase, as newspaper columnist, 47
Williams, Fannie Barrier: as magazine and newspaper contributor, 9, 88, 173; use of recirculation, 44
Williams, Florence, as newspaper columnist, 9
Woman's Era, The (Boston, MA; 1894–1898), 49–50, 173. *See also* Ruffin, Josephine St. Pierre